Kingdom on the Mississippi Revisited

Kingdom on the Mississippi Revisited

NAUVOO IN MORMON HISTORY

EDITED BY

Roger D. Launius and
John E. Hallwas

University of Illinois Press URBANA AND CHICAGO

Library of Congress Cataloging-in-Publication Data

Kingdom on the Mississippi revisited : Nauvoo in Mormon history
edited by Roger D. Launius and John E. Hallwas.
    p.   cm.
Includes bibliographical references and index.
ISBN 0-252-02197-5 (alk. paper). — ISBN 0-252-06494-1 (paper :
alk. paper)
   1. Mormon Church—History. 2. Nauvoo (Ill.)—Church history. I.
Launius, Roger D. II. Hallwas, John E.
BX8615.I3N38   11996
289.3'77343—dc20   95-14673
                                       CIP

To the memory of
T. Edger Lyon
and Richard D. Poll,
scholars who understood the importance
of Nauvoo in Mormon history

Contents

Acknowledgments

As in any book numerous debts were incurred over the course of its production. We acknowledge the support and encouragement of a large number of people associated with the study of Mormon history and want to thank many individuals who contributed to the completion of this project. Of course, Richard L. Wentworth and Elizabeth G. Dulany of the University of Illinois Press provided encouragement and ideas for proceeding with the work. We also wish to thank Jane Mohraz, whose fine editorial work made this book much better than it would otherwise have been. In addition to the individual essay authors, who deserve much credit for whatever success this book might have, several individuals offered suggestions that helped us more than they will ever know: James B. Allen, Lavina Fielding Anderson, Leonard J. Arrington, Milton V. Backman Jr., Alma R. Blair, Peter Blodgett, Martha Sonntag Bradley, Richard L. Bushman, Paul M. Edwards, Jeffery O. Johnson, Danny L. Jorgensen, Glen M. Leonard, F. Mark McKiernan, W. Grant McMurray, Max H. Parkin, Isleta L. Pement, D. Michael Quinn, Michael S. Riggs, Ronald E. Romig, Donald R. Shaffer, Steven L. Shields, A. J. Simmonds, E. Gary Smith, W. B. Spillman, Grant Underwood, Clare D. Vlahos, Edward A. Warner, David J. Whittaker, and Kenneth H. Winn.

Our thanks are also gratefully given to the editors of the various journals in which these essays originally appeared for permission to reprint them: *Brigham Young University Studies, Dialogue: A Journal of Mormon Thought,* the *Illinois Historical Journal,* the *John Whitmer Historical Association Journal,* the *Journal of Mormon History,* the *Utah Historical Quarterly,* and *Western Illinois Regional Studies.* Without their assistance, this book could not have been completed.

Introduction

ROGER D. LAUNIUS AND
JOHN E. HALLWAS

Nauvoo, Illinois, located on a bend in the Mississippi River in Hancock County, is as much a state of mind as it is a physical place. Today a small community of less than fifteen hundred residents, without access to major highways, railroads, or airports, Nauvoo appears peaceful and almost parklike. Part of it is devoted to an idealized reconstruction of the early town, a Mormon city of the 1840s, which draws visitors from around the world. To the thousands of Mormons who come to Nauvoo each year, however, it is much more than a pleasant setting or an American historic site. It represents a seedbed from which sprang many important doctrinal concepts, a place where their religion took shape. Considered from that perspective, the rise and fall of Mormon Nauvoo was a sacred episode, a refiner's fire in which pioneers of the church encountered opposition and demonstrated their spiritual superiority. In the 1840s they engaged in a conflict with non-Mormons that led to casualties on both sides. One of those casualties was Joseph Smith Jr., the Mormon prophet, who was lynched in nearby Carthage, Illinois, the county seat, while awaiting trial in 1844 for crimes both real and imagined. The impact of that struggle is still present in the attitudes and perspectives of modern Mormons. The town's early history is regarded as a kind of verification of religious truth, and Nauvoo is central to Mormon identity.

To many historians and others outside of the church, Nauvoo is important simply because the Mormons who lived there in the 1840s struggled with other Americans in the region over fundamental questions of ideology, leading to violence and, eventually, to an evacuated city and a mass migration to the West. For these non-Mormons and religious scholars, the conflict of the 1840s raises fascinating and significant questions about American frontier culture and the place of the early Latter-day

Saints in the development of the nation, questions that will forever be associated with the quiet, richly historic village.

The story of Mormon Nauvoo began during the bitter winter of 1838–39, when some five thousand Latter-day Saints crossed the Mississippi River from Missouri and settled in western Illinois. Led by their prophet, Joseph Smith Jr., the Mormons built one of the most impressive and powerful cities in the region, the community of Nauvoo, erected on a limestone flat by the banks of the Mississippi River some fifty miles north of Quincy.[1] Throughout the first half of the 1840s Hancock County was dominated by Nauvoo, with its wealth, population, cultural achievements, and military and political power. For most of the Saints, the rise of this mighty religious commonwealth was the fulfillment of the shattered dreams of previous church-dominated communities in Kirtland, Ohio, and Independence and Far West, Missouri. They believed that God had finally enabled them to begin the establishment of his kingdom on earth, a utopia they called Zion.[2]

Nauvoo was, in essence, a boomtown, and no one was a greater booster than the Mormon prophet. In December 1841 he wrote to Edward Hunter, a recent convert to Mormonism from Pennsylvania, about the city. "There are scarcely any limits which can be imagined to the mills and machinery and manufacturing of all kinds which might be put into profitable operation in this city," he boasted, "and even if others should use a mill before you get here, it need be no discouragement to either you or Brother Buchwalter, for it will be difficult for the mills to keep pace with the growth of the place. . . ."[3] Although Nauvoo never developed a sound economic basis, Smith's enthusiasm seemed justified, for Nauvoo's population doubled every year between 1839 and 1842 and continued to increase until 1846. The city eventually became the second largest in Illinois, rivaling Chicago, and, as a result, political and economic influence emanated from it.

While headquartered in Nauvoo, Smith expressed many innovative theological ideas, some of which revolved around rituals to be conducted in a majestic temple built in the city. Excavation for the foundation of this temple began as early as the fall of 1840, but the real impetus to build the temple came on January 19, 1841, when Smith proclaimed a revelation commanding the building's aggressive construction.[4] Mormons worked on the religious building with zest for the next five years. Built of gray limestone, the temple came to dominate Nauvoo from its perch atop the bluffs overlooking the city. It stood 165-feet high, measured 88 by 128 feet, and cost something over $1 million—an enormous sum at the time. The demands of temple construction, as well as all the other building taking place in Nauvoo, strained the resources of the Mormons almost to the breaking point, but it also sent an ominous signal to other residents of Hancock County about what the Mormons could accomplish. It revealed something of the numerical and economic strength of the community and symbolized the religious, especially theocratic, tendencies of the Saints. They were willing to sacrifice everything they had to accomplish the work that was defined by the institutional church. The building, never completed during Joseph Smith's lifetime, was first used for meetings on October 5, 1845, just a few months before the majority of the Saints began leaving Nauvoo on the exodus to the Great Basin. The Saints abandoned the temple in 1846, and it was gutted by fire in 1848 and knocked down by a tornado in 1850.[5]

Without question the Nauvoo period was the most fertile time for the development of Smith's unique doctrinal conceptions. During that era his ideas concerning the hierarchical nature of eternity, the multiplicity of gods, the possibility of progression to Godhood, celestial and plural marriage, baptism for the dead, and various Mormon temple endowments all came to fruition.[6] Some of these ideas were well outside the mainstream of American religious thought. One of them, plural marriage, scandalized most non-Mormons and some Mormons and became a rallying point for opposition to the movement.[7]

In and of themselves, however, Mormon theological ideas would not have sparked the violent confrontation that took place in Hancock County during the mid-1840s. However, the Mormon theocracy established in Nauvoo greatly disturbed, and in some cases terrified, the other residents of Hancock County. As a group of non-Mormon leaders stated in resolutions passed at an 1841 convention, "With the peculiar religious opinions of the people calling themselves Mormons, or Latter-Day Saints, we have nothing to do—being at all times perfectly willing that they shall remain in the full possession of all the rights and privileges which our constitution and laws guarantee," but "in standing up as we do to oppose the influence which these people have obtained, and are likely to obtain, in a political capacity, over our fellow citizens and their liberties, we are guided by a desire to defend ourselves against a despotism, the extent and consequences of which we have no means of ascertaining."[8]

Smith, in fact, had sought to establish control over very nearly every arena of his followers' activity during the decade following the formation of the church in 1830, and by the time Nauvoo was founded he had been largely successful. Marvin S. Hill has recently argued persuasively that these efforts should be viewed as an attempt to escape from American pluralism and secularism. According to Hill, the early Mormon attempt to develop a communal utopia under theocratic control during the 1830s and 1840s was partially a reaction against the increasing importance of democratic, competitive, and secular tendencies as well as the overall decline of religion in American life. The Mormon church therefore "sought to revitalize this magical world view [like that in medieval society], combine it with elements of more traditional Christianity, and establish a theocratic society where the unconverted, the poor, and the socially and religiously alienated could gather and find a refuge from the competing sects and the uncertainties they engendered. His [Smith's] efforts to do so would bring him into conflict with leaders and others of the established order who were otherwise-minded." [9] The emerging emphasis on personal freedom, as expressed in Jacksonian democracy, and the increasing tolerance and individualism found in other religious denominations caused enormous anxiety for Smith and many of his followers, who felt increasingly alienated.[10] The erection of a strong theocratic organization to counter these external pressures seemed imperative. Consolidation of authority therefore became an early and persistent goal of the Mormon leadership.

Juxtaposed against Smith's search for authority and control was the ideology of republicanism. Arising out of the American religious-political-social revolution that occurred in the eighteenth and early nineteenth centuries, republican ideology prompted Americans to move away from the traditional, patriarchal structure of authority that had been so present in the colonial era and toward a much more individualistic and egalitarian social order.[11] As one leading religious scholar has noted, the republican vision "defended the same classless view of society, hostility to rank and privilege, rejection of the wisdom of the ages, and buoyant confidence in the 'newly discovered capacity of human beings to develop constructively under the conditions of freedom.' Just as it was ordinary people who ensured the defeat of aristocratic values in American politics under Jeffersonian banners, so it was outsiders, interlopers, and marginal men who created the turmoil, defined the issues, formed the organizations, and preached the gospel that captured the hearts and minds of so many citizens in the following century."[12]

The non-Mormon residents of Hancock County embraced republican ideology, and they recognized that Nauvoo was a hierarchical, collectivistic, and authoritarian community outside the American political consensus. In addition to specific concerns that grated on the republican residents of the region, the general control of Nauvoo's civil affairs by religious leaders violated the separation of church and state, a concept vehemently insisted on by leaders of the Jacksonian era.[13] As one non-Mormon from the area said of the Mormons in the *Alton Telegraph,* "Their religious and political creed[s] are identical, and as directly at variance with the spirit of our institutions as any system that man could possibly devise."[14] In Nauvoo, social and political order ultimately rested on divine order, which was an Old World idea that had led to the establishment of state religions in Europe and to the rise of organized religious persecution there.[15]

The result was far-ranging political conflict that began soon after the Saints arrived in Illinois and lasted until they had largely removed themselves in 1846. Always ideologically motivated, the tragic conflict was violent at times. It led to the deaths of Joseph Smith Jr. and his brother Hyrum, the murders of several other lesser figures on both sides, numerous raids on property and persons, and at least one full-fledged battle—the Battle of Nauvoo in September 1846. Finally, Brigham Young led the majority of the Mormons to the Great Basin and created a theocracy modeled on what had been attempted in Nauvoo.

Since the 1840s Mormons have viewed Nauvoo as pivotal in the development of their religion, a crucial experience for the growth, organization, and doctrines of the Latter-day Saint faith.[16] As one of the best general histories of Mormonism indicates, the community's significance centers on what the Mormon prophet accomplished there:

> At Nauvoo Joseph Smith reached the zenith of both his temporal and spiritual influence. As a secular leader he became mayor of one of the two largest cities in Illinois, editor of its newspaper, a leading entrepreneur, and a candidate for the presidency of the United States. As a spiritual leader he announced important new doctrinal ideas, began the erection of a magnificent temple, introduced a sacred temple ceremony that helped increase brotherhood and spirituality among the Saints, and laid the foundation for expanding the Kingdom worldwide. His tragic martyrdom in 1844 became a rallying point for a greater spiritual unity among the Saints and strengthened the Kingdom instead of destroying it as his antagonists had hoped.[17]

Furthermore, Smith has been regarded within the church not as a martyr to theocracy, despite the fact that non-Mormons killed him because he represented that nondemocratic system, but as a martyr to the divine mission of the church and even, ironically, as a martyr to freedom of religion. Nauvoo is the sacred context of that martyrdom.

Historical writing about Mormon Nauvoo has consequently been voluminous. Almost all of it has been by Mormons, although some regional and local historians not affiliated with the church have occasionally turned their attention to the subject when it is a part of their larger area of study.[18] Much of the writing about Nauvoo that has emerged out of the Mormon movement has been celebratory in character. The books of E. Cecil McGavin, Elbert A. Smith, N. B. Lundwell, and Mabel

A. Sanford, for example, are blatantly stylized and create a sentimental view of the community as the epitome of religious virtue.[19] Broader church histories have also often presented celebratory images of Nauvoo and of people and events in the church there. *Essentials in Church History,* written in 1922 by Joseph Fielding Smith, a grandson of Hyrum Smith, emphasized the heritage of Nauvoo as the culmination of Joseph Smith's prophetic ministry while mourning his murder at the hands of evil men.[20] *The Story of the Church,* written in 1934 by Inez Smith Davis, a granddaughter of Joseph Smith who became a part of the Reorganized Church based in the Midwest, applauded the innocence of the Saints in Nauvoo but emphasized the disorganization there following the deaths of the Smith brothers in 1844.[21]

Without question, the wellspring from which all studies of the subject emanate has been the work of B. H. Roberts. A towering intellect inside the Mormon faith, Roberts almost singlehandedly fashioned the central theses that have guided studies of the subject to the present.[22] Roberts first explored the topic in a series of articles for a church-sponsored periodical, the *Contributor,* in the 1880s. That study, probably because of its author's personal interests in politics and theology and the trends historians emphasized then, concentrated on political controversies and doctrinal developments.[23] Revised and published as *The Rise and Fall of Nauvoo* in 1900, his study defines and systematizes a powerful thesis: Nauvoo was a community of innocent refugees persecuted for their religion by evil and designing outsiders. He sets this up by recounting, in "Evangeline" fashion, the expulsion of the French Catholic Acadians from their homes in Nova Scotia by a prejudiced, oppressive, and Protestant British government, which he then compares with the conflict between the Mormons and non-Mormons in western Illinois, condemning the "United States, the boasted asylum for the oppressed of all nations," for the intolerance of the Illinois frontier.[24]

That Nauvoo study formed the basis of his interpretation of the era that appeared in *A Comprehensive History of the Church of Jesus Christ of Latter-day Saints,* published at the centennial of Mormonism's founding in 1930. It was the central work of his historical studies.[25] Never an advocate of detached analysis, Roberts confesses in the introduction that "this *History* is pro-Church of the Latter-day Saints."[26] Throughout the six volumes he forthrightly defends the Mormon religion and in his discussion of Nauvoo argues that the Saints were innocent victims of religious persecution by anti-Mormons in western Illinois. While Roberts admits that some of the actions of individual members might have occasionally been unwise or indiscreet, he never seriously questions the actions of the church hierarchy and never sincerely considers the perspective of those outside the faith. Although he was probably not intentionally trying to distort history, Roberts's background and perspectives led him to discount all but a pro-Mormon church position, and his interpretation of the Nauvoo experience, as one scholar concluded for all of his work, saw "the past as a struggle between 'bad guys' and 'good guys,' between 'fiends' and 'saints.' "[27]

J. Reuben Clark—a constitutional lawyer, Republican diplomat, Mormon church official, and political adversary of Roberts—observed that his contemporary's historical writing was "the work of advocate and not of a judge, and you cannot always rely on what Brother Roberts says. Frequently, he started out apparently to establish a certain thesis and he took his facts to support his thesis, and if some facts got in the way it was too bad, and they were omitted."[28] As an example, in his edited work —the *History of the Church of Jesus Christ of Latter-day Saints,* compiled from the writings of early church leaders and published under Joseph Smith's name—Roberts altered a biographical statement about Sidney Rigdon to create a negative impression, even though the original writer had intended just the opposite. Roberts apparently thought that modification of the historical record was necessary to present an image of Rigdon as an unrighteous apostate because he had split with Joseph Smith over polygamy in Nauvoo and had challenged Brigham Young for leadership of the movement after Smith's death in 1844.[29] Although Clark and many other Mormon officials practiced the same type of special pleading and ignoring of information contrary to preconceptions about the church's special place in the world, the quest for the "noble dream" of functional objectivity in historical writing has been a persistent aspect of professional scholarship in the twentieth century.[30] Roberts did did not even attempt to attain it, and in this failure he has more in common with the "gentleman scholars" of the nineteenth century, who conscientiously shaped their historical narratives to reflect their value systems, than with the academics who wrote in the first half of the twentieth century.

Since the 1950s many of Roberts's successors in the Mormon historical enterprise have been academically trained, and they have generally pursued Mormon studies within the rather broad constraints of, and in general concordance with, the trends of the larger discipline. In the early 1970s this approach came to be called the "new Mormon history." In the words of Paul M. Edwards, it represented "a decided shift away from polemics designed as either attacks on or defense of the Mormon movement," and many within the church championed it as an approach that went beyond the assumptions of faith:

This ["new Mormon history"] is not to be understood as lacking faith, being unfaithful, or going beyond faith. Rather it is an affirmation that one moves through reason and understanding to a larger faith. It suggests that doubt and unanswered questions are not issues of weak faith but the consideration of faithful persons seeking to know that which they do not understand. This assumption arises within historians and is based on their understanding of humans, and their own personal relationship with God. Thus they work fully aware that their faith is personal, not historical.[31]

Despite this shift, the themes the so-called new Mormon historians have emphasized in their study of the Nauvoo period, as well as their preconceptions, have been shaped by the long shadow of B. H. Roberts's work. Indeed, many of them overtly trace modern scholarship about Mormon Nauvoo to Roberts. Richard D. Poll argued in a 1978 bibliographical essay that Roberts's editing of the *History of the Church of Jesus Christ of Latter-day Saints* is "the point of departure for almost any study of the Nauvoo era of Mormon history."[32] Richard L. Bushman put a slightly different spin on this debt by suggesting in 1970 that works on Mormon Nauvoo departed little from themes introduced by Roberts, but "as is always the case in the writing of history, the emphasis makes the difference."[33] The emphasis of the "new Mormon history" has indeed been somewhat different, in many instances rejecting simplified, apologetic history for a more academically respectable approach, but still, many of Roberts's basic assumptions—such as Mormon innocence and religious persecution—remain as unsupported but unquestioned facets of Mormon scholarship.

There have been a handful of truly significant historical studies of Nauvoo published since Roberts did his work. Probably the most meaningful was Robert Bruce Flanders's *Nauvoo: Kingdom on the Mississippi*. Interested in government, politics, economics, and Mormon institutions, Flanders—even though his 1965 book is incomplete because of its intentional disregard of social and religious issues—stood the sacred history approach on its head and opened an avenue of exploration that extended beyond Roberts. Flanders, who is not a member of the Utah Latter-day Saint church, said that he wrote of Joseph Smith not as a religious leader but as a "man of affairs—planner, promoter, architect, entrepreneur, executive, politician, filibusterer—matters of which he was sometimes less sure than he was those of the spirit." He also described Mormon Nauvoo as a western boomtown, not as a religious "city on a hill," and viewed Smith as a theocratic leader bent on fashioning "the Kingdom of Heaven into a kingdom of this world."[34] Implied but not emphasized is Smith's ultimate responsibility for the confrontation that erupted in Hancock County. Flanders "secularized and humanized Nauvoo's story to remove it from the celebratory aura of sanctioned interpretations," according to Glen M. Leonard, and in the process he charted a path that most historians inside the Mormon church have been unwilling and perhaps ill-equipped to follow.[35]

The historian Klaus J. Hansen has suggested that while Latter-day Saint scholars admit there is much to admire in Flanders's secular emphasis, they could not have written it because they have an especially difficult time overcoming their predispositions to view the church, its leaders, and its institutions as always righteous and just. Unlike Flanders, wrote Hansen, "Utah Mormons cannot admit a major flaw in Nauvoo, for these were the very practices and doctrines [Brigham] Young transplanted to the Rocky Mountain kingdom."[36] For inheritors of the Mormon legacy, Nauvoo was the first major explication of their vision of the world, and they tend to see this significance first. Most historians who are Mormons have accepted traditional church interpretations, and some have never even considered going beyond them because of their religious convictions. As Ronald K. Esplin comments in his essay published in this volume, "Nauvoo was, and is, and will be important to Latter-day Saints because it was *the* City of Joseph. It was the city he built, where he lived and acted, where he died. Above all, it was the city where he fulfilled his religious mission. . . . In a very real sense, his other labors were prologue."[37]

The reaction to Flanders's emphasis on the secular aspects of life in Nauvoo led David E. Miller and Della S. Miller to publish in 1974 a history of the Mormon era of Nauvoo that emphasized the social and religious aspects of community life.[38] The Millers created a sympathetic portrait of the Saints as a group in the process of becoming a people, a metamorphosis that started in Nauvoo but was only completed in the valley of the Great Salt Lake. Relying on the Roberts edition of the Joseph Smith history, on Hancock County records, and on the Mormon microfilm collection available at Southern Illinois University at Edwardsville, they intended *Nauvoo: The City of Joseph*, according to Glen M. Leonard, as "an alternative to the polemical work of B. H. Roberts, the sentimental recitals of E. Cecil McGavin, and the secular analysis of Robert B. Flanders."[39] Not entirely successful in this task, the Millers wrote a book that is part guidebook, part social history, and part theological tract—and it was much more satisfying to members of the Mormon church than the Flanders study was. The most that can be said for this book was stated by Leonard, when he concluded that it "will serve a useful purpose until a needed comprehensive study of the Nauvoo period appears."[40]

Such a comprehensive study, however, has not appeared. T. Edgar

Lyon—a longtime research historian for Nauvoo Restoration, Inc., the organization managing the Latter-day Saint historic sites in Nauvoo —had been recruited in the mid-1970s to write such a volume as part of a projected sixteen-volume sesquicentennial history of the Mormon church. His death in 1978 sidetracked that effort until Glen M. Leonard, director of the LDS Museum of Church History and Art in Salt Lake City, agreed to carry on with the project using Lyon's research as a beginning point. However, the Lyon/Leonard collaboration has yet to appear.[41]

There has been a large outpouring of historical work on Nauvoo, though, much of it appearing in regional and Mormon-oriented journals. Indeed, most of what we now know about the Saints in Nauvoo has appeared in hundreds of scholarly articles in the periodical literature. Special issues of *Dialogue: A Journal of Mormon Thought*, the *Journal of the Illinois State Historical Society*, *Brigham Young University Studies*, and *Western Illinois Regional Studies* have been devoted to scholarship on Mormon Nauvoo. Isolated articles dealing with the Nauvoo experience have appeared in each of those same journals at other times, as well as in the *Journal of Mormon History*, the *Utah Historical Quarterly*, the *Journal of the Early Republic*, the *Illinois Historical Journal*, the *John Whitmer Historical Association Journal*, *Church History*, and *Sunstone*.[42] Most of those articles have never been reprinted, however, and are not known to readers other than specialists in Mormon history.

The essays in this volume are some of the more insightful and significant historical work on the Latter-day Saints in Nauvoo. They are also representative of the debates raging in Mormon circles over the nature and purpose of historical inquiry. This dialectic has ensured that the idiosyncratic nature of Nauvoo scholarship, with strong feelings on all sides, has continued to be expressed.[43] The partisan nature of many of the essays is typical of the work published in Mormon studies and reflects B. H. Roberts's continued influence.

All of the essays in this collection are reprints of important studies that offer a gradually altered frame of reference to the study of Nauvoo over a thirty-year period. This collection is something more than a potpourri of studies loosely organized around the theme of Nauvoo, for they ask in their own way several essential questions about Mormon identity: Who were the Nauvoo Mormons? Were they essentially Jacksonian Americans or did they embody some other weltanschauung? Why did Nauvoo become such a protracted battleground for the Saints and the non-Mormons in the region? And, finally, what is the larger meaning of the Nauvoo experience for the various inheritors of the legacy of Joseph Smith Jr? The essays were published between 1960 and

1992 by various scholars with different perspectives. The authors represent younger and older scholars; Mormon, Reorganization, and non-Mormon views; academic, public, and nonaffiliated historical positions; and secular universities and church institutions. They dwell on political, social, economic, religious, and cultural themes in their various analyses. All present important components of the complex society that was Nauvoo. Few of the individual authors would agree with all of the interpretations included in this volume, and indeed some of their views and voices are mutually exclusive.

There is a rough chronology to the essays reprinted in this book. We open the collection with Ronald K. Esplin's discussion of the career of Joseph Smith, whose words and actions provide the key to the meaning of the Nauvoo experience for faithful members of the Mormon church. Ranging broadly, Esplin provides the necessary preliminary analysis of Mormonism as it came to Nauvoo and developed under Joseph Smith in the city by the Mississippi. It is a warmhearted essay, very much from a Mormon perspective; as such, it represents some of the very best of what has been called "faithful history." It points up well the partisan and committed style of scholarship that has been so much a part of Mormon historical studies. James L. Kimball Jr. and Hamilton Gardner offer important discussions of the development of the Nauvoo charter, the legal bulwark that the Saints used to protect themselves from what they considered persecution by evil opponents of an innocent people, and the Nauvoo Legion, the Mormon military organization that so terrified the non-Mormon community and created a sense of false security for the Latter-day Saints. The Gardner essay takes a detailed look at the Nauvoo Legion, the military arm of the community that was such a critical component in the Mormon conflict. It shows, much like Kimball's essay about the Nauvoo charter, that the local militia functioned like most other militia units in the state at the time. The real difference was how the Mormons used it. If it is true that the charter was a wall to defend "Zion," the Legion provided the troops guarding the wall. Klaus J. Hansen's important 1960 essay first raised the specter of the secret Council of Fifty formed by Joseph Smith in Nauvoo and charged with bringing about the political kingdom of God on earth. It speaks fundamentally to Mormonism's goal of creating a separate people who were God's chosen followers, living apart from the world.

Four essays in the volume deal with everyday life in Nauvoo. Kenneth W. Godfrey's piece, first delivered as a presidential address to the Mormon History Association in 1984, raises some important and provocative questions about the social construction of Nauvoo and the nature of everyday life. Godfrey's social history argues that with all of the apartness from mainstream American society that the Mormons explicitly established for themselves in Nauvoo in the 1840s, they still lived their lives very much as those around them did. Much additional work on this issue is required, however. The essay by Terence A. Tanner describes the all-important printing establishment in Nauvoo as a means of creating Mormon identity and communicating ideals and issues. Marvin S. Hill has long been associated with challenging analyses of Mormon development, and his essay here argues the centrality of religious life to the Mormons of Nauvoo. He emphasizes that the Saints did not separate society, economics, politics, and culture from religion in Nauvoo. Using plural marriage as a vehicle, Kathryn M. Daynes explores important themes of social, family, and women's history in her contribution to this volume. Her assertion that Joseph Smith instituted plural marriage to provide a test for leaders after the defections of Kirtland and Far West is a thought-provoking, if difficult to prove, thesis that deserves sustained investigation.

Two essays comment directly on the conflict between Mormons and non-Mormons in Hancock County in the mid-1840s. Robert Bruce Flanders, whose *Nauvoo: Kingdom on the Mississippi* is the benchmark book on the community, argues in a relatively little-known essay that Joseph Smith was an emergent Jacksonian and that Mormonism was enmeshed in worldly concerns and bound to clash with nontheocratic America. In a somewhat complementary study, John E. Hallwas asserts that the non-Mormons outside Nauvoo were imbued with a republican ideology that celebrated the Constitution and individual rights—an ideology that was threatened by the theocratic society in Nauvoo. His analysis provides a useful counterpoint to the "faithful history" approach of so much scholarship about Mormon Nauvoo.

Two other studies focus on matters that followed the killing of Joseph Smith in 1844. Davis Bitton reviews the mythmaking that took place among the Mormons as a result of the assassinations in his examination of the poetry and prose inspired by the tragic event. Smith was apotheosized, and his death was viewed as a matter of cosmic significance. To a very real extent, if Smith had not been killed by a mob in Carthage in 1844, the Mormon movement would have had to invent something akin to his assassination to cement their emerging identity as a persecuted, righteous people. In another "faithful history" essay, Marshall Hamilton examines the often violent relations between Mormons and non-Mormons from the time Joseph Smith and Hyrum Smith were killed in Carthage to the time most of the Nauvoo Saints left for the Great Basin in 1846.

Finally, two studies focus on the impact Smith and the Nauvoo experience had on other notable figures. Valeen Tippetts Avery and Linda

King Newell explore the relationship between Brigham Young and Emma Smith, the two individuals most affected by the murder of Joseph Smith in 1844. Young became head of the Latter-day Saint church and struggled to ensure its viability by handling onslaughts from within and outside the organization. Emma Smith, as the prophet's widow, found herself displaced and feared she would be dispossessed. The two contended over assets and images for the rest of their lives, in the process developing a deep mutual dislike. Roger D. Launius explores the impact the Nauvoo experience had on Joseph Smith III, the son of the prophet who later headed the Reorganized Church and took it in some very different doctrinal directions.

The studies presented here constitute a small portion of those that might have been chosen for this volume. The editors' criteria for choosing these particular essays and omitting many others centered on three factors: the essays had to be of importance to the various historical stages of Mormon Nauvoo; they had to reflect a perspective and emphasize a theme that was not duplicated by other essays in the volume; and they had to be thorough, well supported, influential, and clearly written.

The essays reprinted in this book are, then, a cross section of the best scholarship, though much of it is partisan, on Mormon Nauvoo. They present themes and issues that must be considered by anyone who tries to understand this important episode in American history. From Esplin's passionate explanation of the career of Joseph Smith, which culminated in Nauvoo, to Flanders's emphasis on secular politics and economics, to Godfrey's primer of Nauvoo society, all of the studies reflect the significance of that now-famous frontier community, which continues to draw scholarly attention and fascinates a broad spectrum of modern-day people.

This collection is closed by a bibliographical essay that explores the major themes and analyzes the historical literature available on the Mormon experience in Nauvoo. As so much of the scholarship reveals, the long shadow of B. H. Roberts's dialectical approach remains. But we would urge historians of Mormonism to move beyond it, to replace the notion of a sacred drama with one that is more complex, multifaceted, and well supported. The view of Nauvoo's early history as a sacred morality play, which coincides with the traditional perspective of the Latter-day Saints, has already been forcefully challenged.[44] The wider historical process in recent decades has also shed much new light on Nauvoo in relation to nineteenth-century culture, American religious history, the Illinois frontier, and the early development of the Mormon church. The shift toward a more contextual understanding of the famous Mormon community will surely continue.

Notes

1. The best introduction to the Mormon experience in Nauvoo remains Robert Bruce Flanders, *Nauvoo: Kingdom on the Mississippi* (Urbana: University of Illinois Press, 1965). See also David E. Miller and Della S. Miller, *Nauvoo: The City of Joseph* (Santa Barbara, Calif.: Peregrine Smith, 1974). For perceptive reviews of the literature on Mormon Nauvoo, see Richard D. Poll, "Nauvoo and the New Mormon History: A Bibliographical Survey," *Journal of Mormon History* 5 (1978): 105–23; and Glen M. Leonard, "Recent Writing on Mormon Nauvoo," *Western Illinois Regional Studies* 11 (Fall 1988): 69–93.

2. William V. Pooley, *The Settlement of Illinois from 1830 to 1850* (Madison: University of Wisconsin Extension Service, 1908), 509; Ebenezer Robinson, "Items of Personal History of the Editor," *The Return* (Davis City, Iowa) 2 (April 1890): 243; Mrs. Paul Selby, "Recollections of a Little Girl in the Forties," *Journal of the Illinois State Historical Society* 16 (1923–24): 168–69; Joseph Smith, *History of the Church of Jesus Christ of Latter-day Saints*, ed. B. H. Roberts (Salt Lake City: Deseret News Press, 1902–12; 6 vols., a seventh volume was published in 1932; reprinted by Deseret Book, 1976, and reissued in paperback in 1978), 3:269–71. Purportedly written by Joseph Smith, the *History* was edited by B. H. Roberts from various Mormon diaries, journals, and records. An intriguing analysis of the development of the Mormon concept of the kingdom of God and its expression in Nauvoo can be found in Klaus J. Hansen, *Quest for Empire: The Kingdom of God and the Council of Fifty in Mormon History* (East Lansing: Michigan State University Press, 1967), 72–89.

3. Smith, *History of the Church*, 4:482.

4. The revelation was first recorded in "Extracts from a Revelation given to Joseph Smith Jr., Jan. 19th 1841," *Times and Seasons* (Nauvoo, Ill.) 2 (June 1, 1841): 424–29. It has been kept in continuous publication, with some alterations, since the Nauvoo era as section 124 of *The Doctrine and Covenants of the Church of Jesus Christ of Latter-day Saints* (Salt Lake City: Deseret Book, 1981) and as section 107 of *Book of Doctrine and Covenants* (Independence, Mo.: Herald Publishing House, 1970). On the Nauvoo temple, see Laurel B. Andrew, *The Early Temples of the Mormons: The Architecture of the Millennial Kingdom in the American West* (Albany: State University of New York Press, 1978), chapters 4–5; and Stanley B. Kimball, "The Nauvoo Temple," *Improvement Era* 66 (November 1963): 973–84.

5. W. Gerard Huslamp, "The Mormon Colony at Nauvoo, Illinois," *Journal of the West* 2 (October 1963): 470; Henry Lewis, *Making a Motion Picture in 1848* (St. Paul: Minnesota Historical Society, 1936), 51; Flanders, *Nauvoo*, 194–96; Smith, *History of the Church*, 7:434–35, 456–65.

6. The literature on many of the theological developments in Nauvoo is extensive. For general introductions, see T. Edgar Lyon, "Doctrinal Development of the Church during the Nauvoo Sojourn, 1839–1846," *Brigham Young*

University Studies 15 (Summer 1975): 435–46; and Larry C. Porter and Milton V. Backman Jr., "Doctrine and the Temple in Nauvoo," *Brigham Young University Studies* 32 (Winter/Spring 1991): 41–56.

7. On the development of plural marriage, see Lawrence Foster, *Religion and Sexuality: Three American Communal Experiments of the Nineteenth Century* (New York: Oxford University Press, 1981); Richard S. Van Wagoner, *Mormon Polygamy: A History* (Salt Lake City: Signature Books, 1986); and B. Carmon Hardy, *Solemn Covenant: The Mormon Polygamous Passage* (Urbana: University of Illinois Press, 1992).

8. Thomas Gregg, "A Descriptive, Statistical, and Historical Chart of the County of Hancock," broadside, 2d edition, February 1, 1846, Archives and Special Collections, Western Illinois University Library, Macomb.

9. Marvin S. Hill, *Quest for Refuge: The Mormon Flight from American Pluralism* (Salt Lake City: Signature Books, 1989), 17.

10. See the argument in Peter L. Berger, *The Sacred Canopy* (Garden City, N.Y.: Doubleday Anchor, 1969), 111–12.

11. William G. McLoughlin, "Religious Freedom and Popular Sovereignty: A Change in the Flow of God's Power, 1730–1830," in *In the Great Tradition: In Honor of Winthrop S. Hudson, Essays on Pluralism, Volunteerism, Revivalism,* ed. Joseph D. Ban and Raul R. Dakar (Valley Forge, Penn.: Judson Press, 1982), 173–92; William G. McLoughlin, *Revivals, Awakenings and Reform: An Essay on Religion and Social Change in America, 1607–1977* (Chicago: University of Chicago Press, 1977); Cushing Strout, *The New Heaven and New Earth: Political Religion in America* (New York: Harper and Row, 1974); Robert N. Bellah, *The Broken Covenant: American Civil Religion in Time of Trial* (New York: Seabury Press, 1975); Perry Miller, *The Life of the Mind in America, from the Revolution to the Civil War* (New York: Harcourt, Brace and World, 1965).

12. Nathan O. Hatch, *The Democratization of American Christianity* (New Haven, Conn.: Yale University Press, 1989), 6.

13. "The Mormons," *Signal* (Warsaw, Ill.), May 19, 1841, 2.

14. Hancock (pseudonym), "Letter to Gov. Ford, No. 5," *Alton Telegraph,* April 5, 1845, 1.

15. Two books argue this case eloquently: Hill, *Quest for Refuge;* and Kenneth H. Winn, *Exiles in a Land of Liberty: Mormons in America, 1830–1846* (Chapel Hill: University of North Carolina Press, 1989).

16. James B. Allen and Glen M. Leonard, *The Story of the Latter-day Saints* (Salt Lake City: Deseret Book, 1976), 171.

17. Ibid., 137.

18. State and local historians, of course, treat the Mormon experience in Nauvoo as part of the larger story they are describing, but it is at best an interlude in, not a centerpiece of, their work. See, for example, Adelaide Albers, Virginia Van Pappelendam, and Marie Worth, *History of Warsaw* (Warsaw, Ill.: Warsaw Bulletin, 1960); Robert M. Lilibridge, "Architectural Currents on the Mississippi River Frontier: Nauvoo, Illinois," *Journal of the Society of Architectural Historians* 19 (October 1960): 109–14; Thomas Ford, *A*

History of Illinois: From Its Commencement as a State in 1818 to 1850 (Chicago: S. C. Griggs, 1854; reprint, with annotation and introduction by Rodney O. Davis and bibliographical note by Terence A. Tanner, Urbana: University of Illinois Press, 1995); Thomas Gregg, *A History of Hancock County, Illinois* (Chicago: Charles C. Chapman, 1880); Thomas Gregg, *The Prophet of Palmyra* (New York: John B. Alden, 1890); Newton Bateman, J. Seymour Curvey, and Paul H. Selby, eds., *Historical Encyclopedia of Illinois and History of Hancock County*, 2 vols. (Chicago: Munsell Publishing, 1921); Harry M. Beardsley, "The Mormons in Illinois," in *Transactions of the Illinois State Historical Society for the Year 1933*, Illinois State Historical Library Publication, no. 40 (Springfield: Illinois State Historical Society, n.d.), 45–54; Orville F. Berry, "The Mormon Settlement in Illinois," in *Transactions of the Illinois State Historical Society for the Year 1906*, Illinois State Historical Library Publication, no. 11 (Springfield: Illinois State Historical Society, 1906), 88–102; Clyde E. Buckingham, "Mormonism in Illinois," *Journal of the Illinois State Historical Society* 32 (June 1939): 173–92; Alexander Davidson and Bernard Stuve, *Complete History of Illinois from 1673–1884* (Springfield: Illinois Journal, 1884); *History of Hancock County, Illinois* (Carthage, Ill.: Board of Supervisors of Hancock County, 1968); Robert B. Howard, *Illinois: A History of the Prairie State* (Grand Rapids, Mich.: William B. Eerdmans, 1972); Grace Humphrey, *Illinois: The Story of the Prairie State* (Indianapolis: Bobbs-Merrill, 1917); John Moses, *Illinois, Historical and Statistical*, 2 vols. (Chicago: Fergus Printing, 1889); Theodore Calvin Pease, *The Centennial History of Illinois*, vol. 2, *The Frontier State, 1818–1848* (Chicago: A. C. McClurg, 1919); Thomas Rees, "Nauvoo, Illinois, under Mormon and Icarian Occupation," *Journal of the Illinois State Historical Society* 21 (January 1929): 506–24; and Willis G. Swartz, "Mormon Life and Doctrine in Illinois and Utah (1840–1860)," in *Transactions of the Illinois State Historical Society for the Year 1926* (Springfield: Illinois State Historical Society, 1926), 65–74.

19. E. Cecil McGavin, *Nauvoo the Beautiful* (Salt Lake City: Wallace and Stevens, 1946); Elbert A. Smith, *Timbers for the Temple: A Story of Old Nauvoo in the Days of Her Glory* (Independence, Mo.: Herald Publishing House, 1922); N. B. Lundwell, *Fate of the Persecutors of the Prophet Joseph Smith* (Salt Lake City: Bookcraft, 1952); Mabel A. Sanford, *Joseph's City Beautiful: A Story of "Old Nauvoo"* (Independence, Mo.: Herald Publishing House, 1939).

20. Joseph Fielding Smith, *Essentials in Church History* (Salt Lake City: Deseret Book, 1922; rev. ed., 1979).

21. Inez Smith Davis, *The Story of the Church* (Independence, Mo.: Herald Publishing House, 1934; rev. ed., 1985).

22. On the life and career of B. H. Roberts, see Brigham G. Madsen, ed., *Studies of the Book of Mormon* (Urbana: University of Illinois Press, 1985), xiii–xxxi; Davis Bitton and Leonard J. Arrington, *Mormons and Their Historians* (Salt Lake City: University of Utah Press, 1988), 69–86; and Truman G. Madsen, *Defender of the Faith: The B. H. Roberts Story* (Salt Lake City: Bookcraft, 1980).

23. Roberts himself was a politician in Utah and served in Congress. See

Davis Bitton, "The B. H. Roberts Case of 1898–1900," *Utah Historical Quarterly* 25 (January 1957): 27–46; and D. Craig Mikkelson, "The Politics of B. H. Roberts," *Dialogue: A Journal of Mormon Thought* 9 (Summer 1974): 25–43. His theological interests were also wide-ranging. The emerging historical profession was deeply imbued with concern for political issues. The graduate seminar room at the Johns Hopkins University, the first institution in the United States to grant a Ph.D. in history, was adorned with a slogan on the wall that read, "History is Past Politics and Politics present History." See the photo of the Johns Hopkins seminar of Herbert Baxter Adams in Wilbur R. Jacobs, *The Historical World of Frederick Jackson Turner* (New Haven, Conn.: Yale University Press, 1968), following 136.

24. B. H. Roberts, *The Rise and Fall of Nauvoo* (Salt Lake City: Deseret News Press, 1900; reprint, 1965), 16.

25. B. H. Roberts, *A Comprehensive History of the Church of Jesus Christ of Latter-day Saints*, 6 vols. (Salt Lake City, Utah: Deseret News Press, 1930). Like much of his earlier work, this effort had begun as a series of articles, this time in *Americana*, appearing monthly between 1909 and 1915.

26. Ibid., 1:vii.

27. Davis Bitton, "B. H. Roberts as Historian," *Dialogue: A Journal of Mormon Thought* 9 (Summer 1968): 38.

28. J. Reuben Clark statement, April 8, 1943, in "Budget Beginnings," 11–12, Box 188, J. Reuben Clark Papers, Harold B. Lee Library, Brigham Young University, Provo, Utah, quoted in D. Michael Quinn, *On Being a Mormon Historian* (Salt Lake City: Modern Microfilm, 1982), 8.

29. Smith, *History of the Church*, 1:120. The incident concerning Rigdon is discussed in F. Mark McKiernan, "The Uses of History: Sidney Rigdon and the Religious Historians," *Courage: A Journal of History, Thought, and Action* 2 (September 1971): 285–90. On the problems of Roberts's editing, see Dean C. Jessee, "The Writing of Joseph Smith's History," *Brigham Young University Studies* 11 (Spring 1971): 439–73; Dean C. Jessee, "The Reliability of Joseph Smith's History," *Journal of Mormon History* 3 (1976): 23–46; and Dean C. Jessee, "Return to Carthage: Writing the History of Joseph Smith's Martyrdom," *Journal of Mormon History* 8 (1981): 3–21.

30. There is a multitude of writing about the historical enterprise and its wrestling with the objective/subjective problem. General studies of the subject can be found in John Higham, *History: Professional Scholarship in America*, 2d ed. (New York: Harper Torchbooks, 1973); and Peter Novick, *That Noble Dream: The "Objectivity Question" and the American Historical Profession* (New York: Cambridge University Press, 1988).

31. Paul M. Edwards, "The New Mormon History," *Saints Herald* 133 (November 1986): 13. See also Richard P. Howard, "New Currents in Mormon History," *Saints Herald* 135 (November 1988): 483.

32. Poll, "Nauvoo and the New Mormon History," 108.

33. Richard L. Bushman, "The Historians and Mormon Nauvoo," *Dialogue: A Journal of Mormon Thought* 5 (Spring 1970): 53.

34. Flanders, *Nauvoo*, vi.

35. Glen M. Leonard, "Remembering Nauvoo: Historiographical Considerations," *Journal of Mormon History* 16 (1990): 33.

36. Klaus J. Hansen, "The World and the Prophet," *Dialogue: A Journal of Mormon Thought* 1 (Summer 1966): 106.

37. Ronald K. Esplin, "The Significance of Nauvoo for Latter-day Saints," *Journal of Mormon History* 16 (1990): 72. This essay appears later in this work.

38. Miller and Miller, *Nauvoo*. This book was based on David E. Miller, "Western Migration of the Mormons with Special Emphasis on the History of Nauvoo" (National Park Service report, 1963, mimeographed).

39. Glen M. Leonard, "Review of *Nauvoo: The City of Joseph*," *Brigham Young University Studies* 15 (Autumn 1974): 126.

40. Ibid., 127.

41. On the sixteen-volume series, see Davis Bitton, "Ten Years in Camelot: A Personal Memoir," *Dialogue: A Journal of Mormon Thought* 16 (Fall 1983): 9–33, especially 14–15; Allen and Leonard, *The Story of the Latter-day Saints*, 639–40; and Leonard, "Recent Writing on Mormon Nauvoo," 69–93, especially 72.

42. For perceptive reviews of the general literature on Mormon Nauvoo, see Poll, "Nauvoo and the New Mormon History"; and Leonard, "Recent Writing on Mormon Nauvoo." A good formal bibliography can be found in Richard Neitzel Holzapfel and T. Jeffery Cottle, *Old Mormon Nauvoo, 1839–1846: Historic Photographs and Guide* (Provo, Utah: Grandin Books, 1990), 237–53.

43. Much of this debate has revolved around the viability of applying the standards of modern historical scholarship, with its emphasis on rationality and secularism, to the Mormon experience. Opponents of this approach, which emerged in the 1980s, argued that it was fundamentally impossible to understand anything important about Mormonism using this approach because of the religion's sacred character. They charged the "new Mormon history" with abandoning the spiritual justifications that explain favorably virtually all of the events of Mormon history, and they argued for the adoption of a more partisan approach. Those committed to the "new Mormon history" resisted this assault, and the result was a drawing of battle lines that became more strident and more legalistic as time passed. For a collection of essays arguing different sides of the debate, see George W. Smith, ed., *Faithful History: Essays on Writing Mormon History* (Salt Lake City: Signature Books, 1992).

44. See John E. Hallwas and Roger D. Launius, *Cultures in Conflict: A Documentary History of the Mormon War in Illinois* (Logan: Utah State University Press, 1995).

1

The Significance of Nauvoo for Latter-day Saints

RONALD K. ESPLIN

Traveling northward up the Mississippi from St. Louis 144 years ago, a river steamer passed dozens of small villages and a handful of emerging metropolises, each with dreams of commercial and economic success. While hardly carbon copies of each other, the river towns shared many features. Most had their wharf and warehouse and Water Street. Many had able, ambitious citizens and visionary leaders working for the future. Few had features not duplicated in another—if not in the next town upstream, then in the one after that.

Nauvoo in many ways resembled its river neighbors. Other river communities boasted a similar mix of shops and commerce—some had even greater variety. There were other Masonic halls and print shops and public inns. Though perhaps no one else had a "Seventies Hall," other cities had buildings that served similar community functions.

Nonetheless, long before tying up at the wharf on Nauvoo's Water Street, the riverboat traveler perceived something different as soon as Nauvoo appeared in sight. From several miles' distance, the passenger could see above the forest the tower of a building unlike any other on the river. Larger than the typical village church and of different design, it announced that here was a people somehow apart. For those who knew the Mormons of Nauvoo, the building with its spire thrusting heavenward indeed symbolized how very much apart they stood.

The temple did not stand in 1839, of course. Even in 1844, the year Joseph Smith died, it was just emerging from view among the trees, and a half-dozen years later it was gone. Yet from its beginning, it was the centerpiece of Nauvoo community and religious life, the focal point of Joseph Smith's religious mission. It quickly assumed enormous meaning to those who looked back to Nauvoo for their religious heritage.

Both before its completion and after its destruction, the Nauvoo Temple served to tie the Latter-day Saints to the City of Joseph and its unique religious significance. Though it functioned only a handful of months and stood only a handful of years, the Nauvoo Temple served then—and still serves today—as a powerful link between the Latter-day Saints and their religious roots.

Nauvoo was, and is, and will be important to Latter-day Saints because it was *the* City of Joseph. It was the city he built, where he lived and acted, where he died. Above all, it was the city where he fulfilled his religious mission, a mission intimately linked to the temple. In a very real sense, his other labors were prologue. Our cultural and religious roots are planted firmly in Nauvoo; it is to the City of Joseph—and the temple that he made its centerpiece—that we must turn to understand our *religious* heritage. That heritage includes economics and politics, the Red Brick Store and Masonic Hall, plural marriage and city building. But more than any other single thing, the focal point was the temple. In spite of his economic, political, military, and civil involvements, Joseph Smith's mission and his legacy were religious: religious power, insight, teachings, and ritual. That mission centered on the magnificent structure on the hill—never finished during his lifetime and demolished soon after his death—which dominated the religious landscape of Nauvoo, just as it did the visual.

"I understand my mission and business," Joseph Smith declared from the pulpit in Nauvoo. No casual remark, this declaration bespoke a hard-won confidence that he at last comprehended fully what God expected of him. It had not always been so. Between the Sacred Grove and Carthage stretched a difficult road as he endeavored to learn his duty. To understand what Nauvoo meant to him—and what he was trying to do there—we must go back.[1]

We can debate *when* Joseph Smith first conceived of or understood this principle or that possibility, or *where* he got the idea for this or the model for that. What is not debatable in either historical or religious terms is that Joseph Smith, like other mortals, only gradually, "line upon line, precept upon precept," comprehended what God expected of him and, more gradually still, found the means to do it.[2] If Joseph Smith in Nauvoo was confident, strong, and fully aware of his responsibilities, he started out, as acknowledged in later scripture, among the "weak things of the world, those who are unlearned and despised."[3]

As a teen, "convicted" of his sins by powerful revivalist preachers, he went to the Sacred Grove, by his own earliest account, not desiring a call from God but seeking forgiveness. He emerged not with clear understanding of future prophethood but, at most, with some glimpse that the religious landscape would change and that he would play some role in it.

Not until visits with Moroni years later did he begin to sense what that role would be. It had something to do with ancient plates, he first learned, though he might have felt his duty was only to obtain them. Eventually he understood that he had both the responsibility and the gift to translate the record. He also learned that anything else must be future. "Pretend to no other gift . . . until my purpose is fulfilled in this," he was told, "for I will grant unto you no other gift until it is finished."[4] This was not simply a matter of timing and priority but also of process; translating prepared Joseph Smith for further responsibility.

As Joseph Smith grew in understanding of his mission, revelation continually stressed something he had first learned from Moroni: all was conditional and depended on his faithfulness. Chastisements and the accompanying solemn warnings revealed instruction and promise, identifying these early years as ones when young Joseph struggled, learned from mistakes, and occasionally took his eye off the mark.

Scriptures preserve many solemn warnings to the young prophet. A person might have revelations and "power to do many mighty works," read a revelation of July 1828, but if he "sets at naught" the counsels of God, he will fall.[5] A similar warning several months later concluded with a promise, one that foreshadowed, even in 1829, what was to come in Nauvoo: if Joseph was faithful, "behold I grant unto you eternal life, even if you should be slain."[6]

The April 6, 1830, organization of the church brought to Joseph and Oliver Cowdery the responsibility to preside over the church, "to lay the foundation thereof, and to build it up," in the words of scripture. Several weeks later, another revelation confirmed that, though he had formerly been called specifically to produce the Book of Mormon, his mission had now expanded. "Thou shalt devote all thy service in Zion," he was told, "and in this thou shalt have strength." This revelation also warned that "in temporal labors" he would not have strength, "for this is not thy calling."[7]

Each step forward provided Joseph Smith an expanded view of what would be expected of him. With the Book of Mormon, priesthood restoration, the organization of the church, and more, the process was the same performance of duty; today was a prerequisite for a more complete understanding of tomorrow. In Nauvoo, Joseph Smith looked back and described his growth and education during this early period. It came, he declared, through "the voice of God" and other messengers, "at sundry times and in diverse places," each "giving line upon line, precept upon precept, here a little, and there a little."[8] This would con-

tinue until at least 1836, when experiences associated with the Kirtland
Temple prepared the prophet to understand more fully and to complete what remained of his life's work.

In New York in December 1830, revelation declared that the Saints
should "assemble together at the Ohio." In January, an expansion of
that instruction affirmed that the move to Ohio was essential so a righteous people might "be gathered unto me," for "there will I give unto
you my life, and there you shall be endowed with power from on high"
—the first intimations of Joseph Smith's temple-related responsibilities.[9]

Once in Ohio, the blessings associated with the "gathering" and the
temple, both foreshadowed in the New York revelations, unfolded only
slowly. Indeed, learning and then implementing all aspects of his temple-
related responsibilities became for Joseph Smith a central concern the
entire last decade of his life, as we shall see. In Kirtland he came to
understand how the gathering and the temple related to Zion and its
power.

Even as Joseph Smith settled in Kirtland, he knew that it was not to
be the only gathering place. Though revelation commissioned Ohio as
the place for "an endowment from on high," Missouri, soon called Zion,
would be the "center place." By the spring of 1831, "the gathering of the
Saints to Zion" was a major topic of discussion.[10] Who would go to
Missouri? When? To what specific part? What about Kirtland? That
summer, at a special conference in Missouri, leaders designated the
center place, dedicated a temple site, and began preparations for the
Saints to gather. From this time forward, Missouri held special importance for Joseph Smith and his people.

As important as Zion in Missouri was, the vital "residue of the work . . .
appointed," to use the words of the scripture, was in Kirtland. Without
question, that "residue" included the temple. In September, as some
Kirtland residents by assignment prepared to move to Missouri, the
word of the Lord declared that Kirtland was to remain an important
"strong hold" for five years. Only after that would all be free to leave for
Zion.[11] Why five years? Five years would see the temple dedicated and
initial ordinances and revelatory experiences completed.

In Nauvoo, the prophet publicly taught concepts related to Zion that
he had clearly understood in Kirtland.[12] The main object of gathering
the people of God in any age of the world, Joseph Smith declared, "was
to build unto the Lord an house whereby he could reveal unto his
people the ordinances."[13] A fullness of priesthood power, of saving ordinances, and of instruction was impossible without a temple; a temple was
impossible without gathering. Gathering and temple provided the foundation for Zion, for building a community bound together by God's law

and enjoyment of his power. It was this—not sword and gun but priesthood power through temple—that would "revolutionize the world."[14]

If Joseph Smith did not understand priorities before, it was made perfectly clear in 1833. In May, Kirtland prepared to construct several important community buildings—one for the presidency, one for education, another for printing—each "wholly dedicated to the Lord from the foundation thereof."[15] Then a June revelation chastened the leaders for not pressing forward with "the building of mine house" as a priority above all others. Though significant, the other buildings could not compare with the commandments to build a house in which, the Lord said, "I design to endow those whom I have chosen with power from on high." After the revelation renewed the commandment, work on the temple began within a week.[16]

Although by 1834 Joseph Smith understood priorities, hard lessons about "timetable" were still ahead: nothing would come as quickly or as easily as he hoped. Zion, he would learn, would be redeemed on the Lord's timetable, not man's, and even an understanding of order and priority did not reveal the timetable.

In 1833, enemies drove the Missouri Saints from their center place. Joseph Smith in 1834 led an armed band from Ohio in the hopes of reinstating the Saints on their Missouri lands. After considerable hardship, Zion's Camp, as it was called, disbanded before entering Jackson County. On June 22, before dismissing his men, Joseph Smith delivered, on the banks of the Fishing River, a pointed revelation. A later revelation suggested that even when the Saints do all in their power to fulfill God's commands, the timetable might be altered by people's opposition. In this case, however, revelation declared that the Saints had not done enough.[17] Because of transgressions, affirmed the revelation, "it is expedient in me that mine elders should wait for a little season for the redemption of Zion." Nor could this occur "until mine elders are endowed with power from on high"—the priority again of the temple.[18]

Though Zion was to wait, Joseph Smith remained optimistic. Writing to church leaders in Missouri two months later, he first reemphasized that the elders must "receive their endowment in Kirtland before the redemption of Zion." He then stated his belief that if the church were united and made every possible effort, Zion might yet be redeemed in two years.[19] For the next eighteen months, the prophet directed all possible resources to complete the temple, with the firm idea of following that up with the "redemption" of Zion. But, as he would learn in the temple in May 1836, the Lord apparently had in mind a different timetable.[20]

It is instructive to see the Prophet Joseph growing through all of this, expanding his knowledge of duty and mission. After expending much energy on church organization before leaving Ohio with Zion's Camp in 1834, he apparently saw his work largely in organizational terms and judged his mission complete. But he returned with a different understanding.

"I supposed I had established this Church on a permanent foundation when I went to Missouri," he told the Quorum of the Twelve in 1835, "and indeed I did so, for if I had been taken away it would have been enough, but I yet live, and therefore God requires more at my hands." The additional requirements were temple related. "There is one great deficiency or obstruction . . . that deprives us of greater blessings," he told the apostles on this occasion, and that is that they must attend to certain "duties" in the temple. He fully understood by 1835 that his work could not be finished or "the foundation of this Church complete and permanent" without temple-related powers, ordinances, and teachings.[21]

Apparently this came home to him with full power only at Fishing River in 1834. When he left for Missouri, he told the Twelve, he thought his mission complete. Two days after the Fishing River revelation, he did not. Cholera struck the camp June 24. Seventy men fell violently ill, Joseph among them, and fourteen died, hastily buried without coffins. "If my work were done," he told his brethren then, "you would have to put me in the ground without a coffin, too."[22] That his work was not finished implied a promise that he would have time to see it through.

As the temple dedication neared in the spring of 1836, attention also turned again to Zion. Since the previous fall, Joseph had contemplated leading an enlarged Zion's Camp to help Missouri Saints recover their Jackson County lands. In October, he had instructed the Twelve to prepare to move their families to Missouri in the spring. On March 13 a council of leaders decided to emigrate by May 15, "if kind providence smiles upon us and opens the way before us."[23] But it was not to be.

Before beginning ordinances in Kirtland, on March 29 the prophet and several associated knelt "in the most holy place in the Lord's house" to be taught by revelation, "concerning our going to Zion, and other important matters." With the appointed day for emigrating fast approaching, he wanted confirmation of the plan. The voice of the Spirit said that if they would humble themselves, fasting and praying in the temple through the night, they would learn his will.[24] Although the diary does not record the answer, the prophet's instructions to the Twelve the next day and his own actions thereafter indicate that the answer removed his personal feeling of urgency about Zion.

It had been necessary to remain in Kirtland until endowed, Joseph affirmed on March 30, but the time was at hand when they could go forth empowered. Modifying the former instruction that the Twelve move to Missouri, he told them they were now "at liberty to go wheresoever they will," to Zion if they pleased or elsewhere. The goal of redeeming Zion remained, but not the urgency.[25]

Joseph Smith also declared to those assembled that, in connection with the dedication of the temple and related ordinances, he had "now completed the organization of the church." Since those present had received all the necessary ordinances and instruction, he continued, they "were now at liberty . . . to go forth and build up the kingdom of God." Had Kirtland Temple experiences ended here, the prophet might have concluded that his work was done.[26]

The following Sunday, one of the most significant events associated with the Kirtland Temple occurred. After preliminaries, Joseph Smith and Oliver Cowdery retreated behind lowered veils for "solemn and silent prayer." "The eyes of their understandings were opened," Joseph reported in his diary, and they saw Christ, acknowledging acceptance of the temple, and then in turn: Moses, with the keys of the gathering of Israel; Elias, with the keys of Abraham; and Elijah with vital keys of redemption and sealing.[27] In 1829, Joseph and Oliver had received the first essential priesthood keys; here, in 1836, they received the last.

The April appearance of Elijah with additional temple-related keys opened the way for—indeed required—expanded temple ordinances. Implementing the ordinances suggested here and passing on the keys received would hereafter be among Joseph Smith's highest priorities.

The prophet could not proceed immediately to discharge his additional responsibilities because the Saints were not yet prepared for further temple experiences. "All these things were to be done in their time, place, and season," George A. Smith later explained. With Kirtland temple ordinances, the Lord proceeded "with such great caution that, at all hazards, a few . . . might be able to understand and obey." Even so, some apostatized because there was too much, some because there was not enough, and "if the Lord had on that occasion revealed one single sentiment more . . . I believe He would have upset the whole of us."[28] Before the Saints were ready for more, Joseph and others were forced to flee Kirtland, leaving the temple behind.

Though the prophet, too, learned "line upon line, precept upon precept," at this point he was clearly well in advance of the Saints. The evidence suggests that he now understood, at least broadly, the full scope of his mission. His challenge changed from learning his duty to doing it—preparing the people to receive the fullness and finding the proper time and place to proceed.

Given the nature of Joseph Smith's calling, it is not surprising that, one month following his arrival in Missouri in March 1838, revelation proclaimed Far West a gathering place and designated a temple site. The revelation required that temple construction begin without delay and that Far West be "built up speedily."[29] No effort, however, could build the temple or the city rapidly enough. Violence first erupted in late summer. Fall saw the imprisonment of Joseph Smith and the Presidency, and during the winter of 1838–39 the Saints were driven from Missouri. Once again obstacles prevented Joseph Smith from completing the indispensable temple-related aspects of his mission.

Joseph Smith's Missouri imprisonment, from November 1838 into April 1839, had a profound impact on his sense of urgency about completing his life's work. He had long been aware of and no doubt considered his own mortality many times as he contemplated his unfolding calling. But this was different. He had narrowly avoided death when first taken, and now "to all human appearance, could not be delivered" alive from his enemies—to borrow Brigham Young's phrase. In July 1838 he had declared, "All the world is threatening my life, but I regard it not, for I am willing to die any time when God calls for me."[30] Now it appeared he would.

Despite his gloomy prospects, Joseph Smith and close associates shared in 1838 an assurance that God would protect him. Too much remained unfinished. Joseph Smith wrote from Liberty Jail that, though their enemies seemed to have triumphed, "we most assuredly know, that their triumph will be but short, and that God will deliver us."[31] Brigham Young, Heber Kimball, and Willard Richard, among others, claimed similar reassurance.[32]

Nevertheless, Joseph Smith did not emerge from Liberty Jail feeling invulnerable. Just as firmly as he believed he would be delivered, he apparently believed he would not live to see forty.[33] While he had thought often of the possibility of death, it is probable that Liberty Jail brought for the first time a conviction that his allotted time was both fixed and short.

In jail, Joseph Smith had long days and weeks to contemplate these things and to review his labors. If he felt satisfaction in the progress through the dedication of the Kirtland Temple, he could have felt only frustration in noting how little more of the essential had been accomplished in the nearly three years since. As he wrote from Liberty Jail in March 1839, "I never have had opportunity to give [the Saints] the plan that God has revealed to me."[34] Pondering past problems, and perhaps his own performance, he concluded that "many things were introduced among the Saints, before God had signified the time, . . . notwithstanding the principles and the plans may have been good." Timing was important.

The Saints must be prepared, and God must approve before pressing forward again, but Joseph felt certain the time was near "when God will signify many things."[35] Freed from prison in April 1839, Joseph Smith arrived among the Saints with an internal agenda, a sense of personal urgency, and a conviction that the city that was to become Nauvoo represented his last opportunity.

With this background, let's pause for a moment before we enter Nauvoo in 1839 to consider later assessments of what the Nauvoo experience meant. The historian Robert Flanders insightfully described Nauvoo as "the first full-scale model" of the kingdom of God as envisioned by Joseph Smith. Using a different metaphor, Richard Anderson described Joseph Smith's Nauvoo program as "a deliberate last will and testament of his work."[36] In this view, Joseph Smith—propelled by premonitions of death—toiled in Nauvoo to complete, whatever the cost, the essential elements of his life's work. If Nauvoo was for Joseph Smith both his "first full-scale model" and his "last will and testament," then we must probe the meaning of Nauvoo to assess him and his life's work properly.

With little understanding of his sense of mission and purpose, critics then and now often measured Joseph Smith's Nauvoo performance by a set of expectations very different from his own. One modern observer, for example, after focusing on what might be called the prophet's "secular" program, concluded that in Nauvoo, Joseph Smith "was losing control of many affairs, and perhaps of himself." This observer could not otherwise understand why the prophet pushed certain things when reason should have dictated caution and suggested the probable disastrous results.[37] From this perspective, Joseph Smith in Nauvoo was a flawed hero in a Greek tragedy moving inexorably to a fate that his own blind actions and imperfect character helped determine. Such an assessment fails to take into account the religious goals, insights, and understandings that influenced—almost compelled—so many Nauvoo decisions. It ignores the religiously based personal timetable and sense of urgency that prodded the prophet in Nauvoo and ignores the perspective from which many of his closest associates evaluated the Nauvoo experience.

Clearly Joseph Smith's Nauvoo was complex. One can find much to criticize and much to admire. Given the prophet's highly visible involvement in business and political affairs, it is tempting to look no further. But in a theocracy where religious belief informed every aspect of life, he was clearly prophet-leader and spiritual mentor as well as political adviser and chief economic booster.

Joseph Fielding represents those who, focusing on the religious meanings, found pattern and purpose in Nauvoo events, even in the problematic ones. "My consolation," he wrote while still mourning the deaths of Joseph and Hyrum, is that they "had done all that they could have done and the Foundation of the great work of the last Days was laid." For Fielding, these reflections "in a great measure took off the Edge of the Grief that I might have felt, for I thought that [Joseph] had . . . fulfilled his own Purposes, and I felt willing to say amen to it." Though Joseph Fielding was an eyewitness to some of the difficulties critics pointed to in criticizing Joseph Smith, the explanation was simple for him: "It seems as though the Lord had pushed things forward rather prematurely on account of the shortness of Joseph's Time."[38]

Now that we have reviewed the prophet's gradually developed understanding of mission, mortality, and personal timetable—especially as they related to temple—we can better understand his Nauvoo "program." We can also see his death as his closest associates did—not as the consequence of misjudgment and events out of control but rather as the result of fearlessly pursuing the essential, regardless of the cost.

When Joseph Smith first entered old Commerce in the spring of 1839, the immediate need was not for a temple city but for refuge. Whatever his hopes, reality dictated that resources be used to regroup and to survive. So enormous was the challenge that, despite the prophet's sense of urgency, the Saints had been in Nauvoo more than eighteen months before revelation authorized the construction of a temple.[39]

During 1839–40, Joseph Smith applied his energies to many projects important to him and the Saints. He laid the foundations of a major city as a new gathering place. He also taught the Twelve many new principles, promising them that "God hath not revealed any thing to Joseph, but what he will make known unto the Twelve." Furthermore, he added, "even the least Saint may know all things as fast as he is able to bear them"—an allusion to temple.[40]

The lack of progress on critical temple-related responsibilities remained a concern, however. In July 1840, the prophet spoke publicly of his dream of building in Nauvoo "as great a temple as Solomon did," adding emotionally that if it should be the will of God "that I might live to behold the temple completed . . . I will say, 'Oh, Lord, it is enough; let thy servant depart in peace.' "[41] Joseph's reaction to a September 1840 blessing his father gave also demonstrates the internal tension he felt. During the deathbed blessing of his children, Father Smith promised that Joseph would live to finish his work. According to his mother, Joseph, upon hearing this, "cried out, weeping, 'Oh! my father, shall I.' 'Yes,' said his father, 'you shall live to lay out the plan of all the work which God has given you to do. This is my dying blessing upon your head in the name of Jesus. . . . for it shall be fulfilled.' "[42] Though Joseph was no doubt reassured by this promise, his sense of urgency remained; he could not shake the conviction that he must press ahead. The time was at hand to emphasize temple again.

In January 1841, Joseph received an important revelation. "I am well pleased with your offering and acknowledgements," it began, "for unto this end have I raised you up, that I might show forth my wisdom through the weak things of the earth." In Nauvoo, indeed since the Kirtland Temple, revelations acknowledged that Joseph "hath sincerely striven to do thy will,"[43] instead of the earlier chastisements and warnings. The prophet's own statements in Nauvoo also reflect a growing confidence that he had done his duty and was acceptable to God.

"Your prayers are acceptable before me," the January 1841 revelation continued, "and in answer to them, I say unto you" proclaim the restored gospel to the world, establish Nauvoo as a cornerstone of Zion, gather the Saints, "and build a house to my name." A temple was imperative, "for there is not a place found on earth that he may come to restore again that which was lost . . . even the fullness of the priesthood." Further, the revelation defined this power, and the ordinances, revelation, and teachings "of my holy house, which my people are always commanded to build" as the essential "foundation of Zion."[44]

The ceremonial laying of the cornerstones of the Nauvoo Temple was the centerpiece of the April 1841 general conference. Substantial construction did not begin immediately, however, because there were limited resources and competing priorities and perhaps because the Twelve, who would become the temple's strongest supporters, were still in England. Upon their return, Joseph Smith called an "extraordinary conference" in August 1841. The time had come, he announced, for the Twelve "to stand in their place next to the First Presidency" and to assist, for the first time, in managing all the affairs of the church.[45] The "business of the church given to the 12"—Willard Richards's phrase[46]—soon included directing resources for the temple.

In Nauvoo, Joseph Smith clearly felt tension between the sense of urgency to complete his work and the relative lack of preparation for the Saints to receive it. Though he had tried "for a number of years to get the minds of the Saints prepared to receive the things of God," he lamented in January 1844 that many still "will fly to peaces like glass as soon as any thing Comes that is Contrary to their traditions. They cannot stand the fire at all."[47] Throughout this period, he labored carefully to prepare the Saints for innovations and succeeded in introducing many. But in some cases he decided to move ahead with those he felt would embrace new teachings, preserve them, and eventually deliver them to the church.

In all of this, he was committed to doing what God required of him—his duty as he understood it—whatever the cost. "The object with me is to obey & teach others to obey God in just what he tells us to do," he taught several months before his death. "It mattereth not whether the principle is popular or unpopular. I will always maintain a true principal even if I Stand alone in it."[48] Understanding that such religiously based imperatives drove him, we can see purpose in Nauvoo decisions and actions that may otherwise seem unwise or premature. This applies, for example, to the introduction of plural marriage.

Inevitably plural marriage brought complications into the prophet's life and into the church, as he knew it would. No explanation for its introduction works as well as the simple one: he believed God required it of him and the Saints. Even so, he would not have introduced it *then*, given other priorities and the certainty of difficulties accompanying it, except that he believed God required it *then*. Though documentation about the precise nature of the imperative is inconclusive, with none from the prophet himself, several witnesses claim that he moved forward in Nauvoo only after an angel declared he must act or his calling would be given to another.[49] He saw it as a necessary use of the "sealing keys" so central to temple and as an essential part of the "restoration of all things." When he did implement in Nauvoo a principle that he had understood for several years, he did so with full understanding of the probable costs. Brigham Young remembers his stating more than once that he was determined to press ahead though it would cost him his life, for "it is the work of God, and He has revealed this principle, and it is not my business to controle or dictate it."[50]

Though perhaps less dangerous, moving ahead with his temple responsibilities presented the prophet a no less difficult challenge. Progress on the structure itself was slow. That winter, after pondering the progress on the temple and renewed forebodings about his death, Joseph Smith made a momentous decision: he would complete, outside the temple, the responsibilities central to his mission. Fearing that construction might require more time than he had, he concluded that a set-apart upper room would have to substitute.[51]

Of necessity, without a temple, only a select few could receive the additional teachings and ordinances at first. But this approach offered the advantage that he could now proceed with the whole program, even though not all the Saints were prepared. Those selected, he made clear, would be a vanguard, not an elite, receiving only "what will be made known to all the Saints . . . so soon as they are prepared to receive, and a proper place is prepared to communicate them,"[52] that is, the temple. The challenge remained of continuing to teach publicly as much as possible to prepare all the Saints—a task actually made more difficult by the inevitable rumors associated with private teachings.[53] There seemed no choice, though. In spite of problems, the work would be advancing again.

Progress, and the arrangement making it possible, provided Joseph Smith a satisfying freedom. Heber Kimball, one of the select group, understood. "Brother Joseph feels as well as I Ever see him," he wrote to Parley Pratt. "One reason is he has got a Small company, that he feels safe in thare ha[n]ds. And that is not all, he can open his bosom to[o] and feel him Self safe."[54]

Throughout the winter and spring of 1842, the prophet prepared for temple ordinances. Perhaps it was no coincidence that in March he published the Book of Abraham, decided to permit the establishment of the Nauvoo Masonic Lodge, and helped organize the Nauvoo Female Relief Society. He might have seen these, along with important public discourses, as playing a role in preparing the Saints.

During this period, Joseph Smith spoke his mind freely to the newly organized Nauvoo Female Relief Society. Its record of his remarks provides a window from which to view him during this season of such importance to his mission. Especially revealing was the meeting of April 28, 1842. He now intended to "organize the Church in proper order," he told the assembled sisters, and that could not be done unless the sisters, too, were properly organized under priesthood—something possible only in connection with the temple.[55]

On this occasion he also shared his premonitions. He would make use of this opportunity with them, he insisted, for "he did not know as he should have many opportunities of teaching them . . . they would not long have him to instruct them—that the church would not have his instruction long, and the world would not be troubled with him a great while . . . he spoke of delivering the keys to this Society—and to the Church—that according to his prayers God had appointed him elsewhere."[56]

Sisters who had heard him three weeks earlier could not have missed his meaning. At a funeral for a young boy, he spoke solemnly of the pain he felt at the passing of his own brothers. Such losses are hard to bear, he said, and sometimes "I should have been more reconciled to have been called myself if it could have been the will of God." "Some has supposed that Br. Joseph could not die but this is a mistake. It is true their has been times when I have had the promise of my life to accomplish such & such things, but having accomplished those things I have not at present any lease of my life & am as liable to die as other men."[57]

As he spoke, he was preparing for the moment, now only days away, when he would at last introduce the ordinances necessary to complete his mission and calling. In early May 1842, Joseph Smith instructed nine close associates in "the principles and order of the Priesthood." This was the occasion of the first full temple ritual or endowment.[58] Finally he was completing what he knew was required of him.

What was still lacking now the prophet might have finished in a relatively short time—and apparently expected to—until realities beyond his control again intervened. Though we cannot here detail the obstacles,[59] we can note that after this promising beginning, he did not return to complete what was begun here until the fall of 1843. In the meantime, as he readjusted his agenda to external realities, one thing remained constant. Knowing that he still had not completed his mission, he again felt a promise of protection until he could.[60]

Another constant throughout this period was work on the temple. Though it was not finished sufficiently for ordinance work during the prophet's lifetime, he continually reminded the Saints of its importance and the promised blessings available to all within.

In September 1843, Joseph Smith returned to the ordinance work begun in the spring of 1842. By December and January, a number of men and women had received temple ordinances at the hands of the prophet. Before the prophet's death, approximately seventy men and women received these ordinances under his direction. By January 1844, nine members of the Quorum of the Twelve, along with some others, had also received the "fullness of the Priesthood" ordinances, essentially completing the prophet's temple-related agenda.[61] At last the stage was set for Joseph Smith's final essential duty.

In the last months of his life, Joseph Smith met frequently with the Twelve and with others who had received temple ordinances, teaching them more fully of temple-related powers, responsibilities, and related doctrine. He also further instructed the Twelve about the importance of finishing the temple.[62]

The climax came in an extraordinary council in late March involving the Quorum of the Twelve and others. Though dozens of reminiscent accounts comment on the council, the Twelve prepared the most detailed account soon after the prophet's death. According to that account, "depressed in Spirit," Joseph Smith opened his heart "concerning his presentiments of the future":

> Brethren, the Lord bids me hasten the work in which we are engaged. . . . Some important Scene is near to take place. It may be that my enemies will kill me, and in case they should, and the Keys and power which rest on me not be imparted to you, they will be lost

from the Earth; but if I can only succeed in placing them upon your heads, then let me fall victim to murderous hands if God will suffer it, and I can go with satisfaction, knowing that my work is done, and the foundation laid on which the kingdom of God is to be reared.

He then rolled the burden of the kingdom onto their shoulders, "for the Lord is going to let me rest a while." That done, he declared: "I feel that I am free. I think God for this deliverance."[63]

As part of this "final charge" to the Twelve, as the apostles later called this council, Joseph Smith conferred "the keys of the sealing power" received from Elijah in 1836 upon Brigham Young, president of the Twelve. The prophet could now declare "that he had conferred upon [them] every key and every power that he ever held himself before God."[64] His life's work was complete.

In the April conference before his death, the prophet testified to the Saints that, far from being, as some charged, "a fallen prophet," he had never been "in any nearer relationship to God than at the present time."[65] A few weeks later, on the eve of his departure for Carthage, George Laub heard him speak for the last time: "The enemy is seeking my life and are laying planns to kill me, but if they kill me they kill an Inocent man. . . . But I have laid the foundation of the work of what the Lord hass gave me to doo, therefore have noe longer leas of my life. I have acco[m]plished my work that was given me & others can build on the same."[66]

The keys, the ordinances, the patterns, the teachings, and the temple—everything was in place. To echo Joseph Fielding, now we see why the Lord "pushed things forward rather prematurely on account of the shortness of Joseph's Time." As Brigham Young reminded the Saints in the Salt Lake Valley as they broke ground for a temple that would continue what the prophet had begun in Nauvoo, though "the enemy had power to kill our Prophet . . . did he not accomplish all that was in his heart to accomplish in his day? He did, to my certain knowledge . . . he had prepared the way."[67] That is why today, though 150 years have passed, Latter-day Saints continue to look back to the City of Joseph—to Nauvoo, its temple, and its prophet-leader—for many of the roots of their religious heritage.

Notes

An earlier version of this essay appeared in the *Journal of Mormon History* 16 (1990): 71–88.

1. For a more detailed discussion and fuller documentation of Joseph Smith's developing understanding of mission leading up to Nauvoo, see

Ronald K. Esplin, "Joseph Smith's Mission and Timetable: 'God Will Protect Me until My Work Is Done,'" in *The Prophet Joseph: Essays in the Life and Mission of Joseph Smith,* ed. Larry C. Porter and Susan Easton Black (Salt Lake City: Deseret Book, 1988), 280–319.

2. *The Doctrine and Covenants of the Church of Jesus Christ of Latter-day Saints* (Salt Lake City: Deseret Book, 1981), sect. 128:21; *Book of Doctrine and Covenants* (Independence, Mo.: Herald Publishing House, 1970), sect. 110:21d.

3. *Doctrine and Covenants* (LDS), sects. 35:13–14, 17, and 124:1; *Doctrine and Covenants* (RLDS), sects. 34:4 and 107:1.

4. *Doctrine and Covenants* (LDS), sect. 5:4; *Doctrine and Covenants* (RLDS), sect. 5:1d.

5. *Doctrine and Covenants* (LDS), sect. 3:1–5; *Doctrine and Covenants* (RLDS), sect. 2:1–3. See also *Doctrine and Covenants* (LDS), sects. 6:18–20 and 20:5–8; and *Doctrine and Covenants* (RLDS), sects. 6:8 and 17:2.

6. *Doctrine and Covenants* (LDS), sect. 5:21–22 (see also verses 31–35); *Doctrine and Covenants* (RLDS), sect. 5:4 (see also verse 6). One month later the Lord told Joseph and Oliver that enemies "can do no more unto you than unto me" (*Doctrine and Covenants* [LDS], sect. 6:29–30; *Doctrine and Covenants* [RLDS], sect. 6:14), that is, take their lives, and even if they did, "you shall dwell with me in glory." Such foreshadowings, coupled with later threats against his life, brought the prophet to face the risks and accept them long before Carthage.

7. *Doctrine and Covenants* (LDS), sects. 21:2 and 24:1, 3–7, 9; *Doctrine and Covenants* (RLDS), sect. 19:1b and 23:1–3.

8. *Doctrine and Covenants* (LDS), sect. 128:21–22; *Doctrine and Covenants* (RLDS), sect. 110:21, taken from a September 6, 1842, letter.

9. *Doctrine and Covenants* (LDS), sects, 37:1, 3, and 38:31–32; *Doctrine and Covenants* (RLDS), sects. 37:1–2 and 38:7. See also *Doctrine and Covenants* (LDS), sect. 39:14–15; and *Doctrine and Covenants* (RLDS), sect. 39:5.

10. Joseph Smith, *History of the Church of Jesus Christ of Latter-day Saints,* ed. B. H. Roberts (Salt Lake City: Deseret News Press, 1902–12; 6 vols., a seventh volume was published in 1932; reprinted by Deseret Book, 1976, and reissued in paperback in 1978), 1:181–82. Purportedly written by Joseph Smith, the *History* was edited by B. H. Roberts from various Mormon diaries, journals, and records.

11. *Doctrine and Covenants* (LDS), sect. 64:21–22; *Doctrine and Covenants* (RLDS), sect. 64:4c-d. For the context, see Smith, *History of the Church,* 1:211.

12. For information on the principles taught in Kirtland and reactions to them, see Ronald K. Esplin, "The Emergence of Brigham Young and the Twelve to Mormon Leadership, 1830–1841" (Ph.D. diss., Brigham Young University, 1981), chapter 5.

13. Joseph Smith sermon, June 11, 1843, in *Wilford Woodruff's Journal, 1833–1898,* 9 vols., ed. Scott G. Kenney (Midvale, Utah: Signature Books, 1983), 2:240. For other accounts of this important sermon, see Andrew F. Ehat and Lyndon W. Cook, eds., *The Words of Joseph Smith: The Contemporary*

Accounts of the Nauvoo Discourses of the Prophet Joseph (Provo, Utah: Religious Studies Center, Brigham Young University, 1980), 209–16.

14. "To the Saints among all Nations," *Times and Seasons* (Nauvoo, Ill.) 4 (May 1, 1842): 201–3; Smith, *History of the Church*, 4:609–10; Joseph Smith sermon, May 12, 1844, in Ehat and Cook, *Words of Joseph Smith*, 267.

15. *Doctrine and Covenants* (LDS), sect. 94:3–12; *Doctrine and Covenants* (RLDS), sect. 91:1–3. See also Smith, *History of the Church*, 1:353.

16. *Doctrine and Covenants* (LDS), sect. 95:1–11; *Doctrine and Covenants* (RLDS), sect. 92:1–2; Smith, *History of the Church*, 1:342, 349.

17. *Doctrine and Covenants* (LDS), sect. 124:49–51; *Doctrine and Covenants* (RLDS), sect. 107:15. The wording suggests that this applied to the prolonged effort of the Saints in Missouri from 1831 on, but for the years up to 1833, apparently the fault lay more with the Saints. See, for example, *Doctrine and Covenants* (LDS), sect. 101:1–10; and *Doctrine and Covenants* (RLDS), sect. 98:1–4b.

18. *Doctrine and Covenants* (LDS), sect. 105:6, 9; *Doctrine and Covenants* (RLDS), sect. 102:2d, 3c.

19. Joseph Smith to Lyman Wight, Edward Partridge, et al., August 16, 1834, in Dean C. Jessee, ed., *The Personal Writings of Joseph Smith* (Salt Lake City: Deseret Book, 1984), 329–31.

20. In 1831, as the Saints first learned of Missouri as the "center place," the Lord made clear that "ye cannot behold with your natural eyes, for the present time, the design of your God concerning those things which shall come hereafter," adding that Zion would be redeemed only "after much tribulation" (*Doctrine and Covenants* [LDS], sect. 58:3; *Doctrine and Covenants* [RLDS], sect. 58:2).

21. Joseph Smith, Diary, November 12, 1835, Archives, Historical Department, Church of Jesus Christ of Latter-day Saints, Salt Lake City, Utah (hereafter LDS Archives).

22. Smith, *History of the Church*, 2:114. After the Fishing River revelation, Joseph Smith felt so strongly about the priority of the temple that he severely reproved the apostles when reports suggested they had inappropriately emphasized redeeming Zion more than temple during their summer mission in the East the following year. See Smith, *History of the Church*, 2:230–40; and Esplin, "Emergence of Brigham Young," 166–67, 213.

23. Joseph Smith, Diary, March 13, 1836. See also ibid., September 24, 1835, and October 5 and 29, 1835.

24. Ibid., March 26, 1836; Jessee, *Personal Writings of Joseph Smith*, 181.

25. Joseph Smith, Diary, March 30, 1836; Jessee, *Personal Writings of Joseph Smith*, 182–83. For the goal or promise relating to Zion, see *Doctrine and Covenants* (LDS), sect. 101:16–17, 20; and *Doctrine and Covenants* (RLDS), sect. 98:4f–g, h.

26. Joseph Smith, Diary, April 3, 1836; Jessee, *Personal Writings of Joseph Smith*, 182–83.

27. Joseph Smith, Diary, April 3, 1836; Jessee, *Personal Writings of Joseph*

Smith, 186–87; this is the original for what is now *Doctrine and Covenants* (LDS), sect. 110.

28. George A. Smith discourse, March 18, 1855, in *Journal of Discourses,* 26 vols. (Liverpool, England: F. D. and S. W. Richards, 1854–86), 2:214–15. See also Brigham Young discourse, April 6, 1853, in *Journal of Discourses,* 2:32. Compare this with *Doctrine and Covenants* (LDS), sect. 50:40; and *Doctrine and Covenants* (RLDS), sect. 50:8d: "Ye are little children and ye cannot bear all things now, ye must grow in grace and in the knowledge of the truth."

29. *Doctrine and Covenants* (LDS), sect. 115:5–12. This also reaffirms Joseph Smith's essential role in the construction of the temple "according to the pattern which I shall show" and as the one holding "the keys of this kingdom and ministry." See verses 14–16, 19.

30. Brigham Young discourse, August 1, 1854, in *Journal of Discourses,* 1:364; William Swartzell, *Mormonism Exposed: Being a Journal of a Resident in Missouri* (Pekin, Ohio: n.p., 1840), 40, quoted in Richard L. Anderson, "Joseph Smith's Martyrdom Prophecies and Submission" (Paper in possession of author, 1988), 3.

31. Joseph Smith to the church, December 16, 1838, later printed in *Times and Seasons* 1 (April 1840): 83. See also his account written after deliverance, *Times and Seasons* 1 (November 1839): 7–8.

32. See Esplin, "Emergence of Brigham Young," 359, n. 73.

33. Upon learning of the prophet's death in 1844, Lyman Wight, Joseph Smith's cell-mate in Missouri, informed Wilford Woodruff "that Joseph told him while they were in joal [jail] that he should not live to see forty years but told him not to reveal it untill he was dead" (quoted in *Wilford Woodruff's Journal,* June 28, 1844, 2:432). Such a presentiment helps account for numerous Joseph Smith statements in Nauvoo about impending death. See Richard L. Anderson, "Joseph Smith's Prophecies of Martyrdom," in *The Eighth Annual Sidney B. Sperry Symposium: A Sesquicentennial Look at Church History* (Provo, Utah: Brigham Young University Press, 1980), 1–14.

34. Joseph Smith to Mrs. Norman Bull, March 15, 1839, in Smith, *History of the Church,* 3:286.

35. "Joseph Smith et al., to Bishop Partridge and the Church, March 25, 1839," *Times and Seasons* 1 (July 1840): 132–33.

36. Robert B. Flanders, "Dream and Nightmare: Nauvoo Revisited," in *The Restoration Movement: Essays in Mormon History,* ed. F. Mark McKiernan, Alma R. Blair, and Paul M. Edwards (Lawrence, Kans.: Coronado Press, 1973), 156; Anderson, "Joseph Smith's Martyrdom," 1.

37. Flanders, "Dream and Nightmare," 152.

38. Andrew F. Ehat, ed., " 'They Might Have Known That He Was Not a Fallen Prophet'—The Nauvoo Journal of Joseph Fielding," *Brigham Young University Studies* 19 (Winter 1979): 153–54.

39. *Doctrine and Covenants* (LDS), sect. 124; *Doctrine and Covenants* (RLDS), sect. 107 (January 19, 1841). Contrast this with Far West, where a temple was announced the month following the prophet's arrival.

40. Comments of Joseph Smith, June 27, 1839, in Ehat and Cook, *Words of Joseph Smith,* 4.

41. Joseph Smith sermon, July 19, 1840, recorded by Martha Jane Knowlton Coray, in Dean C. Jessee, ed., "Joseph Smith's 19 July 1840 Discourse," *Brigham Young University Studies* 19 (Spring 1979): 394. See also Ehat and Cook, *Words of Joseph Smith,* 418.

42. Lucy Mack Smith, *Biographical Sketches of Joseph Smith the Prophet and His Progenitors for Many Generations* (Liverpool, England: Published for Orson Pratt by S. W. Richards, 1853; reprint, New York: Arno Press and New York Times, 1969), 267.

43. *Doctrine and Covenants* (LDS), sect. 109:68. See also *Doctrine and Covenants* (LDS), sect. 132:53, 57.

44. *Doctrine and Covenants* (LDS), sect. 124:1-3, 25-28, 34, 39-44; *Doctrine and Covenants* (RLDS), sect. 107: 1, 10, 12. For any concerned that the temple should instead be built in Jackson County, LDS verses 49-51 explain why, given the circumstances, the Lord would "require that work no more" at the present.

45. "History of Brigham Young," 2, Brigham Young Papers, LDS Archives. For a full discussion of this meeting and the sources for it, see Esplin, "Emergence of Brigham Young," 501-4.

46. Willard Richards, Diary, August 16, 1841, Willard Richard Papers, LDS Archives.

47. Quoted in *Wilford Woodruff's Journal,* January 21, 1844, 2:342-43.

48. Ibid., February 21, 1844, 2:351.

49. Danel W. Bachman, "A Study of the Mormon Practice of Plural Marriage before the Death of Joseph Smith" (M.A. thesis, Purdue University, 1975), 74-75.

50. Brigham Young Discourse, October 8, 1866, Brigham Young Papers.

51. The previous year Joseph Smith had begun temple-related baptisms for the dead without a temple. *Doctrine and Covenants* (LDS), sect. 124:28-35, authorizes such baptisms ("which belongeth to my house") outside the temple under certain circumstances. Though not his preference, the prophet now extended this model to include other ordinances. Before the completion of the St. George Temple in 1877, temple ordinances in early Utah were also performed outside temples, first in dedicated rooms and then in a building erected for the purpose.

52. Smith, *History of the Church,* 5:2. Compare this with the prophet's public teaching of some temple-related principles, on July 16, 1843, followed by the declaration "that he could not reveal the fullness of these things untill the Temple is completed" (Ehat and Cooks, *Words of Joseph Smith,* 233).

53. For a brief discussion of how private teachings complicated Nauvoo society, see Ronald K. Esplin, "Joseph, Brigham and the Twelve: A Succession of Continuity," *Brigham Young University Studies* 21 (Summer 1981): 32-36.

54. Heber C. Kimball to Parley P. Pratt, June 17, 1842, Parley P. Pratt Papers, LDS Archives.

55. Minutes of the Nauvoo Relief Society, April 28, 1842, LDS Archives.

56. Ibid.

57. Quoted in *Wilford Woodruff's Journal*, April 9, 1842, 2:167–68.

58. Smith, *History of the Church*, 5:2.

59. Difficulties with John C. Bennett erupted less than ten days after the
 endowments. His excommunication for moral failings prompted a pub-
 exposé" of, among other things, supposed temple-related ritual, making it difficult to continue and, for a season, diverting attention and resources.
In addition to the always heavy demands on him as father, city-father
(replacing John C. Bennett as mayor of Nauvoo), and spiritual head of his
people, there were also unusual demands, such as time spent in hiding to
avoid Missouri enemies and, on one occasion, capture and escape. That
some of those closest to the prophet were not prepared in 1842 to receive
the ordinances also influenced the timetable.

60. Statements to that effect can be found throughout this period. He
told the newly organized Relief Soceity that "inasmuch as the Lord Almighty
has preserved me until today, [he] will continue to preserve me until I fully
accomplished my mission in this life" (Minutes of the Nauvoo Relief Society,
August 31, 1842). In January 1843 he announced that he understood his
mission and that with God as his shield, "I shall not be Sacrificed until my
time Comes then I shall be offered freely" (quoted in *Wilford Woodruff's
Journal*, January 22, 1843, 2:217). "I defy all the world, and I prophecy they
never will overthrow me till I get ready," he declared later that year (Diary
of Joseph Smith kept by Willard Richards, October 15, 1843, Joseph Smith
Papers, LDS Archives). "I cannot lie down until my work is finished," he
said in the spring of 1844, followed the next month by the declaration that
"God will always protect me until my mission is fulfilled" (*Times and Seasons*
6 [August 15, 1844]: 617; Thomas Bullock Minutes, May 12, 1844, LDS
Archives).

61. See "A Summary of Data on the Individuals Who Received the Endow-
ment before Ordinance Work Began in the Nauvoo Temple," in Andrew F.
Ehat, "Joseph Smith's Introduction to Temple Ordinances and the 1844
Mormon Succession Question" (M.A. thesis, Brigham Young University, 1982),
102–3. For a brief overview of ordinance work for the Twelve, see Esplin,
"Joseph, Brigham and the Twelve," 314–16.

62. Esplin, "Joseph, Brigham and the Twelve," 315–17.

63. Undated Certificate of the Twelve, [fall or winter 1844–1845], Brigham
Young Papers. For another version, see Orson Hyde, "Rigdon Trial Minutes,"
Times and Seasons 6 (September 15, 1844): 651.

64. Undated Certificate of the Twelve.

65. Quoted in *Wilford Woodruff's Journal*, April 6, 1844, 2:374.

66. George Laub's account of the June sermon as published in Eugene
England, ed., "George Laub's Nauvoo Journal," *Brigham Young University
Studies* 18 (Winter 1978): 160.

67. Brigham Young discourse, April 16, 1853, in *Journal of Discourses*, 1:132.

2

The Nauvoo Charter: A Reinterpretation

JAMES L. KIMBALL JR.

The Church of Jesus Christ of Latter-day Saints originated in western New York and encountered historic trials and stresses in Ohio and Missouri, but it was in western Illinois that the doctrines and teachings of the church became "set" in basic form and outline. It was also in Illinois that Joseph Smith and his people endeavored to erect a virtual city-state to benefit the church temporally as well as spiritually.

Located on a horseshoe bend in the Mississippi River, Nauvoo, or "beautiful situation or place," had great physical attributes, both real and potential. But the choice of the area as headquarters of the "kingdom" was a result of special concessions granted to the city by the Illinois General Assembly on December 16, 1840, in the form of a city charter.[1]

Among other powers, the Nauvoo City Council was granted authority to pass any laws not repugnant to the Constitution of the United States or the constitution of Illinois. This provision exempted the city fathers from the necessity of adhering to state laws in enacting ordinances, thereby making the Mormon capital truly a state within a state. The Nauvoo city charter also authorized a "city militia," to be composed of citizens between eighteen and forty-five years of age, a city university under control of the city council, and a municipal court with the power to issue writs of habeas corpus.

Clothed with such rights, the Saints felt safe from the fiery darts of their enemies in Missouri and elsewhere. Miscarriages of justice and persecutions would be banished forever, they thought. By the bountiful blessings of the charter, the church would be able to continue the building of the kingdom in long-sought-for peace and security.

Historians have variously disagreed in their views of the charter. The Illinois governor Thomas Ford described its provisions as "unheard of, and anti-republican in many particulars; and capable of infinite abuse by a people disposed to abuse them."[2] Mormon writers, however, have usually viewed the charter as "in some respects unusual, but . . . purely republican."[3] Most Mormons who have written on the subject character- ize the charter as "the most liberal ever granted to any American city."[4] A comparison of the Nauvoo city charter and other Illinois city charters is therefore a prerequisite to understanding the affairs of Mormon Nauvoo and the precedents the Nauvoo charter set for the future history of the church.

Although Illinois had been a state since 1818, the general assembly saw no town or settlement important enough to merit city status until March 1837, when Chicago was chartered as a city.[5] In July of that year, a city charter was also granted to Alton, Chicago's closest rival in popula- tion.[6] Galena achieved city status two years later,[7] followed in 1840 by Springfield, the new state capital, and Quincy, the largest Illinois settlement on the Mississippi River.[8]

The Twelfth Illinois General Assembly, which met from 1840 to 1841, created the Nauvoo city charter in December 1840, and it became effec- tive February 1, 1841.[9] The charter contained twenty-eight sections, to which were attached (in accordance with section 13) the thirty-nine sec- tions of article 5 of the Springfield charter. Neither the longest nor the shortest city charter, the Nauvoo incorporation document was similar in many respects to the other five Illinois city charters granted by the legislature. The Nauvoo charter was the only one of the six, however, to designate the portion of another city charter as a part of its enumerated powers.

All six charters illustrate early nineteenth-century tendencies toward democratization in government. All of the charters, for example, author- ized short terms for city officials: one year in Chicago, Alton, and Galena, and two years in Nauvoo, Springfield, and Quincy.

Suffrage qualifications imposed by the Nauvoo charter were the same as those set forth in Alton's charter—sixty-day residence in the city and six-month residence in the state. Other charters required longer city residence, U.S. citizenship, or ownership of property.

The Nauvoo charter was silent on qualifications for political office, whereas all other city charters (except Chicago's) insisted on U.S. citi- zenship, in addition to certain residence qualifications. The absence of required qualifications for office proved a double boon for the city, since able converts from Canada and England could be pressed into the service of municipal government when desirable. (Of those elected as the first city officers, William Law, a wealthy convert from Canada, be- came one of the nine councillors; British-born John Taylor was one of the city councillors at the time of Joseph Smith's death in 1844).[10] Moreover, the Mormon practice of sending out missionaries meant that many general and local leaders would be absent for varying periods of time in obedience to the call. The elimination of residence requirements for office allowed these leaders to assume an active role in city affairs immediately upon their return to Nauvoo. Apostles Wilford Woodruff and Willard Richards are cases in point. Both were elected city councillors on October 30, 1841, after serving as missionaries for more than a year in Britain. Elder Richards had never been to Nauvoo before the previous August, and Apostle Woodruff returned to the city only three weeks before his election.[11]

The Nauvoo charter had one provision that was significantly different from those of all the other six charters of the period, and that was the section allowing the city council not only to appoint city officers (common in many charters) but also "to remove them from office at pleasure."[12] This feature pointedly illustrates the Mormon wish to protect themselves against any contingency that might seem inimical to their existence as a people in a city of their own creation.

More important than those privileges, however, were the powers contained in the provisions dealing with city government, municipal justice, education, and the militia. Unlike any of the other city councils in Illinois, the Nauvoo City Council was composed of both aldermen and councillors, plus a mayor. The larger number of members on the city council (initially four aldermen and nine councillors) was also unlike the usual pattern of chartered city government found in the state.[13]

Additional research needs to be done to ascertain the exact functions and procedures of the city council, but certain facts do emerge clearly. The right granted to the Nauvoo City Council to pass any ordinance not repugnant to the Constitution of the United States or that of Illinois enabled the Nauvoo City Council to stand in a federated position with the general assembly of the state. Ordinances passed by the Nauvoo City Council could also be in direct violation or disregard of state law and still be valid in Nauvoo provided they did not conflict with the specific powers granted the federal and state governments by their constitutions.[14]

Although this provision seems unusual, the same delegation of authority was also in three of the other five city charters granted up to that time. Legally, Galena, Quincy, and Springfield, as well as Nauvoo, were not bound by state laws or regulations. Since the provision was not unique, we must consider not only its content but also its implementation and the degree to which others assessed its significance.[15]

The Nauvoo Municipal Court was actually the third such city court created by the Illinois General Assembly. The other two were in Chicago and Alton. The court in Nauvoo differed from those of Chicago and Alton, among other ways, in the method of selecting judges. Whereas appointment by the government and approval by the general assembly were authorized for Chicago and Alton, the principal Nauvoo judge was elected mayor of the city. Also, the courts of Alton and Chicago convened under one judge, but the Nauvoo Municipal Court was conducted by the mayor as chief justice and the aldermen as associate justices. The jurisdiction was complex. According to section 16 of the charter, the mayor and aldermen were named justices of the peace in Nauvoo, with jurisdiction in both civil and criminal cases arising under the laws of the *state*. Like justices elsewhere, they held commissions issued by the governor. But, according to section 17, the mayor of Nauvoo was given "exclusive jurisdiction of all cases arising under the ordinances of the corporation." From the mayor's decisions relating to city ordinances, or from any justice-of-the-peace decisions of the mayor or alderman, "appeals . . . may be had to the municipal court." The mayor and aldermen, sitting together as the municipal court, thus heard appeals from their individual decisions. From the municipal court, appeals were taken to the Hancock County Circuit Court, "*Provided,* That the parties litigant shall have a right to trial by jury of twelve men in all cases before the municipal court."

The city courts in Chicago and Alton enjoyed concurrent jurisdiction with the circuit courts of their respective counties in both civil and criminal matters. This authority allowed them to bypass the local circuit courts and left the power of ultimate appeal to the state supreme court. In contrast, the Hancock County Circuit Court was the next avenue of appeal from a decision rendered by the Nauvoo Municipal Court. Legal appeal procedure in Nauvoo, as defined by the legislature, thus had an extra step, a process that might impede or slow justice rather than speed or simplify its motions.

The conclusion might be reached, therefore, that the main value of the court to the Mormons lay in the power the city (rather than the state) had in the selection and appointment of judges. But such was not the case. Rather, its principal value to the Latter-day Saints was its vested right to issue writs of habeas corpus "in all cases arising under the ordinances of the city council."[16] The Saints in Nauvoo were thus free to seek action in courts that were sympathetic to the cause of Zion.

The early nineteenth century was a testing ground on which local units of government—town and county—competed for power and influence with state governments. The privileges and rights of the courts were sought on every level and once gained were not readily given up.

Although the federal courts had the power to grant writs of habeas corpus and state legislatures could delegate such authority, they rarely did so. Before the Nauvoo charter, however, there was precedent for granting city courts the authority to issue writs of habeas corpus. An amendment made on June 1, 1839, to the Alton charter provided that "the judge of the municipal court of the city of Alton shall have power . . . to issue writs of *Habeas Corpus* . . . with the jurisdiction of said court; and the same proceedings shall be had thereon before said judge and course as may be had . . . before the circuit judges and circuit courts of this state."[17] Alton's court thereby limited the power of the Madison County Circuit Court. In Alton and Nauvoo, then, the lesser government unit had influence over the greater one, at least for a time. The Nauvoo court, contrary to previous widespread view, did have state precedent to follow. Although some of its provisions were unique, the powers of the court were well hedged and easily within the era's allowable range of acceptance.

The provision of the Nauvoo charter that authorized the University of the City of Nauvoo did have certain distinctive characteristics. For other colleges in Illinois, all of which were then chartered by the legislature, the boards of trustees were named in the legislative act, but for the University of the City of Nauvoo the city council possessed the authority of initial and perpetual appointment. The university thus became a *city* university.[18] To this writing, no evidence has been found to indicate that the city council imposed any requirements of church membership or activity for university students or faculty.

The members of the board of trustees for the university were also members of the city council, demonstrating clearly the tight control thought desirable by city officials. The trustees had power to adopt any "laws" necessary for the "*welfare and prosperity*" of the university, provided such "laws" were not contrary to the state and federal constitutions. Again, near-autonomous control over city affairs was vouchsafed to the Nauvoo City Council.

Certain powers granted the University of the City of Nauvoo did, however, resemble powers given earlier to Fairfield Institute in Fairfield, Illinois. That institution, founded in 1837, was also granted broad powers to legislate for the "*welfare and prosperity*" of its "collateral institutions, for public instruction." One of the sponsors of both charters was the enigmatic John C. Bennett, M.D.,[19] and he might have been responsible for the similarities in the charters. Baptized a Mormon in 1840, the opportunistic physician was handpicked by Joseph Smith to carry the Nauvoo charter proposals to the state legislature.

Bennett might also have been instrumental in preparing the militia provision of the Nauvoo charter. In the 1830s and 1840s, state authorities encouraged the organization of volunteer military companies, but such units were generally organized on a county rather than a city level. Section 25 of the Nauvoo charter authorized the formation of a military body to be known as the Nauvoo Legion. The unit officers, as with other militia officers in the state, were to receive their commissions from the governor.[20] The charter also created a "court-martial" to be "composed of the commissioned officers of said legion, and constitute the law making department, with full powers and authority to make, ordain, establish and execute all such laws and ordinances as may be considered necessary." Like the city council and university trustees, the court-martial could frame any ordinance not contrary to the Illinois or national Constitution. As a result, the Nauvoo Legion was not obliged to follow state laws regarding military procedure, and in this sense the military body was free from state jurisdiction.[21]

As with the university, a question can be raised about Bennett's influence on the militia provisions of the charter. Shortly after his arrival in Fairfield, Wayne County, Illinois, he and several other individuals were instrumental in obtaining a charter from the legislature in 1837 for incorporating an independent militia company to be known as the "Invincible Dragoons." Within this incorporation act, as within the Nauvoo charter, there was a provision for a court-martial consisting of the "commissioned officers of the corporation; which court shall have full power . . . to pass all such by-laws . . . necessary for the regulation, government and prosperity . . . of the corporation, its officers and privates." Moreover, the power of court-martial for both the dragoon unit and the Nauvoo Legion was limited only by the Constitution of the United States and the Illinois Constitution.[22]

The resemblance between the two charters seems more than coincidental. If one accepts Bennett as the source of the Nauvoo Legion, that section of the charter was not Mormon at all but had its origins in an act passed before the Saints migrated to Illinois. It is ironic that Bennett, who became such a foe of the Mormons, might have been responsible for much of the criticism that the Mormons received on account of the Nauvoo Legion.

The provisions of the Nauvoo charter that have been most often criticized for the power given to the Mormons actually followed provisions of other city charters granted by the Illinois legislature in the early nineteenth century. The charters for Nauvoo, Springfield, and Quincy had almost identical sections devoted to the legislative powers of the city council, for example. Indeed, more than fifty of the fifty-seven sections of the Nauvoo charter were similar to those of other Illinois city charters.

In the autumn of 1840, the Mormon leaders presumably consulted all the previous city charters of the state prior to composing one for Nauvoo. The Mormons might have devised a charter meeting their particular needs even if Dr. Bennett had not come to Nauvoo, but the coincidental arrival of a person who had detailed knowledge of other charters was fortuitous and timely. Later, both Bennett and Joseph Smith claimed credit for the charter. Bennett stated, "I wrote and procured the passage of the . . . charters." Joseph Smith asserted, "The city charter of Nauvoo is of my own plan and device. I concocted it for the salvation of the Church."[23] Whatever merit these assertions may have, the Nauvoo charter provisions were not, as some historians have said, "unheard of." Based solidly on precedents not termed "anti-republican" until the Mormons obtained and used them, the Nauvoo charter still fell short of supplying the Saints with what they so dearly desired. The fault of the city charter lay not so much in its content as in the manner in which it was interpreted and used by the city council. In the wake of the Mormon removal from Illinois, to which the Nauvoo charter had contributed, the Constitutional Convention of 1869 adopted a section that would prohibit the granting of similar charters. The Illinois General Assembly, said the new constitution of 1870, "shall not pass local or special laws . . . granting to any corporation, association or individual any special or exclusive privilege, immunity or franchise whatever."[24] With this action the nineteenth-century Mormon era in Illinois came to an end.

Notes

An earlier version of this essay appeared in the *Journal of the Illinois State Historical Society* 64 (Spring 1971): 66–78.

1. The manuscript copy of the Nauvoo charter, signed by Governor Thomas Carlin, Speaker William L. D. Ewing, and Lieutenant Governor S. H. Anderson, is in the Illinois State Archives, Springfield. The printed transcript appears in several sources, including *Laws of Illinois,* 12 G.A., 52–57; Joseph Smith, *History of the Church of Jesus Christ of Latter-day Saints,* ed. B. H. Roberts (Salt Lake City: Deseret News Press, 1902–12; 6 vols., a seventh volume was published in 1932; reprinted by Deseret Book, 1976, and reissued in paperback in 1978), 4:239–48.

2. Thomas Ford, *History of Illinois: From Its Commencement as a State in 1818 to 1847* (Chicago: S. C. Griggs, 1854), 265.

3. George Q. Cannon, *Life of Joseph Smith, the Prophet* (Salt Lake City: Juvenile Instructor Office, 1888), 341.

4. John Henry Evans, *Joseph Smith, an American Prophet* (New York: Macmillan, 1933), 151. See also Inez Smith Davis, *The Story of the Church* (Inde-

pendence, Mo.: Herald Publishing House, 1934), 260. Those who hold this position might have taken their cue from Joseph Smith, who considered it to be "one of the most liberal charters of the most plenary powers ever conferred by a legislative assembly on free citizens" (Smith, *History of the Church,* 4:268).

5. *Laws of Illinois,* 10 G.A., 81.

6. Ibid., 10 G.A., Special Session, 29.

7. Ibid., 11 G.A., 25.

8. Ibid., 11 G.A., Special Session, 15, 122.

9. Ibid., 12 G.A., 52.

10. *Times and Seasons* (Nauvoo, Ill.) 3 (February 15, 1842): 287; Smith, *History of the Church,* 6:445.

11. Smith, *History of the Church,* 4:402, 429, 442.

12. *Laws of Illinois,* 12 G.A., 53.

13. *Times and Seasons* 2 (February 1, 1841): 309. By December 1841, however, there were eight aldermen and sixteen councillors. Two aldermen and four councillors represented each ward (*Times and Seasons* 3 [December 15, 1841]: 638).

14. *Laws of Illinois,* 12 G.A., 53.

15. See Robert Bruce Flanders, *Nauvoo: Kingdom on the Mississippi* (Urbana: University of Illinois Press, 1965); and James L. Kimball Jr., "A Study of the Nauvoo Charter, 1840–1845" (M.A. thesis, University of Iowa, 1966). The same legislature that granted broad city council power in the Nauvoo charter repealed that section from the Quincy charter (*Laws of Illinois,* 12 G.A., 58).

16. *Laws of Illinois,* 12 G.A., 55.

17. *Incorporation Laws of Illinois,* 11 G.A., 240. The lack of sympathy for a court such as the one in Alton is demonstrated by an amendment to the incorporation act, which provided for the referendum to be held on the question of whether the Alton Municipal Court should be abolished (*Incorporation Laws,* 11 G.A., 241). In August 1839, the citizens of Alton voted to do away with the court (Cecil K. Byrd, *A Bibliography of Illinois Imprints, 1814–1848* [Chicago: University of Chicago Press, 1966], 111).

18. Nauvoo had the only city-operated university in Illinois; the prevalence of city-operated institutions elsewhere in the nation is not known.

19. *Incorporation Laws,* 11 G.A., 124–25. J. C. Bennett was listed as a member of the governing body of the institute. See also Smith, *History of the Church,* 4:168, 169, 172, 177; and John C. Bennett, *The History of the Saints; or, an Expose of Joe Smith and Mormonism* (Boston: Leland and Whiting, 1842), 17.

20. *Laws of Illinois,* 12 G.A., 57. The law authorizing the organization of volunteer companies went into effect March 2, 1837 (ibid., 10 G.A., 165–66). One of these volunteer companies was the Carthage Greys (named after the Hancock County seat).

21. Ibid., 12 G.A., 57.

22. *Incorporation Laws of Illinois,* 11 G.A., 45. J. C. Bennett is the first man named in the list of incorporators, but the Commission Records, which enumerates commissioned officers of the dragoons, does not list "J. C. Bennett" or any variant thereof (Commission Records, 17:109, Illinois State Archives, Springfield). The dragoons were mounted troops.

23. Bennett, *History of the Saints,* 193; Smith, *History of the Church,* 4:249.

24. Art. 4, sec. 22.

3

The Nauvoo Legion, 1840–45: A Unique Military Organization

HAMILTON GARDNER

By the spring of 1839 the Mormons who had been driven out of the state of Missouri had, for the most part, taken refuge in Illinois, where the people extended a sympathetic welcome. The center of their new home was the small town of Commerce on the east bank of the Mississippi in Hancock County. The name of the post office there was changed to Nauvoo on April 21, 1840, and soon thereafter the citizens petitioned the Illinois legislature for a municipal charter. By an act approved December 16, 1840, by Governor Thomas Carlin, the legislature, of which Abraham Lincoln was a member, granted the city of Nauvoo a charter containing some unusually liberal provisions. It was made effective as of the first Monday in February 1841.

One section of that charter authorized the formation of a local militia to be called the Nauvoo Legion. Since the adoption of the Constitution of the United States in 1789, the militia of the states and territories had been governed by law. In no sense had it functioned sui generis. As early as the Second Congress the militia provisions of the Constitution[1] were implemented by an act approved by President George Washington.[2] That act served as the basic charter of the U.S. militia and remained in force without substantial amendment until shortly after the turn of the twentieth century. It provided for the enrollment of "each and every free able-bodied white male citizen ... of the age of eighteen years, and under the age of forty-five years" and required that each man furnish his own arms, ammunition, and equipment. The militia was to "be arranged into divisions, brigades, regiments, battalions and companies, as the legislature of each state shall direct"—a division to be commanded by a major general, a brigade by a brigadier general, a regiment by a lieutenant colonel (later amended to colonel), a battalion by a major, and a company by a captain. No provision was made for a rank higher than major general. The law also prescribed the office of state adjutant general, appointed by the governor of each state, to whom a yearly strength return was to be submitted.

When Illinois became a state on December 3, 1818, its militia organization was governed by article 5 of the state constitution:

Sec. 1. The militia of the State of Illinois shall consist of all free male able bodied persons, negroes, mulattoes and Indians excepted, resident of the State, between the ages of eighteen and forty-five years, except such persons as now are, or hereafter may be exempted by the laws of the United States or this State, and shall be armed, equipped, and trained as the General Assembly may provide by law.

Sec. 2. No person or persons, conscientiously scrupulous of bearing arms shall be compelled to do militia duty in time of peace, provided such person or persons shall pay an equivalent for such exemption.

Sec. 3. Company, battalion and regimental officers, staff officers excepted, shall be elected by the persons composing their several battalions and regiments.

Sec. 4. Brigadier and Major Generals shall be elected by the officers of their brigades and divisions respectively.

Sec. 5. All militia officers shall be commissioned by the Governor, and may hold their commissions during good behavior, or until they arrive at the age of sixty years.

Sec. 6. The militia shall, in all cases, except treason, felony or breach of the peace, be privileged from arrest during their attendance at musters and elections of officers, and in going to and returning from the same.[3]

That constitutional provision was still in effect, without change, in 1840. Most of the militia statutes then in force can be found in the Militia Code of 1833.[4] The code was amended in 1837, 1839, and 1843 and recodified in the *Revised Statutes of 1845* without substantive change.[5]

The 1845 code also closely followed the 1792 act of Congress. As for universal military obligation, it provided that "all free white male inhabitants, resident in this State, who are or shall be of the age of eighteen, and under the age of forty-five years . . . shall severally and respectively be enrolled in the militia . . . and every such person . . . shall . . . provide himself with a good musket, fuzee or rifle. . . . The field officers . . . shall be armed with a sword and a pair of pistols, and the company officers with a sword" (section 1).

Section 2 provided for the organization of the militia in divisions, brigades, regiments, battalions, and companies, according to counties, with Hancock County in the Third Brigade of the Fifth Division. Section 3 set out the officers of the militia, with a major general to head a division; a brigadier general, a brigade; and a colonel, a regiment. It contained no authorization for a rank higher than major general and limited the number of staff officers allowed. A state adjutant general was to be appointed by the governor (section 4), and his duties were prescribed in section 65. Regimental, battalion, and company officers were to be elected by their enrolled enlisted men, and general officers by their commissioned subordinates. Exact rules for conducting the elections were enumerated in sections 7, 11–14, 21, 75–76. An annual muster was required for each regiment in September (section 25) and for each battalion and company in April (sections 26 and 27), in addition to "drill musters" (section 31).

Courts of inquiry and courts-martial were set up for the purpose of investigating and trying military derelictions (sections 37–42), and fines for nonattendance and other offenses were stated (section 32). Provision was made for inducting the militia into state service at the call of the governor (sections 43–50, 52). The authorized uniform of militia officers was to conform to that of the regular army (section 55). Certain independent companies and separate battalions might be formed (sections 8–10, 83) and adopt a constitution and bylaws (sections 76–84).

Such were the federal and state constitutional and statutory foundations of the Nauvoo Legion, which was authorized in section 25 of the Nauvoo city charter, granted by the Twelfth Illinois General Assembly:

> Sec. 25. The City Council may organize the inhabitants of said city, subject to military duty, into a body of independent military men to be called the "Nauvoo Legion," the Court Martial of which shall be composed of the commissioned officers of said Legion, and constitute the law making department, with full powers and authority to make, ordain, establish, and execute, all such laws and ordinances as may be considered necessary for the benefit, government, and regulation of said Legion; *Provided*, said Court Martial shall pass no law or act repugnant to, or inconsistent with, the Constitution of the United States or of this State; and; *Provided, also*, that the officers of the Legion shall be commissioned by the Governor of the State. The said Legion shall perform the same amount of military duty as is now or may be hereafter required of the regular militia of the State, and shall be at the disposal of the Mayor in executing the laws and ordinances of the City Corporation, and laws of the State, and at the disposal of the Governor for the public defence, and the execution of the laws of the State or of the United States, and shall be entitled to their propor-

tion of the public arms; and *Provided, also,* that said Legion shall be exempt from all other military duty.[6]

Apparent at once to the military student is the incongruity of the provision that made the commissioned officers into a body with extensive law-making powers and called, inexactly, the "Court Martial." In the U.S. Army a court-martial has always been a judicial entity, functioning only (1) to hear the cases of military accused of violating the Articles of War, (2) to determine innocence or guilt, and (3) to fix the prescribed sentence. It accesses and exercises no legislative duties whatsoever. Neither does an army court-martial perform any executive functions; those remain attributes of command. A further departure from customary militia practice was granting authority to the mayor to call out the Nauvoo Legion to enforce city laws. (The later exercise of this prerogative proved to be one of the direct causes for the suppression of the Nauvoo Legion.) In considering the peculiar nature of these provisions, we must not forget they were approved by the Illinois legislature.

The Nauvoo City Council implemented this legislative grant of power in an ordinance passed on February 8, 1841:

Sec. 1. Be it ordained by the City Council of the City of Nauvoo, of the inhabitants of the City of Nauvoo, and such citizens of Hancock county as may unite by voluntary enrollment, be, and they are hereby organized into a body of independent military men, to be called the "Nauvoo Legion," as contemplated in the 25th section of "An act to incorporate the City of Nauvoo," approved December 16, 1840.

Sec. 2. The Legion shall be, and is hereby divided into two cohorts; the horse troops to constitute the first cohort, and the foot troops to constitute the second cohort.

Sec. 3. The general officers of the Legion shall consist of a lieutenant-general, as the chief commanding and reviewing officer, and president of the court martial and Legion; a major-general, as the second in command in the Legion, the secretary of the court martial and Legion, and adjutant and inspector-general; a brigadier general, as the commander of the first cohort; and a brigadier general, as commander of the second cohort.

Sec. 4. The staff of the lieutenant-general shall consist of two principal aides-de-camp, with the rank of colonels of cavalry, and a guard of twelve aides-de-camp, with the rank of captain of infantry; and a drill officer, with the rank of colonel of dragoons, who shall likewise be the chief officer of the guard.

Sec. 5. The staff of the major-general shall consist of an adjutant, a surgeon-in-chief, a cornet, a quarter-master, a paymaster, a commissary, and a chaplain, with the rank of colonels of infantry; a surgeon for each cohort, a quarter-master-sergeant, sergeant-major, and chief musician, with the rank of captains of light infantry, and two musicians, with the rank of captains of infantry.

Sec. 6. The staff of each brigadier-general shall consist of one aide-de-camp, with the rank of lieutenant-colonel of infantry, provided that the said brigadiers shall have access to the staff of the major-general, when not otherwise in service.

Sec. 7. No officers shall hereafter be elected by the various companies of the Legions, except upon the nomination of the court-martial; and it is hereby made the duty of the court-martial to nominate at least two candidates for each vacant office, whenever such vacancies occur.

Sec. 8. The court-martial shall fill and supply all officers ranking between captains and brigadier-generals by granting brevet commissions to the most worth company officers of the line, who shall thereafter take rank, and command according to the date of their brevets, provided that their original place in the line shall not thereby be vacated.

Sec. 9. The court-martial, consisting of all the military officers, commissioned or entitled to commissions, within the limits of the city corporations, shall meet at the office of Joseph Smith, on Thursday, the 4th day of February, 1841, at 10 o'clock A.M.; and then and there proceed to elect the general officers of the Legion, as contemplated in the 3rd section of this ordinance.

Sec. 10. The court-martial shall adopt for the Legion, as nearly as may be, and so far as applicable, the discipline, drill, uniform, rules, and regulations of the United States army.

Passed February 8, 1841.

John C. Bennett, Mayor.

James Sloan, Recorder.[7]

Responsibility for this ordinance rested, of course, with the municipal council, not with the state legislature.

Even though the last paragraph asserted that the Legion should conform to the "discipline, drill, uniform, rules, and regulations of the United States army," it contained several military anomalies. The most unorthodox provision was the elaboration of the court-martial system. Not only was the court-martial authorized to enact military laws and regulations, as originally provided, but it was now empowered to nominate officers for original commissions and promotions. Unquestionably, this method of electing officers represented a departure from the procedure practiced universally in the militia of the states and territories. Whether it actually violated the United States Act of 1792, the constitution of Illinois, and the Illinois Militia Code is a legal question not of particular importance here, because it was accepted by the state militia authorities.

Although sections 8 to 10 and 83 of the Militia Code authorized the formation of independent companies and separate battalions, and sections 76 and 84 empowered those units to adopt constitutions and by-laws for their "regulation and government," the city militia ordinance contemplated a military setup vastly larger than a company or battalion. As a matter of practical fact, no such thing as an *independent* unit has ever existed in the armed forces of the United States, whether civilian militia or the professional army. Each body is a component part of an overall organization, subject to command and discipline in accordance with federal and state constitutions and laws. (This very independence later proved to be one of the factors that brought about the undoing of the Nauvoo Legion.)

The nomenclature was in some respects also unique. Ancient Rome first used the term *legion,* applying it to a body of about ten thousand soldiers. A *cohort* was one-tenth of a legion. Major General Henry Knox, secretary of war in the cabinet of President Washington, directed on December 27, 1792, that both the army and the militia be divided into legions and sublegions, but the plan was never implemented in the militia and had only indifferent success with the regulars. It was discarded officially May 30, 1796.[8] The cohort was never used. Just why these titles were adopted in Nauvoo is not known. Similarly, the special staff function of "drill officers" has never been used in the U.S. Army, since all officers in command of units, large or small, are presumed to be qualified to drill and train them.

The ordinance specified that the commander of the Nauvoo Legion was to hold the rank of lieutenant general. Since the city charter granted by the legislature was silent on that point, it became a subject of bitter dispute later. Except for George Washington, no officer in the U.S. Army, either regular or militia, had held the permanent lineal rank of lieutenant general up to that time.[9] In 1847 Winfield Scott received the honorary rank of brevet lieutenant general for his service in the Mexican War,[10] but he did not acquire higher command functions, for in the line he remained a major general. In the Civil War it required a special act of Congress to promote Ulysses S. Grant to the permanent rank of lieutenant general.[11] The act of 1792 provided for no rank beyond major general. The highest rank mentioned in the Illinois Constitution and statutes was that of major general, in command of a division. The matter may be considered academic, however, because Illinois Adjutant General Moses K. Anderson recommended that Joseph Smith be appointed a lieutenant general; Secretary of State Lyman Trumbull issued the commission; and Governor Thomas Carlin signed it. Just why all this was done still remains unexplained.

The original city militia ordinance did not mention age limits for military obligation in Nauvoo, but the question was clarified on February 20, 1841, when the court-martial adopted a resolution fixing the usual limits of eighteen and forty-five years. This same enactment set up a scale of fines for nonattendance at musters and ceremonies.[12]

The organization of a military force usually starts with lower echelons and proceeds upward; this method seems to have been followed in the early stages of the Nauvoo Legion. "The Legion at its organization," Joseph Smith stated, "was composed of six companies."[13]

The official records of commissions issued to Illinois militia officers were maintained in the office of the state adjutant general and are now in the Illinois State Archives. Although they are not complete for the period 1840 to 1845, rosters containing data on almost one thousand officers, including those of the Nauvoo Legion, were made available for this study.[14] Unfortunately, the muster rolls and returns showing the names and numbers of noncommissioned officers and privates have not been preserved.

One of the earliest rosters of officers in the original Nauvoo Legion companies and battalions was dated "Springfield March 23rd 1841" and certified as correct by Adjutant General Anderson.[15] The list contains the names and ranks of seventy-six officers, many of whom subsequently became important figures in Utah history. At least five were members of the Mormon Battalion in the Mexican War.[16]

The high command of the Nauvoo Legion was activated Thursday, February 4, 1841, at "a court-martial, composed of the commissioned officers of the state of Illinois, within the city of Nauvoo, assembled at the office of Joseph Smith." One lieutenant general, one major general, and two brigadier generals, all church leaders, were elected "by unanimous vote of the court-martial."[17] Joseph Smith was chosen lieutenant general; John C. Bennett, major general; and Wilson Law and Don Carlos Smith, brigadiers.[18]

With a nucleus of four companies each, regimental organizations were effected May 1 and July 3. The following officers were elected:

> FIRST COHORT. *First Regiment*—George Miller, colonel; Stephen Markham, lieutenant colonel; William Wightman, major. *Second Regiment* —George Coulson, colonel; Josiah Ells, lieutenant colonel; Hyrum Kimball, major. . . .
> SECOND COHORT. *First Regiment*—Charles C. Rich, colonel; Titus Billings, lieutenant colonel; John Scott, major. *Second Regiment*—Francis M. Higbee, colonel; Nelson Higgins, lieutenant colonel; Aaron Golden, major. *Third Regiment*—Samuel Bent, colonel; George Morey, lieutenant colonel; William Niswanger, major.[19]

As far as is known, the Nauvoo Legion held its first parade and review on Tuesday, April 6, 1841.[20] Later in the year similar ceremonies were conducted by the commanding general, but no muster rolls or strength reports of these assemblies are now in the adjutant general's files.

On August 10 the Nauvoo Legion headquarters issued a general order reporting the death of Brigadier General Don Carlos Smith, the youngest brother of Joseph Smith. The younger Smith had headed the Second Cohort, whose commissioned officers elected Charles C. Rich to fill the vacancy caused by his death.[21]

Other Nauvoo Legion officers elected about the time Smith died are listed in an unsigned letter to the adjutant general, dated August 11, 1841. Among them were "Sidney Rigdon, Judge Advocate of the Nauvoo Legion"; "Samuel Hix, Armour-bearer to the Major General of the Nauvoo Legion"; "Brigham Young, H. C. Kimball, P. P. Pratt, Orson Pratt, Orson Hyde, John E. Page, Assistant Chaplains of the 1st Cohort;" and "John Taylor, W. Woodruff, W. Smith, W. Richards, G. A. Smith, & W. Marks . . . Assistant Chaplains, 2 Cohort." Eleven of these twelve chaplains were members of the Quorum of Twelve Apostles of the Latter-day Saints church; Marks, though a high church official, was not an apostle.[22]

The last list of commissions in the file of the adjutant general for 1841 contains the names of Wilson Law, Hyrum Smith, William Law, George Miller, A. P. Rockwood, Lyman Wight, and George Robinson—all brevet major generals.[23] Others on the roster were Edward Hunter (later of the Mormon Battalion), designated "Herald and Armor Bearer to Lieut Gen," and John Taylor, judge advocate.[24]

Such were the beginnings of the Nauvoo Legion of Illinois. As of September 11, 1841, its strength was 1,490 men.[25] During 1842 the citizens of Nauvoo continued to expand their militia; by May 7 the Nauvoo Legion had twenty-six companies and "about two thousand troops."[26] On that date Lieutenant General Smith held a parade and review in honor of distinguished visitors, including Judge Stephen A. Douglas. Shortly thereafter, Major General John C. Bennett was excommunicated from the church, ousted from the office of mayor of Nauvoo, and shorn of his military rank. Wilson Law was elected major general in his place, with an August 13 date of rank. The report to the adjutant general of Law's election was made on August 17, by James Sloan, " 'War Secretary' of the Legion."[27]

The files of the adjutant general's office contain numerous other 1842 rosters of officers elected and commissioned. A June 16 roster included Sloan as "War Secretary to the Major General"; "James Brown [subsequently captain, Company C, Mormon Battalion], Lieutenant Colonel 4 Regiment, 2 Cohort"; "William Pitt [an early band leader in Utah], Musician to the Nauvoo Legion"; and "Charles C. Rich, Brevet Major General June 3, 1842."[28] Commissions were also issued in that month to "George Cooke—Surgeon General of the Nauvoo Legion—with the title Major General" and "Hiram Kimball Major General."[29]

The year 1843 witnessed still further growth of the Nauvoo Legion. On April 24 Secretary of War Sloan sent the adjutant general a list that contained the name of Nelson Higgins (later captain of Company D in the Mormon Battalion), who was to be commissioned "Colonel, 2 Regiment, 2 Cohort—from July 30th 1843"; and on May 6 Hosea Stout, an early attorney general of the Utah Territory, became colonel of the Fifth Regiment, Second Cohort.[30]

Late in the year, in view of impending trouble, Joseph Smith, as mayor of Nauvoo, instructed Major General Law to hold necessary portions of the Nauvoo Legion in readiness "to compel obedience to the ordinances of said city and secure the peace of the citizens."[31] The instructions were repeated in substance on December 18, 1843.[32]

It is virtually impossible, because of a lack of relevant data, to judge the Nauvoo Legion as a military unit with respect to efficiency, discipline, equipment, armament, uniforms, and readiness for field service. The remaining records of the state adjutant general supply no information on the number and nature of drills and musters or maneuvers—if any. Nor is anything known of the state of discipline in the Nauvoo Legion. In general, discipline in the militia of the United States during this period was not conspicuous for its effectiveness. Yet it is reasonable to assume that the requirement of strict obedience to leadership in the church hierarchy probably also manifested itself in the Nauvoo Legion.

As for the state of training, any conclusions must remain highly speculative. In 1843 Nauvoo still stood on the edge of the western frontier. It might be inferred, therefore, that the native-born Americans, who almost exclusively constituted the membership of the Nauvoo Legion, knew how to shoot and had some skill in horsemanship. If the Nauvoo Legion had taken to the field for extended service, it would no doubt have stood out as a notable exception to the other militia of the time.

No reliable facts are available about the auxiliary services of the Nauvoo Legion—supply, ordnance, or medical care. The Illinois Militia Code required uniforms similar to those of the regular forces. Whether the Nauvoo Legion wore uniforms at its parades and reviews is unknown, and photography was not sufficiently advanced to leave any evidence on the point. If the Nauvoo Legion behaved in accordance with the practice of contemporaneous militia bodies, however, the high-ranking officers probably appeared in colorful and flamboyant dress, while the enlisted men made shift with such homemade accoutrements and clothing as they could piece together. For the most part the militiamen supplied their own weapons; the War Department and the state of Illinois did furnish some armament. Governor Thomas Ford stated that "the Legion had been furnished with three pieces of cannon and about two hundred and fifty stand of small arms; which popular rumor increased to the number of thirty pieces of cannon and five or six thousand stand of muskets."[33]

In one characteristic, however, the fully developed Nauvoo Legion stood out as unique among U.S. militia organizations: the large proportion of generals to privates. Although the Illinois Militia Code provided for only six major generals (to command the state's six divisions), the Nauvoo Legion had at least thirteen officers of that lofty rank and an even greater number of brigadiers. One of Utah's most distinguished soldiers, Brigadier General Richard W. Young, declared that "the Nauvoo Legion was a very top heavy corps. The staffs of the general officers were unusually large and somewhat fantastic."[34]

The troubles of the Mormon people erupted with violence in 1844. This study is not concerned with these difficulties except as the Nauvoo Legion was involved. With the influx of new converts Nauvoo had experienced a phenomenally rapid growth. It now claimed to be the largest city in Illinois, with a population of at least twelve thousand and perhaps as high as twenty thousand. The Nauvoo Legion had mushroomed in proportion, attaining an estimated five thousand members. The non-Mormon citizens in the surrounding area looked with some apprehension at the Mormons' independent armed body, which Governor Ford called "a military force at their own command."[35]

Not only was persecution raging from without, but serious defections were occurring within the church itself. Already John C. Bennett and Sidney Rigdon had apostatized. They were soon followed by Wilson Law and William Law, the former being the Nauvoo Legion's ranking major general. Soon thereafter, with several members of the Higbee and Foster families, the Laws started a newspaper called the *Expositor*. The city council regarded the first and only edition of June 7 as so scurrilous that on June 10 it declared the paper a public nuisance and authorized the mayor to have it abated. The mayor directed the city marshal to destroy the *Expositor* press and to order Jonathan Dunham, acting major general, to use the Nauvoo Legion in assisting the marshal, "if called upon to do so."[36] By eight o'clock that night the marshal reported back to the mayor that he had destroyed the newspaper's press and equipment.

So far as the Nauvoo Legion was concerned, this event marked the beginning of the end. Anti-Mormons accused it of being the instrument used to suppress the *Expositor.* According to Governor Ford, the "rejected Mormons" went to Carthage, where they took out warrants against the mayor and council for riot; these officials were arrested but were released by the city court on a writ of habeas corpus. Meanwhile, the greatest excitement prevailed. The Nauvoo Legion was called out, and the city was placed under martial law. Finally, Governor Ford personally went to Hancock County, where a force of armed Illinois militia, estimated at between sixteen hundred and eighteen hundred men, had mobilized—still small when compared with the Nauvoo Legion.

From Carthage the governor sent word to Smith and the council that if they surrendered, they would be protected. Otherwise, he said, "the whole force of the States would be called out . . . to compel their submission."[37] As a result, Joseph Smith and his brother Hyrum agreed to submit to arrest on charges of inciting a riot and went to Carthage, where they were incarcerated in the Hancock County jail. On June 27, having ordered most of the militia disbanded, Governor Ford went to Nauvoo, accompanied by two of the three Illinois militia companies still on active duty. While he was gone, the prisoners at Carthage, who were under the ostensible protection of the Carthage Grays (a local militia company), were attacked by a mob of approximately two hundred armed men, and Joseph and Hyrum Smith were killed.[38]

The death of the leader of the Latter-day Saints marked the virtual end of the Nauvoo Legion. Only two documents concerning the unit are in the files of the adjutant general after that time. The first is related to Brigham Young's succession to the command of the organization (see figure 3–1).[39] The other is a roster listing commissions for one major and seventeen junior officers.[40]

The bitter feeling that now ran rampant in the Nauvoo area was reflected in high places in the state, and, in January 1845, the Illinois legislature repealed the city charter. That action terminated the legal authority of the Nauvoo Legion, and it became officially dead.

But the Latter-day Saints did not forget their military unit in "Nauvoo the Beautiful." In 1849, three years after leaving Illinois for a new home in the Rocky Mountains, they formed the provisional State of Deseret and created, as part of the government, a comprehensive militia force, called unofficially the Nauvoo Legion. The title became legal in 1852 through one of the earliest statutes of the newly founded Utah Territory. The Nauvoo Legion flourished under that name until 1870, when its activities were prohibited by proclamation of the territorial governor, J. Wilson Shaffer. Congress finally abolished the Nauvoo Legion in 1887, but it was revived in 1894 as the National Guard of Utah.

ADJUTANT GENERALS OFFICE
SPRINGFIELD SEPT 23RD 1844

Officers Names	Rank	Cohort	Date of Rank
Brigham Young	Lieut General	Nauvoo Legion	31st August 1844
Charles C. Rich	Major General	"	"
Jonathan Dunham	Brigadier Gen	2 Cohort Nauvoo Legion	14th Sept 1844

I hereby certify the foregoing list of officers to be correct as appears from election returns filed in my office

M K Anderson Adjt Gen
By James Shepherd

Indorsed   1844 Militia Returns Nauvoo Legion Dec 16

Figure 3-1

Notes

An earlier version of this essay appeared in the *Journal of the Illinois State Historical Society* 55 (Summer 1961): 181–97.

1. Art. 1, sec. 8; Art. 2, sec. 2; and the Second Amendment.
2. *U.S. Statutes at Large* 1 (May 8, 1792): 271–74.
3. Published as part of *Revised Statutes, 1845* (Springfield, Ill.: State of Illinois, 1845), 36.
4. The Illinois Militia Code of 1833 was printed separately and not included in the *Revised Statutes* of that year.
5. *Revised Statutes*, 355–78, deals with the Illinois military forces in eighty-five sections.
6. *Laws of Illinois, 1840–1841*, 57. The entire charter is also set forth in Joseph Smith, *History of the Church of Jesus Christ of Latter-day Saints*, ed. B. H. Roberts (Salt Lake City: Deseret News Press, 1902–12; 6 vols., a seventh volume was published in 1932; reprinted by Deseret Book, 1976, and reissued in paperback in 1978), 4:239–46.
7. Smith, *History of the Church*, 4:293–94.
8. William Addleman Ganoe, *The History of the United States Army* (New York: Macmillan, 1942), 99–103.
9. It is a matter of almost universal knowledge that on June 15, 1775, the Continental Congress designated George Washington as commander in chief of the American Revolutionary Army with the rank of general. It is less well known that President John Adams on July 3, 1798, commissioned Washington a lieutenant general in the U.S. Army. The first president held this rank until he died on December 14, 1799 (Francis B. Heitman, *History Register*

and Dictionary of the United States Army from Its Organization September 29, 1789, to March 2, 1903 [Washington, D.C.: Government Printing Office, 1903], 1:1004–7).

10. Ibid., 1:870.

11. The act was approved on February 28, 1864 (Ulysses S. Grant, *Personal Memoirs of U. S. Grant* [New York: Charles L. Webster and Co., 1885–86], 2:114–15; *U.S. Statutes at Large* 13 [February 29, 1864]: 11–12).

12. Smith, *History of the Church,* 4:300.

13. Ibid., 4:296.

14. I am greatly obliged to Margaret C. Norton, former assistant state archivist of Illinois, who very courteously furnished a microfilm of these returns to me. Excerpts from the original records of the adjutant general will be cited hereafter as Ill. AGO.

15. Ill. AGO.

16. For a brief history and bibliography of the Mormon Battalion, see the "Report of Lieut. Col. P. St. George Cooke of His March from Santa Fe, New Mexico, to San Diego, Upper California," ed. Hamilton Gardner, *Utah Historical Quarterly* 22 (January 1954): 15–40. This is a reprint from House Executive Document 41, 30 Cong., special session, 1848, 551–63.

17. The details are set forth in Smith, *History of the Church,* 4:295–96.

18. The commissions for Law and the two Smiths are listed on a March 10 roster certified by Adjutant General Anderson and filed March 20, 1841; Bennett's commission was recorded on a roster dated February 16 and filed June 14. All the commissions were effective as of February 5. Ill AGO.

19. Smith, *History of the Church,* 4:353, 382.

20. Ibid., 4:326, 382.

21. Ibid., 4:400, 414.

22. Ill. AGO, "filed October 16, 1841."

23. Ill. AGO, "filed December 14, 1841."

24. Ibid.

25. Smith, *History of the Church,* 4:415.

26. Ibid., 5:3.

27. Ill. AGO.

28. Ill. AGO, June 6, 1842.

29. Adjutant General to the Secretary of State, June 20, 1842, in Ill. AGO.

30. Ill. AGO.

31. Smith, *History of the Church,* 6:104.

32. Ibid., 6:120.

33. Thomas Ford, *History of Illinois: From Its Commencement as a State in 1818 to 1847* (Chicago: S. C. Griggs, 1854), 268.

34. Richard W. Young, "The Nauvoo Legion," *The Contributor* (Salt Lake City) 9 (Winter 1888–89): 42. This was an official publication of the church, later suspended. General Young's articles deal primarily with the Indian campaigns in early Utah. A grandson of Brigham Young's, he graduated

from West Point, class of 1882, and from Columbia Law School. Upon retirement in 1889, he practiced law in Salt Lake City but returned to active duty during the Spanish-American War, serving in the Philippines with the Utah Volunteer Batteries. During World War I, he again became colonel and brigadier general, Fortieth Division, in France. He died in 1920.

35. Ford, *History of Illinois,* 265. On the population of Nauvoo, see the *Dictionary of American History* (New York: Scribner's, 1940), 4:68.

36. Smith, *History of the Church,* 6:432. See also Ford, *History of Illinois,* 323-32.

37. Ford, *History of Illinois,* 332. See also Ford's letter to Smith in Smith, *History of the Church,* 6:533-37.

38. George R. Gaylor, "Governor Ford and the Death of Joseph and Hyrum Smith," *Journal of the Illinois State Historical Society* 50 (Winter 1957): 391-411.

39. Ill. AGO, September 23, 1844.

40. Ibid., December 12, 1844.

4

The Political Kingdom of God as a Cause of Mormon-Gentile Conflict

KLAUS J. HANSEN

The afternoon of October 30, 1838, saw one of the most brutal butcheries of men and children ever to occur in the annals of the state of Missouri. At about four o'clock, relates Joseph Young, one of the eyewitnesses, "a large company of armed men, on horses" advanced toward a mill on Shoal Creek, where about thirty Mormon families had gathered for refuge. Defenseless, the Saints scattered, some into the woods, others into a blacksmith shop. Overtaken by the mob, nineteen men and boys were killed, a dozen wounded. One nine-year-old boy had found refuge under the bellows. Discovered by a mobster, the child was killed by a gun-blast to the head. Boasted the butcher afterwards, "Nits will make lice, and if he had lived he would have become a Mormon."[1]

The shots of the Haun's Mill massacre were to keep ringing in the ears of the Saints, reminding them that Satan was fighting with real bullets against the kingdom of God, a kingdom that, if not of this world, nevertheless marched vigorously and militantly in it. Persecution, then, was to be expected. It had been with the church from the publication of Joseph Smith's first revelation; it was to continue throughout the history of the church in the nineteenth century. Joseph himself was to seal his testimony with his blood. Even the exodus to the Rocky Mountains would not silence the voice of persecution. Not until the Saints submitted to the government demands for the abolition of plural marriage was the conflict between the church and the world to diminish, finally to end.

To the faithful Saint, the problem of historical causation found a simple and straightforward answer. As already implied, Satan would inevitably have to oppose the work of God; this opposition became in itself one of the touchstones for the divinity of the work; and the blood of the martyrs was transformed into seed for the church.

In addition to such considerations, the historian should search for other objective, historical elements of causation. In the history of Mormon-Gentile relations, one of the most significant institutions contributing to the conflict has so far received altogether too little, if any, attention. This institution is the political kingdom of God.

First of all, then, the development of the political kingdom of God in Mormon history will have to be outlined. Space limitations will obviously limit the comprehensiveness and scope of this investigation, a task made even more difficult by the fact that large stretches of the course of the political kingdom of God are still uncharted.[2] However, a sampling of incidences of conflict at certain crucial periods of church history suggests general trends.

It should be remembered that in history beliefs are as important as facts. Whether Joseph Smith actually planned treasonable action against the United States fades into a pale academic question before the bullets of assassins who believed that this was so, irrespective of fact. Likewise, the political kingdom of God caused persecution more by its distorted image in the eyes of its enemies than by the actual ideals and realities it represented in the eyes of its adherents and defenders.

The strong emphasis on the millennial kingdom in Mormon thought has led some writers to believe that the idea of a political kingdom preceding the Second Coming of Christ was never entertained by the Saints. Mormonism was not to establish a temporal kingdom but to wait for Christ.[3] This erroneous notion might have arisen partly because it is extremely difficult to differentiate between the apocalyptic kingdom and its predecessor. Since the one was to lead to the other, they were to be almost identical in nature, at least theoretically. The main difference between the two was mostly a matter of chronology. The one would be the kingdom militant, struggling against a hostile world; the other was the kingdom victorious, having subdued all its enemies. The political kingdom, then, was organized because the Mormons did not believe that, without some preparation, they could wait for Christ to establish his world government. The Saints might have believed in miracles, but they were also of a practical mind and thus believed in aiding the Lord as much as they could. Seen in this context, the efforts of the Saints to establish a political kingdom in preparation for the apocalyptic kingdom became the application of the belief that, while individuals can accomplish nothing without the aid of the Lord, God only helps those who help themselves. John Taylor expressed this idea in his remark, "It is not all a matter of faith, but there is some action required; it is a thing that we have to engage in ourselves."[4]

Thus, the Saints had been engaged in temporal matters almost from the day the church was founded. They had gained experience in government in Kirtland, Missouri, in Nauvoo, and, most of all, in Deseret. "The Time will come," predicted George Q. Cannon at a missionary conference in 1862,

> when . . . [the elders] will be called to act in a different ambassadorial capacity. The nations are not going to be all destroyed at once, as many have imagined; but they are going to stand and continue to some extent with their governments; and the kingdom of God is not all the time to continue its present theological character alone, but is to become a political power, known and recognized by the powers of the earth; and you, my brethren, may have to be sent forth to represent that power as its accredited agents. . . . Young men now here today may be chosen to go forth and present God's kingdom. You may be called to appear and represent it at the courts of foreign nations.[5]

Cannon failed to tell his audience that the kingdom of God had already embarked on its political course almost twenty years earlier.

In the spring of 1844, Reuben Hedlock, president of the British mission, received a letter from Brigham Young and Willard Richards in which the writers informed him that "the kingdom is organized; and although as yet no bigger than a grain of mustard seed, the little plant is in a flourishing condition, and our prospects brighter than ever."[6] Such news must have seemed strange to a man who had been actively engaged in furthering the "kingdom" for some time, unless the term *kingdom* expressed here a more specific meaning than in its usual context, which equated it with the church in both its spiritual and temporal manifestations. Young and Richards were, indeed, referring to the political kingdom of God, whose governing body had been organized on March 11, 1844, as the Council of Fifty by the Prophet Joseph Smith himself.[7] According to one of its members, this council was "the Municipal department of the Kingdom of God set up on the Earth, and from which all Law emanates, for the rule, government & control of all Nations Kingdoms & toungs and People under the whole Heavens."[8] To prepare itself for this ambitious mission, the council, under the leadership of Joseph Smith, met regularly in Nauvoo to discuss principles of government and political theory. Before the prophet's death, "a full and complete organization" of the political kingdom of God had been effected.[9] The basic law of this world government, received through revelation, resembled the Constitution of the United States.

In keeping with a strong Mormon emphasis on the doctrine of individual rights, non-Mormons were to represent the Gentiles in the government of the kingdom. Whether Gentiles actually sat as members of the Council of Fifty is difficult to ascertain, but the possibility points up a significant distinction between the church and the political kingdom. When, after the death of Joseph Smith, George Miller and Alexander Badlam wanted to "call together the Council of Fifty and organize the Church," the apostles George A. Smith and Willard Richards could inform the two petitioners "that the Council of Fifty was not a Church organization." Membership in that group was irrespective of religious beliefs; "the organization of the Church belonged to the Priesthood alone."[10] If the distinction between the church and the political kingdom seemed important in one sense, in another it was highly theoretical, for the leading officers of both organizations were identical.

When David Patten became the first apostolic martyr of the church at the battle of Crooked River in Missouri in October 1838, the doctrine of the political kingdom of God apparently had not been fully formulated. Yet even at this time the suspected Mormon ambitions to establish a political kingdom of God figured prominently in the expulsion of the Saints from Missouri. The testimonies of a number of apostate Mormons before Judge Austin A. King in Richmond, Ray County, in 1838 insisted that Joseph Smith had in mind to establish a temporal kingdom of God. These testimonies, given by enemies of the church, can hardly be considered accurate and unbiased. Some of them are obvious distortions of Joseph's plans, such as George M. Hinkle's assertion, "The general teachings of the presidency were, the kingdom they were setting up was a *temporal* as well as a spiritual kingdom; that it was the little stone spoken of by Daniel. Until lately, the teachings of the church appeared to be peaceable, and that the kingdom was to be set up peaceably; but lately a different idea has been advanced—the time had come when this kingdom was to be set up by forcible means, if necessary."[11] In the light of subsequent events, the temporal if peaceful plans of Joseph Smith cannot be denied.

That Joseph Smith insisted on leadership in both spiritual and temporal matters also caused some internal difficulties in the church. Refusal to acknowledge the authority of the church in temporal matters played an important role in the excommunication of Oliver Cowdery. Answering charges "for virtually denying the faith by declaring that he would not be governed by any ecclesiastical authority or revelations whatever in his temporal affairs,"[12] Cowdery declared:

> The very principle of . . . [ecclesiastical authority in temporal affairs]
> I conceive to be couched in an attempt to set up a kind of petty

government, controlled and dictated by ecclesiastical influence, in the midst of this national and state government. You will, no doubt, say this is not correct, but the bare notice of these charges, over which you assume a right to decide is, in my opinion, a direct attempt to make the secular power subservient to church direction—to the correctness of which I cannot in conscience subscribe—I believe that the principle never did fail to produce anarchy and confusion.[13]

Few of the Saints shared Cowdery's objections, however. Neither did the temporal claims of Joseph Smith deter the influx of converts to the city of Nauvoo after the expulsion of the Saints from Missouri, in spite of the fact that civil and ecclesiastical government were practically identical in that city. To the faithful Saints, who were building the kingdom of God by building their city, it might have been difficult to imagine how it could have been otherwise. They would therefore see no incongruity when their prophet made the celebration of the eleventh anniversary of the organization of the church the occasion for not only laying the cornerstone of their new temple but also showing himself as head of the Nauvoo Legion in an impressive display of newly acquired temporal power. Carried away by their enthusiasm, the Saints believed that in time this power would be able "to rescue the American Republic from the brink of ruin."[14] Exulted the *Latter-day Saints' Millennial Star*, "Nauvoo . . . is the nucleus of a glorious dominion of universal liberty, peace and plenty; it is an organization of that government of which there shall be no end—of that kingdom of Messiah which shall roll forth, from conquering and to conquer until it shall be said, that '*the kingdoms of this world are become the kingdoms of our Lord, and of His Christ,*' 'AND THE SAINTS OF THE MOST HIGH SHALL POSSESS THE GREATNESS OF THE KINGDOM UNDER THE WHOLE HEAVEN.' "[15]

The editor of the *Latter-day Saints' Millennial Star* most likely did not know that shortly before this article appeared Joseph Smith had received his revelation concerning world government and the organization of the Council of Fifty.[16] Gentiles, of course, were even less informed about Joseph Smith's plans for the organization of the political kingdom of God. After the Council of Fifty had been organized in 1844, however, its existence might have been kept secret for a while, but not its activities, for it was this council that organized and supported Joseph's candidacy for the presidency of the United States as one of several alternatives for the possible establishment of the political kingdom. Negotiations were also entered in with Sam Houston for the acquisition of a large tract of land in the Texas region as an alternate possibility for the settling of the Saints and the establishment of the kingdom of God.

Furthermore, scouting expeditions were sent west to explore yet another possible location for the future kingdom.

The secrecy of Council of Fifty deliberations might well have been a protective measure against the possibility of misunderstanding by not only the Gentiles but the Saints as well. Benjamin F. Johnson, one of the charter members of the Council of Fifty, declared that only after attending some of its meetings did he and his associates begin "in a degree to understand the meaning of what he [Joseph Smith] had so often publicly said, that should he teach and practice the principles that the Lord had revealed to him, and now requested of him, that those then nearest to him in the stand would become his enemies and the first to seek his life."[17] But secrecy, to some degree, destroyed its own purpose, for it contributed to false rumors and half truths that, in the eyes of the Gentiles and apostates, gave the political kingdom a sinister and subversive aspect. The opposition that led directly to the assassination of the prophet was partly caused by rumors "that the Mormons entertained the treasonable design, when they thought strong enough, of overthrowing the government, driving out the old population and taking possession of the country, as the children of Israel did in the land of Canaan."[18] The Law brothers and Robert D. Foster, in the Nauvoo *Expositor*, objected to, among other things, "any man as king or lawgiver in the church" Wilson Law, after his excommunication, even made an attempt to obtain a warrant against Joseph Smith for treason on the ground that on one occasion, while listening to the prophet preaching from Daniel 1:44, he heard him declare "that the kingdom referred to was already set up, and that he was the king over it."[19] Governor Ford, in his *History of Illinois*, gives a highly imaginative account of Joseph's temporal aspirations, the source of which must ultimately be sought in the secret deliberations of the Council of Fifty:

It seems, from the best information that could be got from the best men who had seceded from the Mormon Church, that Joe Smith about this time conceived the idea of making himself a temporal prince as well as spiritual leader of his people. He instituted a new and select order of the priesthood, the members of which were to be priests and kings temporally and spiritually. These were to be his nobility, who were to be the upholders of his throne. He caused himself to be crowned and anointed king and priest, far above the rest; and he prescribed the form of an oath of allegiance to himself, which he administered to his principal followers. To uphold his pretensions to royalty, he deduced his descent by an unbroken chain from Joseph the son of Jacob, and that of his wife from some other renowned personage of Old Testament history. The Mormons openly denounced the government of the United States as utterly corrupt, and as being about to pass away, and to be replaced by the government of God, to be administered by his servant Joseph.[20]

Had fact and fiction, curiously intermingled in this document, been separated, and had Governor Ford and the enemies of Mormonism been informed of the truth concerning the kingdom of God—that it was to be established entirely by peaceful, legal means and that the Saints believed worldly governments would dwindle of their own accord, or rather by their wickedness—persecution would most likely have been just as relentless. Theocracy, no matter what form, was highly obnoxious to most mid-nineteenth-century Americans. The Saints themselves were not unaware that kingdom building was a major cause for persecution and to a large degree responsible for the death of Joseph Smith. E. W. Tullidge, writing in the *Latter-day Saints' Millennial Star,* observed, "It is because there has, day after day, and year after year, grown up and fast spread in America a realization, and with it a fear of the empire-founding character of 'Mormonism' and the 'Mormons,' that this Church had such heartrending pages in its history. It is because of the growth of this presentiment and fear that a Joseph, a Hyrum, a Parley, a David Patten, and many others of the chief Elders and Saints have been directly or indirectly martyred."[21] Martyrdom, however, contrary to Gentile hopes and expectations, proved no deterrent to Mormon ambitions of building the kingdom. If anything, the Saints continued their efforts with renewed vigor.

How deeply the idea of the establishment of a theocratic kingdom of God had been embedded in Mormon thinking was revealed by the succession controversy and its resulting schisms. Alexander Badlam and George Miller, as mentioned earlier, wanted to "call together the Council of Fifty and organize the Church." Lyman Wight, who led a colony of Saints to Texas, likewise considered the authority of the Council of Fifty superior to that of the Quorum of the Twelve and lamented the fact that the reorganization of the church had not taken place under the leadership of the legislature of the kingdom of God.[22] Splinter groups, such as the Hedrickites, Morrisites, Bickertonites, and Brewsterites, attempted to establish theocratic governments. Gladden Bishop, who attracted a group of Wisconsin Saints to his cause after the death of the prophet, organized, according to one observer, "what he calls the Kingdom of God, and it was the queerest performance I ever saw."[23] James Strang, one of the most vociferous claimants to the mantle of the prophet, insisted on the establishment of not only a church but also a political kingdom of God and had himself installed as king of a theocratic community on Beaver Island. Even if Strang had been a member of the Council of Fifty himself, his organization looked like a highly garbled product of that council. That Strang claimed two former members of Joseph's legislature of the kingdom as his followers would suggest that any similarities between Smith's ideas of the kingdom and those of a self-styled successor were more than coincidental.

It seems only logical to assume, then, that Brigham Young, whose claim as the rightful heir to the mantle of the prophet was sustained by a special conference of the church held in Nauvoo on August 8, 1844, would continue the organization of the political kingdom of God. Under his practical leadership, the Council of Fifty assumed the responsibility of directing both the politics and administration of the government of Nauvoo. Even more important, the group resumed its earlier activities of looking for a place where the Saints could settle peacefully and establish the kingdom of God without Gentile interference. As a result, the Council of Fifty was to organize and direct the exodus of the Saints to the Rocky Mountains.

Notes

This is a revised excerpt from an earlier version, which appeared in *Brigham Young University Studies* 2 (Spring/Summer 1960): 241–60. Note 2 represents the scholarship on the kingdom of God and the Council of Fifty in 1960. The facts and arguments advanced in the essay published here were fleshed out and elaborated on in my book *Quest for Empire: The Political Kingdom of God and the Council of Fifty in Mormon History* (East Lansing: Michigan State University Press, 1967; rev. ed., with a new preface, Lincoln: University of Nebraska Press, 1974). D. Michael Quinn, "The Council of Fifty and Its Members, 1844–1945," *Brigham Young University Studies* 20 (Winter 1980): 163–93, reported on the discovery of additional sources and fragments in 1980, refining and adding to but not significantly altering the earlier factual basis, though he questioned the centrality of the Council of Fifty in Mormon history, especially after 1850 (the period covered in the second half of my essay, not reprinted here). Other important works stressing the significance of the political kingdom of God are Jan Shipps, *Mormonism: The Story of a New Religious Tradition* (Urbana: University of Illinois Press, 1985); Marvin S. Hill, *Quest for Refuge: The Mormon Flight from American Pluralism* (Salt Lake City: Signature Books, 1989); and John L. Brooke, *The Refiner's Fire: The Making of Mormon Cosmology, 1644–1844* (New York: Cambridge University Press, 1994).

1. Quoted in William Mulder and A. Russell Mortensen, eds., *Among the Mormons: Historic Accounts by Contemporary Observers* (New York: Alfred A. Knopf, 1958), 103.

2. Various aspects of the political kingdom of God have received attention. See Hyrum Andrus, *Joseph Smith and World Government* (Salt Lake City: Deseret

Book, 1958); Alfred Bush and Klaus J. Hansen, "Notes Toward a Definition of the Council of Fifty," 1957, typescript, Special Collections, Harold B. Lee Library, Brigham Young University, Provo, Utah; James R. Clark, "Church and State Relationships in Education in Utah" (Ph.D. diss., Utah State University, 1958); James R. Clark, "The Kingdom of God, the Council of Fifty, and the State of Deseret," *Utah Historical Quarterly* 26 (April 1958): 130–48; and Klaus J. Hansen, "The Theory and Practice of the Political Kingdom of God in Mormon History, 1829–1890" (M.A. thesis, Brigham Young University, 1959).

3. See G. Homer Durham, *Joseph Smith, Prophet-Statesman* (Salt Lake City: Deseret Book, 1944), 101; Therald N. Jensen, "Mormon Theory of Church and State" (Ph.D. diss., University of Chicago, 1938), 20; and J. Keith Melville, "The Political Ideas of Brigham Young" (Ph.D. diss., University of Utah, 1950), 11.

4. *Journal of Discourses*, 26 vols. (Liverpool, England: F. D. and S. W. Richards, 1854–86), 9:341.

5. *Latter-day Saints' Millennial Star* (Liverpool, England) 24 (February 15, 1862): 103.

6. Ibid., 23 (July 6, 1861): 422.

7. This is the date given in Joseph Smith, *History of the Church of Jesus Christ of Latter-day Saints,* ed. B. H. Roberts (Salt Lake City: Deseret News Press, 1902–12; 6 vols., a seventh volume was published in 1932; reprinted by Deseret Book, 1976, and reissued in paperback in 1978), 6:260–61. For reference to a revelation concerning the organization of this body received by the prophet as early as April 7, 1841, see "Minutes of the Council of Fifty," April 10, 1880, typed manuscript, Special Collections, Harold B. Lee Library. The official name of the council apparently was to be kept a secret. "General Council," "Council of the kingdom," "Council of the Gods," and "Living Constitution" are some of the names applied to the council in the literature referring to it. "Council of Fifty," referring to the approximate number of members, appears to have been used most frequently and was therefore adopted to identify the council in this essay.

8. John D. Lee, *A Mormon Chronicle: The Diaries of John D. Lee, 1848–1876,* 2 vols., ed. Robert Glass Cleland and Juanita Brooks (San Marino, Calif.: Arthur H. Clark, 1955), 1:80.

9. *Journal of Discourses,* 17:156.

10. Smith, *History of the Church,* 7:213.

11. U.S. Congress, Senate, *Testimony in Trial of Joseph Smith, Jr., for High Treason,* 26th Cong., 2d sess., 1841, Senate Doc. 189, 23. Parley P. Pratt, referring to this investigation, wrote in his autobiography that "this court of inquisition inquired diligently into our belief of the seventh chapter of Daniel concerning the kingdom of God, which should subdue all other kingdoms and stand forever. And when told that we believe in that prophecy, the court turned to the clerk and said: 'write it down; it is a strong point of treason.' Our lawyer observed as follows: 'judge you had better make the Bible treason.' The court made no reply" (quoted in Smith, *History of the Church,* 3:212).

12. B. H. Roberts, *A Comprehensive History of the Church of Jesus Christ of Latter-day Saints,* 6 vols. (Salt Lake City: Deseret News Press, 1930), 1:431–32.

13. Quoted in ibid., 1:433.

14. *Latter-day Saints' Millennial Star* 3 (August 1842): 69.

15. Ibid., 69.

16. "Minutes of the Council of Fifty."

17. Benjamin F. Johnson to George S. Gibbs, n.d. [written between April and October 1903], transcript of letter, 9, Special Collections, Harold B. Lee Library.

18. LeRoy Hafen and Carl C. Rister, *Western America: The Exploration, Settlement, and Development of the Region beyond the Mississippi,* 3d ed. (New York: Prentice-Hall, 1950), 335.

19. *Latter-day Saints' Millennial Star* 24 (June 7, 1862): 359.

20. Thomas Ford, *History of Illinois: From Its Commencement as a State in 1818 to 1847* (Chicago: S. C. Griggs, 1854), 321–22.

21. *Latter-day Saints' Millennial Star* 23 (February 23, 1861): 125.

22. Joseph Smith III and Heman C. Smith, *History of the Reorganized Church of Jesus Christ of Latter Day Saints,* 4 vols. (Lamoni, Iowa: Herald Publishing House, 1896–1911), 2:90–91.

23. Sarah Scott to her mother Abigail Hall, March 31, 1848, in George F. Partridge, ed., "The Death of a Mormon Dictator: Letters of Massachusetts Mormons, 1843–1848," *New England Quarterly* 9 (December 1936): 614.

5

The Nauvoo Neighborhood: A Little Philadelphia or a Unique City Set upon a Hill?

KENNETH W. GODFREY

A recent bibliographical search disclosed that over 450 books about Joseph Smith, including his sojourn in Nauvoo, are housed in the Historical Department Library of the Church of Jesus Christ of Latter-day Saints, while an additional 120 books, articles, dissertations, and theses have been published on the Nauvoo period alone. Yet most serious students are left with the feeling that there is still Nauvoo gold left to be mined and that somehow we have not fully understood the "City Beautiful" and its charisma. In this essay I focus on the Nauvoo neighborhood and what life was like among the common folk by examining some of the "structures of everyday life."[1]

It is highly probable that if the researcher were to ask a Mormon which nineteenth-century American city had three-quarters of its taxable property valued at over fifty dollars, while at the same time at least a third of its inhabitants were ill-housed, ill-clothed, and ill-nourished; which was in the process of establishing libraries, promoting the arts, and improving health and sanitation; which had citizens devoting themselves to cultural and philosophical matters; which had many craftsmen banded together in associations; which was operating under a liberal city charter; and which had leaders preaching and supporting temperance, while at the same time many of the citizens were looking forward to the Second Coming of Christ, the answer probably would be Nauvoo or Salt Lake City. However, this is James McGregor Burns's description of Philadelphia just before 1800.[2]

It would appear, then, that in many respects life among the common people of Nauvoo was similar to that in other American communities. Peter Gay in his study of life during what we call the Victorian era tells us that hundreds of small towns were "exploding into sprawling, thriving, miserable bustling urban agglomerations."[3] Thus while Nauvoo was also experiencing great growth because of the Mormon concept of the gathering, it was neither unique nor unusual, if Gay's findings are correct.

How Nauvoo's People Made a Living

By means of a thorough search of newspapers, diaries, journals, and the *History of the Church*, I have been able to identify over two hundred different occupations among the citizenry of Nauvoo. With the help of Mervin Hogan and James Kimball Jr., I determined that of 1,348 Masonic Lodge applicants in Nauvoo, at least 38 percent considered themselves farmers, while just under 10 percent listed their occupations as carpenters.[4] Moreover, there were comparatively large numbers of stonemasons, shoemakers, laborers, bricklayers, blacksmiths, and stonecutters. If all of the construction-related occupations were added together, almost 35 percent of Nauvoo's men were engaged in such endeavors. Over two-thirds of the male citizenry thus were either farmers or what would be known today as blue-collar workers.

Some of the most colorful and unusual Nauvoo occupations might include river boat captain (there were at least four), gatherer of rags, soap works manager, portrait painter, seller of palm leaf hats, seller of brass clocks, seller of alum salt, carrier of water to the store for use in the endowments, broadsword teacher, spy, fisherman, trapper, coal miner, matchmaker, dentist, seller of chestnut trees, comb seller, and purveyor of mercury to kill bedbugs. (Bedbugs were prevalent enough that the Nauvoo *Neighbor* frequently ran articles that gave instructions on how to get rid of them. The Saints were to put a small quantity of mercury into a tumbler, break into the mercury the white of two eggs, mix together, and apply with a feather. This mixture was guaranteed to remain for years and sooner or later the bedbug would encounter it and would not "endure it in an instant.")[5] Other occupations included auctioneer, tavern owner (there were at least four), coffin maker, seller of garden seeds, elderberry salesman, cheese merchant, and seller of facsimiles of the Kinderhook plates, which represents perhaps the second attempt to make money from Mormon memorabilia (selling the Egyptian mummies was probably the first).[6]

James Kimball Jr. has shown that 35 percent of the Nauvoo Masonic applicants were between the ages of twenty and twenty-nine, almost 40 percent between the ages of thirty and thirty-nine, almost 20 percent between the ages of forty and forty-nine, and only 6 percent fifty or over, suggesting something about the age of Nauvoo's work force. My own studies have shown that at least 50 percent of the time men in their early twenties were likely to be found working on the temple, in the stone quarry, or on a force or as bodyguards or engaged in founding their own businesses. Women in Nauvoo often taught school, cultivated gardens, or did sewing to supplement the family income.[7] These men and women who made up Nauvoo's work force often had unusual names that sometimes bore a striking resemblance to their occupations. For example, James Twist was a cordwainer, William Winterbottom was a cotton spinner, Forrester Harwood made cabinets, Martin Littlewood laid bricks, and Burr Frost cut wood. It would have been nice if John Fido had trained dogs, Joseph Outhouse made "johns," Joseph DeForest cut down trees, and James Rodeback trained horses, but they did not in fact have trades that so closely resembled their names. Not a few people in Nauvoo banded together and purchased community lots that they would then farm, sharing the produce. In this manner the poor were at least able to keep from starving.[8]

It is important to note that almost all of Nauvoo's work force was engaged in more than one occupation. It appears that to make a living, the Saints had to do many things. It should also be noted, however, that this was typical for other Americans as well. According to James E. Davis, it was not until the 1860s that people generally had only one occupation at a time.[9] Before that decade many, if not most, Americans were jacks-of-all-trades.

Nauvoo also had its wealthier residents, such as William Law, who owned mills, land, and other businesses. The city had at least 10 doctors, at least 6 lawyers, and more than eighty schoolteachers. Other Mormons made their living publishing books, newspapers, and pamphlets; managing drugstores and dry goods stores; or manufacturing furniture, carriages, and weapons. Thus the city also had its share of those considered white-collar workers.

Strikingly, the occupations of Nauvoo's citizenry ran almost parallel, in both percentages and varieties, to those listed and discussed by James E. Davis in his book *Frontier America*.[10] Even his section titled "Defending the Garden," as well as the one that discusses newspapers, sounds very much as if he had studied Nauvoo.[11]

It is apparent from studying Nauvoo's occupations that a good number of its citizenry were willing to do almost anything to make a living. While Nauvoo had its poor and those who struggled against poverty, the percentage of those engaged in blue-collar occupations was probably no higher than in other American communities.

Nauvoo's Economic Associations

As was true in other growing American municipalities, Nauvoo's citizens often banded together according to occupations to set prices, establish standards of quality, and police their particular vocation. Research has been able to establish the existence of at least eighteen such associations. George Miller served as president of the well-known Nauvoo House Association, which sold hay, oats, wheat, corn, potatoes, wood, pork, beef, and houses. The lesser-known Botanic Association, founded to collect herbs and roots for the good of the Saints, was presided over by John Young. George Harris was president of the Nauvoo Coach and Carriage Manufacturing Association, and business was so good that Hosea Stout tells us that the Quorum of the Twelve Apostles appointed a committee from its own members to regulate the regulators. Some of Nauvoo's women organized to promote home industry and manufacturing. The Twelve appointed three sisters to superintend this association, which began on March 13, 1845, and was first organized in the Evans Ward, only six miles from Nauvoo. The schoolteachers of Nauvoo organized an association, which began on August 30, 1843, to ensure the uniformity of standards, textbooks, and curriculum. The famous Nauvoo Agriculture and Manufacturing Association operated under a charter to build a dam across the Mississippi. The dam was to consist of three piers forty feet long, ten feet wide, fifteen feet apart, and twelve feet deep. This dam was intended to foster the development of mills and other machinery and was to run from the shore to the island. Another dam was to be built a mile upriver so the water level could be maintained to drive the mill wheels. The dam, when finished, would have had fifty-three wheels and would have cost $15,000. Those involved in this association, which was often divided, envisioned a cotton factory, two gristmills, one sawmill, a paper mill, and a carding machine powered by the dam. Other associations included the Temperance Society, the Tailors, the Brick Layers, the Potters, the Coopers, and the Shoemakers.[12]

The shoemakers calculated that Nauvoo residents spent $40–50,000 annually for boots and shoes, and they believed that most of this money was spent in cities other than the Mormon capital. By organizing their association, they hoped they could keep the cash from leaving Nauvoo.

Nauvoo, then, was not unlike other American cities in that its residents and leaders saw the need to regulate and cooperate and to establish guidelines for those trades that involved large numbers of people. Its associations were similar to those in other American cities of comparable size and age.

Death and Disease

Not a few historians have emphasized the unhealthy nature of the Nauvoo climate. It appears from reading the diaries and journals of Nauvoo's residents that few, if any, families completely escaped the grim reaper. That death was a frequent guest in many homes did not seem to lessen the sorrow and pain that accompanied each visit.

Some American community historians have been able to verify that women and children seemed the most susceptible to death and disease. In contrast, a study of reported deaths in Nauvoo and its environs discloses that almost the same number of men and women died while the Saints resided in that city. Also striking about Nauvoo's deaths is the number of children in those families who also succumbed. It seems that often when death came calling, more than one family member answered. Another stunning point is that almost half of all the reported deaths in Nauvoo were among children below the age of ten. It was indeed a challenge to reach maturity. Ten percent of all deaths occurred among the residents between the ages of twenty and thirty, with another 13 percent of the deaths among those people who were fifty and over. The lowest death rate was between the ages of thirty and fifty. The historian must be cautious in compiling death statistics, however, because many of Nauvoo's citizens would simply build their own coffins when their children died and would bury the children in their own backyards.[13] Often these deaths went unreported.

Of those who died in Nauvoo under the age of eight, over 20 percent succumbed from diarrhea, 20 percent from fever, nearly 20 percent from canker, and 13 percent from the measles. A comparatively large number of others died from whooping cough, the bloody flux, and tuberculosis. Over a tenth of the adults died from diarrhea, tuberculosis, or canker. Somewhat fewer died from whooping cough, measles, and mumps.

It would appear that from at least 1840 onward the death rates and the causes of death in Nauvoo were not much different from those in the rest of the country. For example, James Burns tells us that the residents of South Carolina most frequently died from cholera, ague, and other fevers.[14] Thus it would seem that after the swamp was drained, Nauvoo was not a more unhealthy place to live than other American communities of similar size.

Nauvoo's School System

Although much has been written about the University of Nauvoo, less is known about the other schools that played a role in the life of Nauvoo's residents. Paul Smith in his master's thesis, titled "A Historical Study of the Nauvoo, Illinois, Public School System, 1841–1845," was able to identify eighty-one people who made at least part of their living teaching school. Of these teachers, forty-eight were males, and thirty-three were females. They taught a total of over eighteen hundred students, and their school terms usually lasted three months. The average student load per teacher was forty-six. Not a few of these educators conducted classes during the summer months as well. Of these eighty-one teachers, less than a tenth had attended a university, and even fewer had earned college degrees. However, many of the teachers had at least a secondary school education. The largest Nauvoo public school, taught and directed by Eli B. Kelsy, had well over a hundred students enrolled, while the smallest had only eleven students. Most if not all of these schools had boards of trustees, usually consisting of three to five persons. Over three hundred of Nauvoo's adult citizenry were thus directly involved in education. There was even one school in the city taught by Charlotte Haven for the children of non-Mormons.[15] The average age of a Nauvoo schoolteacher was twenty-seven, the youngest teacher being only sixteen and the oldest forty-one. The cost of attending a Nauvoo school ranged from $1.50 to $3.00 per term, and some of the residents paid tuition with produce.

One old resident in his later years recalled what one of the schools in Nauvoo looked like:

> The [school]house was built of rough logs, which were put up in such a bungling style that one would suppose that some person had done the carpenter work himself. Where the logs crossed each other at the corners that were from six inches to two feet too long. The crevices between the logs had been chinked with clay, which was still remaining, except such portions as had been knocked out by the boys. The concern was roofed over with clap-boards, but had no ceiling. The floor was made of puncheons which had been smoothed but very little, and the desks and seats were made of the same material, supported by legs polished with an axe and put in with an auger. The door swung on large wood hinges secured by pins. There were two windows in the house, with one being two panes in depth; room had been made for them by cutting out a log on each side. The architectural bounty of the building was finally completed by the fire-place. This was a huge pile built of timber and rocks, and would accommodate a back log six feet in length, with a large quantity of finer wood.[16]

Textbooks used in the schools included several standard references, spelling books, grammar books, histories, and readers. The scriptures were also sometimes substituted as readers. Jesse N. Smith, who years

later became president of an Arizona stake, recalled that "in 1843, for a
short time, I attended a school kept by a Miss Mitchell in Hyrum Smith's
brick office. Passing the Prophet's house one morning, he called me to
him and asked what book I read in at my school. I replied, 'The Book of
Mormon.' He seemed pleased, and taking me into the house gave me a
copy of the Book of Mormon to read in at school, a gift greatly prized by
me."[17] Classes were usually held six hours a day, and discipline sometimes included whipping. Joseph Smith III, during his 1885 visit to
Utah, recalled the following in conversing with his Nauvoo schoolteacher,
Howard Coray:

> In our opening conversation I had mentioned the name of Jack Allred
> and asked if he remembered him and the time when he, as Teacher
> Corey [*sic*], had whipped Jack with the sturdy switch I had cut and
> whipped me with the slender one Jack had procured. At first he
> looked a little mystified, but laughed with me as I related the incidents.
> I told him I had always been curious to know why he punished us
> that way.
>   "Well," he answered, "I felt that a boy who when sent out to get a
> switch to be punished with was honest enough to cut one of a proper
> size, was not at heart a bad boy, that his misdemeanor was doubtless
> due to a bad influence, and that his companion needed the heavier
> thrashing."[18]

James A. Monroe, a teacher who kept a diary, detailed some of his
teaching goals:

> April 22, 1845. This being the first day [of school] everything, of course,
> was to be arranged as far as commencement. I think, however, I was
> enabled to give them some instruction. But I think I never felt my
> inability and incapacity of instructing children as they should be in-
> structed so much as I did today. Perhaps the reason was, partly, be-
> cause I took more than ordinary interest in their advancement and
> also that I was reading a work for the benefit of teachers and saw so
> many requisites to constitute a good teacher that I almost despaired
> of even being able to come up to the standard. . . .
>   To day Frederick was unable to comprehend the philosophy of
> carrying for every ten in multiplication. I have promised to explain it
> to him in the morning. I think I shall accomplish two ends by the
> operation: first, I shall teach the principle and thus render his future
> work more easy and delightful; and secondly, I shall, I think, gain his
> affection and impress upon his mind the fact that I am his friend and
> desire his improvement. . . .
>   April 23, 1845. I am exceedingly happy . . . to be able to say that I
> have not spent this day in vain, having excited some degree of inter-

est in most of my scholars, in the pursuit of two stories, one on the "Consequences of idleness" and the other on "The advantages of industry." . . . I presume I have not yet succeeded in making my school room a place of happy resort, sufficiently to induce my scholars to deny themselves much in order to be present early.[19]

In a letter to the editor of the Nauvoo *Neighbor,* a resident described his visit to the school taught by Joseph and Adelia Cole. Signing his name Othello, he wrote:

On Friday last through the politeness of Mr. Joseph M. and Miss Adelia Cole, I received an invitation to attend a public examination of their seminary. Quite a number of our citizens were in attendance, and appeared to be well pleased with the order of their exercises during the afternoon. Various questions were propounded on Astronomy, Geography, Arithmetic and Grammar, which were answered with readiness by the pupils, which proved that the instructors had used every exertion to cultivate the minds of those who had been placed under their care, and give them a knowledge of the different sciences. . . . The central table was then loaded with compositions written by the pupils on the subject, "Does the merchant enjoy a greater degree of happiness than the farmer." . . . After exercises were concluded, Sidney Rigdon, esq., was called upon, who addressed the school in a very appropriate and able manner. The pupils of the Nauvoo Seminary number about 135.[20]

James A. Monroe, and perhaps some others, also offered evening classes for adults. They studied singing, theology, reading, writing, spelling, grammar, geography, chemistry, philosophy, and astronomy.[21]

Residents of Nauvoo could take advantage of other, less formal educational pursuits. The Nauvoo Library and Literary Institute encouraged reading and promoted culture among Nauvoo residents. Those who belonged to the institute heard lectures on sundry subjects and could borrow books from a library of well over two hundred volumes.[22]

Diaries, journals, and newspaper advertisements give further insight into the range of books that graced Nauvoo homes. The researcher is struck by the fact that few if any of Nauvoo's books were novels. Rather, works of geography, grammar, language, or theology make up the bulk of the list. However, Nauvoo's citizenry did read such newspapers as the *New York Herald,* the *Chicago Democrat,* and of course the *Times and Seasons,* the *Wasp,* and the Nauvoo *Neighbor,* all of which contained some fiction. There were also a few books of poetry in the Saints' houses.

The Seventies Quorum also had, by Nauvoo standards, a rather imposing library. Furthermore, the Seventies were to "gather many antiquities, with various books, charts &c., to deposit in the library for the advancement of art and science, which, with just principles, will so heart and hand unto perfection, being built upon truth. . . ."[23]

Private libraries in Nauvoo included those of James Ivins, Sidney Rigdon, and John Grey, which were housed in their homes, as well as the George Gee Library. Joseph Smith himself had a private collection of over fifty books.

When Nauvoo's private and quasi-public book holdings are compared with libraries found among people with similar backgrounds, educational attainments, and financial resources, the private libraries in Nauvoo are not altogether unimpressive. Though the libraries and intellectual pursuits of the Saints do not compare with those existing in Europe's or even America's chief cultural centers, they do bear witness that the Saints were trying to increase their knowledge of the world.[24]

Recreation Nauvoo Style

Nauvoo's residents, like other Americans, had some time for recreational activities. Levi Hancock was often found playing his violin for his friends, while Hosea Stout talked about the doctrine of Christ's mission with Brigham Young one evening until 11:00.[25] Those who held the office of seventy in the Melchizedek priesthood had a quorum meeting each Tuesday commencing at 7:00 P.M. A Dr. Smith gave a free lecture at the Nauvoo Library and Literary Institute entitled the "New French System of Medical Practice," while on another occasion a twenty-three-piece vocal and instrumental group performed for Nauvoo's citizenry.[26] Charlotte Haven, while spending several winter months in Nauvoo, attended two balls, the dancing school, and the theater, where she saw Erastus Snow play the leading role. She also spent one evening in the parlor watching fires on the prairie and tells us that she could count ten to twenty.[27]

In the summer of 1845, a grand concert of vocal and instrumental music was held in the Nauvoo concert hall, where the Nauvoo choir and band performed. The choir sang such songs as "Strike the Cymbal," "Heavenly Visions," "Jerusalem," and the "Dedication Hymn." The band's renditions included a violin trio, a grand slow march, and an overture. Bishop Newel K. Whitney gave a dinner for the Smith family in the Mansion House, and at least forty-six Smiths and their in-laws came. Nauvoo bishops also were invited, as were the apostles Brigham Young and Heber C. Kimball.[28]

Citizens of the "City Beautiful" had other activities in which they could participate. For example, Nauvoo had at least one zoological exhibition that people who could afford to pay fifty cents could attend; children's admission was twenty-five cents.[29] W. M. Keith sponsored a concert of instrumental and vocal music at the brick store, while the Nauvoo lyceum, presided over by Gustave Hill, frequently sponsored debates especially tailored for the men of the city. George Watt gave free lectures on phonography or writing, while the Fourth of July celebration in 1843 was held to raise funds for George J. Adams to use on his pending trip to Russia. The next day over thirteen hundred people assembled to hear Orson Hyde discuss his mission to Palestine.[30]

Some of Nauvoo's games included kissing, one of which held that if a boy could catch a girl with a red kernel of corn during harvest time, he could kiss her. (If a young lady was caught with a black kernel, she received a spanking.) One card game was called Grab. Cards were alternately placed on a table, and when cards of equal value appeared, the first person to grab them was allowed to keep them. They also played rhymes, enigmas (perplexing riddles), and conundrums (riddles that had to be answered with a pun). The children played with wagons, rag dolls, and spinning tops and often were found engaged in such games as leap frog, Anti-I–Over, follow the leader, blind man's bluff, and fox and geese.[31]

Baseball was played in Nauvoo and was called Old Cat. One Old Cat had only a pitcher, a catcher, and one base, while Two Old Cat had two bases, and so on, according to the number of players. The batter would hit the ball and run to the base. The player was out when the ball was caught in the air or on one bounce. The ball was most often an old rag, wrapped tightly with a string, and the bat was a trimmed hickory stick. Bases were usually piles of straw or rocks.[32]

Nauvoo citizens also bowled. Ninepins and tenpins were the most popular forms. The wooden pins were nine inches high and arranged ten inches apart. They were placed in a square or triangle, depending on the number used. The foul line was twenty to forty feet from the pins. A wooden ball was rolled down alleys, which were smooth areas in the open air. Bowling was so popular and had so many devotees that the city regulated it.

The new cotillion dance was also found in Nauvoo. Theatergoers saw such plays as *Pizarro, The Orphan of Geneva, Douglas, The Idiot Witness, Damon and Pythias, The Virginians, The Iron Chest,* and *William Tell.*[33]

Other Nauvoo recreational activities included hunting, fishing, shooting, wild berry picking, honey gathering, walking in the woods, girl watching, loafing, telescope viewing, braiding, and weaving. People could also go to the Lyon drugstore and purchase not only ice cream but also bread, cakes, cookies, jellies, and candy. Nauvoo promoters anticipated at least two parks, one to be called the Kimball Gardens and another to be named Park Place.[34]

At least three bands filled the Nauvoo air with their music. There was the Nauvoo brass band, the quadrette band, and the E. P. Duzette band. Citizens were also entertained by watching Indian tribes perform some of their ancient dances. Some of the favorite songs of this period were "The Seer," written by John Taylor, "Hail Columbia," "Parting Hymn," "The Morning Breaks, the Shadows Flee," "The Voice of the Prophet Comes to Me," and "O My Father." One Nauvoo resident, Joel H. Johnson, wrote 736 songs, most of which are found only in his journal. It was reported that two girls on at least one occasion beautifully sang "The Battle of Michigan." A popular short song of tobacco chewers, titled "We Three Brothers," began "We three brothers, be in one cause, Bill puffs, Tom snuffs, and I chaws."[35] Often, with the exception of the last ditty, these songs were sung for the enjoyment of the community by the Nauvoo choir, which was directed by B. S. Wilbur and had twenty-five female singers and fifteen male voices. The editor of the *Times and Seasons,* commenting on music in Nauvoo, wrote, "We are pleased to see the laudable zeal manifested by some of our *musical* friends, to bring about a uniform and tasteful style of sacred singing. Among a people emigrated from different countries, with different prejudices and habits as we are, this is no easy task, and we can but admire the improvement made. . . ."[36] The Nauvoo Stake also had a choir, as did the University of Nauvoo Music Lyceum.

Religious Worship in Nauvoo

Public worship in Nauvoo seems to have revolved around the Prophet Joseph Smith and around one's own family. Religious services were often held, especially during the winter months, in the home of the Mormon leader. Saints who were not able to get into his crowded house listened to him preach through open windows.[37] Families often held meetings in their homes, and such meetings frequently involved serving hot bread and other refreshments as well as bearing testimony and publicly praising individuals.[38] Adopted family members were frequently in attendance, which made some gatherings rather large.[39]

In meetings held by the Seventies, instructions were given by those who presided over the quorum. For example, Israel Barlow, one of the presidents, in what was described as a "mild and impressive manner," postulated the following: "Spirits are created the same as lighting a Candle. By applying a Candle to a lighted one you obtain light and do not diminish from the Candle previously lighted. It still burns. This is my opinion. I believe Adam had a father as much as we had."[40] Joseph Smith himself on March 20, 1842, a Sabbath, told the Saints that "the Lord takes many away even in infancy that they may escape the envy of man, and the sorrows and evils of this present world; they were too pure, too lovely, to live on earth; therefore if rightly considered instead of mourning we have reason to rejoice as they are delivered from evil, and we shall soon have them again." Continuing, Joseph declared that all men should take warning "and not wait for the death bed to repent, as we see the infant taken away by death, so may the youth and the middle aged, as well as the infant suddenly be called into eternity." He then said that all children are redeemed by the blood of Jesus Christ and that the moment they leave this world they are taken to the bosom of Abraham.[41]

When the weather allowed, Sunday meetings were held in the grove. The authorities sat on a portable stand, known as the stage or platform, while the audience rested on bricks, split logs, or the grass.[42] Usually Sabbath worship involved what was referred to as a spiritual meeting in the morning, followed by a business meeting in the afternoon. Only those in good fellowship were allowed to attend the business meeting, and on at least one occasion three people were flogged because they refused the request of the police to leave.[43] Heber C. Kimball, preaching at one of these services, told the people not to sleep so much. (Today's reader is left uncertain as to whether he meant in the meeting itself or at home.) He also instructed the Saints to do away with their grog shops, which numbered at least four in Nauvoo, their bad houses, and drunkenness and to stop frolicking and dancing. It was also during the Nauvoo period that Parley P. Pratt published his pamphlet *A Treatise on the Regeneration and Eternal Duration of Matter* and his brother Orson saw his *Several Remarkable Visions and the Late Discovery of Ancient American Records* printed in England.[44] Finally, to demonstrate the content of at least one sermon delivered in a Mormon meeting, note the following words by Parley P. Pratt: "Words are but signs of ideas; and if the Deity would communicate ideas to mankind by words, he must of necessity do it according to the laws of language; otherwise the communication would be unintelligible or indefinite, and therefor[e] unprofitable. The prophetical and doctrinal writings contained in the Bible are mostly adapted to the capacities of the simple and unlearned—to the common sense of the people. They are designed to be understood and practised; without which no one can profit by them."[45]

It becomes obvious from reading Mormon diaries that the Saints looked forward to these meetings and loved to hear their prophets preach.[46] Others who instructed the Saints were not always on the mark when it came to doctrine. Almon Babbitt, for instance, stood and told the Saints one March morning that "he only lacked one thing of being a god. He had almighty will and if he only had almighty power to execute his will he would be a god." Brigham Young then followed Babbitt and said that men ought not to scratch themselves to death in trying to carry their will into effect before they have power, which is knowledge. A mechanic could make any kind of mechanism when he knew how and not before, the new Mormon leader declared.[47]

Private religious life among Nauvoo Mormons included prayer—secret and family—administrations to the sick by both men and women, gospel discussions in the home, missionary testimonials, fasts and prayer meetings, religious music sung "with much feeling" all evening, and Wednesday or Friday night prayer meetings. Returning missionaries were often invited into the homes of the Saints, where after a meal they would recount their experiences to the delight of young and old. Even events thought to be entirely social had religious overtones and played a great role in uniting the Latter-day Saint people and in preserving the way of life they were just then in the process of developing. Bridge parties were sometimes held where gospel subjects were discussed between dancing, eating, and playing games of various sorts.[48] The Latter-day Saints during the Nauvoo period were just beginning to formulate a kind of religious life, both public and private, that has become familiar and traditional.

Clothing, Food, and Lodging

It is probable that not everyone donned striped pantaloons and linen jackets, as Joseph Smith sometimes did. We do know that Sidney Rigdon wore gold glasses and had one of the city's first stoves in his home.[49] Stoves were still rather rare because they had only come into use in America in the late 1830s, helping to free women from certain vexing aspects of cooking.[50] It is no wonder then that the Rigdon stove is frequently mentioned in Mormon diaries. At least one Nauvoo house had a table, three chairs, a coffee pot and coffee mill, a tin dipper, a bake kettle, a red chest, a box of crockery, and a bedstool and was heated by a fireplace. People often dressed in silk, satin, muslin, and crepe; wore dress shawls, gloves, hosiery, and palm leaf hats; used lisle thread; purchased music boxes and accordions; and prized watches and clocks.[51]

A Nauvoo meal might incorporate turkey roasted on a string suspended from the mantel, with a pan suspended under the turkey to catch the drippings for gravy. Other meats would include chicken, beef, and venison. Vegetables consisted of peas, beans, tomatoes, and corn. Mormon families often served hot biscuits, roasted potatoes, corn bread, bacon, butter, and cheese.[52] Families usually ate in the same room where the food was prepared and cooked, indicating that the average home in Nauvoo was rather small.

By the 1840s ready-made clothing was beginning to penetrate America's rural towns and cities. But Mormon girls, as early as their fifth year, began to weave thread into cloth,[53] and women often made their own sheets, blankets, towels, and rugs, as well as family clothing.

In 1842 axes were selling in Nauvoo for $16 a dozen, beans were 40 cents a bushel, coal $14 a ton, coffee 13 cents a pound, chocolate 13 cents a pound, feathers 16 cents a pound, cornmeal 25 cents a bushel, dry apples 50 cents a bushel. It was estimated that a rather large family could live on $176 a year.

To beautify their homes, people in Nauvoo were encouraged to plant and cultivate fruit and shade trees, vines, and fig trees and to build fences and line them with peach and mulberry trees. They were also inspired to border their garden walks with currant, raspberry, and gooseberry bushes. That the residents surrounded their houses with rose and prairie flowers and grape vine porches helped make the city beautiful. Those who needed help with their landscaping and design were urged to contact a Mr. Sayers.[54] Israel Barlow loved the orange day lilies that beautified his Nauvoo home so much that he dug them up and took them to Utah with him.[55] Although Nauvoo might not have reached the degree of beauty that its leaders desired, the people were attempting to make it live up to its name.

City Ordinances and Life in Nauvoo

A careful reading of Nauvoo's city ordinances reveals some of the problems that confronted the inhabitants. As in other American cities, the problem of dead animals challenged the city fathers. By late 1842 they had passed an ordinance that required that carcasses either be taken out of the city limits and disposed of or be buried at least three feet underground. There was a statute that forbade nude swimming within the city limits, while another required that all newcomers to the city register with the city constable. An additional law required people to be in their homes after 9:00 P.M. and to remain there until after sunrise.[56] Another ordinance forbade people to spread contagious diseases or to keep any animals for exhibition or for any purpose that might excite passions or affect decency, virtue, or modesty. Still another ordinance forbade the residents to allow cows, calves, sheep, goats, or dogs to run at large in the city.

Marriage in Nauvoo

Early in Nauvoo's history the city council passed a law that declared that all males over the age of seventeen and females over the age of fourteen could contract marriage, provided it was solemnized by a minister of the gospel, the city mayor, an alderman, or a justice of the peace. The Mormon historian Lyndon W. Cook reports that there were 2 civil marriages in Nauvoo in 1839, 27 in 1840, 45 in 1841, 58 in 1842, 128 in 1843, 128 in 1844, and only 28 in 1845. Of these marriages, only 4 were performed by the prophet himself, 41 were performed by members of the Smith family, and almost 80 of these unions were performed by members of the Quorum of the Twelve.[57]

Nauvoo's newspapers frequently included advice, or "a whisper," to husbands and wives. Such advice included such salient tips as not to expect perfection, not to point out a husband's faults, to use gentleness and love, not to jest about the bonds of the married state, to consult one's wife on all occasions, to leave male companionship and cleave unto one's wife, and never to witness a tear from one's wife with apathy or indifference. Wives were admonished to study their husbands' character, beware of the first dispute, conceal defects from husbands, make themselves alluring to their husbands, always be cheerful, and let husbands think they are good husbands.[58]

After marriages were performed, the bride and groom and the invited guests often had loaf cake, or bridal cake, wine, beer, or some other liquid refreshments. On a few occasions the wedding party included dancing.[59] After the introduction of the endowment in 1842, many, if not most, Mormon weddings were religious in nature and were for eternity as well as for this life. Before the Nauvoo Temple was completed, these weddings often took place in the upper room of private houses or in secluded places in the evening hours. Of course plural marriages were always secret and were often contracted in fields or woods or in draped upper rooms of special homes.[60]

Civil marriages were not unlike those performed in the rest of America, but eternal marriages made marriage in Nauvoo not only unique but secretive as well. Because so much has been written on plural marriage, I will not comment any further on that aspect of matrimony.

Crime in Nauvoo

As the city grew, so did residents' concern for their safety. Although diaries do not reveal an inordinate amount of uneasiness regarding life and property, the leading newspapers and non-Mormon books lead the historian to believe that Nauvoo was a veritable stink hole of debauchery and violence. For example, J. W. Gunnison informs us that "horse thieves and house-breakers, robbers and villains, gathered there to cloak their deeds in mystery, who, caring nothing for religion, could take the appearance of baptism, and be among, but not of them."[61]

Joseph Smith himself declared in the pages of the Nauvoo *Neighbor* that the city was infected "with a set of blacklegs, counterfeiters, and debauchees," while Wilford Woodruff informs us that a villain by the name of Rocky Mountain terrified some Latter-day Saint residents of Montrose.[62] However, it is difficult for the historian to determine just how much crime there was in Nauvoo and whether it was more frequent and more serious than in other American cities of comparable size. That Nauvoo was a frontier city might have influenced the level of violence. The church's own *Times and Seasons* declared that a "gang of thieves had inflicted Nauvoo, so that the Saints had to lock their doors, and secure their cattle and hogs."[63]

Living so close to the river and the Iowa frontier must have increased the chances of escaping with one's life and booty. The researcher does learn that two Mormons, a father and a son, were kidnapped, taken to Missouri, imprisoned, and held without warrant by a man named Eliot, which produced both fear and outrage on the part of the citizenry.[64] In April of 1844 the Rollison and Finch Store was robbed. A suspect was subsequently caught and severely beaten in the woods in the hope that he would reveal the names of his accomplices.[65] A converted murderer, Jeremiah Smith, settled in Nauvoo until his past became known, as did the notorious criminal Joseph H. Jackson.[66]

David Holman and James Dunn were part of a group bound together by secret oaths, obligations, and penalties that held it was right to steal from anyone who did not belong to the church so long as one-third of the booty was consecrated for the building of the temple.[67] These men, it was said, were also involved in making counterfeit money. When this was found out, they not only were denounced and forcefully expelled from the home of Hyrum Smith but also were cut off from the church. Oliver Olney, to cite yet another specific case, was tried for stealing goods from the store of Moses Smith and was convicted and fined.[68] Early in 1841 two men entered a stable where Joseph Smith kept his horses, cut off their tails, manes, and ears and in other ways maimed them.[69] At one 1841 church conference Alanson Brown, Joseph Holbrook, John Telford, James B. T. Page, and William H. Edwards were convicted of larceny and were expelled from the church.

Later in the Nauvoo experience, Charles Crisman, who was purportedly a Mormon elder, was arrested for stealing three wagonloads of iron from the railroad between Meredosia and Jacksonville, which caused the anti-Mormon press to publish many articles implicating all the Mormons in Illinois and Iowa.[70] When the Mormon Therin Terrill was arrested, having in his possession twelve American half-dollars and eight Spanish quarter-dollars, all counterfeited, the boy stated that he had been given the money by another Mormon, George Reader.[71] Finally, Albert G. Hyde, a church member, was apprehended for stealing horses in McDonough County.[72]

It is apparent that there was some crime in Nauvoo, perpetuated by Mormons and non-Mormons alike. However, after its initial settlement, Nauvoo probably had no more crime than other frontier towns of similar size, but there was more publicity when a criminal act occurred. For example, the execution of the infamous Hodge brothers, who were convicted of murder and hanged in the city of Nauvoo, was publicized in many, if not most, of the nation's newspapers. Furthermore, it was even reported that in an effort to protect themselves, their homes, and their property, Nauvoo women banded together and put tar and feathers on some undesirables who came into the city.[73]

My own great-great-grandfather, Charles Shumway, in an 1842 report written in his own hand, stated that he was part of a large group of men called "the guard," which had some interesting adventures with criminal types. He further reported that there were not only gamblers but also other ruffians who frequented the city's streets, especially near the waterfront.[74]

In spite of such specifics, a careful study of the records reveals there was probably less crime, less fear of crime, and safer streets in Nauvoo than in many other American cities. The diaries of Hosea Stout, who was Nauvoo's chief of police, reveal that weeks went by without any mention of a crime in the "City Beautiful." Most police activity revolved around protecting the citizenry from the non-Mormons, who by 1844 wanted to drive the Saints from the state. It is thus apparent that the bulk of Nauvoo's inhabitants lived in comparative peace and safety within the limits of the city.

Conclusion

It is striking that in spite of the rhetoric, the publicity, and the tendency of students of Nauvoo history to emphasize the bizarre, the spectacular, and the unique, life in Nauvoo was for the most part much like that in other American cities. Daily life revolved around making a living, having enough to eat, and being free from sickness. When there was time left over for recreation or pursuits of the mind, it was appreciated and welcomed. People seemed to find great comfort in visiting and socializing. That the common bond of the gospel brought them closer is evidenced by the fact that discord was not more prevalent. Studies of the Nauvoo neighborhood might not win awards or sell as many books as those that emphasize the seamy side of the city's daily activities, but such studies probably provide a more accurate picture of life as the majority experienced it. While the leaders of the church and its thinkers labored in the belief they were building a place of refuge, a kingdom, a Zion, or unique city set upon a hill, it becomes obvious that life among the common folk was structured around family and work, punctuated with periods of recreation. That they had joined a cause they believed was destined to revolutionize the world and prepare it for the Second Coming of the Savior gave them hope in time of despair, peace in the face of death and tragedy, and purpose as they struggled.

Still, their homes were typical American homes, furnished like average American homes of the period; their education was like that of other Americans; and they had average death rates and crime rates. They married, worried about their children, and recreated as other Americans did. Their newspapers published much the same news that other periodicals in the United States did. Thus it can be safely stated that Nauvoo had more in common with other American communities than it had differences.

Notes

An earlier version of this essay appeared in the *Journal of Mormon History* 11 (1984): 78–97.

1. Ferdinand Braudel, *The Structures of Everyday Life* (New York: Harper and Row, 1979), examines the social history of people during the Middle Ages. Such studies are now very fashionable.

2. James McGregor Burns, *The Vineyard of Liberty* (New York: Alfred A. Knopf, 1982), 116–17.

3. Peter Gay, *The Bourgeois Experience: Victoria to Freud,* vol. 1, *Education of the Senses* (New York: Oxford University Press, 1984), 50.

4. These figures are from a study of Nauvoo Masonic Lodge applicants, compiled by Mervin B. Hogan, and were shared with the author by James L. Kimball Jr.

5. *Neighbor* (Nauvoo, Ill.), July 2, 1845.

6. I have compiled a list of occupations from advertisements in the *Wasp,* the Nauvoo *Neighbor,* the Masonic list compiled by Hogan, and the diaries of Nauvoo's citizens.

7. This information was compiled from over a hundred diaries dating from the Nauvoo period.

8. *Neighbor,* January 1, 1845.

9. James E. Davis, *Frontier America, 1800–1840: A Comparative Demographic Analysis of the Settlement Process* (Glendale, Calif.: Arthur H. Clark, 1977), 151–54.

10. Ibid.

11. Ibid., 157, 144.

12. For information on these associations, see the *Neighbor,* September 27, 1843; April 20, 1844; and January 28, February 4, March 11, March 13, March 25, May 23, June 4, June 11, 1845. See also Joseph Smith Collection, folder 3, box 3, Archives, Historical Department, Church of Jesus Christ of Latter-day Saints, Salt Lake City, Utah. It is interesting that most of these associations sprang into existence after the murder of Joseph Smith and under the presidency of Brigham Young. They were all short-lived.

13. See, for instance, John Brown, Diary, Archives, Historical Department, the Church of Jesus Christ of Latter-day Saints, Salt Lake City, Utah (hereafter LDS Archives). Published death statistics and reports must be supplemented by research in diaries and other unpublished materials.

14. Burns, *Vineyard of Liberty,* 395.

15. Paul T. Smith, "A Historical Study of the Nauvoo, Illinois, Public School System, 1841–1845" (M.A. thesis, Brigham Young University, 1969), 82–98.

16. O. T. Conger, ed., *Autobiography of a Pioneer, Rev. Samuel Pickard* (Chicago: Church and Goodman, 1866), 36–37, cited in Arthur R. Jones, "A Historical Survey of Representative Recreation Activities among the Mormons of Nauvoo, Illinois, 1839–1846" (M.S. thesis, Southern Illinois University, 1970), 35.

17. Jesse N. Smith, "Recollections of the Prophet Joseph Smith," *Juvenile Instructor* 27 (January 1, 1892): 24, quoted in ibid, 46.

18. Mary Audentia Anderson and Bertha Audentia Anderson Hulmes, eds., *Joseph Smith III and the Restoration* (Independence, Mo.: Herald Publishing House, 1952), 349, quoted in ibid., 48.

19. James A. Monroe, Diary, 1841–45, 101–3, microfilm copy in Lovejoy Library, Southern Illinois University, Edwardsville, Illinois, quoted in ibid., 149–50.

20. *Neighbor,* December 13, 1843.

21. D. Garron Brian, "Adult Education in the Church of Jesus Christ of Latter-day Saints" (Ph.D. diss., University of Chicago, 1956), 55, quoted in Smith, "A Historical Study of the Nauvoo, Illinois, Public School System," 32.

22. Kenneth W. Godfrey, "A Note on the Nauvoo Library and Literary Society," *Brigham Young University Studies* 14 (Spring 1974): 386–89.

23. *Times and Seasons* (Nauvoo, Ill.) 6 (February 1, 1845): 797.

24. For a discussion of libraries in France during the eighteenth and nineteenth centuries, see Robert Darnton, *The Great Cat Massacre and Other Episodes in French Cultural History* (New York: Basic Books, 1984), 215–56. Burns, *Vineyard of Liberty,* tells us that America in the early nineteenth cen-

tury was not as sophisticated intellectually and culturally as would be the case later.

25. Juanita Brooks, ed., *On the Mormon Frontier: The Diary of Hosea Stout, 1844–1861,* 2 vols. (Salt Lake City: University of Utah Press, 1964), 1:51.

26. *Neighbor,* September 23, 1845, July 3, 1945, October 2, 1844.

27. William Mulder and A. Russell Mortensen, eds., *Among the Mormons: Historic Accounts by Contemporary Observers* (New York: Alfred A. Knopf, 1958), 121–22.

28. *Neighbor,* July 16, 1845.

29. Ibid.

30. *Neighbor,* July 16, 1845, July 4 and 5, 1843.

31. Jones, "Representative Recreation Activities," 100–101. See also T. Edgar Lyon, "Recollections of 'Old Nauvooers': Memories from Oral History," *Brigham Young University Studies* 18 (Winter 1978): 143–50.

32. Jones, "Representative Recreation Activities," 91.

33. Ibid., 97; *Neighbor,* September 6, 1843, May 1, 1844.

34. Jones, "Representative Recreation Activities," 41.

35. *Wasp* (Nauvoo, Ill.), August 20, 1842.

36. *Times and Seasons* 3 (January 15, 1842): 664.

37. Mulder and Mortensen, *Among the Mormons,* 118.

38. Mary Richards, Diary, February 19, 1847, LDS Archives. See also Kenneth W. Godfrey, "Winter Quarters: Glimmering Glimpses into Mormon Religious and Social Life," in *The Eighth Annual Sidney B. Sperry Symposium: A Sesquicentennial Look at Church History* (Provo, Utah: Brigham Young University Press, 1980), 149–61.

39. Ora H. Barlow, ed., *The Israel Barlow Story and Mormon Mores* (Salt Lake City: Publishers Press, 1968), 210–12. See also Kenneth W. Godfrey, "Religious Training among the Mormons, 1830–1900: A Mother's View" (Paper presented at the Family History and Heritage Symposium, Brigham Young University, March 27, 1974).

40. Barlow, *Israel Barlow Story,* 213.

41. *Times and Seasons* 3 (April 15, 1842): 751.

42. Barlow, *Israel Barlow Story,* 26. See also Jones, "Representative Recreation Activities," 37, 41.

43. Brooks, *On the Mormon Frontier,* 1:63.

44. For a complete treatment of Mormon pamphlets published during the Nauvoo era, see David J. Whittaker, "Early Mormon Pamphleteering" (Ph.D. diss., Brigham Young University, 1982).

45. Parley P. Pratt and Elias Higbee, "An Address," *Times and Seasons* 1 (March 1840): 68.

46. Those who were not members of the church were not always as impressed with the talks of Mormon leaders and often wrote to relatives in the East criticizing the theology they heard in Nauvoo.

47. John Brown, Autobiography, LDS Archives.

48. Godfrey, "Religious Training among the Mormons."

49. *Times and Seasons* 2 (January 1, 1841): 260; Joseph Smith to Moses Nickerson, November 19, 1833, in Dean C. Jessee, ed., *The Personal Writings of Joseph Smith* (Salt Lake City: Deseret Book, 1984), 302, reveals that Sidney Rigdon suffered from weak eyes.

50. Burns, *Vineyard of Liberty,* 394–95.

51. Barlow, *Israel Barlow Story,* 192. From descriptions of Mormon homes found in contemporary records, it becomes obvious that Nauvoo Restoration, Inc., and its refurbished homes might have led tourists to believe that the Mormons were more prosperous when they were in the City of Joseph than was really the case.

52. Mulder and Mortensen, *Among the Mormons,* 184–85. See also the sermon by Jedediah M. Grant, May 30, 1855, in *Journal of Discourses,* 26 vols. (Liverpool, England: F. D. and S. W. Richards, 1854–86), 3:11.

53. Burns, *Vineyard of Liberty,* 394–95.

54. *Times and Seasons* 3 (February 1, 1842): 686.

55. Barlow, *Israel Barlow Story,* 197.

56. *Wasp,* October 1, 1842; *Neighbor,* June 29, 1843, July 5, 1843.

57. Lyndon W. Cook, *Civil Marriages in Nauvoo, 1839–1845* (Provo, Utah: Liberty Publications, 1980).

58. *Neighbor,* September 16, 1843.

59. *Times and Seasons* 3 (February 15, 1842): 701.

60. For the pain and difficulties associated with such courtships and marriages, see *An Intimate Chronicle: The Journals of William Clayton,* ed. George D. Smith (Salt Lake City: Signature Books, 1991), 105, 106, 110.

61. John W. Gunnison, *The Mormons, or Latter-day Saints, in the Valley of the Great Salt Lake* (Philadelphia: J. B. Lippincott, 1860), 117.

62. Wilford Woodruff, Diary, May 22, 1839, LDS Archives.

63. *Times and Seasons* 2 (November 1, 1840): 204.

64. *Illinois Statesman,* January 15, 1844. For additional information on crime in Nauvoo, see Kenneth W. Godfrey, "Crime and Punishment in Mormon Nauvoo," *Brigham Young University Studies* 32 (Winter and Spring 1991): 195–228.

65. Ibid., May 22, 1844. See also Kenneth W. Godfrey, "The Counselor, the Colonel, the Convict, the Columnist: A Most Unlikely Quartet" (Paper presented at the Mormon History Association meeting, Ogden, Utah, May 8, 1982).

66. Joseph Smith, *History of the Church of Jesus Christ of Latter-day Saints,* ed. B. H. Roberts (Salt Lake City: Deseret News Press, 1902–12; 6 vols., a seventh volume was published in 1932; reprinted by Deseret Book, 1976, and reissued in paperback in 1978), 5:333–34. See also B. H. Roberts, *A Comprehensive History of the Church of Jesus Christ of Latter-day Saints,* 6 vols. (Salt Lake City: Deseret News Press, 1930), 2:224n, 313n.

67. Smith, *History of the Church,* 5:269.

68. *Wasp,* March 29, 1843.

69. *Times and Seasons* 2 (January 15, 1841): 288.

70. *Missouri Reporter,* June 23, 1845.

71. *Signal* (Warsaw, Ill.), June 4, 1844.

72. *Quincy Whig,* April 22, 1846.

73. Douglas Knox to Willard Richards, July 25, 1844, Willard Richards Papers, LDS Archives.

74. Kenneth W. Godfrey, *Charles Shumway: A Pioneer Life* (Provo, Utah: J. Grant Stevenson, 1974), 99A.

6

The Mormon Press in Nauvoo, 1839–46

TERENCE A. TANNER

Officially organized a short time after the publication of the first edition of the Book of Mormon in 1830, the Mormon church was to rely heavily on the printers' art in its formative years. Surprisingly, considering the importance of the Nauvoo experience in the history of the Mormons, the Mormon printing office in Nauvoo has received little scholarly attention.[1] Although a complete history of the Nauvoo printing office and its numerous publications is beyond the scope of this essay, I have tried to provide a broad outline of its history and to suggest its significance in the development of the peculiar sense of identity so important to the growth of the Church of Jesus Christ of Latter-day Saints.

The first church-sponsored printing office was established in 1831 in Independence, Missouri. The office was destroyed in 1833, and a new printing office was established in Kirtland, Ohio. This office also was destroyed. The church procured yet another press and reestablished its printing office in Far West, Missouri.[2] When the Mormons in Far West were surrounded by Missouri militia on October 30, 1838, William Miller took the precaution of burying the press and types in the front yard of Brother Dawson's farm to protect them from destruction.[3] After the Mormons fled Missouri, Mormon leaders returned to Far West in April 1839, in fulfillment of one of Joseph Smith's prophecies, and uncovered the press and brought it to Illinois.

Shortly after Joseph Smith purchased the site of Commerce, Illinois, the church leaders decided that a new periodical, to be called the *Times and Seasons*, should begin publication. It was decided that the printing equipment should be turned over to two young printers in the church, Ebenezer Robinson and Don Carlos Smith. Due to the financial condition of the church, Robinson and Smith were informed that they would have to operate the press without assistance from the church but that they could keep the profits arising out of the operations.[4]

Only twenty-two at the time, Ebenezer Robinson had already labored for a number of years as a printer for the church. Born in 1816 in Oneida County, New York, Robinson spent his early apprenticeship working for newspapers in New York State and Ohio. In May 1835, he moved to Kirtland, Ohio, and obtained employment in the Mormon printing office of F. G. Williams & Co. Although not himself a Mormon, he wrote to his sister that "Mormon money [was] as good as anybody's money" and that he was engaged by the month and received room and board from his employers.[5]

Although skeptical at first, Robinson became impressed by his Mormon employers and friends and was eventually baptized by Joseph Smith in October 1835. In his autobiography, Robinson relates how almost immediately after being received into the church, he was called into the office of his employers and informed that his services were no longer required but that if he was willing to work for $11 a month—presumably a significant reduction in his wages—he would be retained. Surprised by this turn of events, Robinson seriously considered leaving Kirtland to seek employment in Columbus, where printers were in demand and commanded higher wages. He prayed to God for guidance and received the answer: "Stay and be happy."[6]

He stayed and shortly thereafter married a young Mormon woman. His involvement with the church grew, and he was ordained an elder in April 1836. Except for two short missionary trips in the spring and fall of 1836, he remained in Kirtland, working in the printing office, until April of 1837, when he and his wife moved to the Mormon settlement in Far West, Missouri. After taking up farming, he was eventually reemployed as a printer when the church established its printing office in Far West in 1838. Drawn into the difficulties in Missouri, he was imprisoned for a short time and finally fled the state in January 1839.

Walking from Far West with three other Mormons, Robinson arrived in Quincy, Illinois, practically penniless. Although Quincy was overrun with laborers and offered little opportunity for employment, Robinson managed to secure work in the printing office of the *Quincy Whig*. He remained in Quincy until May 1839, when he moved to the newly established Mormon settlement in Commerce, Illinois.[7]

His partner, Don Carlos Smith, the youngest brother of the Prophet Joseph Smith, was also born in 1816.[8] One of the first to convert to his brother's newly founded church, Don Carlos was ordained into the priesthood at the age of fourteen. In the fall of 1833, he began his apprenticeship as a printer in the newly established church printing office in

Kirtland, Ohio, and he became friends with Ebenezer Robinson when Robinson joined the establishment in 1835. When the printing office in Kirtland was destroyed in 1837, Don Carlos Smith moved his family to New Portage, Ohio, and spent most of 1838 on a mission. He finally arrived in Far West in December 1838, just before the exodus of the Mormons from Missouri.

When the printing equipment was turned over to these two friends in June of 1839, their first task was to clean from the press and type the Missouri dirt that covered them. Discovering that some of the type had been destroyed by dampness, they were forced to secure an additional $50 worth of type on credit from Dr. Isaac Galland of Montrose, Iowa, the notorious land speculator who had sold Joseph Smith thousands of acres in the "half-breed" tract to which he did not hold clear legal title. After procuring the type from Galland, Robinson and Smith borrowed $50 from a Mormon brother to purchase a supply of paper. At this time, the only room they could obtain for the printing office was a basement in an old warehouse on the bank of the river. The room had no floor, and they were forced to work on ground kept constantly damp by the water trickling down from the bank side—Joseph Smith in his *History of the Church* described the room as one "through which a spring was constantly flowing." Under these rather difficult circumstances, the partners prepared a prospectus for the new paper in July 1839.[9] Also in July, after printing the prospectus, they began to print copies of the first issue of the paper, but after only two hundred copies had been printed, both printers were taken ill with a swamp fever then sweeping through town. At the time they became ill, they had already wet down enough paper to print an additional two thousand, and this paper soon mildewed and was lost. A Mormon by the name of Francis Higbee tried to be of assistance. He wet down even more of the remaining paper stock, but he proved unequal to the task of printing, and that paper was also lost. Subscription money eventually began to come in response to the prospectus and the sale of the two hundred copies printed before they took ill, and with these funds the printers were able to have built a "cheap frame building one and a half stories high" into which they moved the printing office. The printers themselves moved into the upper portion of the building and were slowly able to recover from their crippling illness.[10]

By November 1839, the two young printers had recovered sufficiently to resume work, and they were fortunate to secure the services of a young apprentice printer by the name of Lyman Gaylord.[11] They reprinted the first number of the paper, substituting November as the publication date on the masthead, and the *Times and Seasons* officially began its life in the world.[12]

The start of the *Times and Seasons* marks an important transition in the history of Mormon journalism. Although the editors were experienced practical printers, neither seems to have been very much interested in theology, and neither held a very high position in the church. Don Carlos Smith, although a member of the prophet's immediate family, does not seem to have been closely associated with the older leaders of the church. Ebenezer Robinson, from what we know of his character, did not appear to have aspirations beyond becoming a successful printer. In contrast to these men, all of the earlier editors of the church newspapers had been men intimately involved in some way with the development of the church; one, Oliver Cowdery, was one of the earliest converts to the church and one of the three witnesses to the Book of Mormon. All of the earlier editors of the newspapers had a personal stake in the theological development of the church, and all had fallen away from the church before the Saints settled in Nauvoo. While it was probably true that Robinson and Smith were chosen to run the newspaper primarily because they were the only experienced printers available at the time in Nauvoo, this turned out to be fortunate for the church. Because these men did not have the aspirations to power that earlier editors exhibited, they served the church more effectively by their natural inclination to avoid the turgid articles on religious questions found in the earlier papers.

While the *Evening and Morning Star,* the first Mormon periodical, is filled with a dark and brooding millennialism and its successor, the *Messenger and Advocate,* is characterized by an incomprehensible religiosity, the *Times and Seasons* is filled with the color of history, even if it was the bloody color of the recent Mormon persecutions in Missouri. Furthermore, it was the most distinctly Mormon of all the church papers. Wayne Ham, in his anthology of selections from church newspapers entitled *Publish Glad Tidings,* remarked of the *Evening and Morning Star* that it provided "very little context . . . in which to understand the development of the church."[13] This is not quite so true of the *Messenger and Advocate,* but what Mormon qualities were to be found in the paper were buried beneath an avalanche of endless lectures on faith and articles on theology. The *Messenger and Advocate* even neglected to inform the church members that Joseph Smith had formed a group called the Quorum of Twelve Apostles to serve as his principal advisers. But with its emphasis on the recent past history of the Mormons, the *Times and Seasons* is unmistakably a Mormon newspaper. There were still to be found in the paper, of course, theologically oriented articles, but these play a relatively minor role in the publication.

Shortly after the editors began publication of the *Times and Seasons,* they announced that they would start publication of a weekly paper of general interest, but they were unable to generate enough subscriptions and the plans were dropped.[14] This meant that the *Times and Seasons* had to serve not only the specific interests of the church but also the general interest of its readers. The marriage of these two elements within one paper served to create a sort of continuum of Mormon existence in which God and mammon, church and state, became one. This joining together of the two worlds was even more pronounced because there was almost no real news of the outside world presented in the paper. Unlike the Oneida Colony's *Free Church Circular,* which John Humphrey Noyes founded not only to promulgate his own views in his community but also to serve as a vehicle to educate the community and keep it in touch with the outside world,[15] the *Times and Seasons* was practically devoid of news of the world outside Nauvoo.[16] The world as presented in the *Times and Seasons* is the Mormon world, and in many ways the newspaper is not unlike any institutional newsletter one might pick up today. Even in terms of its historical articles on the Missouri persecutions, the principle that became quickly established was that the Mormons were persecuted not for what they had done but for what they were. The audience for the *Times and Seasons* was wholly and exclusively Mormon; its message wholly and exclusively Mormonism.

Now that the periodical was finally begun, the editors turned their attention to the need in the church for a new edition of the Book of Mormon, as well as a new edition of the Doctrine and Covenants and a Mormon hymnal.[17] In April 1840, Robinson and Smith ran an advertisement in the paper asking for a loan of $1,000 to print these books.[18] The response was such that the next month they lowered the request to $500.[19] Considering the unlikely prospect of raising this kind of money from Mormons who had only recently been driven from their homes in Missouri, the editors finally gave up the whole idea. However, Ebenezer Robinson received what he described as a "manifestation from the Lord," which told him the course to pursue. He approached Joseph Smith and told him that if Smith could put up $200, he and Don Carlos Smith could get an additional $200 and that they would then print two thousand copies of the Book of Mormon and give Joseph Smith the plates. Joseph Smith agreed to this plan, but two weeks later informed the printers that he had been unable to raise the necessary funds. Robinson and Smith, meanwhile, had managed to borrow at least $145—at 35 percent interest—and they told Joseph Smith that they would go ahead on their own if he would allow them to print four thousand copies of the book, to which Joseph Smith agreed.[20]

In June 1840, Ebenezer Robinson set off for Cincinnati with the $145. After losing $23 of this money in what he referred to as a "mock auction" in St. Louis, Robinson, considerably the wiser, arrived in Cincinnati. After purchasing $17 worth of paper to be shipped back to Nauvoo, Robinson contracted with the firm of Shepard & Sterns to stereotype the plates for the Book of Mormon. Although the total cost of stereotyping the plates, printing, and binding the book far exceeded the money he carried in his pockets, Robinson negotiated for the completion of two thousand copies of the book, instead of the planned four thousand copies, partly through credit terms and partly by offering to work in the printer's office until the book was completed. Robinson was able to sell somewhere around a thousand copies from Cincinnati, enough to meet his immediate obligations. With the money he cleared over and above his initial expenses, he secured a stereotype foundry, binding equipment, and other supplies sufficient to start a job printing office upon his return to Nauvoo.[21] He also seems to have purchased a stock of patent medicines, for after his return to Nauvoo in the fall of 1840, the paper ran a series of advertisements informing the readers that Gridley's Salt Rheumatic Ointment, Bliss' Purgative Bilious Pills, and Vancouver's Powders for the Cure of Fever and Ague could all be had at the office of the *Times and Seasons.*[22]

Flush with Robinson's success in Cincinnati and eager to put the new equipment to use, the printers announced in November 1840 that plans were underway to print a new edition of the Latter-Day Saints hymn book, and appeals were made to all to send copies of their favorite hymns to Emma Smith, wife of the prophet, who was compiling the work.[23] Also, at this time, the proprietors were shepherding through the press the first edition of the *Journal* of Heber C. Kimball, one of the first Mormon elders to travel on a mission to England. This work, published over the imprint of Robinson and Smith in January 1841, although carrying the date of 1840 on the title page, is the earliest extant book known to have been printed in Nauvoo.[24]

That Kimball's *Journal* was the first work to be produced in Nauvoo is not really surprising. It was edited and prepared for the press by Robert B. Thompson, Joseph Smith's personal secretary, so there can be little doubt that its publication was important to Joseph Smith. This book not only addressed itself to regular Mormons, encouraging them in their faith by offering them an account of one of the church's true successes, the missionary effort in Great Britain, but also spoke to those men close to Joseph Smith in the Quorum of Twelve. Most of these men would be tested in their faith by overseas missions, just as Kimball had. In his introduction to the *Journal,* Thompson, undoubtedly acting for Joseph Smith, spoke directly to these men when he wrote, "The Elders of Israel would do well to copy the example [of Kimball], and I hope they will be able to receive some instruction from a perusal of this work, particularly those, who may visit Great Britain, which may be of some value to them. One great cause of his usefulness was, that he attended closely to the commandment of heaven, and without intermeddling with many abstruse and dark passages, which are only a source of speculations, and tend to strife rather than salvation."[25]

Not long before this book was published, the newspaper had celebrated its first anniversary, and the proprietors decided that, beginning with the second volume, the paper would be published semimonthly instead of monthly.[26] This fact, coupled with the start-up of the job printing office, led the partners to decide that it would be best to divide the labor and dissolve the partnership. Don Carlos Smith would maintain control of the newspaper, and Ebenezer Robinson would take over the job printing office by himself.[27]

In the months following his breaking off from Don Carlos Smith, Robinson enjoyed continuing sales of his edition of the Book of Mormon and published two volumes of poetry, one by James Mulholland,[28] a young Mormon who had died not long after arriving in Nauvoo, and another by the Mormon poet Eliza Roxey Snow.[29] He also published Emma Smith's *Collection of Sacred Hymns, for the Church of Jesus Christ of Latter Day Saints.*[30] The *Times and Seasons* office also published a volume of poetry by one "Omer," the pseudonym of a young printer in the office by the name of Lyman Omer Littlefield.[31]

To help with the editorial burden at the *Times and Seasons,* Don Carlos Smith announced in May 1841 that Robert Thompson, personal clerk to Joseph Smith, would join him as assistant editor.[32] Unfortunately, Don Carlos Smith died on August 7, 1841, and Ebenezer Robinson was forced to resume control of the paper in cooperation with Thompson.[33] This new partnership had barely gotten underway, however, when Robert Thompson himself died at the end of August, at the age of thirty.[34] There is an interesting anecdote concerning Robert Thompson recorded in the diary of Oliver Huntington. Thompson had apparently been working as a clerk for Joseph Smith in so steadfast and serious a manner that Joseph Smith became concerned about him and took him aside and said, "Robert, I want you to go and get on a bust, go and get drunk and have a good spree. If you don't you will die." "Robert Thompson did not do it," Huntington reported soberly. "He was a very pious exemplary man and never guilty of such an impropriety as he thought that to be. In less than two weeks he was dead and buried."[35]

With Thompson's death, all of the editorial duties of the *Times and Seasons* fell solely on Ebenezer Robinson's shoulders. He somehow managed to keep up with his job printing and was even busy preparing to print a new edition of the Doctrine and Covenants.[36] Much to his surprise, he began to hear some whispers of displeasure with the manner in which he conducted his business.[37] At a meeting of the Quorum of Twelve held on November 20, 1841, the leaders expressed unhappiness with the way in which Gustavus Hills was conducting the editorial department of the newspaper.[38] This is curious, though, because Gustavus Hills was not announced as having any connection with the paper until January of 1842, almost two months later.[39] It is possible, of course, that Hill had been unofficially acting as editor of the paper to allow Robinson time to attend to the job printing. Anyway, at a meeting ten days later, the Twelve voted that Robinson be asked to give the printing of the *Times and Seasons* to Willard Richards. The Twelve further voted that, if Robinson did not comply with this request, Willard Richards was to procure another press and establish a rival church paper.[40] When Joseph Smith reported all of this to Robinson, he was a little surprised and somewhat bewildered, for he could not imagine any reason for these feelings on the part of men with whom he had always been friendly.

In the midst of all of this uncertainty, Joseph Smith received a revelation that was to complicate Ebenezer Robinson's life further. Early in December of 1841, the Lord instructed Joseph Smith to move Nancy Marinda Hyde, wife of Orson Hyde, then on mission to Palestine, into the home of Ebenezer Robinson, located in the printing complex he had built for himself in the spring of 1841.[41] Needless to say, Robinson was none too happy about this, but he complied and took Nancy Hyde into his home.

The storm building over the printing establishment finally broke on January 28, 1842, when Joseph Smith received another revelation, this one instructing the Twelve to take over the operation of the printing establishment.[42] God had spoken, and Robinson knew it was pointless to resist. Keeping his wits, though, he agreed to turn over the newspaper office to the Twelve only on the condition that they buy out his entire establishment, including stereotype foundry, bindery, stationery store, and buildings. Although this was a bit more than they had originally wanted, the Twelve finally agreed and instructed Robinson to make out an invoice for the sale.[43]

About a week later, Robinson presented the Twelve with an invoice amounting to $6,000 for the operation and buildings. He received in return some cash, some credit against the Book of the Law of the Lord in the Temple, some livestock, and several shares in the Nauvoo House.[44]

The transfer of all of this property took place in the winter, however, and Robinson was having some difficulty locating suitable quarters for his family. He notified Willard Richards that he would require a little more time to find a new place to live, but, according to Robinson, Richards responded, "You must get out tonight or I will put you in the street." Brother Richards's anxious desire to have Robinson out of the house did not apply, however, to Nancy Marinda Hyde, who had been moved into the house in December by celestial fiat. According to the account in Robinson's autobiography, "That evening Willard Richards nailed down the windows, and fired off his revolver in the street after dark, and commenced living with Mrs. Nancy Marinda Hyde, in the rooms we had vacated in the printing office building where they lived through the winter. His family was residing at the time in Massachusetts, and Elder Orson Hyde was absent on mission to Palestine."[45]

In reflecting back on these events many years after the fact, Robinson concluded that the printing office was taken away from him due to the envy of the leaders of the church. By the standards of contemporary journalism, the *Times and Seasons* would have to have been counted a resounding success. Although the precise size of the subscription list of the paper is not known, it must have been in excess of two thousand and perhaps as large as five thousand.[46] It might well have seemed only natural to the church leaders that if anyone was to profit from operating the church newspaper it should be the church. Moreover, a number of members of the Twelve had had experience running the church newspaper in Great Britain. Such a simple answer is complicated, however, by the fact that at this time it was very difficult to differentiate between church finances and the personal finances of Joseph Smith. In fact, Ebenezer Robinson recounted his surprise at discovering that the bill of sale he made out for the establishment listed Joseph Smith as the principal rather than the Quorum of Twelve.[47] Furthermore, Robinson was preparing another edition of the Book of Mormon, and it may well be that Joseph Smith was no longer satisfied to watch others profit from his own work and wished the income from the sales of the new edition for himself.[48] When the new edition finally did appear in the summer of 1842, it carried as publisher the name of Joseph Smith.

If it is fairly certain that the ownership of the printing office passed to Joseph Smith at this time, one is still left with the question of why the Quorum of Twelve was anxious to have control of the newspaper wrested from Ebenezer Robinson. Discounting the possibility that they were acting only at the behest of Joseph Smith—which is probably unlikely— part of the answer is to be found in the role of the Twelve. Several factors are important to keep in mind about the Twelve Apostles at this time. First, Smith began a careful program in the summer of 1841 to turn more and more of the responsibility for everyday affairs of the church over to the Twelve, including maintaining records of tithing. All of the key members of the Quorum of Twelve had been tested in their faith by Smith and had spent long and lonely years on missions in Europe. They had, so to speak, paid their dues and now wished to enjoy the fruits of their newfound power.[49] Although Ebenezer Robinson was a good Mormon, he clearly was not a part of that group, and yet he held a position in the church that was potentially of great power. It is not unreasonable to assume that the Twelve wanted to have one of their own in control of the newspaper and printing office.

Second, it is worth noting that Smith was in 1843 to formally announce his plans for establishing the political kingdom of God on earth and would shortly thereafter create a highly secret body in Nauvoo known as the Council of Fifty, which was to act as the main governing body for the kingdom. Although we know very little about the history of the Council of Fifty, we do know that the Quorum of Twelve was the heart of the group.[50] It is not inconceivable that Joseph Smith had discussed his ideas for the political kingdom in some detail with Brigham Young and others as early as the fall of 1841.[51] If he had, this could well have added to the Twelve's desire to secure the all-important printing office for itself under its own control.

Third, it is almost certain that Joseph Smith had informed most of the members of the Twelve about the doctrine of plural marriage and that most of them had already taken plural wives or would soon do so. Because this was still a carefully guarded secret in Nauvoo, the Twelve might well have felt uncomfortable about having somebody other than itself in the potentially powerful position of editor of the church paper. On this point, it should be noted that there is some evidence that both Ebenezer Robinson and Don Carlos Smith had known something of the doctrine of plural marriage and were adamantly opposed to it.[52]

When Ebenezer Robinson gave up the newspaper establishment, the editorial duties passed to Joseph Smith. Unfortunately for Smith, however, he announced his taking over control of the paper just a bit too soon. In the issue of February 15, 1842, there appeared a valedictory article signed by Ebenezer Robinson announcing that he was giving up the paper and an unsigned article by Smith regarding his having taken over the editorial duties.[53] In this same issue there appeared a short notice that Gilbert H. Rolfe had married Eliza Jane Bates. Rolfe was an apprentice printer in the newspaper office, and the announcement of his nuptials was apparently used as the occasion for a practical joke. Filled with puns of various printer's terms, the announcement read in part that "on receipt of the above notice, we were favored with a rich and delightful loaf of cake—by no means *below* the medium *size;* which makes us anxious that all their acts through life may be *justified;* and when life wanes and they find a peaceful abode in the 'narrow house,' may the *many outs and ins* they have made, leave to the world an abundant posterity to celebrate their glorious example."[54]

It may be somewhat difficult to understand how this notice could have offended anyone, but for Joseph Smith any reference to marriage that was even slightly off-color must have caused consternation. He took every opportunity to deny that the church favored anything other than the purely monogamous life and the usual attitudes toward sex. When the Warsaw *Signal* picked up on the announcement,[55] Smith inserted a notice in the next issue that he was taking full editorial control and that he could not be held responsible for anything that had appeared in earlier issues.[56] The next issue of the paper carried a letter from Ebenezer Robinson exonerating Smith from any responsibility in the publication of the marriage notice and also carried a letter from Lyman O. Littlefield, another young typesetter in the office, stating that he had been the author of the notorious marriage notice and that Smith had not seen it in proof and was to be held blameless.[57]

Upon Joseph Smith's assumption of the editorial chair of the *Times and Seasons,* the history of the press in Nauvoo entered a new period. Smith began his editorship by publishing his translation of several papyri that had come into his possession in 1835. Purportedly written in the hand of the Prophet Abraham, the text of the Book of Abraham, as translated by Smith out of the Egyptian, appeared in the *Times and Seasons* accompanied by a series of remarkable engravings. This work, embodying Joseph Smith's concept of the plurality of God and the notion that the earth had been "organized" rather than "created," became one of the primary religious documents of Mormonism and was later published in the Pearl of Great Price.[58]

Perhaps the most important change in the printing establishment as far as ordinary Nauvoo citizens were concerned, however, was the establishment of the weekly newspaper called the *Wasp.* It had been the dream of Ebenezer Robinson and Don Carlos Smith almost from the beginning of their careers in Nauvoo to publish a weekly paper that would be dedicated to news, literature, the arts, and other matters normal to most newspapers. Although, as mentioned earlier, they had advertised as early as April 1840 that they intended to publish a weekly to be called the *News,* they were unable to secure the necessary subscribers and thus dropped the plan. Don Carlos Smith made one more attempt later on to start a weekly newspaper in Nauvoo, but this also died for want of subscribers.[59] The *Wasp*, however, seems to have begun publication without any regard to subscribers. At least no serious effort was made to enroll subscribers. There is no indication that a prospectus was ever issued for the paper, and the *Times and Seasons* carried no announcement of any kind concerning the establishment of the paper beyond a short notice requesting agents of the paper to act as agents for the *Wasp*.[60]

This unusual circumstance can be explained by remembering that Joseph Smith himself had just begun acting as editor of the *Times and Seasons*. Sensitive as he was to the rumors circulating in and around Nauvoo concerning his and other leaders' polygamous behavior, as witnessed by his reaction to the rather innocuous marriage notice mentioned earlier, Smith was beginning to be very seriously concerned about the behavior of John C. Bennett. Bennett, a notorious rogue and opportunist, had befriended the Mormons shortly after their expulsion from Missouri and had managed to worm his way into a position of some authority in Nauvoo, serving as both mayor of Nauvoo and general in the Nauvoo Legion. A close associate of Joseph Smith, Bennett had learned of the doctrine of plural marriage and quickly took it up in earnest, baldly attempting the seduction of any number of women in Nauvoo. Joseph Smith realized that Bennett was becoming an embarrassment and would have to be cut away from the church. But Smith must have also realized that Bennett was unlikely to take his fall meekly and would undoubtedly return the favor by attacking the church and unmasking the doctrine of plural marriage.[61] As the new editor of the official church newspaper, Smith was not in the best position to defend himself and the church against Bennett and the anti-Mormon forces of the Warsaw *Signal* and other papers that would certainly pick up on Bennett's charges. Also, the *Times and Seasons* was distributed outside of Nauvoo, and Smith would not have wanted any hint of these troubles to appear in the newspaper being used to help gain converts to the faith and new settlers for Nauvoo. What he needed was another journalistic medium, not immediately associated with him, which could take the low road, so to speak, and engage in what was certain to be a polemical war. Thus, the *Wasp* was rather hurriedly planned, and William Smith, another of the prophet's brothers, was named its editor. It began publication in April 1842, and less than a month later John C. Bennett was disfellowshipped. When he did begin his attacks on "Old Joe" and the church, they were largely answered in the pages of the *Wasp*.

With the publication of the *Wasp*, the *Times and Seasons* no longer had to fulfill a double function, and it shed whatever news-oriented qualities it had. It did not, however, become the kind of religious paper that its predecessors had been. Rather, it became even more concentrated

on church history and began publishing a long series of articles prepared by Smith on the history of his revelations and the early history of
the church.[62]

Joseph Smith remained as editor of the *Times and Seasons* until the
close of the third volume. In the first issue of the fourth volume, on
November 15, 1842, he announced that he was turning over the paper
to John Taylor.[63] Smith's career with the *Times and Seasons* ended on a
note quite similar to that on which it opened—the marriage notice. Just
before he gave up the printing office, there appeared on the streets of
Nauvoo, over the imprint of "J. Smith, printer," a curious thirty-seven-
page pamphlet by one Udney Hay Jacob entitled *An Extract from a Manuscript Entitled the Peace Maker. Or the Doctrines of the Millennium: Being a
Treatise on Religion and Jurisprudence. Or a New System of Religion and Politics.
For God, My Country and My Rights. By Udney Hay Jacob, an Israelite, and a
Shepherd of Israel.* A short note on the verso of the title page explained
that the author was not a Mormon, although the book had been printed
on their press for convenience. It added about the author, "But the
public will soon find out what he is, by his work." What in fact the
public found out was that the author had written a sophisticated treatise
advocating polygamy in lieu of divorce as a solution for marital difficulties.[64] Fawn Brodie, in her biography of Joseph Smith, *No Man Knows
My History,* suggested that he published this book "to break the ground
before sowing broadcast the seeds of his new doctrine" of plural marriage.[65] If this is true, Smith must have found the ground to be rather
hard, for he shortly published the following notice in the *Times and
Seasons:* "There was a book printed at my office, a short time since,
written by Udney J. Jacob, on marriage, without my knowledge, and
had I been apprised of it, I should not have printed it, not that I am
opposed of any man enjoying his privileges, but I do not wish to have
my name associated with the author's, in such unmeaning rigmarole of
nonsense, folly, and trash."[66] The doctrine of plural marriage was destined to remain an official secret for some time to come.

The man to whom Smith turned over the editorial duties of the
Times and Seasons, John Taylor, was born in England in 1808. He immi-
grated to Canada and was there baptized a Mormon in 1836. He went
west to Utah in 1846, and after the death of Brigham Young in 1877, he
became the third president of the church. Not long after taking over the
Times and Seasons, Taylor also took over the editorial duties at the *Wasp,*
which he changed to the *Neighbor* in May 1843. He remained in control
of both papers until they ceased publication.

When he first took over the printing establishment, Taylor was joined
by Wilford Woodruff, who acted as a sort of business manager for the

operation. Woodruff was born in Connecticut in 1807 and was converted to Mormonism in 1833. Because of his missionary duties, Woodruff avoided most of the difficulties in Missouri. His partnership with John Taylor lasted until February 1844, when he left Nauvoo to go on mission to England, where he remained until 1846. He also went to Utah, in 1889 became the fourth president of the church, and in 1890 issued the manifesto ending the practice of polygamy in Utah.

It certainly cannot be considered accidental that the men who succeeded Joseph Smith and Brigham Young as presidents of the church had earlier served in responsible positions in the printing office. But perhaps it would be more correct to say that it was no accident that the men who took over the printing office from Smith in 1842 were trusted associates and prominent members of the Quorum of Twelve and the Council of Fifty.[67] Having taken the printing office away from Ebenezer Robinson, Joseph Smith and the Quorum of Twelve made certain that the operation of the office would henceforth remain closely integrated with the highest levels of church leadership.

By 1844 Nauvoo could boast a population in excess of ten thousand inhabitants and had become the second largest city in Illinois. In part due to the prosperity of the town, and in part due to the perception that the Mormons tended to vote in a block and wielded immense political power in the county, if not the state, citizens in the neighboring town of Warsaw, Illinois, were beginning to become rather vocal in their opposition to the Mormons. It is also possible that they had become aware of the political ramifications of Joseph Smith's kingdom of God and perhaps even learned of the establishment of the Council of Fifty. Of course, they knew something of the sexual activities of the Mormon leaders and appeared to have direct knowledge of the text of the revelation on polygamy that Smith had showed to his own wife in 1843. These factors, and others too complicated to dwell on here, added fuel to the constantly growing fires of anti-Mormonism in Illinois, and the Warsaw newspaper, called the *Signal*, was only too happy to constantly keep all of this before its readers.[68]

Although this is sketchy at best, some of the animosity against the Mormons exhibited in the Warsaw *Signal* can be understood as a kind of journalistic envy.[69] Journalism in Illinois was hardly an easy life, few papers survived for very long, and those that did had difficulty. Editors and publishers were constantly on the move looking for a community that would actually support a newspaper. Warsaw, strategically located on the Mississippi River about twenty miles south of Nauvoo, was like almost every other town in Illinois in that its citizens had come west looking for a green pasture in which to thrive—most, of course, found

only failure. Newspapers served their communities not only as pur-
veyors of news but more important as boosters, constantly plugging for
railroads and other internal improvements that would ensure the town's
continued growth and prosperity.

If the citizens of Warsaw could feel jealous about the growth and
prosperity of Nauvoo, it can be imagined how much more so the editor
of the *Signal* must have felt. The circulation of the *Signal* seems to have
always been less than a thousand subscribers, and the paper was always
seriously in debt and, in fact, had ceased publication on several instances,
usually to be revived by dire warnings of how its permanent demise
would further the Mormon desire to take over the county.[70] While one
cannot dismiss the other factors that played a role in Warsaw's growing
animosity toward Nauvoo, neither can one dismiss outright the possibility that the Warsaw *Signal* used the "Mormon menace" to its own advantage and to further its own growth.

Although the *Times and Seasons* and the *Neighbor* were not themselves
necessarily openly hostile to Warsaw, one is struck in perusing the Nauvoo
papers by the fact that there is almost no mention of Warsaw at all. No
ads and almost no news about the second largest town in the county.
The insular qualities of the Mormon newspapers not only served to seal
off Nauvoo residents from outside influences but also possibly caused
their neighbors in Warsaw to feel that the rumors of the Mormon conspiracy to take over the county were true.[71]

This sentiment was only strengthened when Joseph Smith announced
in 1844 that he was presenting himself as a candidate for the presidency
of the United States. Smith had prepared a campaign document carefully outlining his views and positions, and in February 1844 fifteen
hundred copies of his *Views of the Powers and Policy of the Government of the
United States* were published in the printing office by John Taylor.[72]
These copies were widely distributed throughout the United States to
various government officials and all of the principal newspaper offices.
Taylor reprinted the text in the *Times and Seasons*—but not in the pages
of the *Neighbor*—on May 15, 1844, and two days later Joseph Smith was
officially nominated by a convention held in Nauvoo.[73]

Just before this convention took place, however, the troubles over the
still secret doctrine of plural marriage reached a point beyond Joseph
Smith's control. Concerned about Smith's economic and political control in Nauvoo and increasingly alarmed by his taking wives, a group of
very prominent Mormons, including Robert D. Foster, William Law,
Wilson Law, Charles Higbee, and Francis Higbee, began to form a dissident group within the Mormon community. When Smith made advances to Wilson Law's wife, Jane, the break became complete.

On the seventh of May 1844, this group brought another printing press to Nauvoo and established a printing office in the house of Robert Foster. Three days later they issued a prospectus for a newspaper to be called the *Expositor.*[74] The prospectus announced the intention of the proprietors to use the paper as a vehicle to denounce the abuse of power by the authorities in Nauvoo and to provide evidence of the "flagrant abuses of moral delinquencies."[75] John C. Bennett had been a thoroughgoing rogue, and while Joseph Smith had been able to fend off his attacks with little difficulty, he realized that he would be unable to turn aside as easily the attacks of men so prominent and respected in his own community. When the first issue of the *Expositor* was published on June 7, 1844, Smith acted quickly to ensure that it would be the last. He went before the city council and had the press declared a public nuisance, and on the evening of June 10 the city marshal of Nauvoo gathered a posse and destroyed the press and distributed the type in the streets.[76]

Such an act could hardly be called uncommon in American history, and Illinois had its share of such outrages, the most famous of which was the destruction of Elijah Lovejoy's *Observer* in Alton a few years before and the murder of Lovejoy himself. But the destruction of the *Expositor* was not the act of an outraged citizenry, shamefully acting on some frenzied impulse. Rather, this was an officially sanctioned act of the city government of Nauvoo itself, and one is hard-pressed to see in it anything other than a flagrant abuse of political power.[77] Joseph Smith had spent a lifetime living by his instincts. In almost every case they had served him well. But by this point it would seem that his instincts had given way to hubris, and he was unable to foresee the ramifications of his act.

There is some irony in the knowledge that Joseph Smith had used the press in Nauvoo to help build up his kingdom, and it was the press in Nauvoo that finally gave Smith over to his enemies, for with his destruction of the *Expositor* office, Smith had effectively delivered himself into the hands of the anti-Mormon forces in Hancock County. A warrant for his arrest was issued shortly after the *Expositor* was destroyed, and although he and his brother Hyrum went so far as to escape across the river into Iowa, they eventually surrendered to authorities in Carthage. On June 27, an anti-Mormon mob stormed Carthage Jail, where Joseph and Hyrum Smith were incarcerated, and murdered the prophet and his brother. John Taylor, who had accompanied the brothers to jail, was wounded during the attack but survived.

With the murder of Joseph Smith, the history of the printing office in Nauvoo enters its final stage. The Mormons remained in Nauvoo for

almost two more years, and the bitter anti-Mormon feelings that had
erupted in June into the violence at Carthage continued in what has
come to be called the Mormon War. Throughout most of this period,
the *Times and Seasons* largely maintained its sedate demeanor, and most
of the news of the violence was carried in the pages of the *Neighbor.*
Curiously enough, during the trial of the persons indicted for the murder of Joseph Smith, neither paper carried any news concerning the
trial. One Mormon in the printing office did issue a pamphlet containing
an account of the murders written by William M. Daniels, but when its
author was brought before the court to testify against the defendants,
his account did not stand up very well under cross-examination.[78] According to an unreliable account provided by Joseph Smith's brother
William, Brigham Young was so outraged by the publication of this
work that he ordered the murder of its author.[79] While this account is
probably false, it does serve to emphasize the attitude of the Mormon
elders and highlights the role assumed by the press during this period.
Shortly after the murder of Joseph Smith, the Saints began making serious plans to leave Nauvoo, but they needed time to avoid reliving their
hasty retreat from Missouri years earlier, and the Quorum of the Twelve
was determined that the temple be completed so the Nauvoo Mormons
could receive their endowments before vacating the city.

In the fall of 1845, John Taylor announced at a church conference
that he thought the time had come to cease publication of the *Times and
Seasons* and *Neighbor.* The Twelve decided that the *Neighbor* should cease
publication immediately and that the *Times and Seasons* should continue
until the current volume was completed.[80] The *Neighbor* abruptly ceased
publication in October 1845, and the *Times and Seasons* finally ended
publication in February 1846.

When the *Times and Seasons* ceased publication, the printing office
was taken over by a Gentile named William Matlack, who began publishing a paper called the *Hancock Eagle* in the interests of the Mormons
who remained in Nauvoo, as well as those non-Mormons, called "new
citizens," who had purchased Mormon property. Matlack died not long
after he took over the office, and the *Eagle* ceased publication in August
1846. With the suspension of the *Eagle,* the Nauvoo printing office passed
out of Mormon hands.

The Mormons fled Missouri in 1839, a motley group of individuals
only loosely tied together by their faith. In Nauvoo, the Mormons pros-
pered, and the institutional church grew strong enough to survive the
murder of its founder. The Mormon sense of identity, deeply involved
with the history of the former-day saints revealed in the Book of Mormon,
was made deeper and stronger during the years in Nauvoo, partly with
the aid of the church printing office. What had happened in Missouri

would never happen again; the Mormons would leave Nauvoo en bloc as a church with their leadership intact and their sense of identity strong.

Notes

An earlier version of this essay appeared in *Western Illinois Regional Studies* 11 (Fall 1988): 5–29.

1. Robert Bruce Flanders makes only passing reference to the printing office and its publication in his *Nauvoo: Kingdom on the Mississippi* (Urbana: University of Illinois Press, 1965). Parry D. Sorensen's *"Nauvoo Times and Seasons," Journal of the Illinois State Historical Society* 55 (Summer 1962): 117–135, is inaccurate and uninformative.

2. For a brief account of all of these printing offices with a bibliography of the productions of the presses, see Peter Crawley, "A Bibliography of the Church of Jesus Christ of Latter-day Saints in New York, Ohio, and Missouri," *Brigham Young University Studies* 12 (Summer 1972): 465–537.

3. Joseph Smith, *History of the Church of Jesus Christ of Latter-day Saints,* ed. B. H. Roberts (Salt Lake City: Deseret News Press, 1902–12; 6 vols., a seventh volume was published in 1932; reprinted by Deseret Book, 1976, and reissued in paperback in 1978), 4:398. Purportedly written by Joseph Smith, the *History* was edited by B. H. Roberts from various Mormon diaries, journals, and records. An interesting account of this work is Jerold Tanner and Sandra Tanner, *Changes in Joseph Smith's History* (Salt Lake City: Modern Microfilm, 1964). William Miller is credited with the act of burying the press by Juanita Brooks, ed., *On the Mormon Frontier: The Diary of Hosea Stout, 1844–1861,* 2 vols. (Salt Lake City: University of Utah Press, 1964), 1:99.

4. Ebenezer Robinson, "Items of Personal History of the Editor," *The Return* (Davis City, Iowa) 2 (May 1890): 257. *The Return* was a monthly periodical edited, published, and printed by Ebenezer Robinson at Davis City, Iowa, from January 1889 to February 1891. Beginning with the April 1889 issue, Robinson published his autobiographical reminiscences, under the title listed here.

5. Ibid., 1 (April 1889): 59.

6. Ibid., 1 (May 1889): 75–76.

7. Ibid., 2 (April 1890): 241–44; 2 (May 1890): 258.

8. The biographical information relating to Don Carlos Smith is taken from Smith, *History of the Church,* 4:393–98.

9. Unfortunately, no separate copy of this prospectus has survived. The text of the prospectus was reprinted in the *Times and Seasons* in the first issue of July 1839 and reprinted again in the November 1839 issue.

10. Ebenezer Robinson, "Items of Personal History of the Editor," *The Return* 2 (May 1890): 257–58. A slightly different account of the establishment of the printing office is given in Smith, *History of the Church,* 4:398. That account essentially ignores Ebenezer Robinson and glorifies Don Carlos Smith's role in the establishment of the printing office.

11. Ebenezer Robinson, "Items of Personal History of the Editor," *The Return* 2 (May 1890): 258.

12. Most of the extant runs of the *Times and Seasons* begin with the November 1839 issue. A copy of the original July 1839 issue can be found in the Library-Archives of the Reorganized Church of Jesus Christ of Latter Day Saints in Independence, Missouri.

13. Wayne Ham, *Publish Glad Tidings: Readings in Early Latter Day Saint Sources* (Independence, Mo.: Herald Publishing House, 1970), 30.

14. A prospectus for this paper, to be called *The News*, was published in the *Times and Seasons* 1 (April 1840): 96. The editors announced in the issue of 2 (December 1, 1840): 240, that publication of *The News* had been deferred "for the present" because of the lack of subscribers. Such "secular" newspapers had been issued as companions to the church's religious paper in Independence, Missouri, and Kirtland, Ohio.

15. Lawrence Foster, *Religion and Sexuality: Three American Communal Experiments of the Nineteenth Century* (New York: Oxford University Press, 1981), 119.

16. This generalization is not meant to imply that there was absolutely no news of the outside world in the *Times and Seasons*, but generally the "news" that was printed was intended to strengthen Mormon views about Nauvoo and the world at large. Of course, nineteenth-century editors had an entirely different sense of "news" than do modern editors and readers, and the *Times and Seasons* was primarily a "religious" periodical.

17. In the *Times and Seasons* 1 (December 1839): 25, the editors printed a resolution of "the Presidency and high council of this place" that "ten thousand copies of a Hymn Book, be printed; also that the Book of Mormon be re-printed in this place, under the inspection of the Presidency, as soon as monies can be raised to defray the expenses." See also Smith, *History of the Church*, 4:49.

18. *Times and Seasons* 1 (April 1840): 91. This advertisement only specifies that the money is to be used for "BOOK printing."

19. Ibid., 12 (May 1840): 112.

20. Ebenezer Robinson, "Items of Personal History of the Editor," *The Return* 2 (May 1890): 258–59.

21. Ibid., 2 (May 1890): 259–62. Robinson's interesting account of the printing of the 1840 edition of the Book of Mormon does not begin to answer all of the questions surrounding that edition. For instance, his account clearly stated that he paid for the binding of two thousand copies of the Book of Mormon in Cincinnati and returned to Nauvoo with about a thousand of these copies. But he had negotiated with Joseph Smith to print four thousand copies. It is possible that Robinson was intending to print the other two thousand copies from the stereotype plates after he returned to Nauvoo. This might possibly help explain the two issues of the book (see Colton Storm, *A Catalogue of the Everett D. Graff Collection of Western Americana* [Chicago: University of Chicago Press for the Newberry Library, 1968],

item #709, which contains a simple description of the two issues), as well as the disputed "index" to the Book of Mormon (see Cecil Byrd's *Bibliography of Illinois Imprints, 1814–1858* [Chicago: University of Chicago Press, 1966], item #511). Answers to these questions await a more detailed study of the operations of the Nauvoo printing office.

22. *Times and Seasons* 1 (November 1, 1840): 208.

23. Ibid., 1 (November 1, 1840): 204.

24. Kimball's *Journal* was advertised as "just published" in the *Times and Seasons* 2 (January 1, 1841): 271.

25. Robert B. Thompson's "Introduction" to Heber C. Kimball's *Journal* (Nauvoo, Ill.: Robinson and Smith, 1840), vi–vii. Kimball's *Journal* has been reprinted in facsimile in *Nauvoo Classics* (Salt Lake City: Mormon Heritage Publishers, 1976).

26. *Times and Seasons* 1 (September 1840): 169.

27. Ibid., 2 (December 15, 1840): 248.

28. James Mulholland's book of poetry, entitled *An Address to America: A Poem in Blank Verse* (Nauvoo, Ill.: Ebenezer Robinson, 1841), was advertised as "just published" on January 1, 1841, in the same advertisement announcing the publication of Kimball's *Journal.* Because Mulholland's work carried only the imprint of Ebenezer Robinson, printing must have begun after the dissolution of the partnership of Robinson and Smith and hence after printing had begun on Kimball's *Journal.*

29. Eliza Roxey Snow, *Time and Change: A Poem in Blank Verse. Also Two Odes, One for the Sons of Liberty, the Other for the Fourth of July* (Nauvoo, Ill.: E. Robinson, 1841).

30. Robinson and Smith announced that they were going to publish this hymn book in the *Times and Seasons* of November 1, 1840. The work was described as "just out of the press" in the *Times and Seasons* 2 (March 15, 1841): 355. The book was published over the imprint of Ebenezer Robinson.

31. Omer, *The Latter-Day Saints: A Poem in Two Cantos* (Nauvoo, Ill.: for the author, 1841). Although no printer is listed on the title page of this work, it can be assigned to the *Times and Seasons* office with some certainty. A long editorial notice of the work appeared in the *Times and Seasons* 2 (June 15, 1841): 449, and the same issue carried an advertisement for the work, noting that it was "for sale at this office, at the stores of J. Smith and C. W. Lyon" (454). Both Byrd, in his *Bibliography of Illinois Imprints,* and Chad Flake, in his *Mormon Bibliography, 1830–1930* (Salt Lake City: University of Utah Press, 1978), were unwilling definitively to assign Littlefield as the author of this work. However, in his autobiography, *Reminiscences of Latter-day Saints* (Logan, Utah: Utah Journal, 1888), Littlefield describes how he came to write a romance entitled "Eliza, or, the Broken Vow," which "Omer" is credited with writing on the title page.

32. *Times and Seasons* 2 (May 1, 1841): 403.

33. Ibid., 2 (August 15, 1841): 517.

34. Ibid., 2 (September 1, 1841): 519.

35. Quoted in Fawn M. Brodie, *No Man Knows My History: The Life of Joseph Smith, the Mormon Prophet,* rev. ed. (New York: Alfred A. Knopf, 1971), 289.

36. Ebenezer Robinson, "Items of Personal History of the Editor," *The Return* 2 (July 1890): 302. Robinson stated that he began the work of stereotyping the hymn book and the Doctrine and Covenants in the spring of 1841. Of course, Robinson was also busy with other job printing work, which included the printing of the stock certificates for the Nauvoo House.

37. Ibid., 2 (September 1890): 324. Here Robinson describes a visit from Joseph Smith in which Smith gave him a warning: "He said: 'The Twelve are wanting to get the *Times and Seasons* from you, and I thought I would tell you, for I am sorry to see any feelings of difference arise between you [and the] brethren who have borne the burden in the heat of the day.'"

38. Smith, *History of the Church,* 4:454.

39. Robinson's announcement of having secured the services of Gustavus Hills, as well as Hills's "Salutary," appeared in the *Times and Seasons* 3 (January 15, 1842): 663.

40. Smith, *History of the Church,* 4:463.

41. Ibid., 4:467.

42. Ibid., 4:503.

43. Ebenezer Robinson, "Items of Personal History of the Editor," *The Return* 2 (September 1890): 325.

44. Ibid., 2 (October 1890): 346. In Smith, *History of the Church,* 4:514–15, Joseph Smith reported that the purchase price was "between 7,000 and 8,000 dollars." Although Robinson was writing of the event many years later, he states in his account that he was referring to his account book, "which I kept at the time, and which is now before me." Thus, I believe, there is little reason to doubt Robinson's account of the transaction.

45. Ebenezer Robinson, "Items of Personal History of the Editor, *The Return* 2 (October 1890): 346–47.

46. I have found no direct evidence of the size of the subscription list of the *Times and Seasons,* but the *Hancock Eagle,* the paper published by William Matlack on behalf of the Mormons after they had begun leaving Nauvoo in 1846, reported in its issue of April 24, 1846, that it had 1,200 subscribers and would thereafter print 2,000 copies. Considering that the population of Nauvoo had seriously declined by April of 1846, it is reasonable to assume that the circulation of the *Times and Seasons* would have been substantially larger than that of the *Eagle.*

47. Ebenezer Robinson, "Items of Personal History of the Editor," *The Return* 1 (October 1890): 346.

48. Under the date of January 17, 1841, Smith, *History of the Church,* 4:494–95, stated that "the Council were unanimously opposed to Robinson's publishing the Book of Mormon and other books."

49. Joseph Smith's warning to Ebenezer Robinson bears repeating: "The Twelve are wanting to get the *Times and Seasons* from you, and I thought I

would tell you, for I am sorry to see any feelings of difference arise between you [and the] *brethren who have borne the burden in the heat of the day*" (Ebenezer Robinson, "Items of Personal History of the Editor," *The Return* 1 (September 1890): 324 [emphasis added]).

50. The best work on the Council of Fifty is Klaus J. Hansen, *Quest for Empire: The Political Kingdom of God and the Council of Fifty in Mormon History* (East Lansing: Michigan State University Press, 1967).

51. The actual revelation concerning the political kingdom was received by Joseph Smith on April 7, 1842.

52. Ebenezer Robinson, "Items of Personal History of the Editor," *The Return* 2 (June 1890): 287. Robinson recounts a conversation with Don Carlos Smith in June 1841, in which he quoted Don Carlos Smith as saying, "Any man who will teach and practice the doctrine of spiritual wifery will go to hell. I don't care if it is my brother Joseph."

53. *Times and Seasons* 3 (February 15, 1842): 696. This notice, headed "To Subscribers," was signed "ed." The editor was listed on page 792 of the same issue as Joseph Smith.

54. Ibid., 3 (February 15, 1842): 701.

55. The fact that the *Signal* picked up on the implications of the marriage announcement is found in a letter by Lyman O. Littlefield published in the *Times and Seasons* 3 (March 15, 1842): 729. Littlefield makes reference to a "very wanton and ungentlemanly attack" on Joseph Smith published in the "last" *Signal*. Littlefield's letter is dated March 14, 1842, but it is not clear to which issue of the *Signal* he was referring. The issue of the *Signal* for March 9, 1842 (i.e., the "last" issue before Littlefield's letter was written) contains no attack on Joseph Smith, nor do the issues of February 16 and February 23. Unfortunately, the issues of March 2 and March 16 are not extant.

56. *Times and Seasons* 3 (March 1, 1842): 710. Curiously, this notice appears under the dateline of "Tuesday, March 15, 1842."

57. Ibid., 3 (March 15, 1842): 729.

58. "From the standpoint of the church which survived him, the Book of Abraham was the most unfortunate thing Joseph ever wrote" (Brodie, *No Man Knows My History*, 174). Eleven fragments of these papyri were discovered at the Metropolitan Museum of Art in 1967 and returned to the Utah church. Unfortunately, scholars working on the papyri confirmed that they were ordinary funeral documents. An extended account of the Book of Abraham papyri can be found in Jerold Tanner and Sandra Tanner, *Mormonism: Shadow or Reality?* rev. ed. (Salt Lake City: Utah Lighthouse Ministry, 1982), 294–369D.

59. Don Carlos Smith published a prospectus for a weekly paper to be called the *Nauvoo Ensign and Zarahemla Standard* in the *Times and Seasons* 2 (June 15, 1841): 453. In the *Times and Seasons* 3 (November 1, 1841): 535, Ebenezer Robinson announced that the proposed weekly had been abandoned.

60. *Times and Seasons* 3 (April 15, 1842): 766. I have been unable to locate any reference to a prospectus for the *Wasp* published in any other

Illinois paper of the period. Prospectuses for both of the weeklies proposed earlier in Nauvoo were published in the *Times and Seasons.*

61. Bennett's main attack against Joseph Smith was published as *The History of the Saints; or, an Expose of Joe Smith and Mormonism* (Boston: Leland and Whiting, 1842). Bennett also published articles in various newspapers, most notably the *Sangamo Journal* (Springfield, Ill.), and gave lectures throughout the East prior to the publication of his book.

62. The publication of Joseph Smith's history actually began a short time before the first issue of the *Wasp* was published. The first issue to contain the history was that of March 1, 1842.

63. *Times and Seasons* 4 (November 15, 1842): 8. At this time, Joseph Smith maintained ownership of the printing office, only leasing it to Taylor and Woodruff for a period of five years (Smith, *History of the Church,* 5:198–99). Smith sold the establishment to John Taylor in January of 1844 (Smith, *History of the Church,* 6:185). Taylor moved the printing office from the corner of Water and Bain streets to the building at Main and Kimball streets in May 1845. Taylor's decision to move the printing office is surprising, despite his announcement that the move was being made to enlarge the establishment, considering that he was certainly aware that time was running out for the Mormons in Nauvoo; the official decision concerning suspending publication of the period was made in October of 1845. I believe Taylor's decision to move the printing office was a direct outcome of the antagonism between Emma Smith and Brigham Young. Joseph Smith sold John Taylor the printing establishment in 1844, but he retained ownership of the property at Water and Bain.

64. An interesting account of Jacob and his work can be found in John E. Hallwas, *Western Illinois Heritage* (Macomb: Illinois Heritage Press, 1983), 79–81.

65. Brodie, *No Man Knows My History,* 298.

66. *Times and Seasons* 4 (December 1, 1842): 32.

67. At a meeting with the Twelve on April 19, 1842, Joseph Smith told John Taylor, "I believe you can do more good in the editorial department than preaching. You can write for thousands to read; while you can preach to but a few at a time. We have no one else we can trust the paper with" (Smith, *History of the Church,* 5:367).

68. Unfortunately, there is no detailed study of the Warsaw newspaper and their editors; only Thomas Gregg has received any real attention, in John E. Hallwas, *Thomas Gregg: Early Illinois Journalist and Author,* Monograph Series (Macomb: Western Illinois University, 1983).

69. Bad feelings among journalists was not unique to Warsaw and Nauvoo. For instance, John York Sawyer, editor of Vandalia's *Illinois Advocate,* made scurrilous attacks on the character of Meinrad Greiner, editor of the *Vandalia Whig & Illinois Intelligencer,* because of their natural economic and political rivalry and Sawyer's anger over having lost to Greiner the contract to print the Illinois laws of 1833.

70. The *Signal* notes in its issue of July 2, 1845, that it had 700 subscribers; in its issue of July 26, 1846, it noted that it had 900 subscribers. Of course, subscribers alone rarely sufficed to keep a newspaper solvent. Most newspaper printing offices relied on job printing as well. One of the difficulties facing the *Signal* was that the Mormons, through their eventual control of the county, were able to secure the lucrative contracts for publication of the county tax delinquent list and for the various county "forms" for their own printing office.

71. Hancock County was one of the very few counties in Illinois that did not have a newspaper office located in its county seat. Although Carthage had been the home of the first paper published in the county, the *Carthagenian,* established in 1836, no paper was published in Carthage from 1837 until 1853. Centrally located in the county away from the Mississippi River, Carthage lacked the natural advantages of both Warsaw and Nauvoo and exercised but economic power in the county.

72. Under the date of February 24, Joseph Smith noted "Fifteen hundred copies of my 'Views' out of press" (Smith, *History of the Church,* 6:224). Smith completed the text of his work on February 7, and it was publicly read for the first time on February 8 (Smith, *History of the Church,* 6:210) and then read to a large public meeting in Nauvoo on February 9 (Smith, *History of the Church,* 6:211).

73. Although the text of Smith's *Views* was not printed in the *Neighbor,* it was advertised for sale by that paper on February 28, 1844.

74. On May 7, Joseph Smith noted, "An opposition printing press arrives at Dr. Foster's" (Smith, *History of the Church,* 6:357). Smith further noted on May 10 that "a prospectus of the *Nauvoo Expositor* was distributed among the people by the apostates" (ibid., 6:363). Dale L. Morgan mistakenly believed that this prospectus "was not printed by the Mormon press in Nauvoo [but] it may have been printed in St. Louis" (*A Bibliography of the Churches of the Dispersion* [N.p, (1953)], 1). As Byrd noted, these two statements in the *History* would "seem to prove incontestably that the *prospectus* was printed in Nauvoo" (*Bibliography of Illinois Imprints,* notes to item #880).

75. Smith, *History of the Church,* 6:443–44.

76. Ibid., 6:432–52.

77. Although Dallin H. Oaks found "considerable basis in the law of their day for their action in characterizing the published issues of the *Nauvoo Expositor* as a nuisance . . . there was no legal justification in 1844 for the destruction of the *Expositor* press" ("The Suppression of the Nauvoo *Expositor,*" *Utah Law Review* 9 [Winter 1965]: 890–91, quoted in Dallin H. Oaks and Marvin S. Hill, *Carthage Conspiracy: The Trial of the Accused Assassins of Joseph Smith* [Urbana: University of Illinois Press, 1975], 26, note 48). Perhaps the case in Illinois that most closely parallels the destruction of the *Expositor* is Lincoln's suppression of the *Chicago Times* during the Civil War, but in that instance the suppression ceased after a relatively short time, and the press itself was not destroyed.

78. William M. Daniels, *A Correct Account of the Murder of Generals Joseph and Hyrum Smith, at Carthage, on the 27th Day of June, 1844* (Nauvoo, Ill.: Published by John Taylor for the Proprietor, 1844). Lyman O. Littlefield was responsible for the publication of this pamphlet. See Oaks and Hill, *Carthage Conspiracy*, 125–36, for an account of Daniels's testimony.

79. William Smith's charges appeared in a letter, dated "Perkins Grove, Sept. 24, 1846," published in the *Sangamo Journal*, November 5, 1846, 3.

80. *Times and Seasons* 6 (November 1, 1845): 1015.

7

Religion in Nauvoo: Some Reflections

MARVIN S. HILL

One has no difficulty finding evidence of religious piety in Nauvoo. The miraculous healings by the Prophet Joseph Smith when fever swept the bottomlands during the first year of settlement, the river baptisms for the dead, the majestic temple gradually taking form high on the bluffs above the town are all reminders that Nauvoo was a religious community and the Mormons a religious people.[1] One might cite Joseph Smith's instructions to the women on March 17, 1842, at the time the Relief Society was established, as evidence of Christian charity and morality. The women were to provoke the brethren to good works by looking to the wants of the poor—searching for "objects of charity . . . to assist by correcting morals and strengthening the virtues of the community."[2] An ardent missionary spirit that filled the minds and hearts of the elders is reflected in Wilford Woodruff's journal on the eve of his mission to England in August 1839: "it is no small trial of faith to leave my family & my all & start on a mission of four thousand miles . . . & that without purse or scrip with the power of disease resting upon me . . . but I do this freely for Christ's sake trusting in him for the recompense of reward."[3]

There was also a Christian millennial hope. John Taylor expressed this in a letter written to his wife in September 1840. He said that when he returned from his mission, they would talk of things old and new and "forget all our troubles & look forward to the day that shall be revealed at the coming of our Lord Jesus Christ with all his saints."[4]

But when I was asked to consider religion in Nauvoo and began looking over my research notes that fill many file cabinets, I found that very few of them deal directly with religious subjects. To be sure, I have a folder on theology and one on Joseph Smith as a religious leader, but the majority of them deal with such topics as "the kingdom," "politics," "business affairs," and "polygamy." There is a folder labeled "Mormon apocalyptic," but much of this material is actually social and political in nature. When I turned to the journals of the elders, I found on the whole very little soul-searching; they were far too busy building the kingdom to have time for religious meditation or introspection. A question now becomes appropriate: in comparison with so much that seems to be secular and worldly, was there much that was religious in Nauvoo?

This is a question that has been asked about Mormonism as a whole and often has been answered negatively. Many are familiar with Bernard DeVoto's disgust with Mormon materialism, its "talents for sugar, rails, and industrials."[5] But, of course, that general point of view goes far back into Mormon history. As early as 1833 Nancy Towles said Mormonism was a "profanation and sacrilege of all religious things."[6] Even Jules Remy, a more perceptive interpreter of Mormonism, said following his journey to Salt Lake City in 1860, "Mormonism is nothing more than the product of calculation . . . or speculation. . . . The thirst for gold . . . was the . . . inspiration of Smith's religious scheme."[7]

Harsh words indeed. Yet it is a judgment that has persisted in somewhat more moderate terms until our own day. One thinks of Fawn Brodie's earthy characterization of Joseph Smith or of numerous articles in popular journals that stress the mundane programs of the Utah church, its banks and business enterprises, or its welfare program.[8] Very little has been written about the religious quality of Mormonism and thus almost nothing about religion in Nauvoo. In a more recent study of Nauvoo, which I think is exceptionally well done, chapter topics include government, the military, land speculation, business, industry, finance, conflict within the kingdom, and the kingdom as empire. Almost nothing here treats religion as such. The orientation is largely economic and political, although the author initially treats the subject in a religious context. A chapter on the Nauvoo House and the Nauvoo Temple is called "A Dwelling for Man and a Dwelling for God" but deals with the activity of building these edifices, not their ultimate religious significance.[9] Clearly, perceptive interpreters have considered Mormonism in Nauvoo to be very worldly.

Notwithstanding this, there have been those from time to time who thought they saw something else in Mormonism besides American materialism. Jules Remy said that what struck him most was Mormonism's universality—"it summons the whole world within its embrace."[10] Richard T. Ely saw this universality as religious, for he said that "according to the Mormons all life is held to be sacred."[11] I like best the way Orson Hyde stated it in his speech before the high priests in Nauvoo in 1845. He said Mormons call "everything an ordinance of religion that can tend to man's perfection and happiness; whether it be to plow and sow the fields, to buy and sell goods, wares and merchandise, houses or lands, to go to the polls and vote, to the prayer meeting, or to the sacrament of the Lord's supper . . . whatever we do we wish to do all to the glory of God."[12]

That, I think, is the essence of Mormonism and helps to explain why it has been so difficult for observers to say much about its religious nature. Mormonism includes so much of the things of this world that critics have not been able to identify its religious qualities. It might be that the inability to identify what is religious in Mormonism grows out of the fact that historians who observe it are victims of their own cultural evolution, that they are post-Reformation in their outlook and tend, whether Catholic or Protestant, to see the sacred and secular as different things. It seems to me that when Joseph Smith in the account of his vision received in 1820 denounced all churches as having a form of godliness but teaching the commandments of men, he was in part criticizing the secularism implicit in a multitude of religious sects. It seems also that in denouncing the prevailing religious establishment he repudiated Protestantism with its strong emphasis on individualistic religion,[13] the idea that salvation comes through a personal confrontation between God and the individual, in which no hireling priest as mediator is necessary. Most of this was spelled out by 1830 or 1831.[14] The Mormon emphasis on personal testimony would seem to be an exception to this generalization, a continuation of the central Protestant thrust. Yet I would argue that primarily the Mormons sought their salvation by different means, by the performance of duties that were essentially social, by ceremonies and rituals that were largely public, by conformity to measurable standards that ranged from baptism by immersion and support for polygamy to abstinence from tea, coffee, alcohol, and tobacco.

Seen in this context, everything that occurred in Nauvoo of a social or political nature was to the Saints essentially religious. These things were religious in a sense that the Yale historian Erwin Goodenough would have understood. In his article "A Historian of Religion Tries to Define Religion,"[15] he maintained that the initial universal quest for religion is the quest for security. Religion is secondarily a search for beliefs that explain and control nature. Goodenough maintained that legalism and orthodoxy provide freedom from doubt. The common denominator, he said, is devotion, commitment, and service to the source of the "unknown terror" in the universe.

Most of the specialists in Mormon history have been aware for years that establishing a political kingdom of God was a central concern of the early Mormons,[16] but few have bothered to ask why this was so. I believe that the social and intellectual taproot of the kingdom was the fear that prevailed among the Saints that the American democracy based, as James Madison saw, on pluralism could not work. The Mormon millennialist faith affirmed that only a government designed and governed under the intimate direction of Almighty God could endure and provide peace and justice on the earth.[17] We have overlooked the fact that millennialist hope grew out of a desire for a termination of social change and social conflict and the establishment of eternal peace.[18] Peace, security, the end of social conflict—these are, in Goodenough's terms, religious desires. Hence, the pursuit of the kingdom might have been as much a quest for refuge as a quest for empire. One recalls Joseph Smith's prophecy at Nauvoo in July 1839 that "the time is soon coming, when no man will have any peace but in Zion and her stakes."[19] Empire seems to have been somewhat incidental to the underlying religious objective. A young man who began his religious search by reacting rigorously against the pluralism of contending sects might conclude it by establishing a kingdom that would, he hoped, bring peace on earth.

A similar point can be made about the Nauvoo Legion, Joseph Smith's military arm of the kingdom. The Mormon people showed no overt tendency toward militarism until they were brutally expelled from Jackson County, Missouri. The Nauvoo Legion was a lawful extension of the county militia organized to protect the Mormons from their violent enemies, but it was also to be an instrument in the hands of the Lord to preserve the nation's liberty and peace on the eve of the millennium. A poem by Eliza R. Snow written in Nauvoo makes this clear:

> Fair, Columbia! rejoice! look away to the West,
> To thy own Illinois, where the saints have found rest;
> See a phoenix come forth from the graves of the just,
> Whom Missouri's oppressors laid low in the dust:
> See a phoenix—a "Legion"—a warm hearted band,
> Who, unmov'd, so thy basis of freedom will stand.
>
> When the day of vexation rolls fearfully on—
> When thy children turn traitors—when safety is gone—
> When peace in thy borders, no longer is found—
> When the fierce battles rage, and the war-trumpets sound;
> Here, here are thy warriors—a true hearted band,
> To thy country's best int'rest forever will stand;
> For *then* to thy stand the "Legion" will be
> A strong bulwark of Freedom—of pure Liberty. . . .
>
> Should they need re-inforcements, those rights to secure,
> Which our fathers purchas'd; and Freedom ensure.
> There is still in reserve a strong Cohort above;
> "*Lo! the Chariots of Israel and horsemen thereof.*"[20]

Another area where the life in Nauvoo has seemed very worldly, but where social control seems to have been the primary objective, was land speculation. It is true, as Robert Flanders has stressed,[21] that the Mormon prophet spent much time as a realtor, buying land in large quantities and selling it at a profit when he could, but it does not seem likely that he profited personally to an exceptional degree. His standard of living was not above that of many others in Nauvoo; as a matter of fact, during the first four years when he lived in a log house, it may have been below that of many of the prominent men.[22] What profits he made were channeled back into the system to pay back debts and to promote the general economy.[23] Land-trading was a means to an end: to keep the kingdom going, to gather the Saints in large numbers, and to gain the benefits of a close-knit and harmonious, self-sustaining social order.

But the Mormons wanted more than peace on earth. They wanted salvation in the next world also. They tended, especially in Nauvoo, to see salvation in terms of prescribed procedures that would lead them to a higher level of achievement and power. Power to become a god was power to control the universe and make all things subject to their will.[24] Security was their aim in this and the next life. Sidney Rigdon spoke to the point when he said at Nauvoo that "it has been a universal mistake to suppose that salvation is distinct from government." He affirmed that when "God sets up a system of salvation, he sets up a system of government . . . I mean government that shall rule over spiritual and temporal things."[25] *Government* and *rule* are the key words here, and they imply social control. If establishing a political kingdom on earth seems to us today to be a radical means to achieve peace, we must not lose sight of the fact that the end—the religious ends—were clearly conservative.

Mario DePillis has argued that Mormonism had its origins in the quest for religious authority.[26] I would add that it was a quest for insight and certainty, however momentary. Relatively few Mormons seemed to care whether what had been prophesied was perfectly consistent with what happened afterward.[27] It did not matter how often the prophet altered or expanded theology;[28] the Saints valued the process of revelation more than the product. Although Joseph Smith revised his revelations from time to time,[29] including the Book of Mormon,[30] few elders ever objected. Only David Whitmer raised it as a major issue, but he had been in the movement from its inception and had been from the first opposed to having Joseph named prophet and seer.[31]

Many of Joseph Smith's earliest revelations were almost routine,[32] consisting of personal advice to individual elders who wished to know their calling in the church. What they wanted was a prophet who would spell out the Lord's will day to day, so all of them could feel that their personal lives were in complete accord with the "unknown terror." Again, it was the process more than the product that was of crucial importance. The multiplication of aspiring prophets following Smith's death in 1844 suggests how important the function of prophecy was to his followers.[33]

There was some wish for comprehensiveness as Jules Remy perceived. He said that the Mormon people wanted what their prophet wanted—a religion that would unite all religions and all nations. Remy quoted Joseph Smith in a significant passage: "if by the principles of truth I succeeded in uniting all denominations in the bonds of love, shall I not have attained a good object? Christians should cease wrangling and contention with each other, and cultivate the principles of union and friendship."[34] Union and friendship, I might add, would promote social peace rather than conflict and make individual differences easier to reconcile. Joseph's antipluralism, so apparent in his first vision,[35] provided one source for his new interpretations of biblical doctrine. His quest for theological inclusiveness in Nauvoo may best be seen in the ordinance of baptism for the dead, which combines a Baptist conception of the need for adult baptism by immersion with a Universalist idea that the gospel ought to save all people. It is significant that in introducing this doctrine, Smith said that the Saints past and present would be fused into a "whole and complete, and perfect union."[36]

Joseph Smith's stress on a universe governed by law, on its ultimate order and rationality,[37] may be seen as another way of guaranteeing security. The promise was that if people obeyed the laws they would gain their desired ends. The emphasis on priesthood held forth the same pledge, that right-thinking and right-acting elders could draw upon divine power and make the universe subject to their needs. Temple ordinances at Nauvoo, under the priesthood, guaranteed salvation, eternal achievement, and eternal union to those who conformed to the outward ordinances and were loyal to the leadership. They promoted group loyalty and subservience and a collective approach to problems met by the group.[38]

Even polygamy, which was introduced as a church institution for the first time in Nauvoo, was largely social in its purpose. The doctrine of plural marriage provided a means by which sex could be regulated under a new order and put to social purposes. The faithful elders were given the privilege of having another wife. Only those whose loyalty was established were initiated,[39] although even some of them rebelled at the idea.[40] The church members who would obey the principle could be depended on to follow without question the leadership of the Twelve Apostles, for outside the Mormon community there were no social sanctions for their innovations. I am saying that in one sense polygamy provided a kind of in-group test and security—those who practiced it were, willy-nilly, totally committed and willing to obey in all things.[41]

Thus, many of the things that we traditionally think of as secular in nature in Nauvoo, and somewhat irreligious, were not that but were designed to promote social control (not necessarily coercion) and social stability. Even Smith's political activities could be interpreted as essentially defensive in nature—a means to ensure security and peace for himself and his people. He acknowledged that when he said, "If I ever get into the presidential chair I will protect the people in their rights and liberties."[42] He said at one time in Nauvoo that he intended to pursue political influence,[43] but it is evident that he did not get embroiled politically until courted by contending political parties and that protection of his people was a major concern.[44] That Mormon involvement in politics may have had the opposite effect, as Thomas Ford has argued,[45] would seem to be one of the many examples of tragedy in early Mormon history. The tragedy was compounded by Ford himself, for he maintained in his *History of Illinois* that "I have nothing to do with religious but only with political considerations connected with this people."[46] Neither Ford nor the people of Hancock County generally appreciated that to the Mormons such a distinction was incomprehensible. Herein was the making of civil disorder and war.

When the Mormons, who were threatened with imminent violence and were disillusioned with state and national governments that seemed too decentralized and ineffectual to protect them from their enemies, loaded their wagons and began crossing the Mississippi River in February 1846, the editor of the *Illinois State Register* said of them, "The universal desire seemed to be to get away to a land of peace."[47] Not all of them sought peace by taking refuge in the Far West, where "none should come to hurt or make afraid."[48] Those Saints who would later join the Reorganization movement remained in Illinois, where they hoped to secure peace by repudiating polygamy and conforming to the prevailing laws of the land.[49] In either case, protection from the "unknown terror," a religious objective, was their ultimate concern.

Notes

An earlier version of this essay appeared in the *Utah Historical Quarterly* 44 (Spring 1976): 170–80. In some respects my views in my book *Quest for Refuge: The Mormon Flight from American Pluralism* (Salt Lake City: Signature Books, 1989) contrast sharply with this essay. Nonetheless, I am content to let it stand with but a few changes. The essay and the book were written from two different perspectives. The essay was from an insider's view, trying to correct some misconceptions I thought I saw at the time. The book was written from an American perspective, trying to tell the Saints why they were so feared and mistrusted; I still think both works serve that purpose.

1. A succinct history of the Mormons in Nauvoo is David E. Miller and Della S. Miller, *Nauvoo: The City of Joseph* (Santa Barbara, Calif.: Peregrine Smith, 1974).

2. See Smith's comments in the "Book of Records Containing the Proceedings of the Female Relief Society of Nauvoo," manuscript, Archives, Historical Department, Church of Jesus Christ of Latter-day Saints, Salt Lake City, Utah (hereafter LDS Archives).

3. Wilford Woodruff, Journal, August 7, 1839, LDS Archives.

4. The letter, dated September 6, from Liverpool, is found among the John Taylor Letters, LDS Archives.

5. Bernard DeVoto, "The Centennial of Mormonism," *American Mercury* 19 (January 1930): 3, 12.

6. Nancy Towles, *Vicissitudes Illustrated, or the Experiences of Nancy Towles, in Europe and America* (Portsmouth, N.H.: n.p., 1833), 15.

7. Jules Remy and Julius Brenchly, *A Journey to Great Salt Lake City* (London: n.p., 1861), xxxi.

8. Fawn Brodie, *No Man Knows My History: The Life of Joseph Smith, the Mormon Prophet,* rev. ed. (New York: Alfred A. Knopf, 1971); representative of a plethora of articles dealing with Mormon material success is "A Church in the News: Story of Mormon Success," *U.S. News and World Report,* September 26, 1966.

9. Robert Bruce Flanders, *Nauvoo: Kingdom on the Mississippi* (Urbana: University of Illinois Press, 1965).

10. Remy and Brenchly, *Journey,* 7.

11. Richard T. Ely, "Economic Aspects of Mormonism," *Harper's Monthly* 106 (April 1903): 669.

12. Orson Hyde, *Speech of Elder Orson Hyde Delivered before the High Priest's Quorum in Nauvoo, 1845* (Liverpool, England: n.p., 1845), 4.

13. Smith condemned the existing Christian churches in what is called his First Vision, which appears in Joseph Smith, *History of the Church of Jesus Christ of Latter-day Saints,* ed. B. H. Roberts (Salt Lake City: Deseret News Press, 1902–12; 6 vols., a seventh volume was published in 1932; reprinted by Deseret Book, 1976, and reissued in paperback in 1978), 1:2–6.

14. As suggested in my "Shaping of the Mormon Mind in New England and New York," *Brigham Young University Studies* 9 (Spring 1969): 351–72.

15. Erwin Goodenough, "A Historian of Religion Tries to Define Religion," *Journal of Religion and Science* 2 (March 1967): 7–22.

16. Brodie, *No Man Knows My History,* made some suggestions along this line, but perhaps the first scholar to make a central point of it was James R. Clark, "The Kingdom of God, the Council of Fifty, and the State of Deseret," *Utah Historical Quarterly* 26 (April 1958): 130–58.

17. Joseph Smith said in 1842 that no man-made government, not even a democracy, could long endure on earth and that the government of God was needed (*Times and Seasons* 3 [July 15, 1842]: 855–56). *Times and Seasons* was published in Nauvoo as a periodical.

18. Suggested in part in Norman Cohn's brilliant work on revolutionary millennialism in medieval and Reformation Europe from the eleventh to the sixteenth centuries (*Pursuit of the Millennium* [New York: Harper, 1961]). Michael Zuckerman, *Peaceable Kingdoms* (New York: Alfred A. Knopf, 1970), 58, explains that during the Great Awakening, revivalists envisioned a millennium where society would be "knit together in sweet harmony."

19. Smith, *History of the Church*, 3:391, but the whole discourse on 390–91 develops this idea. For an opposing view, see Klaus J. Hansen, *Quest for Empire: The Kingdom of God and the Council of Fifty in Mormon History* (East Lansing: Michigan State University Press, 1967).

20. Eliza R. Snow, "The Nauvoo Legion," *Times and Seasons* 2 (July 1, 1841): 467.

21. Flanders has an entire chapter on this (*Nauvoo*, 115–43).

22. Smith lived in a small log cabin until 1843, when the Mansion House, which served as a hotel as well as the Smith residence, was finished. Smith's estate at his death included substantial real estate, but this was because no distinction was made in the kingdom between his personal things and those of the church. Emma was able to secure much property that Brigham Young asserted belonged to the church.

23. Smith's entrepreneurial activity in Nauvoo has yet to be fully studied; however, a preliminary examination of this material suggests to me that Smith served partly as a banker in Nauvoo, that is, a central figure in the process of exchange, advancement of credit, and the like, although there was no bank as such. Further, he made a significant effort to pay his old debts from Kirtland and seems often to have made land available at low prices to the poor. Somebody had to pay for all of this, and prices might have been high to those who could afford to pay. I do not believe his economic activities can be divorced from the total social ideal.

24. Note, for example, Smith's promise to the missionaries in July 1839 that as "the legates of heaven" if they will "fulfill the purposes of God in all things," the power of the priesthood would rest upon them and "kings bow to the sceptre of Immanuel . . . Zion shall blossom as a rose, and the nations flock to her standard" (Smith, *History of the Church*, 3:394–95).

25. Rigdon's address, given in 1844, appeared in *The Prophet*, June 8, 1844, 2. This newspaper was published by William Smith, the prophet's brother, in New York.

26. Mario S. DePillis, "The Quest for Religious Authority and the Rise of Mormonism," *Dialogue: A Journal of Mormon Thought* 1 (Spring 1966): 68–88.

27. There were always dissenters who were exceptions to these generalizations, yet for the majority of Mormons they hold true. Smith prophesied that unless the people of New York City, Albany, and Boston accepted the

gospel, their cities would be destroyed, but not even John Whitmer made
an issue of the failure of this prophecy (*History of John Whitmer* [Salt Lake
City: Modern Microfilm, n.d.], 9). Smith affirmed in a revelation in 1833
that there would be no other place for the gathering except Jackson County,
but later Far West, Nauvoo, and Zarahemla in Iowa were designated (*The
Doctrine and Covenants of the Church of Jesus Christ of Latter-day Saints* [LDS]
[Salt Lake City: Deseret Book, 1968], sects. 101:20, 114:17, and 125:2; *Book of
Doctrine and Covenants* [RLDS] [Independence, Mo.: Herald Publishing House,
1970], sect. 98:4h). Smith indicated after the failure of Zion's Camp that
Zion would be redeemed in two years, once the armies of Israel had built
up their strength, but when migrating Saints met resistance and all the
Mormons were expelled from Clay County, he gave up the project (*Doctrine
and Covenants* [LDS], sect. 105:26–30; *Doctrine and Covenants* [RLDS], sect.
102:8; Smith, *History of the Church*, 2:145, 455). I have spelled out this episode in detail with documentation in my "Role of Christian Primitivism in
the Origin and Development of the Mormon Kingdom, 1830–1844" (Ph.D.
diss., University of Chicago, 1968), 149, 161–62.

28. The doctrines of plurality of gods and polygamy were highly controversial in the church and violated deeply rooted traditions or social norms.
Nonetheless, the prophet's conception of the nature of the individual became more positive after the Book of Mormon was published, and the
conception of Zion underwent considerable change, from a particular place
in Missouri to the idea that all of America was Zion. Baptism for the dead
was an innovative doctrine that came late in the prophet's career but did
not stir great resistance. Meanwhile, despite the fact that it was the product
of revelation, the administrative structure of the church underwent considerable elaboration, with only minor resistance, during the prophet's lifetime.
I touch on several doctrinal innovations in "Role of Christian Primitivism,"
while Dennis Michael Quinn deals with organization changes in "Organizational Development and Social Origins of the Mormon Hierarchy, 1832–1932:
A Prosopographical Study" (M.A. thesis, University of Utah, 1973).

29. A comparison of the Book of Commandments with later editions
makes this clear. Compare 129 with sect. 8 of the current edition; 58 with
25:9; 93 with 42:39; and 95 with 43:79, where the latter version indicates that
the Saints were to adhere to the laws of the land. See also 160 and compare
with 64:30.

30. See also Richard P. Howard, *Restoration Scripture: A Study of Their
Textual Development* (Independence, Mo.: Herald Publishing House, 1869),
26–29.

31. David Whitmer, *An Address to All Believers in Christ* (Richmond, Mo.:
n.p., 1887), 32–33.

32. See, for example, *Doctrine and Covenants* (LDS), sects. 12, 14, 15, 16,
23, 26, 31, 34, 53, 55, 79, 80, 92; and *Doctrine and Covenants* (RLDS), sects. 11,
12, 13, 14, 21, 30, 33, 53, 55, 78, 79, 89.

33. Almost all of the successors to Smith claimed to be prophets, includ-

ing James J. Strang, James C. Brewster, William Smith, Charles B. Thompson, and Sidney Rigdon, as well as others. Perhaps David Whitmer is an exception, for he was reluctant to seize the mantle, and so was Brigham Young in the earliest years, maintaining that his role was to fulfill the prophet's purposes, not replace him.

34. Remy and Brenchly, *Journey,* xxvii.

35. See my "Role of Christian Primitivism," 53–56. I have also commented on this point in my "Secular or Sectarian History, a Critique of *No Man Knows My History,*" *Church History* 43 (March 1974): 84–85.

36. "Journal History of the Church of Jesus Christ of Latter-day Saints," May 15, 1840, LDS Archives.

37. *Doctrine and Covenants* (LDS), sect. 130:20, indicates that all blessings are predicated on obedience to law.

38. Some discussion of the temple endowment appears in B. H. Roberts, *A Comprehensive History of the Church of Jesus Christ of Latter-day Saints,* 6 vols. (Salt Lake City: Deseret News Press, 1930), 2:133–36. Compare with Brodie, *No Man Knows My History,* 279–83.

39. Stanley S. Ivins, "Notes on Mormon Polygamy," *Western Humanities Review* 10 (Summer 1956): 229–39; Hill, "Role of Christian Primitivism," 253.

40. Among the rebels were William Law, one of Smith's counselors, and Ebenezer Robinson, an editor of the *Times and Seasons.*

41. See Hill, "Secular or Sectarian History," 93–95.

42. Smith, *History of the Church,* 6:188.

43. In February 1843 Smith said, "'Tis right, politically, for a man who has influence to use it, as well as for a man who has no influence to use his. From henceforth I will maintain all the influence I can get" (Smith, *History of the Church,* 5:286). Earlier in the year Smith had said, perhaps with some justification, that "the 'Mormons' were driven to union in their elections by persecution, and not by my influence" (ibid., 5:232).

44. The Mormons were the objects of considerable political propaganda as soon as they entered the state since the political parties were evenly balanced (Flanders, *Nauvoo,* 212–16; Hill, "Role of Christian Primitivism," 239–40).

45. Thomas Ford, *A History of Illinois: From Its Commencement as a State in 1818 to 1854* (Chicago: S. C. Griggs, 1854). He argued this throughout his account of the Mormon difficulties, but see especially 262, 269, 362, 413.

46. Ibid., 262.

47. *Illinois State Register,* March 13, 1846.

48. This line is found in William Clayton's hymn, "Come, Come Ye Saints."

49. An excellent chapter by Alma Blair on the origin of the Reorganized Church is in F. Mark McKiernan, Alma R. Blair, and Paul M. Edwards, eds., *The Restoration Movement: Essays in Mormon History* (Lawrence, Kans.: Coronado Press, 1973), 207–30.

8

Mormon Polygamy: Belief and Practice in Nauvoo

KATHRYN M. DAYNES

> And when I saw a funeral, I felt to envy the
> corpse its situation, and to regret that I was not
> in the coffin.
> —Brigham Young
>
> It made my flesh crawl.
> —John Taylor
>
> [It] had a similar effect to a sudden shock of a
> small earthquake.
> —Helen Mar Whitney

Such were the reactions of three Latter-day Saints when introduced to plural marriage. Despite their initial feelings, however, these Saints not only entered into plural marriage during Joseph Smith's lifetime but also became three of its most outspoken advocates. How could people in Nauvoo, whose traditions and feelings were puritanical and monogamous, eventually accept and practice plural marriage?[1] What social functions did it serve?

The answer can, in part, be found in the theory that new ideologies are produced and, more important, accepted in societies undergoing severe stresses and strains. Relationships between people may be seen as an exchange, and a person will invest in the relationship as much as the outcome seems worth. The certainty of the outcome, however, varies from one relationship to another. The more uncertain the outcome of an exchange relationship, the more likely that relationship will include moral obligations—socially legitimated definitions of individual or collective responsibility. As such, they stabilize relationships by making outcomes more predictable. Moreover, the less predictable the outcome of a relationship, the greater the likelihood that social exchange will be sustained by various symbols, including rituals. In short, the outcome of relationships is made more certain by moral obligations and rituals which are a part of a belief system—the ideology—that maintains cohesion within a group. During times of severe environmental changes, however, the moral duties of the past may prove impossible, unnecessary, or inadequate to the new situation; the opportunity is thus provided for a community to accept new beliefs.[2]

The Saints experienced such "severe environmental changes" during the apostasies of 1837–39, the forced abandonment of Kirtland, and the expulsion from Missouri. These crises demonstrated the inadequacy of the moral obligations and rituals within the group to maintain cohesion and thus created the climate in which plural marriage became acceptable. The social problems caused by disloyalty among church leaders are directly linked to the social solutions provided by accepting new family forms with their accompanying covenants.[3]

New ideologies tend to be produced for either the most impersonal of relationships or the most personal; they tend to deal with the state or with the family.[4] During his lifetime, Joseph Smith developed ideologies relating to both. The purpose of this essay, however, is to analyze the conditions that made acceptance of plural marriage possible as well as the social functions it served, not to explore how the new family beliefs developed or why plural marriage was chosen. (Jan Shipps has persuasively dealt with the latter question.) In Kirtland, Mormons began living through "a latter-day recapitulation of the ancient Patriarchal Age," so, not surprisingly, the new family pattern embedded in the developing theology was the plural marriage practiced by the patriarchs Abraham, Isaac, and Jacob.[5] Moreover, the new family beliefs were connected to the developing temple rituals, which were initiated in the Kirtland Temple.[6]

The theological continuity between Kirtland and Nauvoo is evident, but the apostasy of many church leaders and the subsequent persecution created a social disjuncture between the two periods. Between 10 to 15 percent of the members in Kirtland alone withdrew from the church from November 1837 to June 1838.[7] More significant, however, was the apostasy of half of the top leadership before the Saints' expulsion from Missouri in 1839.[8] Of the First Presidency, Oliver Cowdery and Frederick G. Williams were no longer in the church. Five of the Twelve Apostles were excommunicated, one was dropped from the Quorum, and one was saved from being disfellowshipped only by a timely reconciliation with the prophet. Of the presidents of Seventy, three of seven were excommunicated. Moreover, all three witnesses to the Book of Mormon left the church. So did three of the six still living eight witnesses; the three who remained were Joseph Smith's father and two brothers.[9] Although some of these men returned to fellowship in the church, apostasy and dissension rent the highest levels of leadership, and, with the exception of Joseph Smith's own family, those who had been instrumental in bringing forth the Book of Mormon left in the crises of 1837 and 1838.

In the wake of this crisis of disloyalty by prominent leaders and the consequent increased persecution of the Saints, the new family beliefs— including plural marriage—created stronger moral obligations among leaders of the church. In some cases, plural marriages created family ties among church leaders, with the strong moral responsibilities that attend familial relationships; in all cases, entering plural marriage was a sign of loyalty to Joseph Smith. Plural marriages were solemnized by a religious ritual involving covenants that bound the families together for eternity, thus emphasizing even more strongly the moral obligations to each other.

Despite the persecution and continuing threats the Saints suffered through the Kirtland period, attempts to introduce plural marriage then were relatively unsuccessful. A belief circulated among some Saints that plural marriage was a correct principle and would be practiced in the church at some future time.[10] Though the belief soured the minds of some, little evidence exists indicating that the belief alone had much impact on the community. Rumors of sexual misconduct did abound, but these did not start the fires of apostasy. Instead, the major objection of dissenters during the late 1830s was "a concentration of authority at the top and authority's increasing control of every aspect of life." Marvin Hill has cogently argued that those who left the church in this period "wanted a more open society, closer to the values and traditions of evangelical Protestantism" than appeared to be the case as the church became more involved in economic and political activities.[11]

This apostasy and the subsequent persecution created a climate conducive to the Saints' accepting plural marriage in two ways. First, those leaders who preferred a more open society were no longer in the church. The contrast between the dissenters and those who entered plural marriage may readily be seen in their approach to marriage. On August 17, 1835, W. W. Phelps presented an article on marriage written by Oliver Cowdery stipulating that "all marriages in the Church of Christ of Latter-day Saints, should be solemnized in a public meeting, or feast, prepared for that purpose."[12] Not only did this article mandate public marriages, but it was also accepted by the church at large through a vote taken at the conference. In presenting this, two future dissenters indicated they preferred religious rituals to be open and policy-making to be democratic. In contrast, high-level leaders in Nauvoo introduced plural marriage to an elite group only, and marriages were always performed out of public view. The society that fostered plural marriage was closed and hierarchical.

Second, having experienced the misery the expulsion from Missouri caused, church leaders who had gone through those trials knew firsthand the results of apostasy. Moreover, those who had endured the considerable suffering and monetary losses of those years had made a large personal investment in the success of the church; hence, their past sacrifices provided an additional reason to continue accepting Joseph Smith's leadership.

Joseph Smith's concern with loyalty, or lack of it, is shown in a letter written to the Saints from Liberty Jail on March 25, 1839. "We have learned by sad experience," he wrote, "that it is the nature and disposition of almost all men, as soon as they get a little authority, as they suppose, they will immediately begin to exercise unrighteous dominion."[13]

Soon after his escape from Missouri on July 2, 1839, he preached a sermon in which he admonished, "Let the Twelve be humble & not be exalted & beware of pride & not seek to excell one above another but act for each others good. . . . Why will not man learn Wisdom by precept & example at this late age of the world & not be oblieged to learn every thing we know by sad experiance. . . . See to it that you do not betray heaven, that you do not betray Jesus Christ, that you do not betray your Brethren, & that you do not betray the revelations of God . . . but whatever you do do not betray your Friend."[14] This theme of loyalty and union among the Saints continued to be included in Joseph Smith's sermons, especially when threats to the church or the prophet were intensified.

Others were also concerned with loyalty. In a letter to his daughter in the summer of 1843, Apostle Heber C. Kimball cautioned:

Let us seek to be true to our integrity, wherever we shall make vows or *covenants* with other. . . . You have some experience, and you see others walking through trouble and sorrow, because those who have *covenanted* to be their friends have betrayed them; for instance, look and see what the Prophet has to pass through. This comes upon him because of the treachery of some who have *promised* to be his friends and the friends of God. We should have no trouble if it were not for such persons. They make league with our enemies, Judas like. Oh, God, save me and my posterity from treachery.[15]

The emphasis on covenants binding people together is clear. That the promises had not always been kept showed how uncertain relationships were. The past crises, as well as the continuing threats to Joseph Smith and the church, produced a climate in which loyalty and the possibility of betrayal were of immediate and vital importance. This created a need for even more binding covenants and rituals.

These covenants, including those of marriage, were inextricably connected to the new temple rituals introduced in Nauvoo. In speaking about these rites, Heber C. Kimball stated, "It is not for us to reproach the Lord's anointed, nor to speak evil of him; all have covenanted not to do it."[16] On another occasion, he said, "Do [this people] hold their covenants sacred, those they made when they received their endowments, when they covenanted not to speak evil of one another, nor of the Lord's anointed, nor of those that lead them."[17] Because the apostasy of so many church leaders had made loyalty uncertain, moral obligations to the community were explicitly stated in the developing rituals, made binding by solemn oaths, and impressed upon the minds of those participating by symbolic penalties.[18] The covenants that bound families together and in turn linked them to Joseph Smith, who had the sole power to administer the sealing ordinances, strengthened the moral obligations among leaders of the church. Within the multiplicity of meanings in these religious rituals was the important social function of building a loyal community.

The act of accepting plural marriage was itself a dramatic sign of loyalty to the community's leader because entering plural marriage caused considerable anguish. Several conflicting pressures that made the decision difficult are illuminated by using a theory developed to explain how belief is related to behavior. Formulated by Icek Ajzen and Martin Fishbein, this theory states that belief and behavior are related but not directly.[19] Attitudes and subjective norms mediate between belief and practice. A person may have a positive or a negative attitude toward any given belief depending on what one believes the outcome of the behavior will be. Whether or not a person engages in a behavior also depends on what one *believes* those significant others want him or her to do. Significant others, such as family and peers, may in fact desire the person to do something different from what he or she believes they want. It is, however, what the person believes about their wishes and motivation to comply with those wishes that influence the eventual decision. One's behavior, then, depends on the relative importance that is given to beliefs about outcome of the behavior and beliefs about what significant others want the person to do.

In Nauvoo, those taught about plural marriage were asked to accept the belief that this type of marriage was necessary to achieve the highest glory in heaven and that they should therefore enter into it. In every recorded case, the initial attitude toward entering plural marriage was negative. Moreover, most of those told to enter into plural marriage had every reason to believe that those significant in their lives would not want them to do so. Men could expect their wives to oppose it, and plural wives could expect suspicion or scorn from those unaware of the new doctrine.

On the positive side, however, were the scriptural arguments: God had "proclaimed against adultery, fornication, and divorce, but never against plurality of wives; and in all cases where his [servants were] faithful—he blessed them for it."[20] More persuasive was the doctrine that "except a man and his wife enter into an everlasting covenant and be married for eternity, while in this probation, by the power and authority of the Holy Priesthood, they will cease to increase when they die; that is, they will not have any children after the resurrection. . . . In the celestial glory there are three heavens or degrees; and in order to obtain the highest, a man must enter into this order of the priesthood."[21] In the 1840s many Saints believed that "this order of the priesthood" meant not only marrying one's spouse for eternity but also entering into plural marriage. To lose the greatest celestial glory when they had invested so many sacrifices in their eternal salvation would have been a bitter blow. "No earthly inducement could be held forth to the women who entered this order," wrote one plural wife. "It was to be a life-sacrifice for the sake of an everlasting glory and exaltation."[22] Moreover, one of the people most significant in their lives wanted them to enter plural marriage. The proposition for many was simply this: if they believed Joseph Smith was a prophet of God, they would take this step. Accepting plural marriage thus became a test of loyalty to the prophet.[23]

This general pattern is illustrated by the accounts left of two individuals who entered plural marriage during Joseph Smith's lifetime. Heber C. Kimball's daughter recorded her father's introduction to that doctrine:

> Father was heard many a time to say that he had shed bushels of tears over this ORDER, the order of "Celestial or plural marriage." . . . When [Joseph Smith] told my father to take a second wife, he requested him to keep it a secret and not divulge it even to my mother, for fear that she would not receive the principle. Father realized the situation fully, and the love and reverence he felt for the Prophet was so great that he would rather have laid down his own life than have betrayed him. This was the greatest test of his faith he had ever experienced. . . . The Prophet told him the third time before he obeyed the command. This shows that the trial must have been extraordinary, for he was a

man who from the first had yielded implicit obedience to every requirement of the Prophet.... [Having entered plural marriage without his wife's knowledge] so worked upon his mind that his anxious
and haggard looks betrayed him daily and hourly ... he would wring
his hands and weep, beseeching the Lord with his whole soul to be
merciful and reveal to his wife the cause of his great sorrow, for he
himself could not break his vow of secrecy.[24]

The difficulty Kimball had in accepting plural marriage is evident. The
greatest trial, however, was in being asked to choose between the two
most important people in his life: his wife and Joseph Smith. Although
the struggle was great, he demonstrated that his loyalty to the prophet
took precedence over other loyalties.

Women, on being commanded to enter plural marriage, experienced
anguish similar to men's. Having plural marriage proposed to them in
terms of loyalty to the prophet, they also struggled with various conflicting
pressures, as Lucy Walker's autobiographical account illustrates. "In the
year of 1842," she wrote,

President Joseph Smith sought an interview with me, and said: "I
have a message for you. I have been commanded of God to take
another wife, and you are the woman." My astonishment knew no
bounds. This announcement was indeed a thunderbolt to me. He
asked me if I believed him to be a prophet of God. "Most assuredly I
do," I replied. He fully explained to me the principle of plural or
celestial marriage. Said this principle was again to be restored for the
benefit of the human family. That it would prove an everlasting blessing to my father's house, and form a chain that could never be broken,
worlds without end.... If you will pray sincerely for light and understanding in relation thereto, you shall receive a testimony of the
correctness of this principle. I thought I prayed sincerely, but was so
unwilling to consider the matter favorably that I fear I did not ask in
faith for light.... I was tempted and tortured beyond endurance until
life was not desirable. Oh that the grave would kindly receive me....
Father, [she prayed] I am only a child in years and experience. No
mother to counsel; no father near to tell me what to do in this trying
hour. Oh, let this bitter cup pass....

The Prophet discerned my sorrow. He saw how unhappy I was,
and sought an opportunity of again speaking to me on this subject....
"I have no flattering words to offer. It is a command of God to you. I
will give you until to-morrow to decide this matter. If you reject this
message the gate will be closed forever against you."...

I felt at this moment that I was called to place myself upon the
altar a living sacrifice—perhaps to brook the world in disgrace and

incur the displeasure and contempt of my youthful companions. . . . Said I, "The same God who has sent this message is the Being I have worshipped from my early childhood and He must manifest His will to me." He walked across the room, returned and stood before me with the most beautiful expression of countenance, and said: "God Almighty bless you. You shall have a manifestation of the will of God concerning you. . . . It shall be that joy and peace that you never knew."

Oh, how earnestly I prayed for these words to be fulfilled. It was near dawn after another sleepless night when my room was lighted up by a heavenly influence. . . . My soul was filled with a calm, sweet peace that "I never knew." Supreme happiness took possession of me, and I received a powerful and irresistable testimony of the truth of plural marriage. . . . As I descended the stairs, Pres. Smith opened the door below, took me by the hand and said: "Thank God, you have the testimony, I too, have prayed." He led me to a chair, placed his hands upon my head, and blessed me with every blessing my heart could possibly desire.[25]

This account reveals several factors that influenced Lucy Walker's decision to enter plural marriage. When first told that she had been commanded by God to become a plural wife, her attitude was decidedly negative. She was "unwilling to consider the matter favorably" and felt her youthful companions would treat her with contempt if she became a plural wife. There were, however, positive inducements. That the outcome "would prove an everlasting blessing to my father's house" might have had some appeal. More important, however, was the knowledge that one of the most important people in her life, the Prophet Joseph Smith, wanted her to take this step. She not only lived in his household and received sustenance at his table but also believed he was the mouthpiece through whom God spoke. She and her family had already sacrificed and suffered by following Joseph Smith. Lucy's father had been shot at the Haun's Mill massacre, and the entire family experienced privation during the Saints' expulsion from Missouri, then sickness and death in Nauvoo. By 1843 Lucy Walker had invested her life in the belief that the church was indeed restored to earth by God and that Joseph Smith was his prophet. The crux of the argument was whether she believed Joseph Smith was a prophet of God. If she believed he was, she would prove her loyalty by obeying the commandment that he said had come from God. Framing the question in terms of loyalty was, of course, a risk. A favorable response, however, would not only prove her loyalty but also increase her commitment to Joseph Smith's prophetic leadership. Entering plural marriage was a sacrifice—one mechanism that increases commitment. "The more it 'costs' a person to do something, the more 'valuable' he will consider it, in order to justify the psychic 'expense.'"[26] Unquestionably the "costs" and psychic "expense" of entering plural marriage were great; hence, the commitment to Joseph Smith's leadership by taking that step would be commensurately increased.

Lucy Walker's negative attitude toward and fears about plural marriage indicate she intended initially to refuse. What brought plural marriage into the realm of possibility were her belief in Joseph Smith as a prophet and the question plural marriage posed about her loyalty to him. In the end, her internal conflict was resolved by a manifestation of "sweet peace," which, being predicted by Joseph Smith, augmented her faith in his prophetic role. It is unclear whether the "joy and peace" she felt were the same as the "testimony of the truth of plural marriage," but the importance of that manifestation and the prophet's influence are shown by her being sealed to Joseph Smith on May 1, 1843.[27]

Numerous other accounts could be similarly analyzed to show how loyalty to Joseph Smith's leadership was a crucial element in accepting plural marriage. When teaching Mary Rollins Lightner about plural marriage, Joseph Smith asked her if she "was going to be a *traitor.*"[28] To Emily Partridge, he said, "Emily if you will not *betray* me, I will tell you something for your benefit."[29] Emily's sister, Eliza, testified that plural marriage "was truly a great trial for me but I had the most implicit confidence in him as a Prophet of the Lord and could not but believe his words and as a matter of course accept of the privileg of being sealed to him as a wife for time and all eternity."[30] John Taylor recalled that Joseph Smith stopped him one day in Nauvoo and said to him, "Those things that have been spoken of must be fulfilled, and if they are not entered into right away, the keys will be turned." Taylor felt that he could not treat lightly the things of God, so he promised to enter plural marriage as soon as he could.[31] Despite the exposé style of her 1842 account, Martha Brotherton confirms this emphasis on loyalty. When she was first approached about plural marriage, an apostle asked if she was willing to do all that the prophet required. Later, according to her account, Joseph Smith tried to persuade her that plural marriage "is lawful and right before God—I know it is. . . . don't you believe in me?"[32]

Loyalty versus betrayal, accepting Joseph Smith as the mouthpiece of God or rejecting his prophetic role—these themes implicitly or explicitly run through account after account. The reasons given for entering plural marriage at Nauvoo do not fit into the four categories one prominent family historian lists as motivations for marriage.[33] First, these were not marriages of convenience arranged for economic or political reasons. One instance may appear at first to fit this category, for Helen Mar Kimball did enter into a plural marriage with Joseph Smith because her father wanted to be connected with that family. The benefits from such a marriage, however, were otherworldly because she took the step to ensure her "eternal salvation & exaltation and that of [her] father's household."[34] Second, sexual attraction is inadequate as a satisfactory explanation. For example, when Heber C. Kimball believed he would be called upon to enter plural marriage, he considered the two elderly Sisters Pitkin because he thought marriage to them would cause his wife the least unhappiness. Instead, Joseph Smith counseled him to marry Sarah Noon, the mother of two daughters whose husband had deserted her.[35] Third, these accounts of entering into plural marriage contain little mention of romantic love. On the contrary, Joseph Smith in the example quoted above told Lucy Walker he had no flattering words to offer. When she consented to be sealed to him, he laid his hands on her head and blessed her, a decidedly unromantic response. Nor were Lucy's words, actions, and feelings any more romantic.[36] Fourth, plural marriages were not contracted because of prospective companionship between bride and groom. Such a relationship might have developed after the marriage, but the Nauvoo accounts give no hint that this was a motivating factor. On the contrary, men like Joseph Smith and Heber C. Kimball demonstrated in both word and deed that the companionship with their first wives was the most important.

According to the accounts of those directly involved, then, plural marriage during Joseph Smith's lifetime was a product not of lust or romantic love but of loyalty—loyalty cemented by sacrifice and sacred covenants that bound families together under solemn moral obligations. Significantly, all were bound to Joseph Smith, for it was through him that the commandments came requiring the sacrifice, and only he had the authority to seal families for eternity.

Obviously, not everyone to whom it was introduced willingly entered plural marriage. Sidney Rigdon and William Marks were two notable leaders who rejected it. Both had experienced the crises of 1837–39, however, and neither opposed Joseph Smith's leadership. In contrast, John C. Bennett had not experienced crises in the church or made sacrifices that would have given him a stake in the church's success. His apostasy and subsequent defamation of Joseph Smith and the church in general created no small storm, but the church successfully weathered it. In fact, as long as plural marriage was a commandment for only some individuals rather than the norm among church leaders, it generally did serve to strengthen the bonds of loyalty to Joseph Smith.

A turning point came when Hyrum Smith read the revelation on plural marriage to the high council on August 12, 1843. Heretofore, Joseph Smith had carefully selected those to whom he introduced plural marriage. He had taught them individually and put plural marriage into a theological context that emphasized the eternal nature of families and the added heavenly glory it would bring. Joseph Smith regarded "everything acording to the circumstances of the case, and every person according to their intrinsic worth."[37] Hyrum Smith, however, was more legalistic. Once he was finally converted to plural marriage, he thought the doctrine was so plain that he could "convince any reasonable man or woman of its truth, purity or heavenly origin."[38] His faith in revelations given through Joseph Smith was implicit, although he seemed to feel they had more authority when written. At his behest the controversial revelation was put on paper, though it was not intended for circulation in the church.

Nevertheless, the authority of the written word was such that Hyrum Smith used the revelation to teach Saints the doctrine. Rumors about the principle led to questions at a high council meeting. Instead of casting plural marriage in terms of loyalty to the prophet, Hyrum Smith returned home to get the revelation so he could read it to the group. After the reading, he said, "Now, you that believe this revelation and go forth and obey the same shall be saved, and you that reject it shall be damned."[39] What had been binding heretofore on only certain individuals was rapidly transformed into the norm for the leadership of the church, making it necessary for leaders to take a stand one way or the other.

In writing of this time, William Marks, president of the stake in Nauvoo, stated, "I saw and heard of many things that was practiced, and taught that I did not believe to be of God; but I continued to do and teach such principles as were plainly revealed, as the law of the church.... Therefore when the doctrine of polygamy *was introduced into the church as a principle of exaltation,* I took a decided stand against it; which stand rendered me quite unpopular with many of the leading ones of the church."[40] Marks thus believed presenting the revelation to the high council introduced the principle of plural marriage as a church doctrine. As such, he felt the need to take a stand. Although he opposed plural marriage, he remained loyal to the church and Joseph Smith. He had been a church leader during the apostasies in Kirtland and knew firsthand the difficulties apostasy could create. His loyal opposition was vindicated when Joseph Smith confessed shortly before his death that "he had done wrong" and desired Marks's help in putting down "this damnable heresy."[41]

Austin Cowles, who had also experienced the crises of the late 1830s but not as a church leader, reacted more precipitously. He indicated that "this revelation with other evidence, that the aforesaid heresies were taught and practiced in the Church, determined me to leave the office of first counselor to the president of the Church at Nauvoo, inasmuch as I dared not teach or administer such laws."[42] Cowles had privately opposed plural marriage earlier,[43] but its presentation to an official body of the church gave it an aura of authority. He felt it was no longer a question of acquiescing to others' practicing it but rather his responsibility to teach and administer the new doctrine. He therefore resigned his office in the church and soon became associated with those opposed to Joseph Smith's leadership.

The revelation also produced a crisis for William Law, counselor in the First Presidency, when Hyrum Smith loaned him a copy of it. Impressing him most forcefully about the document was that it "authorized certain men to have more wives than one at a time, in this world and in the world to come. It said this was the *law*—and commanded Joseph to enter into the *law*.—And also that he should administer to others."[44]

William Law also regarded the revelation as making plural marriage the norm for the church leadership. Like many others to whom plural marriage was presented, he struggled between his negative attitude toward it and his loyalty to Joseph Smith. He and his wife, he later recalled, "were just turned upside down by it; we did not know what to do."[45] Even before this, however, Law had found himself in conflict with the prophet over political and economic matters.[46] Many of his associates shared his economic interests, which conflicted with those of Joseph Smith.[47] Moreover, Law had not experienced firsthand the 1837–39 crises in the church, having gathered with the Saints only in Nauvoo.[48] In the end, Law resolved his struggle by rejecting Joseph Smith's leadership. He wrote, "Fearful and terrible, yet most distressing have been the scenes through which we have past, during the last few months. . . . Had it not been for the goodness of God, surely we had been lost, overwhelmed, swallowed down in the vortex of iniquity, through our religious zeal we harkened to the teachings of man, more than to the written word of God."[49] This description of his struggle is similar to that of others asked to accept plural marriage. In the end, he chose those associates with whom he shared economic interests, but the struggle had been great, and his reaction against the prophet was commensurate with the suffering that struggle had caused him. "My heart was burning," he recalled years later; "I wanted to tread upon the viper."[50] He had not conspired to take Joseph Smith's life, but his actions began the series of events that led to the prophet's death.

The covenants of loyalty were not enough. Joseph and Hyrum Smith were killed in Carthage by a militia turned mob, and the community of Saints became divided. One group continued these covenants and rituals, binding together ever-increasing families of plural wives and adopted sons. The sacred covenants could not forestall all dissension, but they did hold a large community together for a hegira into the wilderness and the conquest of a dry, mountainous land.

Another group eventually coalesced around the standard of "moderate Mormonism" and loyalty to a lineal priesthood.[51] Still they could not escape the effects of plural marriage. The polygamy of Utah Mormons became a negative reference, and the Reorganization developed an identity by rejecting it.

To understand plural marriage in Nauvoo, we should not judge it by its immediate rejection by the Reorganized Latter Day Saints or its eventual repudiation by the Latter-day Saints. To understand plural marriage in Nauvoo is to see it in the context in which it was lived, not just the continuing threats to Joseph Smith and to the community but also those continuing threats of the excruciating experiences of Liberty Jail and the Extermination Order. Divisions in the leadership had created the crises in both Kirtland and Missouri; the solution was to strengthen those bonds among the leaders. Plural marriage, with its sacred covenants and rituals superimposed on already strong moral obligations to family members, increased commitment. Its acceptance demonstrated undeviating loyalty to the prophet. In short, plural marriage cemented loyal relationships among church leaders at the time when the Mormon great apostasy threatened disintegration of the leadership and destruction of the church.

Notes

An earlier version of this essay appeared in the *John Whitmer Historical Association Journal* 8 (1988): 63–75. The author wishes to express her appreciation to Jan Shipps, Ian Barber, Marvin Hill, and Thomas Alexander for insightful comments and suggestions made during preparation of this essay.

1. Excellent works dealing with plural marriage in the Nauvoo period include Lawrence Foster, *Religion and Sexuality: Three American Communal Experiments of the Nineteenth Century* (New York: Oxford University Press, 1981); and Danel W. Bachman, "A Study of The Mormon Practice of Plural Marriage before the Death of Joseph Smith" (M.A. thesis, Purdue University, 1975).

2. Robert Wuthnow, "Comparative Ideology," *International Journal of Comparative Sociology* 22 (September–December 1981): 122–23. The strain theory of ideology as refined by Wuthnow is more appropriate for analysis of the Mormon situation than the interest theory of ideology. Interest theory, developed by Marxists, posits that the ruling class develops and disseminates an ideology that rationalizes its class interest to maintain its rule.

3. The interpretation presented in this essay differs from Foster's in that it views changes in the traditional family, the fluidity of Jacksonian society, and the context of escalating tension and increasing separateness of the Mormons in Nauvoo (see Foster, *Religion and Sexuality*, 3–20, 130–43) to be necessary but not sufficient causes for the acceptance of plural marriage by Mormon society. These factors were all present in Kirtland and Missouri, but introducing plural marriage there was relatively unsuccessful. The argument in this essay presumes social institutions serve social purposes. For the intellectual and theological development of plural marriage, see Danel W. Bachman, "New Light on an Old Hypothesis: The Ohio Origins of the Revelation on Eternal Marriage," *Journal of Mormon History* 5 (1978): 19–32; and Foster, *Religion and Sexuality*, 10–18, 125–147.

4. Wuthnow, "Comparative Ideology," 123.

5. Jan Shipps, *Mormonism: The Story of a New Religious Tradition* (Urbana: University of Illinois Press, 1985), 61.

6. Richard P. Howard, "The Changing RLDS Response to Mormon Polygamy: A Preliminary Analysis," *John Whitmer Historical Association Journal* 3 (1983): 19–21, 24, correctly connects plural marriage to the temple rituals, but these began in Kirtland. See Andrew F. Ehat, "Joseph Smith's Introduction of Temple Ordinances and the 1844 Mormon Succession Question" (M.A. thesis, Brigham Young University, 1982), 169.

7. Milton V. Backman Jr., *The Heavens Resound: A History of the Latter-day Saints in Ohio, 1830–1838* (Salt Lake City: Deseret Book, 1983), 328.

8. Based on biographical profiles of the General Authorities listed in D. Michael Quinn, "Organizational Development and Social Origins of the Mormon Hierarchy, 1832–1932: A Prosopographical Study" (M.A. thesis, University of Utah, 1973), 248–91.

9. Ibid., 248–87; Lyndon W. Cook, *The Revelations of the Prophet Joseph Smith* (Salt Lake City: Deseret Book, 1985), 14, 42–43, 104–107, 109–11, 156, 256, 276; Donald Q. Cannon and Lyndon W. Cook, eds., *Far West Record: Minutes of the Church of Jesus Christ of Latter-day Saints, 1830–1844* (Salt Lake City: Deseret Book, 1983), 146–50, 166–78, 266, 294–95; Parley P. Pratt, *Autobiography of Parley Parker Pratt* (Salt Lake City: Deseret Book, 1979), 168.

10. Franklin D. Richards to Joseph F. Smith, July 5, 1881, Archives, Historical Department, Church of Jesus Christ of Latter-day Saints, Salt Lake City, Utah (hereafter LDS Archives), quoted in Bachman, "A Study of the Mormon Practice of Plural Marriage before the Death of Joseph Smith," 89; *Latter-day Saints' Millennial Star* (Liverpool, England) 40 (December 16, 1878): 788; Dean R. Zimmerman, *I Knew the Prophets: An Analysis of the Letter of Benjamin F. Johnson to George F. Gibbs, Reporting Doctrinal Views of Joseph Smith and Brigham Young* (Bountiful, Utah: Horizon, 1976), 38; Oliver H. Olney, *The Absurdities of Mormonism Portrayed* (Hancock County, Ill.: n.p., 1843), 5.

11. Marvin S. Hill, "Cultural Crisis in the Mormon Kingdom: A Reconsideration of the Causes of Kirtland Dissent," *Church History* 49 (September 1980): 291, 296. That plural marriage was a factor in the apostasy is argued

by Max H. Parkin, "The Nature and Cause of Internal and External Conflict of the Mormons in Ohio Between 1830 and 1838" (M.A. thesis, Brigham Young University, 1966), 162–74, 348; and Bachman, "A Study of the Mormon Practice of Plural Marriage before the Death of Joseph Smith," 77–90. Bachman calls this "the First Hierarchical Split over Plural Marriage," but his purpose is to detail evidence about plural marriage in Kirtland, not to assess its importance among the range of factors causing the apostasy. Parkin lists plural marriage as one factor in the conflict at Kirtland, but, in fact, it appears to be relatively unimportant in relation to the other social, economic, and political factors he recounts. Foster accepts, though tentatively, that plural marriage was a cause of the apostasy (*Religion and Sexuality,* 138, 302).

12. *Book of Doctrine and Covenants* (Independence, Mo.: Herald Publishing House, 1970), sect. 111:1. See also Joseph Smith, *History of the Church of Jesus Christ of Latter-day Saints,* ed. B. H. Roberts (Salt Lake City: Deseret News Press, 1902–12; 6 vols., a seventh volume was published in 1932; reprinted by Deseret Book, 1976, and reissued in paperback in 1978), 2:243–47. See also Cook, *Revelations of Prophet Joseph Smith,* 295, 348–49, 359–60.

13. Smith, *History of the Church,* 3:299–300.

14. Andrew F. Ehat and Lyndon W. Cook, eds., *The Words of Joseph Smith: The Contemporary Accounts of the Nauvoo Discourses of the Prophet Joseph* (Provo, Utah: Religious Studies Center, Brigham Young University, 1980), 7–8.

15. Helen Mar Whitney, "Scenes and Incidents in Nauvoo," *Woman's Exponent* 11 (August 1, 1882): 40 (emphasis added).

16. Helen Mar Whitney, "Scenes and Incidents from H. C. Kimball's Journal," *Woman's Exponent* 12 (August 1, 1883): 34.

17. *Journal of Discourses,* 26 vols. (Liverpool, England: F. D. and S. W. Richards, 1854–86), 4:46. For similar statements, also see ibid., 3:269 and 6:124.

18. Increase M'Gee Van Dusen, *A Dialogue between Adam and Eve, the Lord and the Devil* (Albany, N.Y.: n.p., 1847), 13. See also John Hyde, *Mormonism: Its Leaders and Designs* (New York: W. P. Fetridge, 1857), 97.

19. This theory is succinctly described in Icek Ajzen and Martin Fishbein, *Understanding Attitudes and Predicting Social Behavior* (Englewood Cliffs, N.J.: Prentice-Hall, 1980), 4–91. It is detailed in Martin Fishbein and Icek Ajzen, *Belief, Attitude, Intention and Behavior: An Introduction to Theory and Research* (Reading, Mass.: Addison-Wesley, 1975). Ajzen and Fishbein developed the theory to predict behavior patterns. In this essay, it is used only to provide categories useful in analysis.

20. George A. Smith to Joseph Smith III, Letter Book, No. 6, 1891, LDS Archives, quoted in Raymond T. Bailey, "Emma Hale, Wife of the Prophet Joseph Smith" (M.A. thesis, Brigham Young University, 1952), 86.

21. Smith, *History of the Church,* 5:391–92.

22. Helen Mar Whitney, "Scenes in Nauvoo after the Martyrdom of the Prophet and Patriarch," *Woman's Exponent* 11 (March 1, 1883): 146.

23. The theory of reasoned action used here assumes people make rational choices within the framework of their own beliefs. This interpretation thus differs from Foster, who writes, "A feeling of intense comradeship, egalitarianism, and exhilaration is experienced as a sense of direct personal contact replaces the institutional constraints that normally separate individuals. Men and women become *malleable, capable of being molded* by their leaders" (*Religion and Sexuality*, 166 [emphasis added]).

24. Helen Mar Whitney, "Scenes and Incidents in Nauvoo," *Woman's Exponent* 10 (October 15, 1881): 74.

25. Quoted in Lyman O. Littlefield, *Reminiscences of Latter-day Saints* (Logan, Utah: Utah Journal, 1888), 46–48. Most of this account is reprinted in Fawn M. Brodie, *No Man Knows My History: The Life of Joseph Smith, the Mormon Prophet*, rev. ed. (New York: Alfred A. Knopf, 1971), 477–79.

26. Rosabeth Moss Kanter, *Commitment and Community: Communes and Utopias in Sociological Perspective* (Cambridge, Mass.: Harvard University Press, 1972), 76.

27. Littlefield, *Reminiscences*, 48.

28. Mary Elizabeth Rollins, Address delivered at Brigham Young University, April 14, 1905, typescript, Mary Elizabeth Rollins Lightner Papers, Archives and Manuscripts, Harold B. Lee Library, Brigham Young University, Provo, Utah (emphasis added).

29. Emily Dow Partridge Young, Diary, photocopy of typescript, 124, Special Collections, Harold B. Lee Library (emphasis added).

30. Eliza M. Partridge Lyman, "Life and Journal of Eliza Maria Partridge Lyman," ca 1874, photocopy of original, 78, Special Collections, Marriott Library, University of Utah, Salt Lake City, Utah.

31. *Journal of Discourses*, 24:231.

32. *Sangamo Journal*, July 22, 1842, quoted in Charles Shook, *The True Origin of Mormon Polygamy* (Cincinnati: Standard Publishing, 1914), 75, 77.

33. Lawrence Stone, *The Family, Sex, and Marriage in England, 1500–1800* (New York: Harper and Row, 1977), 271–72.

34. Helen Mar Kimball Smith Whitney, Statement, March 30, 1881, holograph, LDS Archives.

35. Whitney, "Scenes and Incidents in Nauvoo," 74. Foster has cogently argued the inadequacy of sexual motivation as an explanation for introducing polygamy (*Religion and Sexuality*, 126).

36. The possible exception is Eliza R. Snow. Having become converted to the principle of plural marriage before she was asked to enter into it herself and having never before married, she was effusive in her praise of the man to whom she was sealed in plural marriage (Eliza R. Snow, "Sketch of My Life," Bancroft Library, Berkeley, California, printed in Spencer J. Palmer, "Eliza R. Snow's 'Sketch of My Life': Reminiscences of One of Joseph Smith's Plural Wives," *Brigham Young University Studies* 12 [Autumn 1971]: 125–30).

37. Brigham Young, Address, October 8, 1866, LDS Archives, quoted in Ehat, "Joseph Smith's Introduction of Temple Ordinances," 58.

38. Andrew Jenson, comp., *Historical Record* 6 (February 1887): 225.

39. Ibid., 227.

40. William Marks, "Epistle of Wm. Marks," *Zion's Harbinger, and Baneemy's Organ* 3 (July 1853): 53 (emphasis added).

41. Ibid.

42. *Expositor* (Nauvoo, Illinois), June 7, 1844, 2.

43. Ebenezer Robinson, "Items of Personal History of the Editor," *The Return* (Davis City, Iowa) 3 (February 1891): 29.

44. *Expositor,* June 7, 1844, 2.

45. "Dr. Wyl and Dr. Wm. Law," *Salt Lake Daily Tribune,* July 31, 1887.

46. Lyndon W. Cook, "William Law, Nauvoo Dissenter," *Brigham Young University Studies* 22 (Winter 1982): 58–62.

47. Robert Bruce Flanders, *Nauvoo: Kingdom on the Mississippi* (Urbana: University of Illinois Press, 1965), 188–89.

48. Cook, "William Law," 48–49.

49. William Law, Diary, January 1, 1844, quoted in Ehat, "Joseph Smith's Introduction of Temple Ordinances," 130.

50. "Dr. Wyl and Dr. Wm. Law."

51. Alma R. Blair, "The Reorganized Church of Jesus Christ of Latter-day Saints: Moderate Mormons," in *The Restoration Movement: Essays in Mormon History,* ed. F. Mark McKiernan, Alma R. Blair, and Paul M. Edwards (Lawrence, Kans.: Coronado Press, 1973), 207–30.

9

The Kingdom of God in Illinois: Politics in Utopia

ROBERT BRUCE FLANDERS

The purpose of this essay is to reexamine, using a political frame of reference, the persistent question of why the Mormons were so ferociously constrained from their attempt to establish at Nauvoo a society that was for them the beginning of the kingdom of God on earth. The "Mormon Question," as it was called in the nineteenth century, remains an important one in a nation concerned with the nature and functional limits of an open society. Interest in Mormon history—along with immigrant, African American, and Indian history—reflects not only an increase in what might be termed "social problem" history but also an increased desire to better understand the dynamics of restriction in American life. The same generation of Americans that drove the Mormons from Missouri to Illinois and from Illinois into the wilderness also uprooted the remaining southeastern Indians and transported them to western reservations, and counted as progressive and liberal the scheme to transport African Americans back to Africa. Was the United States, as exemplified by Illinois in the late Jacksonian period, really a "promised land" for the Mormons to establish God's kingdom in the "last days"? Or was it rather a cursed land? Within Mormon society and within the hearts and minds of individual Mormons, it was a dilemma never fully resolved.

A comparison of Nauvoo with other contemporary communitarian societies that were also religiously heterodox but did not suffer persecution in the same manner suggests the Mormon community was, in important ways, essentially different. Nauvoo was larger and growing more rapidly. The community of Swedish Jansonites at Bishop Hill, Illinois, in the north-central part of the state, numbered only 780 people at the most. The Jansonites were mobbed once; but the continued existence of the community was never seriously threatened from the outside, probably because it was no threat. Illinoisans did not fear the Jansonites as they feared the Mormons. Nauvoo had its thousands and talked stridently of tens of thousands to come. A comparison of the Mormons and other religious utopian societies, such as the Amana Church Society, the Harmonists, the Shakers, the Separatists of Zoar, and the Perfectionists of Oneida, suggests that the Mormon endeavors were of an entirely different order of magnitude.

Less tangible differences existed between Mormons and other communitarian groups. The less committed a society was to typical middle-class American goals and values, the more likely it was to be free from outside interference. The German Pietist communities provide a good example. They were exclusive and separate, if not always ascetic; they were walled off by the barrier of language and by a pious, peasant, Christian communism; and they were nonpolitical. They did not generally seek participation in the mainstream of American life. The Mormons, conversely, were more typically American in significant ways. They were of westering New England stock, Puritan in religious background, and lower middle class rather than peasant and proletarian in outlook. They were typical old stock American farmers, artisans, and small entrepreneurs.[1] The Mormons were committed to group development to be sure, but they were also committed to upward socioeconomic mobility for themselves as individuals. In their politics, in their attitude toward the national issues of the day, and in their understanding of American history, they were Jacksonian Democrats.[2] Nor was the Mormon group life and collectivist spirit as unusual in American history as might be supposed. Pioneering by groups was common; from Massachusetts and Virginia in the seventeenth century to Illinois in the nineteenth, many towns were settled by groups moving en masse. The Mormons were welcomed to Illinois in 1839 as yet another group of pioneering, colonizing fellow Americans for whose contribution the Prairie State hungered.

Many of the things that Joseph Smith wanted for Nauvoo were typical of the time and place: population growth, commercial and industrial development, economic security and a modicum of prosperity (including an increment of property values), and freedom under the law to live and worship as they pleased. If Mormon evangelical zeal is defined as the Gentiles were wont to define it—as aggressive and successful promotion of Mormon enterprise—it was as American as apple pie. The Mormons shared a typical American ambitiousness. Nauvoo was growing more rapidly than any other city in the state, and, said the Saints, that was only the beginning. The Illinoisans, whose frontier boosterism and expansiveness in 1839 masked apprehension about the current depression, the state debt, and the future in general, watched Nauvoo grow and began to be disquieted.

The Nauvoo city charter, a typical charter for the time and place, was manipulated in practice to produce a quasi-independent municipal government that seemed to rival the sovereignty of the state itself. Some in the region said that, using that autonomy, Nauvoo sheltered cutthroats and desperadoes from the Illinois government. "They murdered many of our best citizens," said a Carthage man bitterly, "and there was nothing (eight ox team [or] a diaper) that they would not steal . . . our lives and property was at the mercy of the worst set of outlaws that ever congregated together . . . and the law could not reach them. . . ."[3] As Smith became unpopular in Illinois, the fact that the Nauvoo Municipal Court protected him from extradition to Missouri by issuing writs of habeas corpus was increasingly irksome. Perhaps the mildest Gentile opinion of the use of the charter to gain unwarranted privilege was an official one expressed in 1842 by Governor Thomas Carlin in a letter to Emma Smith: "I have examined both the Charters and the city ordinances upon the subject and must express my surprise at the extraordinary assumption of power by the board of aldermen as contained in said ordinance!"[4]

The most far-reaching consequence for Mormon life in Illinois was the church's involvement in a complex process of political action. Nothing could have been more typically American than their use of the power of their numbers, actual and potential. Nor could anything have been more hazardous. Bishop George Miller, on a mission in Kentucky in 1844, was adjured that it was acceptable for him to preach, but if he preached "political Mormonism," the Negroes would hang him to an apple tree.[5] Mormon political ambition, founded as it was on a powerful religious base and in the hands of a powerful leader like Smith, sounded the tocsin in Illinois. Ambition in an ambitious country could be a fault as well as a virtue.

Politics may be broadly defined as the pursuit and exercise of power. Political action by individuals, groups, and corporations has ever been the essence of American self-government. However, the political power of religious leaders and corporations to be found in the Puritan Commonwealth of Massachusetts and in the established churches of all the colonies was eroded by eighteenth-century secularism and further reduced by the American Revolution. The churches were disestablished, and separation of church and state became an enduring objective of American republicanism. Despite the revival of religion in the early nineteenth century, from which the Mormon church benefited, separation of church and state continued to be axiomatic. The idea of a kingdom of God on earth persisted, especially where the Puritan influence was strong, but the notions of conjoining civil and ecclesiastical rule were generally left by Protestants at the level of allegory and apocalypse. Nor was the Catholic church, by then growing in America, aggressive on the subject.

The Mormons, however, believed that the latter-day restoration of the gospel brought to an end such "spiritualizing" of the kingdom of God. "Now, when we speak of the Kingdom of God," wrote Apostle Parley P. Pratt, "we wish it to be understood that we mean His organized government on the earth. . . . Four things are required in order to organize any kingdom in heaven or on the earth: namely, first, a king; secondly, commissioned officers duly qualified to execute his ordinances and laws; thirdly, a code of laws by which the subjects are governed; and fourthly, subjects who are governed. Where these exist in their proper and regular authority there is a kingdom. . . . In this respect the Kingdom of God is like other kingdoms. . . ." Apostle John Taylor added, "The Lord is that king; his people are his subjects, his revealed will is the law of the kingdom; the Mormon priesthood is the administrator of those laws." The Mormon priesthood, said Brigham Young, is a "perfect system of government."[6]

Such a view of government within the kingdom had its external counterpart, albeit somewhat less simplistically conceived, in the intention to use political power to abet and protect the kingdom. There would be government and politics in the Mormon utopia, both managed by God's priests. To most Mormons, such an arrangement might have seemed simply expedient for survival. Beyond that, the nascent idea that the Church of Jesus Christ of Latter-day Saints should be established as the American national church was not only visionary but revolutionary as well. It may be that the bitter anti-Mormon antagonism of Christian clergy and laity developed in part not because they did not believe in the literal establishment of God's kingdom but because in their hearts they wished they did.[7]

Although the Mormon expulsion from Missouri set the stage for political involvement in Illinois, it also suggested making a cautious beginning, as is illustrated by the following. In the spring of 1839, when the Mormons first arrived in Illinois as refugees, Lyman Wight, an outspoken Mormon apostle, publicly attacked Democratic Governor Lilburn Boggs of Missouri, the Missouri Democratic Party, and Democrats in general. He even called the powerful and prestigious Senator Thomas Hart Benton a demagogue. Wight's remarks, reported in the *Quincy Whig,* caused a stir in Democratic circles right up to the governor's mansion in

Springfield, which was occupied by a Democrat, Thomas Carlin. Joseph Smith's response revealed his concern over Wight's outburst. In two letters (dated May 11 and May 16) to the *Quincy Whig*, he expressed a strictly nonpartisan position for the church. It was Elder Wight's privilege, he said, to express his opinion on either political or religious matters, but "we profess no authority in the case whatever, [and] we have thought, and still think, that it is not doing our cause justice to make a political question of it in any matter whatever." The Missouri barbarities were not the responsibility of any party or religion, said Smith, but were committed by a mob "composed of all parties." By the same token, Smith continued, members of all parties and religious societies had befriended the exiled Saints in Illinois, and, he said, "Favors of this kind ought to be engraven on the rock, to last forever." Smith wrote Lyman Wight privately, "We do not at all approve of the course which you have thought proper to take, in making the subject of our sufferings a political question. At the same time ... we ... feel ... a confidence in your good intentions."[8] Smith would soon alter his apolitical view of the situation.

Both Whigs and Democrats wooed the Mormon vote between 1839 and 1842; however, the Saints went solidly Whig in the elections of 1840 and 1841. By 1842 the Democrats had succeeded in turning this preference around. Stephen A. Douglas was especially influential in the reversal. Douglas was a leader in the Democratic party and a newly appointed Illinois supreme court justice, whose circuit, by choice, included Nauvoo. Of a visit Douglas made in May 1841, Smith wrote in the Nauvoo *Times and Seasons*, "I wish, through the medium of your paper, to make known that, on Sunday, last, I had the honor of receiving a visit from the Hon. Stephen A. Douglas, Justice of the Supreme Court, and Judge of the Fifth Judicial Circuit ... and Cyrus Walker, Esq., of Macomb, who expressed great pleasure in visiting our city, and were astonished at the improvements which were made. ... Judge Douglas expressed his satisfaction of what he had seen and heard respecting our people. ..."[9]

In 1842, as the state gubernatorial campaign got under way, Smith announced that the Mormon vote would go for the Democrats. He explained that in 1840 the Saints had voted for William Henry Harrison "because we loved him—he was a gallant officer and a tried statesman." He did not mention that at the time of the presidential campaign there was a lingering Mormon reaction against the Democratic government in Missouri. Nor did he mention his own bitterness toward President Martin Van Buren, who had refused to act on Mormon claims for damages against the state of Missouri. Now it was 1842; Harrison was dead, and, said Smith, "All of his friends are not ours." He added, "In the next canvass, we shall be influenced by no party consideration. ... so the partizans in this county, who expect to divide the friends of humanity and equal rights, will find themselves mistaken—we care not a fig for Whig or Democrat; they are both alike to us, but we shall go for our friends, or tried friends, and the cause of human liberty which is the cause of God."[10] Smith's views had changed dramatically in three years. By now the Mormons were eager to obtain the aid of both state and federal governments, and the growing Mormon community was widely expected to be an important element in the future of Illinois politics. Smith announced that the Mormons would vote as a bloc, that they had no party loyalties or interests, and that they would, in effect, sell to the highest bidder, which at the moment was the Democratic party.

The death of the Democratic gubernatorial candidate, Adam Snyder, early in the 1842 campaign did not change the Mormon commitment, despite the fact that Thomas Ford became the new candidate. Ford had said publicly that Joseph Smith was an impostor and a scoundrel and pledged if elected to seek alteration or repeal of the Nauvoo charter. Although the Mormon vote was too small to play a significant role in Ford's subsequent election, he carried Hancock County (where Nauvoo was located) 1,174 to 711. Inasmuch as Hancock was previously a Whig county, the result showed the Mormon vote to have been solidly Democratic.

Not surprisingly, apprehension about "political Mormonism" gained momentum during 1842. Whig politicians and newspapers were understandably bitter. The *Peoria Register and Northwestern Gazetteer* editorialized on January 21, 1842, "As we at various times expressed ourselves pretty decidedly against political tendencies of this sect. . . . we have no recollection anywhere of a movement similar to that of the Mormon prophet. We trust that all parties will see its dangerous tendency, and at once rebuke it." The following day the *Quincy Whig* described Smith's support of the Democrats as a "highhanded attempt to seize power and to tyrannize over the minds of men" and concluded that "this clannish principle of voting in a mass, at the dictation of one man, and this man who had acquired an influence over the minds of his people through the peculiar religious creed which he promulgates, is so repugnant to the principles of our Republican form of Government, and that its consequences . . . will be disagreeable to think of—bitter hatred and un-relenting hostility will spring up, where before peace and good will had an abiding place."

In 1842 the idea of the Mormons as a political power became established in the state, in the nation, and in the minds of Mormons themselves. The *Niles National Register* reported on August 6 that the Mormons had "six thousand votes under their immediate control, sufficient to give them the balance of power between the parties in the state. It is alleged they have found out how to make profitable use of this power." Although such an assessment of Mormon votes was a wild exaggeration, no accurate figure was available to counter it. The specter of "political Mormons" was enlarged in the fall of 1842, when, in his *History of the Saints,* John C. Bennett charged that they had "a vast and deep-laid scheme . . . for conquering the states of Ohio, Indiana, Illinois, Iowa, and Missouri, and erecting upon the ruin of their present governments a despotic military and religious empire. . . ."[11] Bennett's intent was to defame and his exaggeration was immense, but the undoubted seriousness of Mormon political intent lent credibility to his accusation.

Criticism in Illinois focused on the Mormon bloc vote and Joseph Smith's ability to manipulate it. As early as 1840 one observer had said, "These remarkable sectaries . . . hold in their hands a fearful balance of political power. . . . Should they ever become disposed to exert their influence for evil, which may Heaven prevent, they would surround our institutions with an element of danger, more to be dreaded than an armed and hundred-eyed police."[12] Smith himself relied on the bloc vote and its power, both at election time and between elections as a bargaining point. During the 1843 congressional campaign Smith offered his vote, and by implication the Mormon bloc, to the Whig candidate, Cyrus Walker, in return for a desperately needed favor. Then by a subterfuge he diverted the Mormon vote to the Democrats. It was a provocative act that made the Whigs rabid and doubtless contributed to the outbreak of violence and depredations against the Mormons soon afterward.[13] It was Smith's last gambit in state politics; within ten months he was dead.

The Mormon bloc vote, with the hopes and dreams that surrounded it, was not the only reason for Mormon-Gentile political conflict. For one thing, voting en bloc was not entirely novel, even for religious groups. The Irish in the Illinois canal counties voted en bloc, and they normally voted Democratic. Of course the Whigs did not like it, but the depth of antagonism against the Catholic Irish was in no way parallel to the hostility toward the Mormons, despite the fact that the Irish exercised the vote without benefit of citizenship. Whigs tended to be less aroused at the Irish than at the Democratic party, which brazenly and successfully defended the legality of the alien Irish vote.[14] Bloc voting was unusual but not unique. It was not the sine qua non of the "Mormon Question."

Mormon unwillingness to identify permanently with either party was, in reality, more provocative than the bloc vote. When the Mormons came to Illinois, it was assumed that they, like the Irish or other groups with a particular identity and self-interest, would become identified with and constituents of one party or the other. Each party hoped to win

Mormon loyalties and votes. In a normal course of events, the Mormons, like the Irish, would have become welded into the federation of groups and interests that composed the Illinois Democratic party.

Another less likely alternative would have been for the church to remain apolitical, a course Smith seemed to prefer at the outset. In such a case, there would have been no "Mormon vote." The Mormons guarded against such an eventuality, however. In urging the Saints to vote unitedly for the Democratic candidate in 1843, Apostle John Taylor told them, "It can serve no good purpose that half the citizens should disfranchise the other half, thus rendering Nauvoo powerless as far as politics is concerned."[15] In the end the Mormons were not assimilable into the structure of party politics. They had no party loyalties, interests, or connections. They gave no party service, contributed no funds, and, perhaps most important, could not be trusted by either party. Smith's quixotic politics were easily interpreted as evidence of insincerity and duplicity. In January 1843, midway between the elections of 1842 and 1843 in which the Mormons played so controversial a role, Smith said that "as my feelings revolt at the idea of having anything to do with politics, I have declined, in every instance, having anything to with the subject. I think it would be well for politicians to regulate their own affairs. I wish to be let alone, that I may attend strictly to the spiritual welfare of the Church."[16] In August of the same year, Smith declared, "I am above the kingdoms of the world, for I have no laws. I am not come to tell you to vote this way, that way or the other. In relation to national matters, I want it to go abroad unto the whole world that every man should stand on his own merits. The Lord has not given me a revelation concerning politics. I have not asked Him for one. I am a third party, and stand independent and alone."[17] Such a characteristic mixture of apparent innocence and naiveté with shrewdness and design enraged the prophet's enemies and added to his reputation for political intrigue.

In the political course they pursued, the Mormons appeared, to those who feared them, to be singularly successful. Nauvoo was safe to follow its own way, protected by its charter and potentially by the Nauvoo Legion. The Democratic majority in the legislature might have despised the Saints, but as beneficiaries of their vote, it was slow to prescribe limits to Mormon power. That power increased every day as new converts thronged to Nauvoo. The Mormon kingdom flourished.

The fundamental Gentile objection to the Mormon religion was not that it was unorthodox but that it was responsible for the alarming successes of the Saints in worldly affairs—it was the wellspring of corporate Mormonism and the Mormon political kingdom. Their analysis was fundamentally correct. At the very heart of the Latter-day Saint gospel was the testimony that the kingdom would "roll forth" to fill the whole earth. As citizens of Carthage and Warsaw watched Nauvoo outstrip the modest proportions of their own towns and saw the city limits of Nauvoo expand into county real estate, the Mormon prophecy alarmed them.

The separation of church and state, by then firmly established, and the secularizing, materialistic values of nineteenth-century America seemed to prescribe some outer limits for the practice of religion. A religious leader was allowed pulpit opinions on affairs of the day, particularly if they coincided with those already held by the congregation. But when a religious leader such as Joseph Smith—regarded as charismatic in the Gentile community and who was regarded as a prophet in the Mormon community—was simultaneously in the temple, in the counting house, in the seat of government, in the land office, and on the stump, it was too much. As de Tocqueville said, "Religions ought to confine themselves within their own precincts; for in seeking to extend their power beyond religious matters, they incur a risk of not being believed at all."[18]

The prevailing Mormon view of the proper role for religion was, of course, exactly the opposite—the "one true Church" was rightly at the heart of all affairs; there was and could be no legitimate separation. Here was the fundamental and irreconcilable conflict. After 1842 it was apparent that accommodation was impossible, and the history of the Mormon kingdom of God in Illinois became increasingly political—not only in the partisan sense but also in the radical sense of a total struggle for power and for survival. A Carthage man put it bluntly: it was to be "war to the knife and knife to the hilt."[19] The conflict was waged on every front, first in the press, in the pulpit, and in political campaigns, and finally in bushwhackings, burnings, and lynchings.

By 1842 the Mormons probably had a sufficient number of votes to take over the Hancock County government. To do so, however, was not their objective. Nauvoo sought separation and independence from county government and law enforcement. When the county sheriff, Jacob Backenstos, was elected by Mormon votes in 1845 and served Mormon interests (albeit entirely legitimate ones), it merely fanned the flames of smoldering civil war. In the state of Illinois, the Mormons could not have won a political struggle in which the "Mormon Question" thus defined was the real issue, as indeed it was by 1843. Outside Hancock County the Mormon vote was minuscule, and Mormon influence was small.

But the ultimate futility of the Mormon political enterprise was not at all clear either to the Mormons or to their Gentile antagonists. The church moved ever deeper into a political maelstrom on a local, state, national, and even supranational level, led on by a combination of circumstance, naiveté, optimism, recklessness, fear, and faith. On one hand, their political response was a predictable one. They were in many ways typical Americans of the time and place, normally Jacksonian Democrats, old-stock citizens, whose grandparents had fought in the War for Independence—a fact to which they frequently alluded. Zeal for territorial expansion and belief in Manifest Destiny were, for example, prototypical of Mormon thinking. Like most citizens, they had great faith in (if small grasp of) the processes of law and politics. And like many a beleaguered minority, they were afraid, but they had the inclination, the hope, and perhaps sufficient power to fight.

On the other hand, the deepening political involvement of the Nauvoo years evidenced a dreamlike, apocalyptic quality that marked it as the politics of utopia. God would open a way. Millenarianism, rather than a sense of process and continuity in history, dominated the Mormon mind. In 1840 Smith wrote in his journal, "Since Congress has decided against us, the Lord has begun to vex this nation, and He will continue to do so except they repent. . . . A hailstorm has visited South Carolina . . . which swept the crops, killing some cattle. Insects are devouring crops on the high lands, where the floods of the country have not reached, and great commercial distress prevails everywhere."[20] In 1843, when Stephen A. Douglas was a guest at his table, Smith said, "I prophesy in the name of the Lord God of Israel, unless the United States redress the wrongs committed upon the Saints . . . in a few years the government will be utterly overthrown and wasted, and there will not be so much as a potsherd left. . . ." He warned Douglas further, "If ever you turn your hand against me or the Latter-day Saints you will feel the weight of the hand of Almighty upon you. . . ."[21] In the same year Smith prophesied that as soon as the temple was completed, the Saints would be gathered into Illinois by the "thousands and tens of thousands." He announced to an inner group of leaders, "From the sixth day of April next [the anniversary of the founding of the Church], I go in for preparing with all present for a mission through the United States, and when we arrive in Maine we will take ship for England and so on to all the countries where we shall have a mind to go. . . . If I live, I will yet take these brethren through the United States and through the world, and will make just as big a wake as God Almighty will let me. We must send kings and governments to Nauvoo, and we will do it."[22] The extravagant self-confidence of Smith and other Mormon leaders, reinforced by the faith and expectations of their followers, knew no bounds. It was in such a temper of mind and heart that the Council of Fifty, an extraordinary group created for strategic planning, proposed to detach Nauvoo from the state of Illinois and make it a powerfully garrisoned independent state under the guise of a federal territory; to launch vast, paramilitary mission-colonizing ventures beyond the western territories of the United States; to create a Mormon state in Texas; and to nominate Joseph Smith for president of the United States.[23] While Smith lived, any and all of these schemes seemed possible, although there are suggestions that in the case of his candidacy, he and other leaders quietly sought to prepare themselves and the Mormon community for failure.

The term *utopian politics* describes the irony of the Mormon situation. American politics was typically the essence of pragmatism; the Mormon millenarian concept of a new heaven and a new earth was speculative, visionary, idealistic, and doctrinaire. Herein lay the Mormon political dilemma. The attempt to translate Smith's apocalyptic social vision— conditioned as it was by Bible literalism and a passion for "true doctrine"— into *political* action created a specter of theocratic tyranny intolerable to Illinoisans (and a minority of Mormons as well). Just as many Saints had faith in their wildest dreams, so did many Gentiles come to have faith, so to speak, in their wildest fears and hastened to crush the Mormon community in Illinois, as it had been crushed in Missouri. The attempts of the state to preserve the life of Joseph Smith and then the city of Nauvoo were feeble, to be sure, but it is not likely that a greater effort would have proved more effectual. Governor Ford later reflected, "[A] cause of mobs is, that men engaged in unpopular projects expect more protection from the laws than the laws are able to furnish in the face of popular excitement.... If the government cannot suppress an unpopular band of horse thieves.... how is it to suppress a popular combination which has the people on its side? I am willing enough to acknowledge that all this is wrong, but how is it to be avoided? ... This brings us to treat of the Mormons."[24]

The literalism of the Mormon doctrine of the kingdom of God on earth was dangerous in America. Fundamentally, the Mormons denied the legitimacy of a pluralistic society—the kingdom was to fill the whole earth. Although Mormonism was a product of a pluralistic society where religious freedom was possible, Mormonism threatened such a society; and so that society denied the Mormons the right to participate in it.

Because the Saints dared to live outside of American law, antagonistic citizens felt justified in doing likewise. "What would be thought," wrote an Illinois editor, "if Baptists, Methodists, Presbyterians, or Episcopalians had military organizations ... ?"[25] The Mormons sought to alter the course of American religious history, a revolutionary endeavor. The result was civil war in Missouri, Illinois, and finally Utah. The Mormons could not be protected by law or government in such conflict, and neither could they win. The most that nineteenth-century America was willing to grant them was well stated in the seventeenth century by the Dutch directors of New Amsterdam when they enjoined Director-General Peter Stuyvesant to be tolerant of religious deviants: "The *consciences* of men, at least, ought ever to remain free and unshackled. Let everyone be unmolested, as long as he is modest; as long as his conduct in a political sense remains irreproachable; as long as he does not disturb others, or oppose the government."[26]

Notes

An earlier version of this essay appeared in *Dialogue: A Journal of Mormon Thought* 5 (Spring 1970): 26–36.

1. Immigrant Mormons, arriving in substantial numbers after 1841, are excluded from these generalizations inasmuch as they did not form the fundamental character of Mormon society in Illinois.

2. Marvin Meyers's *The Jacksonian Persuasion: Politics and Belief* (Stanford, Calif.: Stanford University Press, 1957) is a provocative study suggesting by implication many parallels with the Mormon persuasion.

3. Dr. Thomas Barnes, Letter, [1897], Manuscript Collection, Illinois State Historical Library, Springfield, Illinois. According to correspondence with Lucinda Martin, the great granddaughter of Barnes (1812–1901), this letter was written in 1897. Martin has the original letter, copies of which are in the Huntington Library and in the Illinois State Historical Library. It should be noted that this letter was written more than fifty years after the events it describes. In 1845 Barnes was secretary of an anti-Mormon society in Carthage, Illinois.

4. Joseph Smith, *History of the Church of Jesus Christ of Latter-day Saints,* ed. B. H. Roberts (Salt Lake City: Deseret News Press, 1902–12; 6 vols., a seventh volume was published in 1932; reprinted by Deseret Book, 1976, and reissued in paperback in 1978), 5:154.

5. George Miller, *Correspondence of Bishop George Miller with the Northern Islander from His First Acquaintance with Mormonism up to Near the Close of His Life, 1855,* comp. Wingfield Watson (Burlington, Wisc.: Wingfield Watson, 1916), 21. A copy of this rare pamphlet is in the Library of the Wisconsin State Historical Society. A more widely available publication containing much the same material is H. W. Mills, "De Tal Palo Tal Astilla," *Publications [of] the Historical Society of Southern California* 10, no. 3 (1915–17): 86–174.

6. Parley P. Pratt, *A Voice of Warning and Instruction to All People, Containing a Declaration of the Faith and Doctrine of the Church of the Latter Day Saints, Commonly Called Mormons* (New York: n.p., 1837), 85; *Times and Seasons* (Nauvoo, Ill.) 4 (December 1, 1842): 24–25; Smith, *History of the Church,* 5:550.

7. See Klaus J. Hansen, *Quest for Empire: The Political Kingdom of God and the Council of Fifty in Mormon History* (East Lansing: Michigan State University Press, 1967), chapter 2 and passim.

8. Smith, *History of the Church,* 3:366–67.

9. Joseph Smith Jr., Letter dated May 6, 1841, *Times and Seasons* 2 (May 15, 1841): 414.

10. Smith, *History of the Church,* 4:479–80.

11. Quoted in ibid., 5:80n.

12. *Quincy Whig,* October 17, 1840.

13. For a detailed description of Mormon political developments in 1842 and 1843, see Robert Bruce Flanders, *Nauvoo: Kingdom on the Mississippi* (Urbana: University of Illinois Press, 1965), 232–39.

14. For a discussion of the alien vote controversy in Illinois, see Frank E. Stevens, "Life of Stephen A. Douglas," *Journal of the Illinois State Historical Society* 16, nos. 3 and 4 (1923): 336–37; and Raymond C. Buley, *The Old Northwest: Pioneer Period, 1815–1840,* 2 vols. (Indianapolis: Indiana State Historical Society, 1950–51), 2:232.

15. *Neighbor* (Nauvoo, Ill.), August 2, 1843.

16. Smith, *History of the Church,* 5:259.

17. Ibid., 5:526.

18. Alexis de Toqueville, *Democracy in America,* 2 vols., trans. Henry Reeve (New York: Harper, 1900), 2:24. Toqueville continued, "The human mind does not consent to adopt the dogmatical opinions without reluctance, and feels their necessity in spiritual matters only. . . . The circle in which [religions] seek to bound the human intellect ought therefore to be carefully traced, and beyond its verge the mind should be left in entire freedom to its own guidance."

19. Barnes, Letter, [1897].

20. Smith, *History of the Church,* 4:145.

21. Ibid., 5:394.

22. Ibid., 5:255–56.

23. Klaus Hansen describes the Council of Fifty as "a political organization [founded by Joseph Smith in Nauvoo] intended to prepare the world for a literal, political government in anticipation of Christ's millennium" (*Quest for Empire,* ii). For a fuller discussion of these matters, see ibid., chapters 4 and 5; and Flanders, *Nauvoo,* chapter 10.

24. Thomas Ford, *History of Illinois: From Its Commencement as a State in 1818 to 1847* (Chicago: S. C. Griggs, 1854), 250–51.

25. *Sangamo Journal* (Springfield, Ill.), June 3, 1842.

26. Quoted in Sidney Mead, *The Lively Experiment: The Shaping of Christianity in America* (New York: Oxford University Press, 1964), 21.

10

Mormon Nauvoo from a Non-Mormon Perspective

JOHN E. HALLWAS

Mormon Nauvoo (1839–46) was a remarkable community because of its religious utopianism and rapid growth, but its historical significance derives primarily from the violence that it provoked, which resulted in the expulsion of the Saints from Illinois. Hence, from a non-Mormon perspective, the community must be understood not in relationship to the Restoration movement but in relationship to the Illinois frontier. The key to Nauvoo's fate is that it was an ambitious theocracy that asserted itself within a Jacksonian social environment deeply devoted to democracy.[1] To understand the community's violent decline, then, we must also comprehend the cultural context in which it arose and the democratic ideology held by the non-Mormons (and dissident Mormons) who opposed it.[2]

The roots of the so-called Mormon conflict of the 1840s are in the American religious-political-social revolution that occurred in the eighteenth and early nineteenth centuries. Briefly, under the influences of the Great Awakening, American political revolution, and Second Great Awakening, there was an enormous shift away from the traditional, patriarchal structure of authority and toward an individualistic, egalitarian social order. As William E. McLoughlin has pointed out, by the Jacksonian era "romantic ideology, romantic nationalism, and romantic Christianity" had gained power, and "the will of the nation came to rest in precisely the same place as the spirit of God, namely, in the people."[3] There was a fusion of temporal and spiritual power in the average citizen as the United States came to embody God's purpose, in the public view, and popular sovereignty became the means of realizing the nation's destiny: to establish a new, divinely sanctioned social order, committed to individual rights. At the same time, of course, with the loss of traditional authority and the lessening of denominational adherence came the growth of dissenting groups, the emergence of ecclesiastical divisions, and the wider toleration of religious differences. Republicanism became the common ideology of the people; individualism became the hallmark of the American character; pluralism—at least with respect to religion—became an acknowledged facet of national life; and the separation of church and state became an increasingly important axiom of democracy.[4]

This great cultural change had an enormous impact on Joseph Smith. Reacting to the sectarianism prevalent in western New York, he became engaged in a quest for authority—a quest that led to his special sense of relation to God.[5] The religious system that emerged as his career unfolded was itself partly an expression of romanticism, a sweeping cultural development characterized by a turning from traditional creeds to individual revelations and speculations, from beliefs based on reason to faith based on experience, from humanistic universalism to cultural particularism (national and religious uniqueness), and from the acceptance of present social conditions to the embracing of utopian social ideals—among other factors. But Mormonism also reflected the religious tradition of Smith's native New England. A providentially created society with a covenanted relationship with God and a morally superior chosen people with a millennial mission were concepts that had originated in colonial Puritan culture and had contributed to America's identity as a redeemer nation before they became part of Smith's ideology.[6] Mormonism also reflected a reactionary pattern of thought that arose among the New England clergy during the revolutionary era: fear of moral degeneracy, demand for a republic of Christian virtue, and identification of America with the millennial kingdom of God.[7] Smith absorbed that perspective too, but he asserted that the Mormons alone were the chosen people, not the American public, and that their development of a new social order, amid the apparent disorder of early nineteenth-century America, would hasten the millennium. The nation would fulfill its divine destiny through the Saints.[8]

Paradoxically, Mormonism was both a romantic rejection of authority, as embodied in the patriarchal Christian tradition—dismissed by Smith as "the Great Apostasy"—and a new, equally romantic assertion of authority, based on the notion that the truth came to the prophet and his church through a unique means, divine revelation to a spiritually sensitive individual. Although the new church reflected democratic values in some ways, the Mormon priesthood elite, created and directed by the prophet as God's agent, made all the important decisions. The church was a theocratic oligarchy.[9] In short, what Joseph Smith did, while Americans were giving birth to a society marked by pluralism, egalitarianism, and individualism, was establish a new source of authority, a new hierarchy, and a new, highly unified community, based on fresh spiritual experience, and he thus rescued Mormon converts from religious uncertainty and social insecurity.[10] But theocratic authoritarianism and popular sovereignty were incompatible, so Smith's extension of his religious ideology into temporal affairs during the Jacksonian era placed the Mormons on a collision course with the rest of America.

Illinois was the locus of that collision. For the most part, the settlement of the state occurred between 1818, when statehood was achieved, and the late 1840s, when all but a few of the state's 102 counties had been established. During that time, Andrew Jackson became immensely popular in Illinois. The courageous, decisive, outspoken Old Hero was the essence of American individualism, and his presidency (1829–37) symbolized the achievement of political power by the common man. He was a forceful spokesman for democratic and egalitarian values, so he seemed to embody the spirit of the people—especially to residents of the West. Jackson's followers established the first true political party in Illinois, and, for a time, no anti-Jackson man could be elected there to a state or national office.[11]

As this suggests, the emerging Illinois commonwealth was deeply infused with the ideals of romantic democracy. In the process of pursuing self-realization in an open society, unencumbered by social class stratification and confining traditions, Illinois settlers commonly experienced a profound sense of freedom. So it was for the British immigrant Morris Birkbeck. He came to the state before Jackson's presidency, and he underwent a kind of romantic rebirth (as an egalitarian frontiersman) in the Illinois wilderness. As he said in *Letters from Illinois* not long after he had arrived, "Liberty is no subject of dispute or speculation among us backwoods men; it is the very atmosphere we breathe."[12] He also described the democratic ideology of early Illinois residents, commenting that they were "the most decided foes of all legitimacy [religious and political establishment], except that of a government appointment by the people"—and they were prepared to fight for their "Republican principles."[13]

Indeed, on the Illinois frontier, freedom was easy to find, and democracy was vigorously advocated by almost everyone; but still, self-government had to be learned. Governor Thomas Ford, who understood the people of Illinois as well as any man of his time, makes this clear in his *History of Illinois,* which is really a case study in the establishment and operation of republican government. As he points out, in early Illinois "the great mass of the people, politicians and all, had a mere selfish destiny in view," and "they did not want government to touch them too closely, or in too many places: they were determined upon the preservation and enjoyment of their liberties."[14] In other words, there was insufficient commitment to the common good and inadequate understanding of the obligations that democratic government imposed on the people. Unfortunately, that was true of both the Mormons and non-Mormons in Hancock County, despite their repeated assertions of republicanism.

* * *

In the scholarship on the Mormon conflict in Illinois, there has been little emphasis on the ideals of the non-Mormon public, as if that public did not have any ideals and simply reacted to Nauvoo out of religious bigotry, political frustration, community competition, and frontier belligerence.[15] But that is to overlook the very essence of the non-Mormon perspective and, ultimately, to ignore the historical significance of Nauvoo. The people of Hancock County, like those throughout the state of Illinois, had a deeply felt democratic ideology, and they continually perceived Mormon Nauvoo in relation to it.

Warsaw was particularly important, for it was the center of anti-Mormon feeling in the 1840s. Like most Illinois towns, it was a cumulative community, a kind of voluntary association devoted to the economic and social advancement of its members. The Warsaw pioneers hailed from a variety of states and countries and had various religious affiliations, so the town was something of a microcosm of pluralistic America. The five hundred or so people who lived there in 1840 were very optimistic about their future, for they recognized the importance of Warsaw's location on the Mississippi River, just below the Des Moines Rapids. Scores of riverboats arrived every month, and shipping was a very important business. By the late 1830s the town had a hotel, a fine brick school, and many substantial homes. It was a progressive community, whose leaders organized a temperance society, an agricultural society, and a library association in 1841.[16] The title of Warsaw's first newspaper, the *Western World,* expressed the community's sense of location in the land of mythic American promise—a place of new beginnings and endless opportunity, where the New World was still new.

More important, Warsaw was a practical exercise in self-government. It was founded (in 1834) and incorporated in the Jacksonian era, when the public—especially in the West—demanded noninterference with popular rights. "Freedom," not "faith," was the shibboleth of the community. In fact, Warsaw was named for the capital of Poland, where heroic freedom fighters had battled against the invading Russians in 1830, so the town's very name symbolized freedom and the willingness to fight for it. An early newspaper article that mentions the naming of the town also refers to "the enlarged patriotism of the proprietors"—that is, their commitment to democratic ideology.[17]

In Warsaw, republicanism was fundamental; it had a religious quality.[18] Common democratic ideals bound the people together, and the rituals of self-government, such as local elections and city council meetings, were symbolic affirmations of those beliefs. Likewise, Fourth of July celebrations—marked by the erection of a liberty pole, patriotic speeches, and a public reading of the Declaration of Independence—affirmed the community's ideological bond through symbolic participation in the origin of the republic.[19] Warsaw was, in a sense, connected with that origin, for it was located where a military outpost named Fort Johnson had been established during the War of 1812—a war popularly regarded as a second assertion of American independence and, hence, an instrument of the nation's democratic mission.[20]

Warsaw's leaders had an enormous interest in politics, government, and history. Local newspapers printed the town's "Corporation Proceedings" (city council meetings) in some detail, as well as numerous articles about the state and national governments and American history, including a locally written patriotic series, "Brief Biography of Eminent Americans."[21] Perhaps the most substantial contribution to the newspaper by a local author was "The Science and Progress of Government," a three-part series that chronicles the rise of republican government and celebrates equal rights, democratic institutions, and America's "glorious mission of political redemption."[22] To the people of Warsaw, the nation had a transcendent value, and republicanism—or American democratic ideology—was the operative faith of their community, shaping their experience and mobilizing their wills.

In the fall of 1843, local leaders formed a civic group called the Warsaw Legislature, which was devoted to their ideology. It was a lyceum in which people of the community acted as a democratic assembly to discuss current issues and propose legislation. They assumed, for purposes of discussion, that Warsaw was a new American "state," the organization's members were the "legislature," and their elected leader was the "governor." The first "governor" was a local lawyer, who delivered his inaugural address on November 17, 1843. He asserted that Warsaw was an expression of republican ideals, a place where "indomitable love of civil and religious liberty . . . acknowledges no restraint inconsistent with the laws of conscience and moral right" and where "the humblest citizen" may express his views of government and aspire to high office. Although he charged his listeners with responsibility to the public, he also celebrated the rights of the individual:

The people of Warsaw have expressed their preference for a representative government. Claiming all political power as inherent in themselves, they have delegated to you their authority.... They have made you their servants, not their rulers:—from them you derive all your power and authority....

As the object of all legislation should be to secure the greatest good of the greatest number, in enacting such laws as you may deem necessary to promote the peace and prosperity of our young state, it should be your aim to employ the least possible coercion upon the will and action of the people.

The rights of conscience should be placed above all human laws; and such acts only as are wrong in themselves, impairing the natural rights of individuals or of society, should justify any restraints upon personal liberty.[23]

By stating that "human laws" were less important that "the rights of conscience," the speaker failed to recognize the deep relationship between such laws and "personal liberty." However, he later reminded his listeners that "the intelligence and virtue of the mass of the people constitute the only base of civil and religious liberty," and he confidently asserted that "our people" possess "all the elements of true greatness"— including love of liberty, perseverance, patriotism, energy, and independence of thought and action. He also declared that "the bold fire of liberty in a heart capable of appreciating its life giving influences" was as unstoppable as the Mississippi River. In Warsaw, freedom was indeed a sacred cause, and surging individualism demanded strict limits on governmental power. All political authority resided in the people and was carefully delegated.

The Warsaw Legislature affirmed the town's commitment to democratic ideology by its very operation within the community as well as by the views of those addressed by the organization. It was an ongoing testament to what the townspeople deeply believed—that the good society arose not through a covenant with God that created a people, as in Nauvoo, but through a contract among individuals that created a government. (That made an enormous difference in what residents of the two communities regarded as tyranny.) The first meeting of the Warsaw Legislature was, in fact, a symbolic reenactment of the establishment of the community, a performance of their democratic cultural myth that reaffirmed their identity as Americans. In his inaugural address, the speaker declared that the people of Warsaw were "gathered from nearly every state in the Union, and from many nations of the Old World" and were making their "first attempts . . . at enlightened self-government." It is clear that the town of Warsaw institutionalized the ideals of its residents, just as Nauvoo institutionalized Mormon ideals. The so-called Mormon conflict of the 1840s was, then, not just a contest for local political control that got out of hand; it was an ideological struggle in which the non-Mormons viewed themselves as the champions of republicanism, standing opposed to those who would subvert that ideology.

It is not surprising that among such people Nauvoo became an issue of fundamental importance. After all, it was a hierarchical, collectivistic, and authoritarian community—and therefore outside the American political consensus. The bloc voting that Joseph Smith encouraged as a means of gaining political advantages for Nauvoo was an affront to the personal independence that Warsaw residents and other non-Mormons felt was essential to popular government. The misuse of the Nauvoo charter to empower the municipal court with excessively broad jurisdiction, so the prophet could avoid trial on state charges, challenged the concept of equality before the law that was a much-respected democratic axiom in early Illinois. In general, the control of Nauvoo's civil affairs by religious leaders, which non-Mormons in Warsaw objected to as early as the spring of 1841, violated the separation of church and state, a concept vehemently insisted on by leaders of the Jacksonian era.[24] As one non-Mormon from the area, who used the pseudonym "Hancock," said of the Mormons in the *Alton Telegraph,* "Their religious and political creed[s] are identical, and as directly at variance with the spirit of our institutions as any system that man could possibly devise."[25] This was an overstatement, but he was essentially right. In Nauvoo, social and political order ultimately rested on divine order, which was really an Old World idea that had led to the establishment of state religions in Europe and, ultimately, to the rise of religious persecution there.

Of course, non-Mormons in Warsaw and other nearby areas did not understand Mormon millennialism or the connection between that doctrine and the American sense of mission. They simply realized that the Nauvoo public did not thoroughly subscribe to democratic values—that, in fact, the community was a theocracy headed by a man whose religious position was the basis of his political and military power. This deviation from democracy became even more alarming to local non-Mormons in the spring of 1842, when the prophet, who was already lieutenant general of the Nauvoo Legion, became mayor of the town and chief magistrate of the municipal court. As one anonymous commentator put it in the Quincy newspaper, "The spectacle presented in Smith's case—of a civil, ecclesiastical, and military leader, united in one and the same person, with power over life and liberty, can never find favor in the minds of sound and thinking Republicans."[26] As this suggests, many nearby people became convinced that if Mormonism succeeded, republicanism would fail, for the two ideologies were contradictory.

Furthermore, the people of early Illinois, like most Americans of the Jacksonian era, had an enormous fear of despotism. That aspect of the American character arose during "the birth of democracy in revolt against tyranny," and it was prevalent until the Civil War.[27] As late as 1858, Abraham Lincoln warned the people of Edwardsville, Illinois—and by extension, all Americans—against "despotism" at the hands of "the first cunning tyrant who rises" if they failed to maintain their "love of liberty."[28] The non-Mormons in Hancock County repeatedly voiced their fear of despotism as they commented on developments in Nauvoo.[29] They even proclaimed their concern in official form, as in these twin resolutions passed at the first anti-Mormon political convention in the summer of 1841:

> Resolved, That with the peculiar religious opinions of the people calling themselves Mormons, or Latter-Day Saints, we have nothing to do—being at all times perfectly willing that they shall remain in the full possession of all the rights and privileges which our constitution and laws guarantee and other citizens enjoy.
> Resolved, That in standing up as we do to oppose the influence which these people have obtained, and are likely to obtain, in a political capacity, over our fellow citizens and their liberties, we are guided only by a desire to defend ourselves against a despotism, the extent and consequences of which we have no means of ascertaining.[30]

Naturally, their fear was amplified when Smith became a candidate for president early in 1844, and it was again increased when dissenting Mormons, who knew about the secret Council of Fifty, revealed the prophet's plan to establish a political kingdom of God, with himself in charge.[31] Indeed, the dissenters themselves accused Joseph Smith of "despotism, engendered by an assumption of power in the name of religion."[32]

Of course, most of the Mormons in Nauvoo failed to see any danger. They thought their system of government was democratic—or at least not inconsistent with democracy—and they repeatedly asserted their republicanism. Joseph Smith himself said on March 7, 1844, "We are republicans, and wish to have the people rule," but he also added, "They must rule in righteousness."[33] The implication was that he, as God's agent, set the parameters of righteousness and that the people therefore ruled—or individuals participated in government—at his pleasure. Moreover, they participated to serve his religious purpose, for he had admitted earlier that the very instrument of government in Nauvoo, the city charter, was his own device, concocted "for the salvation of the Church."[34] In short, despite his apparent commitment to republicanism, the prophet established a theocratic government in Nauvoo.[35] It is not surprising that Joseph Smith as presidential candidate openly campaigned for what he called "theodemocracy" in the spring of 1844.[36] He did not realize that democracy and theocracy were incompatible. He failed to understand that in the United States not only must religion be free from political authority but also politics must be free from ecclesiastical authority. There could be no religious denomination behind the government and no religious purpose for the government. Of course, Smith's theocratic views were echoed by Brigham Young—who flatly declared that "the government belongs to God"—and by other Mormon leaders, although they also proclaimed their republican sentiments as well.[37]

One of the unfortunate ironies of the Mormon experience in Illinois was that Joseph Smith's fear of mobocracy (as well as his desire for social unity) caused him to establish Nauvoo as a theocratic, militaristic city-state, which in turn aroused the non-Mormons' deepest fears and led to the very mobocratic attacks he hoped to avoid. Indeed, the man who delivered the speech on liberty and self-government to the Warsaw Legislature quoted above was William N. Grover, who became increasingly alarmed by Nauvoo's challenge to democratic ideology and went to Carthage the following June, with some other non-Mormons, and murdered the prophet.[38] In the process, of course, he and the other mobocrats violated the very ideals to which they subscribed, and they so forcefully polarized the Mormons and non-Mormons in Hancock County that effective self-government came to an end there. They also turned public sentiment against themselves, made Smith into a martyr, and obscured the ideological significance of their cause.

* * *

If the unrestrained popular will, which tramples on the rights of individuals and minorities, is the characteristic problem of democracy, the abuse of authority by religious leaders is the characteristic problem of theocracy. This is exemplified by Joseph Smith's suppression of religious and political dissent in Nauvoo, which culminated in the *Expositor* affair. The entire matter has not received adequate discussion by historians.

The affair began in the spring of 1844, when a group of Mormons broke with the prophet and founded a new, reformist church. They did not hesitate to make their reasons public, and they met with some initial success, as revealed by this brief, non-Mormon newspaper account of May 15:

The New Church appears to be going ahead. On last Sunday, there were about three hundred assembled at Mr. Law's house in Nauvoo, and [they] listened with much seeming pleasure to a sermon from Elder Blakely [James A. Blakeslee], who denounced Smith as a fallen Prophet. He treated the Spiritual wife doctrine without gloves, and repudiated Smith's plan of uniting Church and State.

After Blakely had concluded, William Law gave his reasons in strong language for leaving the false prophet.

Francis M. Higbee, then read a series of resolutions which set forth the reasons for withdrawing from Joe. After this a number of affidavits were read testifying to Joe's villainy, and showing the evils under which a huge portion of the citizens are obliged to labor.

The new church and those opposed to Mormonism in Nauvoo, are said to be strongly in favor of repealing their Charter, it having been made an instrument of oppression rather than a benefit.[39]

Earnest, well-informed, and influential dissent had come to Nauvoo, and it was both religious and political. The dissenters, led by William Law, who was counselor to the prophet in the church presidency and one of the foremost leaders in the community, had been scandalized by the secret practice of polygamy, and they had objected to it and to some other new doctrines. They had also criticized the prophet's subversion of democratic ideology. As Lyndon W. Cook has pointed out, William Law asserted that Smith "was totally ungovernable and defiant and was determined to obey or disobey the law of the land at his convenience" and that he "united church and state, both as mayor of Nauvoo (in the passage of city ordinances and the use of police power) and as an influential religious leader by manipulating or seeking to manipulate politicians for private purposes."[40] Since Law was a prominent businessman, committed to free enterprise, he also objected when Smith tried to control the economic activities of the Mormon people by ecclesiastical authority. According to Cook, Law's "democratic spirit" and "individualism" prevented him from assuming the kind of "total submission" to Smith that was characteristic of most other Mormons.[41] That was probably true of the other dissenters as well. As their disenchantment with Smith's leadership grew, so did their determination "to break the *yoke of tyranny*" that had fallen upon the people of Nauvoo.[42] The dissenter Charles Foster put it this way in a letter to the Warsaw *Signal:* "We verily believe in the sentiment that 'Resistance to tyranny is obedience to God,' and with the arms and heart that God has given us, we will fearlessly and faithfully maintain our rights."[43]

Before they had separated from Smith to form a new church, the dissenters had attempted to achieve reform by objecting to specific doctrines and policies, but their views had been rejected by the prophet. He began to treat them as enemies, attempting first to silence them by intimidation. As he said at a meeting on March 7, "I will wage an eternal warfare with those that oppose me. . . . I will disgrace every man by publishing him on the house top, who will not be still and mind his own business."[44] But the would-be reformers refused to be silenced. Soon, in a speech on March 24, Smith accused the leading dissenters of conspiring to kill him, his immediate family, all of his relatives, and the heads of the church.[45] No charges of that sort were filed, but Smith's public portrayal of them as potential mass murderers and enemies of the people opened the floodgates of slander and incited persecution. Men who had been regarded as upright Mormons were suddenly defamed as "thieves, counterfeiters, bogus-makers, gamblers, debauchers, murderers, and all that is vile," as Willard Richards put it in a letter to James Arlington Bennet.[46] John Taylor launched a campaign of vilification against them in the pages of the Nauvoo *Neighbor*, hoping to discredit them and drive them from the community. Some of the dissenters were threatened, and several were excommunicated. Rather than leave, however, they decided to remain and express their views. After all, they hoped to attract members to the Reformed Church, as they called it, from among the Nauvoo public.[47] They had to stay. As all Mormon and Illinois historians know, they established a newspaper called the *Expositor*, which was to be the organ of their cause.

At that point, Nauvoo was on the verge of becoming more deeply American. Civil rights were being tested in a theocratic environment, and if the dissenters succeeded in firmly establishing a dissenting minority in the community—regardless of whether they ever removed Smith from political power or curbed his plans for a temporal kingdom—the town's role as a unified separatist community was at an end. Indeed, Nauvoo's symbolic identity as Zion was shattered by the very notion that the Mormon community was apparently not the divinely inspired ensign of peace and freedom but a place of discord and loss of freedom, not the one true church but two rival churches, led by men who were outspokenly opposed to one another. No wonder the Reformed Church, which was planning to launch a newspaper and had appointed a committee "to visit the different families in the city, and see who would join," created a crisis for the prophet.[48] At stake was the Mormon antipluralistic notion that within the emerging kingdom of God only one church had cultural legitimacy—and that church must be under the control of God's prophet. Religious freedom and Mormon separatism were incompatible.

More deeply, at stake was Smith's vision of a dichotomous America:

.the millennial kingdom of God versus Babylon (the evil kingdom of men), the children of God versus the children of the devil. That perspective made the building of Zion imperative and democracy there impossible, for it labeled critics as enemies of the community (the kingdom), eliminating the right to disagree. As John Taylor said in attempting to justify the suppression of the dissenting newspaper, "Are a virtuous people to be condemned because they have the moral courage to put a stop to blacklegs, counterfeiters, and the veryest schophants and snakes that ever poisoned community."[49] If Zion had serious shortcomings and opponents of Smith had anything constructive to offer by way of reform, Nauvoo was part of imperfect America after all—not a bastion of virtue in a corrupt nation but a place where moral, social, and political problems existed and public pressure could bring change. Thus, the dissenters did threaten the community—not by planning to assassinate its leaders but by undermining its ideological foundation.

The prophet's destruction of the *Expositor* was not just a temporarily successful effort to suppress religious and political dissent; it was an unsuccessful attempt to maintain his authority against individualism and his community against pluralism—the very aspects of American society that had created the religious uncertainty and rampant sectarianism that had troubled him years earlier. Moreover, because Smith had virtually consolidated all local power in himself, the destruction of the press was indeed *his* act. The Nauvoo City Council was under his unofficial control, and the council's minutes reveal that he personally and vigorously spearheaded the drive for declaring the *Expositor* a nuisance and having it destroyed. At the June 8 city council meeting, which was continued on June 10, he called for its destruction at least four times. He even asserted that the dissenters wanted to incite violence against Nauvoo—an irrational claim, considering that the organizers of the new church and their families were part of the community. "What the opposition party want is to raise a mob on us and take the spoils from us, as they did in Missouri," he said, appealing to the fears of his listeners, and he added that he "would rather die tomorrow and have the thing smashed, than live and have it go on, for it was exciting the spirit of mobocracy among the people, and bringing death and destruction upon us."[50] Ironically, the *Expositor* was probably doing the opposite—defusing hostility by creating the hope among non-Mormons that the dissenters would curb Smith's power and that Nauvoo would cease to be so threatening to democratic ideology. Indeed, Thomas Sharp, the leading anti-Mormon and a relentless agitator, hoped that the newspaper would divide the community and thus end its theocratic separatism: "We say success to the new undertaking—for a kingdom divided against itself cannot stand."[51]

In any case, it was not the newspaper but Smith's destruction of it that incited the mob.

After the city council consented to what the prophet wanted done, he acted as mayor to order the city police to destroy the press, and then he acted as lieutenant general of the Nauvoo Legion to provide military support for the institutionalized violence. Smith had clearly violated the dissenters' constitutional right to due process of law as well as their right to publish their views, but of course he was exonerated by the local court, where he was chief magistrate. In short, the prophet's actions in the *Expositor* affair were clear evidence that in Nauvoo *he* was the repository of governmental authority and that local institutions served the people only insofar as they served his purposes. He was indeed "ungovernable," as William Law so clearly recognized.

All of this received the most intense criticism from non-Mormons, including the following biased but astute analysis in the Warsaw *Signal:* "Why did he [Smith] fear the Nauvoo Expositor, if he were an innocent and abused man? He had a press under his own control, by which he could defend himself from all unjust aspersions. But no! he knew that this press, located in the midst of his followers, would open the eyes of the honest portion of them to his villainous practices. . . . Why stake so much upon the destruction of this press, if he did not deem that either his power, or it, must be crushed."[52]

Although the non-Mormons inaccurately perceived the prophet as a villain, they understood correctly that he ultimately did not trust the people. In this case, he did not trust them to evaluate competing claims about his religious leadership and his governance of the community and to make up their own minds. He asserted his power by eliminating the dissenting press and thereby made it impossible for the Nauvoo public to consider the issues any further and determine where they stood and what they might want him to do. Against the democratic ideology that was the very basis of community in Warsaw, he had committed the ultimate sin: overt suppression of civil rights to maintain his sovereignty. Although non-Mormons there and elsewhere in Hancock County were not directly affected—because they were not residents of Nauvoo—they had identified deeply with the dissenters, who had become surrogates for them in the battle against Smith's theocratic city-state. And they felt threatened, for they knew that the powerful Mormon leader could dominate Hancock County institutions in a similarly high-handed manner. Some of them therefore took up arms and resorted to mob violence, incited by the inflammatory articles in Thomas Sharp's Warsaw *Signal.*

*   *   *

The Hancock County violence of the mid-1840s was, then, firmly based on a clash of values. This is not to deny that factors discussed by other scholars—such as non-Mormon political frustration and Mormon misuse of the Nauvoo charter—contributed to the eruption of violence, but most of those matters are related to the underlying ideological conflict. Even the charge of religious persecution, which the Mormons leveled against their critics and which the non-Mormons denied, takes on a new significance in this light. Since there was ultimately no separation between the government and the church in Nauvoo, non-Mormon opposition to Mormon antirepublican behavior was regarded as religious persecution by Smith and his supporters. By the same token, the Mormons' ambitious, repressive theocracy was perceived as a threat to the democratic ideology that was so deeply held in Warsaw. In short, ultimate values were at stake on both sides. Although the Mormons and non-Mormons had much in common ideologically,[53] this fundamental conflict of values led to violence, for it was symbolized by the struggle for political control of the county, in which the non-Mormons were defeated, and it was again symbolized by the struggle of the dissenters (non-Mormon surrogates) against theocratic despotism, which ended in a more disturbing kind of defeat.

Unfortunately, the two groups shared one crucial shortcoming. The Mormons, with their cultural particularism, and the non-Mormons, with their Jacksonian individualism, were insufficiently committed to the social whole, the common welfare. Each group readily, almost eagerly, perceived the potential threat from the other group (theocratic despotism, mobocratic violence) because that threat verified its own sense of identity as the politically righteous opposite. Although the leaders of both groups viewed themselves as defenders of republicanism, democratic values, and the Constitution, they were in reality defenders of their own rights, which is not the same thing. For example, after Smith had denounced the reformist church leaders as enemies of the community, convicted them without due process of law, destroyed their newspaper, and declared martial law in Nauvoo, he ironically called on "lovers of liberty" to punish those "who trample under foot the glorious Constitution and the people's rights."[54] Likewise, the Nauvoo *Neighbor* editor, John Taylor, cried out, "Let us enjoy our religion" and "the *rights of Americans*" in the same article in which he attacked the dissenters as "wicked and malicious" and justified the destruction of the *Expositor*.[55] His comments too are deeply ironic: he called for freedom of religion while praising an attack on religious dissenters by a repressive government that did not achieve the separation of church and state upon which religious freedom rests. In the same way, the Warsaw *Signal* editor, Thomas Sharp, asserted that the non-Mormons stood for "virtue and liberty" and "our political rights" in the same article in which he summoned his readers to take up arms against the "band of villains" in Nauvoo.[56] He thus employed the rhetoric of republicanism to incite mobocratic behavior, ironically revealing that a newspaper could be detrimental to democracy. The leaders in both communities cherished their own freedom, but their self-interested, localistic republicanism—modified by Jacksonian individualism in Warsaw and by Mormon cultural particularism in Nauvoo—engendered a shallow commitment to pluralistic America and its democratic institutions, which make freedom possible. So when viable opposition to their political will arose and actions that aroused their fear developed, both groups readily suppressed the liberty of others in a misguided effort to secure their own.

Oddly enough, one man who was caught in the middle and criticized by both groups had the right perspective. Thomas Ford was not only one of the finest nineteenth-century governors of Illinois but also an experienced judge with an extreme dislike of unlawful violence and considerable insight into frontier people and communities. He forcefully decried both the constitutional violations in Nauvoo, connected with the *Expositor* affair, and the subsequent mobocratic actions of the non-Mormons. His letter "To the Mayor and Council of the City of Nauvoo," dated June 22, 1844, in which he censured the Mormon leaders for their civil rights violations, and his broadside letter "To the People of Warsaw, in Hancock County," dated July 25, 1844, in which he criticized their mob violence, are two of the finest historical documents of the Mormon conflict. In the former, he sternly told the Nauvoo leaders, "Your conduct in the destruction of the press was a very gross outrage upon the laws and the liberties of the people," and in the latter, he warned the Warsaw mobocrats against further illegal actions, asserting that "mob violence" was "threatening our fair form of government."[57]

Like Abraham Lincoln, Ford was an advocate of procedural democracy and had a tremendous sense of commitment to the social whole and to the maintenance of democratic institutions. As he said to the citizens of Warsaw in a letter dated January 29, 1844, which discusses the growing antagonism between the Mormons and the non-Mormons, "I am bound by the laws and the constitution to regard you all as citizens of the state, possessed of equal rights and privileges; and to cherish the rights of one as dearly as the rights of another."[58] For Ford, as for Lincoln, the love of liberty did not mean simply insisting upon it for yourself or your community but prizing it as the sacred right of all people, whether they supported or opposed your own values. Unfortunately, that high standard of democratic obligation was not matched by the leaders on either side of the conflict, and, consequently, Mormon Nauvoo became an American tragedy.

Notes

An earlier version of this essay appeared in the *Journal of Mormon History* 16 (1990): 53–69.

1. Shortly after this essay was prepared for the May 1989 Mormon History Association meeting in Quincy, Illinois, two books appeared that relate directly to matters discussed here: Marvin S. Hill, *Quest for Refuge: The Mormon Flight from American Pluralism* (Salt Lake City: Signature Books, 1989); and Kenneth H. Winn, *Exiles in a Land of Liberty: Mormons in America, 1830–1846* (Chapel Hill: University of North Carolina Press, 1989). Hill maintains that the Mormons rejected American pluralism, strove to establish a theocratic government, and were persecuted for their antipluralism. Winn argues that the Mormons felt alienated in what they thought was a corrupt America, strove to reestablish communal republicanism, and were regarded as antirepublican subversives by non-Mormons. My essay has much in common with both books, but it differs from them as well. More narrowly focused, it centers on two related matters: Mormon Nauvoo as a challenge to non-Mormon ideology, and the Reformed Church in Nauvoo as a challenge to Mormon ideology. In any case, the essay has been revised since being delivered to reflect the books by Hill and Winn and to provide some additional evidence about the ideological conflict from contemporaneous documents.

2. I use *democratic ideology* and *republicanism* interchangeably in this essay, although the latter was the common term used by Americans in the revolutionary era and afterward to denote a system of values that centered on the individual's relation to America, the new democratic social order. Freedom, equality, virtue, independence of thought and action, and devotion to the common good were key values of republicanism. See Gordon S. Wood, *The Creation of the American Republic, 1776–1789* (Chapel Hill: University of North Carolina Press, 1969), 416–90; and Bernard Bailyn, David Brion Davis, David Herbert Donald, John L. Thomas, Robert Wiebe, and Gordon S. Wood, *The Great Republic: A History of the American People* (Boston: D. C. Heath, 1977), 291–97. By the Jacksonian era, that ideology had taken on an even deeper significance, chiefly through the communal and utopian dimensions of town development, the widespread sense of participation in the American democratic mission, the mythologizing of the revolutionary past, and the celebration of individual rights.

3. William G. McLoughlin, "Religious Freedom and Popular Sovereignty: A Change in the Flow of God's Power, 1730–1830," in *In the Great Tradition: In Honor of Winthrop S. Hudson, Essays on Pluralism, Volunteerism, Revivalism,* ed. Joseph D. Ban and Raul R. Dakar (Valley Forge, Penn.: Judson Press, 1982), 175.

4. Ibid.; William G. McLoughlin, *Revivals, Awakenings and Reform: An Essay on Religion and Social Change in America, 1607–1977* (Chicago: University of Chicago Press, 1977); Wood, *Creation of the American Republic;* Cushing Strout, *The New Heaven and New Earth: Political Religion in America* (New York: Harper and Row, 1974); Robert N. Bellah, *The Broken Covenant: American Civil Religion in Time of Trial* (New York: Seabury Press, 1975); Perry Miller, *The Life of the Mind in America, from the Revolution to the Civil War* (New York: Harcourt, Brace and World, 1965).

5. Mario S. DePillis, "The Quest for Religious Authority and the Rise of Mormonism," *Dialogue: A Journal of Mormon Thought* 1 (Spring 1966): 68–88.

6. David Brion Davis, "The New England Origins of Mormonism," *New England Quarterly* 26 (June 1953): 147–68; Ernest Lee Tuveson, *Redeemer Nation: The Idea of America's Millennial Role* (Chicago: University of Chicago Press, 1968); Bellah, *Broken Covenant;* J. F. MacLear, "The Republic and the Millennium," in *The Religion of the Republic,* ed. Elwyn A. Smith (Philadelphia: Fortress Press, 1971), 183–216; J. F. MacLear, "New England and the Fifth Monarchy: The Quest for the Millennium in Early American Puritanism," *William and Mary Quarterly,* 3d ser., 32 (April 1975): 223–60; Gustav H. Blanke and Karen Lynn, " 'God's Base of Operations': Mormon Variations on the American Sense of Mission," *Brigham Young University Studies* 20 (Fall 1979): 83–92.

7. Strout, *New Heaven and New Earth;* Nathan O. Hatch, *The Sacred Cause of Liberty: Republican Thought and the Millennium in Revolutionary New England* (New Haven, Conn.: Yale University Press, 1977).

8. Klaus J. Hansen, *Quest for Empire: The Kingdom of God and the Council of Fifty in Mormon History* (East Lansing: Michigan State University Press, 1967); Gordon S. Wood, "Evangelical America and Early Mormonism," *New York History* 61 (October 1980): 359–86; Winn, *Exiles in a Land of Liberty.*

9. Thomas F. O'Dea, *The Mormons* (Chicago: University of Chicago Press, 1967).

10. Wood, "Evangelical America and Early Mormonism"; Winn, *Exiles in a Land of Liberty.*

11. Thomas Ford, *A History of Illinois: From Its Commencement as a State in 1818 to 1847* (Chicago: S. C. Griggs, 1854); Theodore Calvin Pease, *The Centennial History of Illinois,* vol. 2, *The Frontier State, 1818–1848* (Chicago: A. C. McClurg, 1919); Rodney O. Davis, "Politics and Law in Frontier Illinois," in *Illinois: Its History and Legacy,* ed. Roger D. Bridges and Rodney O. Davis (St Louis: River City Publications, 1984), 47–56.

12. Morris Birkbeck, *Letters from Illinois* (London: Taylor and Hessey, 1818), 70.

13. Ibid., 24.

14. Ford, *History of Illinois*, 90.

15. See, for example, George R. Gaylor, "A Social, Economic, and Political Study of the Mormons in Western Illinois, 1839–1846: A Re-evaluation" (Ph.D. diss., Indiana University, 1955); Kenneth W. Godfrey, "Causes of Mormon–Non-Mormon Conflict in Hancock County, Illinois, 1839–1846" (Ph.D. diss., Brigham Young University, 1967); Annette P. Hampshire, *Mormonism in Conflict: The Nauvoo Years* (New York: Edwin Mellen Press, 1985).

16. John E. Hallwas, "Warsaw: An Old Mississippi River Village," *Illinois Magazine* 18 (December 1979): 8–15; John E. Hallwas, *Western Illinois Heritage* (Macomb: Illinois Heritage Press, 1983), 37–48.

17. "Sketches of Hancock County," *Western World* (Warsaw, Ill.), April 7, 1841, 1.

18. I do not use the term *civil religion* because it is a controversial concept with several meanings, as Russell E. Richey and Donald G. Jones point out in "The Civil Religion Debate," introduction to *American Civil Religion* (New York: Harper and Row, 1974), 3–18. However, republicanism in Warsaw corresponds roughly to what they categorize as "folk religion," which has been described by Will Herberg as "the American Way of Life," a common democratic faith, in his classic study *Protestant-Catholic-Jew: An Essay in American Religious Sociology* (1955; rev. ed., Garden City, N.Y.: Anchor Books, 1960), 75–81. I prefer simply to depict the manifestations of democratic ideology in Warsaw and assert its profound moral seriousness for the people of that community.

19. "Our Anniversary," *Warsaw Message*, 26 July 1843, 1.

20. Warsaw's heritage includes two military outposts: Fort Johnson, erected there by Zachary Taylor in 1814 and destroyed later that year, and Fort Edwards, erected there in 1817 and used by federal troops to support the fur trade until 1824 (Hallwas, "Warsaw"). Early Warsaw residents tended to confuse those two forts, which preceded the establishment of their community, but they knew about them (the ruins of Fort Edwards stood until the mid-1840s). The forts provided the community with a sense of historical connection to American military operations in the West and, ultimately, to the War of 1812. On the War of 1812 as a "Second War for Independence," a struggle for "the perpetuation and growth of free institutions," see, for example, Benson J. Lossing, *The Pictorial Fieldbook of the War of 1812* (New York: Harper and Brothers, 1868), 1067–69.

21. As early as 1840, the *Western World* regularly carried articles entitled "Corporation Proceedings," "Illinois Legislature," and "Twenty-Sixth Congress." That practice was continued by later newspapers. The series devoted to "Brief Biography of Eminent Americans" appeared in the Warsaw *Signal*, starting with "John Adams" and "John Quincy Adams" on May 19, 1841.

22. Cleon [pseudonym], "The Science and Progress of Government: An Essay in Three Parts," *Warsaw Message*, January 7, 1843, 4; January 21, 1843, 4; January 28, 1843, 4.

23. "State of Warsaw Association, Inaugural of Gov. Grover," *Warsaw Message*, November 29, 1843, 1–2.

24. "The Mormons," *Signal* (Warsaw, Illinois), May 19, 1841, 2.

25. Hancock [pseudonym], "Letter to Gov. Ford, No. 5," *Alton Telegraph*, April 5, 1845, 1.

26. "The Mormons," *Quincy Whig*, May 22, 1844, 1.

27. Arthur M. Schlesinger Jr., *The Age of Jackson* (Boston: Little, Brown, 1946), 517.

28. Abraham Lincoln, "Speech at Edwardsville, Illinois, September 11, 1858," in *Abraham Lincoln: His Speeches and Writings*, ed. Roy P. Basler (Cleveland: World Publishing, 1946), 473.

29. "Our Position—Again," *Signal*, June 16, 1841, 2.

30. Thomas Gregg, "A Descriptive, Statistical, and Historical Chart of the County of Hancock," broadside, 2d edition, February 1, 1846, Archives and Special Collections, Western Illinois University Library, Macomb.

31. George T. M. Davis, *An Authentic Account of the Massacre of Joseph Smith, the Mormon Prophet, and Hyrum Smith, His Brother, Together with a Brief History of the Rise and Progress of Mormonism, and All the Circumstances Which Led to Their Death* (St. Louis: Chambers and Knapp, 1844), 7–8; Ford, *History of Illinois*, 321.

32. "Introductory," *Expositor* (Nauvoo, Illinois), June 7, 1844.

33. Joseph Smith, *History of the Church of Jesus Christ of Latter-day Saints*, ed. B. H. Roberts (Salt Lake City: Deseret News Press, 1902–12; 6 vols., a seventh volume was published in 1932; reprinted by Deseret Book, 1976, and reissued in paperback in 1978), 6:237.

34. Ibid., 4:249.

35. Robert Bruce Flanders, *Nauvoo: Kingdom on the Mississippi* (Urbana: University of Illinois Press, 1965); Hill, *Quest for Refuge*.

36. Joseph Smith to the editor of the *Washington Globe*, April 15, 1844, in *Neighbor* (Nauvoo, Illinois), April 17, 1844, 2.

37. Smith, *History of the Church*, 6:322.

38. Grover was not convicted, but there is convincing evidence that he participated in the murders at Carthage. See Dallin H. Oaks and Marvin S. Hill, *Carthage Conspiracy: The Trial of the Accused Assassins of Joseph Smith* (Urbana: University of Illinois Press, 1975), 118–19, 126, 147–55. A man of much patriotic fervor, Grover read the Declaration of Independence to the Warsaw populace after community leaders had erected a liberty pole to mark the Fourth of July 1843 ("Our Anniversary," 2). In his inaugural speech to the Warsaw Legislature later that year, he referred to the "military organization and discipline" of "the Nephites" (i.e., the Nauvoo Legion of the Mormons) and then proposed the organization of the Warsaw militia as a "guaranty of our rights" ("State of Warsaw"). He became a leader in that militia, which contributed to the formation of the mob that stormed Carthage Jail the following June.

39. "The New Church," *Signal*, May 15, 1844, 2.

40. Lyndon W. Cook, "William Law, Nauvoo Dissenter," *Brigham Young University Studies* 22 (Winter 1982): 56.
41. Ibid., 55, 70.
42. William Law to the editor of Rock Island *Upper Mississippian,* August 1844, in "The Dissenters," *Signal,* September 18, 1844, 2.
43. Charles A. Foster to the editor, April 29, 1844, *Signal,* May 8, 1844, 2.
44. Smith, *History of the Church,* 6:239.
45. Ibid., 6:272. It is impossible to know for sure what kind of information Smith had received, but M. G. Eaton and A. B. Williams had recently published in the Nauvoo *Neighbor* affidavits about a conspiracy (ibid., 6:278–80). Williams's source of information was Joseph H. Jackson, "an adventurer and a desperate character," according to the Hancock County historian Thomas Gregg (ibid., 6:149). Jackson had come to Nauvoo in 1843, joined the church, and apparently engaged in counterfeiting. In the spring of 1844, he broke with the prophet and associated himself with the dissenters. He later published an exposé in which he accused Smith of masterminding the counterfeiting and conspiring to kill Governor Boggs of Missouri, the Reformed Church leader William Law, and others (Joseph H. Jackson, *A Narrative of the Adventures and Experience of Joseph H. Jackson of Nauvoo* [Warsaw: n.p., 1844]). Obviously, Jackson was adept at spinning tales of conspiracy.

In his affidavit published in the Nauvoo *Neighbor* on April 17, 1844, Williams asserted that Jackson had told him on March 15 "that Doctor Foster, Chauncey L. Higbee, and the Laws were red hot for a conspiracy, and he should not be surprised if in two weeks there should not be one of the Smith family left alive in Nauvoo" (Smith, *History of the Church,* 6:278). As this suggests, Jackson evidently learned of "a conspiracy" and then drew his own wild conclusions about what might result from it. He probably became aware of the dissenters' plans to expose Smith and curb his power and then misstated the matter as a conspiracy to commit murder.

M. G. Eaton's affidavit appeared on the same page of the Nauvoo *Neighbor,* and it confirms this view. He went to a meeting of a few dissenters, along with Jackson, and simply heard complaints about "the spiritual wife system" and comments that some dissenters feared for their lives because of their opposition to Smith. Eaton made no assertions about proposed violence against the prophet, but he mentioned that "I heard said Jackson say that the Laws were ready to enter into a secret conspiracy tooth and nails" (Smith, *History of the Church,* 6:280).

Smith evidently heard of the matter from others as well (Smith, *History of the Church,* 6:280–81). It is likely that in the highly charged atmosphere of Nauvoo in the spring of 1844 the secret meetings of the dissenters were exaggerated into a conspiracy to commit murder. The ultimate basis for such reports was perhaps Smith himself for he viewed critics as enemies and enemies as a personal threat. In a speech on December 29, 1843, he spoke about "the ungrateful treachery of assassins" and asserted, "My life is in danger" and "I am exposed to far greater danger from traitors among ourselves than from enemies without" (Smith, *History of the Church,* 6:152). That speech did much to create an atmosphere in which opposition to the prophet would be construed as a murder conspiracy.

In any case, in the spring of 1844 Smith used the incredible story of a mass murder conspiracy to turn the community against his critics.

46. Smith, *History of the Church,* 6:517.

47. Isaac and Sarah Scott letter, June 16, 1844, in George F. Partridge, ed., "The Death of a Mormon Dictator: Letters of Massachusetts Mormons, 1843–1848," *New England Quarterly* 9 (December 1936): 596.

48. Smith, *History of the Church,* 6:347.

49. "A Question," *Neighbor,* June 16, 1844, 2.

50. Smith, *History of the Church,* 6:441–42.

51. "The Nauvoo Expositor," *Signal,* May 15, 1844, 2.

52. "From Nauvoo," *Signal,* June 19, 1844, 2.

53. R. Laurence Moore, "How to Become a People: The Mormon Scenario," in *Religious Outsiders and the Making of Americans* (New York: Oxford University Press, 1986), 25–47; Winn, *Exiles in a Land of Liberty.*

54. Smith, *History of the Church,* 6:499.

55. "Retributive Justice," *Nauvoo Neighbor,* June 12, 1844, 2.

56. *Signal,* broadside, June 14, 1844. Included in the microfilm copy of the *Signal,* Illinois State Historical Library, Springfield.

57. Quoted in Smith, *History of the Church,* 6:534; Thomas Ford, "To the People of Warsaw in Hancock County," July 25, 1844, copy in Archives and Special Collections, Western Illinois University Library, Macomb.

58. Thomas Ford letter (addressee's name omitted), January 29, 1944, *Signal,* February 14, 1944, 2.

11

The Martyrdom of Joseph Smith in Early Mormon Writings

DAVIS BITTON

The assassination of Joseph Smith and Hyrum Smith in Carthage, Illinois, on June 27, 1844, continues to arouse interest and emotion among the Latter-day Saints. Tourists by the tens of thousands flock to Carthage Jail each year to climb the narrow stairs and examine the upper room where the prophet and patriarch were ensconced at the time of their death. Artists early began to portray the incident as a kind of passion play—the forces of evil marshaled against those of good. C. C. A. Christiansen and Philo Dibble, for example, did paintings of church history scenes and did not overlook this emotion-packed event. The painter Gary Smith has devoted his talent to a series of paintings on the martyrdom.[1] Nor have writers overlooked the event.[2]

The martyrdom literature I consider here was written in the weeks and months immediately following the event. Several diaries and autobiographies made mention of the martyrdom, as did a few surviving letters. Poetry began to appear almost immediately. It included Eliza R. Snow's "The Assassination of Gen'ls Joseph Smith and Hyrum Smith," published on July 1, 1844, just four days after the event; the anonymous (Alexander Neibaur?) "Lamentation of a Jew among the Afflicted and Mourning Sons and Daughters of Zion, at the Assassination of the Two Chieftains in Israel," published on July 15; W. W. Phelps's "Praise to the Man," which appeared on August 1; Charles Rogers's "On the Death of the Prophet," appearing on August 10; Parley P. Pratt's "Cry of the Martyrs," published September 2; Catherine Lewis's "On the Death of the Prophet and Patriarch," published September 28; Sylvester Hulet's "O Earth Attend," published December 15; John Taylor's "The Seer," which appeared January 1, 1845; and John Taylor's "O Give Me Back My Prophet Dear," which came out on August 1, 1845. A few other published poems of 1844 and 1845, while not dealing with the martyrdom specifically, are so closely related in mood and subject as to be considered part of the same corpus. These include Eliza R. Snow's "To Elder John Taylor," her "Lines Written on the Birth of the Infant Son of Mrs. Emma Smith, Widow of the late General Joseph Smith," and W. W. Phelps's "A Voice from the Prophet." Unpublished martyrdom poetry included William I. Appleby's "Lines Suggested by the Reflections of the Calls and Martyrdom of the Prophet and Patriarch"; William Hyde's "On the Death of Joseph and Hyrum Smith"; and Nelson W. Whipple's "The Two Martyrs."[3]

The Mormon poets tried to convey their grief, their sense of loss—not only their individual bereavement but also that of the entire community. Among the poems, only those of William Hyde and William Appleby attempt to convey their personal reaction. Hyde, preaching the gospel in Vermont, heard the news from a stranger:

> I listened to this stranger's tale
> Until my strength did almost fail;
> My blood did chill within my vein,
> From weeping I could not refrain.

The more general grief was conveyed by the anonymous Jew in a poetic prayer to God:

> How can we, a people in sackcloth,
> Open our lips before thee?
> . . . .
> Our eyes are dim, our hearts heavy;
> No place of refuge being left.

Charles Rogers, addressing Joseph Smith, wrote:

> We feel thy loss, tears of sadness
> Fill every eye in Zion's land;
> We would have met thy fate with gladness,
> Could we have staid thy murderers hand.

There can be no doubting the sincerity of these emotions, but imagery or concrete figures enter into the works only rarely. For comparison consider some of the simple, straightforward prose statements that describe individual reactions to the news. Here, for example, is Warren Foote's journal entry of June 28:

> Elihu Allen and I were working in the harvest field cutting his wheat when about three o'clock P.M. my wife came out and told us that word had just come that Joseph Smith and brother Hiram was shot in Carthage Jail yesterday afternoon. I said at once, "that it cannot

be so." Yet it so affected us that we dropped the cradle and rake and went home. We found that the word had come so straight that we could no longer doubt the truth of it. We all felt as though the powers of darkness had overcome, and that the Lord had forsaken His people. Our Prophet and Patriarch were gone! Who now is to lead the Saints? In fact we mourned "as one mourneth for his only son." Yet after all the anguish of our hearts, and deep mourning of our souls a spirit seemed to whisper "All is well. Zion shall yet arise and spread abroad upon the earth, and the kingdoms of this world shall become the Kingdom of our God and his Christ." So we felt to trust in God.[4]

Jacob Gibson observed the "distress and mourning, tears and weeping." He went on to tell of the meeting in the public square and the desire of some to avenge the murders. The speaker—probably Willard Richards—told them to "be still and know that God raineth." The bodies of the dead prophets were brought for viewing, but here Gibson's emotions overcame him. With unrefined eloquence he wrote, "But I cant describe the Sean no, no, no."[5]

Also in Nauvoo was Benjamin F. Cummings, who said, "In vain would it be for me to attempt to describe the feeling of consternation, dismay, and anguish that the sad intelligence produced. Never did man feel a greater sorrow for the loss of human friends that [than] was felt for these two men."[6] Arouet L. Hale, who later played the snare drums at the funeral ceremony, noted, "To See Stout men & Women Standing around in groops Crying & morning for the Loss of their Dear Prophet & Patriarch was Enough to break the hart of a Stone."[7] Sixteen-year-old John Lyman Smith, a cousin of the prophet, said, "I could not weep for the fountain was dried up, for I would gladly have given my life for them, but so it was & it is not for me to judge for God Doeth all things well."[8]

In a letter dated June 30 Vilate Kimball wrote to her "Dear Dear Companion" who was preaching in the East, "I saw the lifeless corpses of our beloved brethren when they were brought to their almost distracted families. Yea I witnessed their tears, and groans, which was enough to rend the heart of an adamant. Every brother and sister that witnesses the scene fe[lt] deeply to sympathyze with them. Yea, every heart is filled with sorrow, and the very streets of Nauvoo seem to morn. Where it will end the Lord only knows." She went on to tell of an omen appropriate to Elizabethan tragedy. When the Nauvoo Legion was called out, ten drums were found with blood on them. "No one could account for it," she wrote. "They examined to see how many there was. They found ten, and while they were examining the eleventh there came a large drop on that." Vilate saw these as dismal omens of death: William Law had brought about the death of two and would not be satisfied until nine more had been murdered.⁹

On July 18, less than a month after the event, Almira Mack, niece of Lucy Mack Smith, wrote to her sister, who had just lost a little son:

> Your trouble, you think, is as much as you can bear; but it is not like Aunt Lucy's. What must have been her feelings at seeing two of her sons brought into the house dead? Murdered by wicked men. When your little boy was sick, you could be with him and administer to his wants, and when he was gone, you could bury him with decency. But this privilege she could not have. . . . These two of the noblest men on earth were slain, and for what? Was it for crimes they had committed? I answer no; but it was because they professed the religion of Jesus Christ.
>
> They were Prophets of the Lord, and they laid down their lives as did the Prophets in ancient days.¹⁰

I am not sure how comforting this kind of comparison was, but there can be little doubt of Almira's perceptions: the deaths were cruel and undeserved; wicked men had murdered noble men.

Lucy Walker Kimball, writing many years later, provides valuable insights into how one person heard the news and reacted to it:

> At the ernest solicitation of Gen. Don Carlos Smith's widow, some time prior to Prest. Smith's death, Prest. Smith consented to me making my home with her, and she was an elder sister to me. We had just retired on the night of 27th June, when there came a loud rap at the door below. News, I cried, and fled down stairs, opened the door. A messenger quietly said Joseph and Hyrum have been murdered. I seemed paralized with terror, had no power to speak or move. Agnes, called out what is the news, receiving no answer, came rushing down to learn the awful truth. When at length we returned to our chamber and on our bended knees poured out the anguish of our souls to that God who holds the destinies of his children in his own hands, for a time it seemed utterly impossible that he would allow his prophet to be slain by his foes.

Lucy Walker in effect then takes us through the sequence of thoughts that rushed through her mind that memorable night as she (and Agnes Smith) wondered why God would allow such a thing to happen:

> Why not? His only begotten Son offered his life as a sacrifice. What did Joseph say when he gave himself up, at the solicitation of those who plead he would not forsake his flock, "If my life is worth nothing to you it is worth nothing to me." He knew well what his destiny was when he gave up the plan of flying to the "Rocky Mountains." How we plead that Father would, as he had done fifty times before, save him

from his foes. But he gave his life chearfully to save the people. He had often said he would not die a natural death but by the hands of his enemies. That he made every preparation for this great sacrifice we well knew, as we called to mind his own words and yet felt unprepared for the blow, when it came. Never was such a night spent since the crucifiction of our Saviour. The Dogs howled and barked, the cattle bellowed and all creation was astir. We kept by the open window with our arms around each other, untill the dawn, witnessing the terrible commotion and calling to mind his profetic words. My soul sikens as I recall the anguish of the whole people as they crowded around his lifeless body and that of his noble brother Hyrum who was so true to him.

This valuable account, full of detail, combines the real experience with the later reintegration that probably could not be accomplished the very night of the martyrdom.[11]

Many of the journal references are recorded by people who were not in Nauvoo at the time of the tragedy. To help promote Joseph Smith's candidacy for the presidency of the United States, almost every available man, including all but three of the apostles, had left on preaching tours and were widely scattered. News traveled slowly. The murder, which occurred on June 27, 1844, was not reliably reported in some places for a week or two or even longer.

Some of the Mormons later told of experiencing premonitions on June 27, which they only later discovered to be the date of the awful event. Here is Erastus Snow's description as found in his later "Autobiography": "Although at that time I was ignorant of the awful tragedy which had occured, I felt resting down upon me a more dreadful pressure of sorrow and grief and sense of mourning, greater than I had ever before felt, but knew not why."[12]

Parley P. Pratt remembered something similar. A day or two before the murder occurred, he was "constrained by the Spirit to start prematurely for home." On a canal boat in New York State, with his brother William as his traveling companion, he had an ominous experience:

As we conversed together on the deck, a strange and solemn awe came over me, as if the powers of hell were let loose. I was so overwhelmed with sorrow I could hardly speak; and after pacing the deck for some time in silence, I turned to my brother William and exclaimed —"Brother William, this is a dark hour; the powers of darkness seem to triumph, and the spirit of murder is abroad in the land; and it controls the hearts of the American people, and a vast majority of them sanction the killing of the innocent. My brother, let us keep silence and not open our mouths."

Pratt went on to state that, according to his calculations, "it was the same hour that the Carthage mob were shedding the blood of Joseph and Hyrum Smith, and John Taylor, near one thousand miles distant."[13]

It was on July 6 that John D. Lee, then preaching in Kentucky, first heard of the murder. That night, as he explained in his journal, he received angelic confirmation when a heavenly messenger uttered these words: "Instead of electing your leader the chief magistrate of the Nation—they have Martyr[e]d him in prison—which has hasten[ed] his exaltation to the executive chair over this generation." When he received the additional confirmation in a letter from Nauvoo, Lee gave vent to his feelings: "The feeling of grief and anguish operated so powerful upon my natural effections as to destroy the strength of mind & rendered it almost impossible for me to fill my appointments."[14]

Orson Hyde later developed this notion of "that awful night" of June 27. Hundreds of miles from the scene of the crime, he said, two apostles became "unaccountably sad" and filled with "unspeakable anguish of heart."[15] He also mentions a president of the high priests who in Kentucky had a vision of the bodies of the two martyrs.

But these were later recollections. Examination of the diaries kept at the time fails to reveal any general awareness of a tragic occurrence on the night of June 27. Many of them simply record routine happenings for that date. The shock and surprise when the news was received a week or so later suggest that the report had not already been conveyed by dreams and visions. Nonetheless, there is no doubt that a mood of heightened concern, even a dread foreboding, was widespread. Letters from Nauvoo expressed fears for Joseph's safety; the possibility of his arrest by Missourians or Illinois lawmen and the danger of mob violence hovered constantly in the background.

In Massachusetts Wilford Woodruff had been hearing rumors for several days. On July 9 he found a detailed report of the martyrdom in the Boston *Times* and recorded it in his journal with this comment: "My prayer is that God will prepare our minds for the worst & that we may maintain our integrity until death, that we may overcome as Jesus has overcome." The news was fragmentary. Woodruff wrote, "We do not obtain one word from any of our friends so that we can obtain any thing correct upon the subject. I hope we may get something soon." He noticed the mob spirit in the country and the outbreak of war between Texas and Mexico, concluding that "the world is shed[d]ing the blood of prophets Patriarch & Saints in order to fill up their cup."[16]

On July 17 Brigham Young arrived in Boston. He and Woodruff walked to the home of a church member at 57 Temple Street, where they could have some privacy. Here is Woodruff's entry: "Br Young took the bed and I the big chair, and I here veiled my face and for the first time gave vent to my grief and mourning for the Prophet and Patriarch of the Church Joseph and Hiram Smith who were murdered by a gentile mob. After being bathed in a flood of tears I felt composed. I have never shed a tear since I heard of the death of the prophet untill this morning but my whole soul has felt nerved up like steel."[17] Heber C. Kimball first heard the news on July 9, when he recorded the following: "The papers were full of News of the death of our Prophet. I was not willen to believe it, for it was to[o] much to bare. The first news I got of his death was on Tuesday morning. . . . it struck me at the heart."[18] The next few days were days of uncertainty. Elder Kimball went on to Baltimore with delegates, apparently still planning to hold a nominating convention for Joseph Smith. On July 12 he and Lyman Wight picked up mail that told them of events in Nauvoo up to June 19, at which time the prophet was still alive and free. Kimball and Wight prayed fervently "that we might hear some definite news." In the evening they picked up a letter that told of events up to June 24, when Joseph and Hyrum were incarcerated in Carthage Jail. "This letter satisfied us that the Brethren ware dead O Lord what feelings we had."[19]

On Sunday, July 14, Kimball went to a church meeting in Philadelphia and told the Saints of the news. He reported, "great sorrow prevailed and agreed to dress in mo[u]rning. O Lord How can we part with our dear Br, O Lord save the Twelve." The next day he left for New York and from there went on to Boston, arriving on July 18. There he found Brigham Young, Orson Hyde, Orson Pratt, and Wilford Woodruff, all of whom, as Kimball noted, "felt Sorrifull for the Loss of our Prophet and Patriarch."[20]

Alfred Cordon, preaching in Canada and upper New York, heard of the event on July 9 but "did not credit the statement as we had heard of their death so many times." Not until July 26 did he read a newspaper account that convinced Cordon and his partner: "we returned to Mr. Parkhurst's very sorrowfull, we did not fully credit the report till now."[21]

James Madison Fisher remarked that "everything seemed to turn as black as ink."[22] H. H. Cluff experienced a "crushing feeling."[23] William Hyde said, "My soul sickened and I wept before the Lord and for a time it seemed that the very Heavens were clad in mourning."[24] In Pennsylvania, William I. Appleby noted in his diary on July 10, "Heard of the murder of Br. Joseph & Hyrum Smith by a Mob at Carthage, Illinois. Staid over night at Br. S. Bringhursts. I could not credit the Report of their deaths at first, indeed I did not want to believe it, and almost hoped against hope."[25]

More than a month after the assassinations, on August 11, Brigham

Young was still moved by accounts of how the news had been received in Nauvoo. Writing to his daughter Vilate, he said, "It has be[e]n a time of mo[u]rning. The day that Joseph and Hyrum ware braught from Cartheg to Nauvoo it was judged by manny boath in and out of the church that there was more then 5 barels of tears shead. I cannot bare to think enny thing about it."[26]

The news eventually reached church members in other parts of the world. One of the last to hear of the martyrdom was Benjamin F. Grouard, who was preaching Mormonism in the Society Islands. After taking passage on a ship to Tahiti on February 1, 1845, he found newspapers telling of the event. He found the account "so contradictory & improbible that I did not know what to believe," but he remembered a dream in which he had seen the bodies of Joseph and Hyrum. Not until February 25, 1845, did Grouard receive reliable news, which led to the following journal entry:

> Tuesday Feb 25th the sad news came fully confirmed. The whale ship Averic had been cast away on Raitea, an Island one hundred miles to the leaward, & consiquently her papers &c cam[e] to Tahiti & among the rest was the governors letter addressed to the citizens of Illinois stating the particulars of the assasination of "Joseph & Hyrum Smith." Though we had been looking for & partialy expected such news from the many flying reports w[h]ich had already come, yet when we were thus fully convinced of its truth it was a dreadful shock to us—one which we were ill prepared to receive. The heartrending anguish it causes us I will not attempt to discribe—: that our beloved prophet & patriarch were gone—gone to return no more—to rejoyce—that we must return to the church & find their places vacant who had blessed us in the name of the Lord & told us to go in peace & prosper, those who held the cause of Zion so close to their hearts, who lived for it, laboured for it, & died for it—that we could see them no more, no more hear their voices till we met them in the celestial kingdom of God it was bitter, bitter, more than words can tell.

He went on to express his indignation toward the murderers, the state of Illinois, and even the United States, concluding, "you have accomplished what you have sought for these last 14 years, & now look out for the judgements of God."[27]

It is in getting beyond factual description associated with expression of grief that the poetic statements are especially effective. Consider, for example, the despicableness of the assassins. Eliza R. Snow in "The Assassination of Gen'ls Joseph Smith and Hyrum Smith" sees the dead martyrs as a sacrifice: "t'appease the ragings of a brutish clan, / That has defied the laws of God and man." Sylvester Hulet's poem calls on the

Saints to "weep o'er the deeds just done by wicked hands." William Hyde describes the assassins as "Those hellish fiends, in hellish form, / Out from their coverts they did swarm." For Nelson Whipple the assassins were "mob[b]ers vile . . . feindish men who left them bleeding on the plain."

Another way of conveying essentially the same idea was to refer not to the assassins but to the crime itself. How horrendous it was. It was "one of the most horible crimes that ever history records," Sally Randall wrote. "Never," she continued, "has thare been such a horible crime commited since the day Christ was crucified."[28] For Sylvester Hulet, "ne'er transpir'd on earth, (nor yet in hell) / A scene more tragic since the Saviour fell." This was not the death of two ordinary men, or even an ordinary murder—if there is such a thing. It had cosmic importance, and the Saints grappled with words as they tried to express how important, how tragic, the event really was.

In the tradition of elegy, some Mormon writers wanted to say something about the character of the departed leaders. It was indeed a heinous crime, committed by diabolical men, but the horror was compounded by the nature of the victims, as John Taylor articulates in "O Give Me Back My Prophet Dear":

> O give me back my Prophet dear.
> And Patriarch, O give them back,
> The Saints of latter days to cheer,
> And lead them in the gospel track.
> But ah! they're gone from my embrace,
> From earthly scenes their spirits fled:
> These two, the best of Adam's race.
> Now lie entombed among the dead.

For John Taylor, in "The Seer," Joseph was "of noble seed—of heavenly birth," and "His equal now cannot be found / By searching the wide world around." Eliza R. Snow put it this way in "The Assassination of Gen'ls Joseph Smith and Hyrum Smith":

> . . . never, since the Son of Man was slain
> Has blood so noble, flow'd from human vein
> As that which now, on God for vengeance calls
> From "freedom's ground"—from Carthage prison walls!

The martyrs were not only great and noble but also innocent, and some writers were anxious to stress this point. For Sylvester Hulet, it was "righteous blood that now stains this guilty land." In "O Give Me Back My Prophet Dear," John Taylor writes:

> Ye men of wisdom tell me why,
> When guilt nor crime in them were found,
> Why now their blood doth loudly cry
> From prison walls, and Carthage ground.

Eliza R. Snow expressed the same idea in "The Assassination of Gen'ls Joseph Smith and Hyrum Smith:

> Once lov'd America! what can atone
> For the pure blood of innocence, thou'st sown?
> . . . .
> Yes, blameless men, defam'd by hellish lies
> Have thus been offer'd as a sacrifice. . . .

Such protestations of blamelessness and innocence might well have been simply the Mormon reaction to the violent denunciations of Thomas Sharp and the anti-Mormon press, but it is hard to overlook the closeness of such an idea in the Mormon mind that the prophet was a sacrificial lamb without spot or blemish in much the same way that the sinless Son of God, Jesus Christ, was a sacrifice by God for the world.

One word with powerful emotional overtones is *blood.* For these writers, some of whom had seen the bodies of the dead martyrs, the word conveyed their grief and outrage. It was innocent blood that would stain Illinois (or would plead unto heaven) and call upon God for vengeance. In her poem dated July 1, 1844, Eliza R. Snow tells how the dead brothers had "seal'd their testimony with their blood." On the very same day, July 1, Sally Randall was writing, "The earth is deprived of the two best men there was on it. They have sealed thare testimony with thare blood."[29] John Taylor's great tribute (now section 135 in the LDS Doctrine and Covenants) stated that Joseph Smith, "like most of the Lord's anointed in ancient times, has sealed his mission and his works with his own blood; and so has his brother Hyrum."

The concept had, of course, been part of Christian experience since the martyrdom of Stephen as recorded in the Acts of the Apostles. W. H. C. Frend's authoritative study *Martyrdom and Persecution in the Early Church* points out how the idea was taken over by persecuted Christians in the second century. They were witnesses, and their death for their faith gave added force to their testimony. They were "sealed" by death. Significantly, they saw their death as an imitation of Christ's death, and they were thought to be taken immediately to heaven or paradise, there out of reach of their enemies, there to plan and work with the Lord for the coming of the millennium. The early Christians drew these ideas not only from the Gospel of John, Acts, and the epistles but also from Maccabean literature, the Maccabees being regarded as the "prototypes of martyrdom" and "prefigurations of Christian martyrdom." Drawing from the biblical passage, early Christians found ample assurance that persecution even unto death was simple evidence that they were God's chosen people.[30]

It should not be surprising that the Mormons tapped these concepts, for they saw themselves as the modern representatives of God's true church on earth. As soon as there was any kind of opposition or harassment, it was quickly viewed as persecution. As soon as there were actual deaths, the victims were praised as "martyrs." I am tempted to see John Foxe's *Book of the Martyrs* as the widely available account that provided the terminology for the Saints, but in point of fact the conceptualization was built into the situation. Every Christian group that has been non-establishment, especially the radical Protestants of the sixteenth century, saw their experience in terms of persecution and the suffering of martyrdom. During the 1830s the Mormons took over this phraseology, finding it especially comforting during the Missouri persecutions. In 1839 Joseph Smith, then safe in Illinois, wrote of those Mormons who had lost their lives: "Although some of our beloved brethren had had to seal their testimony with their blood and have died martyrs to the cause of truth; yet, short though bitter was their pain, / everlasting is their joy."[31]

The paradigm by which Joseph Smith's death would be explained and rationalized was thus already present in the minds of Mormons. God's people have always been persecuted; martyrs are the highest kind of Saints who pay the ultimate price; they seal their testimony with their blood; they then pass beyond the power of their enemies, and God's cause on earth continues and will still ultimately triumph. These ideas were applied to the death of the prophet and patriarch. The elements were already floating in the atmosphere from which the surviving Saints would construct their comforting explanation after the tragic deaths in June of 1844. Like all martyrs, the dead prophet and patriarch had been innocent victims. Their blood was the confirming seal on their life's mission. "The blood of the martyrs is the seed of the church," said an old Christian maxim. This very expression was used by the artist C. C. A. Christensen as the caption for his dramatic painting of the assassination scene.[32]

A related idea is that of *sacrifice*—that somehow, with full knowledge of their impending fate, the brothers voluntarily returned to give their lives for their people. As the "Lamentation of a Jew" put it, addressing God:

> O look in righteousness upon thy faithful servants,
> Who have laid bare their lives unto death,

Not withholding their bodies:
Being betrayed by false brethren and their lives cut off.
Forbidding their will before thine:
Having sanctified thy great name,
Never polluting it;

Ready for a sacrifice;—standing in the breach,
Tried, proved, and found perfect.
To save the blood of the fathers;
Their children, brothers, and sisters. . . .

John Taylor wrote in "The Seer," "The saints, the saints, his only pride, / For them he liv'd, for them he died!" In this connection the Saints remembered Joseph's statements, now canonized: "I am going like a lamb to the slaughter; but I am calm as a summer's morning; . . . I shall die innocent, and it shall be said me—He was murdered in cold blood."[33] That he willingly laid down his life for others found expression in Sally Randall's letter just four days after the murder: "He gave himself up to die for the church that they might not be destroid for it seamed all they wanted was to kill him and they have done it. . . ."[34]

The comparison that came most naturally to mind when Mormons sought to explain the greatness of their departed prophet was the comparison with Jesus Christ. Not that anyone suggested in so many words that Joseph was divine; he was not considered by Mormons then or now as one of the persons in the Godhead or Trinity. But in certain respects he did serve as a kind of Christ-figure. Notice the parallels. Joseph had laid down his life voluntarily, shedding his blood for his people. If he was not specifically sinless, he was at least "innocent." His role had been that of a mediator between God and humanity. As the anonymous Jewish poet wrote in "Lamentation of a Jew," "There is none to stand between and inquire." Joseph Smith was one among a class of men known as prophets, to be sure, but for the Latter-day Saints he was both the latest and greatest of the prophets. He was among a class of martyrs, but here too there was an evident feeling that this martyrdom could stand comparison with none other except the crucifixion of Christ. Hence the several references to the claim that never since Calvary had blood so noble been shed, never since Calvary had there been such a heinous crime, and the like. Now Joseph was in the courts on high—with the gods—planning for his brethren, pleading their cause in the courts above. Such images come close to an apotheosis of Joseph Smith.

It is evident that the martyrdom literature was attempting several things. It was an expression of grief, in both prose and poetry. It was an effort to condemn the assassins and deplore the shame of the country that had allowed such a thing to occur. It was an effort to proclaim in ringing words the greatness, the nobility, and innocence of the martyrs, who had sealed their testimony with their blood and whose work would continue in the courts on high while the church would continue its onward course below. But as we have noticed, it was especially an effort to state in words the significance of the mission of Joseph Smith. What had he done that was so great? What was his real contribution that deserved memorializing in stone? Not merely that he was innocent and noble or that he had died—this would not be enough. We find in most of the martyrdom poems succinct statements of what his significant achievement was. Here is a passage from Eliza R. Snow's "The Assassination of Gen'ls Joseph Smith and Hyrum Smith":

> Oh wretched murd'rers! fierce for human blood!
> You've slain the prophets of the living God,
> Who've borne oppression from their early youth.
> To plant on earth, the principles of truth.
> . . . .
> We mourn thy Prophet, from whose lips have flow'd
> The words of life, thy spirit has bestow'd—
> A depth of thought, no human art could reach
> From time to time, roll'd in sublimest speech,
> From the celestial fountain, through his mind,
> To purify and elevate mankind:
> The right intelligence by him brought forth,
> Is like the sun-beam, spreading o'er the earth.

In "Praise to the Man" by W. W. Phelps, Joseph was the one anointed by Jesus, who communed with Jehovah and who opened the last dispensation. John Taylor described Joseph as follows in "The Seer":

> With Gods he soared, in the realms of day;
> And men he taught the heavenly way.
> . . . .
> The chosen of God, and the friend of men,
> He brought the priesthood back again,
> He gazed on the past, on the present too,
> And open'd the heav'nly world to view.

Such efforts to capture in poetic form the greatness and significance of Joseph Smith's mission have continued to the present.

The topical nature of the martyrdom poetry is especially apparent in the sense of outrage, the grief, the verbal spitting on the vile assassins, the disgust at a country in which such a thing could take place, the praise of the dead brothers as God's noblemen. Of all the themes found in the poetry, most immediate to the needs of the Saints in the days, weeks, and months following the event was the question of what they should do. The poetry, which might well have fanned the flames of anger, instead counseled patience while at the same time calling for divine retribution or vengeance.

In some ways, of course, it is artificial to separate prose and poetry when the function was the same: to provide catharsis and meaning. One of the most famous statements, indeed the only one that has become effectively canonized by its inclusion in the LDS Doctrine and Covenants (section 135), was written by John Taylor. The words are familiar to all Latter-day Saints:

> Joseph Smith, the prophet and seer of the Lord, has done more, save Jesus only, for the salvation of men in this world, than any other man that ever lived in it. In the short space of twenty years he has brought forth the Book of Mormon, which he translated by the gift and power of God, and has been the means of publishing it on two continents; has sent the fullness of the everlasting gospel which it contained, to the four quarters of the earth; has brought forth the revelations and commandments, which compose this Book of Doctrine and Covenants, and many other wise documents and instructions for the benefit of the children of men; gathered many thousands of Latter-day Saints; founded a great city, and left a fame and name that can not be slain. He lived great, and he died great in the eyes of God and his people, and like most of the Lord's anointed in ancient times, has sealed his mission and works with his own blood; and so has his brother Hyrum. In life they were not divided, and in death they were not separated!

These words are carefully chosen. The phrases mount to a crescendo until in the concluding paragraph we read: "They were innocent of any crime, as they had often been proved before, and were only confined in jail by the conspiracy of traitors and wicked men; . . . and their innocent blood, with the innocent blood of all the martyrs under the altar that John saw, will cry unto the Lord of hosts, till he avenges that blood on the earth. Amen." These same ideas, as we have seen, were expressed in the martyrdom poetry as early as August 1844, and some of them were in the letters and diaries following the event. By the time twelve months had passed, it was time for a restatement—a kind of official, scriptural summing up.

The letters and diaries reporting reactions here should be compared not with great funeral orations of Ciceronian eulogies but with other letters and diaries. Several of the examples we have looked at are moving in their simplicity and concreteness. Nonetheless, if we compare any of the Mormon poetry with "When Lilacs Last in Dooryard Bloom'd," it is apparent that the Mormons had no Walt Whitman. The sincerity of the Saints' emotions is unquestionable. Nor is the truth of the religious claims at issue. Powerful religious faith does not in itself ensure great art. According to critical standards, the Mormon martyrdom poetry may be deficient in tone and concreteness and uninteresting in rhythm and rhyme, but it represented, in Wordsworth's phrase, the "spontaneous overflow" of human emotions deeply moved. One Mormon woman close to the event, Sarah Griffith Richards, found that the words that came to her again and again were those of John Milton in "On the Late Massacre in Piedmont":

> Avenge, O Lord, thy slaughtered saints, whose bones
> Lie scattered on the Alpine mountains cold,
> Even them who kept thy truth so pure of old
> When all our fathers worshiped stock and stones. . . .

Perhaps in the interest of fairness, also, the basis of comparison should be shifted. Of the hundreds or thousands of poems denoting death and paying tribute to departed loved ones, not many are truly memorable. At the deaths of Abraham Lincoln and John F. Kennedy, there were great quantities of verse, some tasteful and eloquent but much of it mediocre. In these instances, the poetic outpouring, good or bad, did help to express feeling and meaning; it represented, in addition, a catharsis for the emotions of all the survivors.

The Mormon martyrdom poetry did this too. More important, it succeeded in expressing in a few pieces that could be read, recited, and sung the basic ideas that helped place the tragedy in perspective. If the diaries and letters were unsurpassed as an account of individual reactions to the sad news, the poetry did something more in its expression not only of grief but also of meaning as it placed the dead leaders in the company of martyrs, denounced the assassins, explained how their testimony gained in force by their death, and even went on to portray the comforting picture of the prophet and patriarch in the councils on high. A literature that does this has not necessarily achieved greatness, but it has accomplished something important. It is, however, in the social historical context, not the literary, that this something important can be most accurately recognized.

Notes

An earlier version of this essay appeared in the *John Whitmer Historical Association Journal* 3 (1983): 29–39 and has been supplemented in *The Martyrdom Revisited* (Salt Lake City: Aspen Books, 1994).

1. These paintings have been conveniently published in color. See Brian Kelley, "The Martyrdom as Seen by a Young Mormon," *New Era* 3 (December 1973): 20–30.

2. Examples include Sandra Petree, "June 28, 1844," *Ensign* 5 (June 1975): 35; and Michael Nibley, "June 27, 1844," in *Poems of Praise*, ed. Edward L. Hart and Marden J. Clark (Provo, Utah: Brigham Young University Press, 1980), 3–35. Other closely related poems in *Poems of Praise* are Sally T. Taylor, "Stephen—The Bodyguard After Carthage"; and John B. Harris, "To Joseph." Prose treatments of the subject range from scholarly treatment by Dallin H. Oaks and Marvin S. Hill, *Carthage Conspiracy: The Trial of the Accused Assassins of Joseph Smith* (Urbana: University of Illinois Press, 1975) to documentary treatment by Keith Huntress, ed., *Murder of an American Prophet: Materials for Analysis* (San Francisco: Chandler Publishing, 1960) to popular treatment by Henry A. Smith, *The Day They Martyred the Prophet* (Salt Lake City: Bookcraft, 1963).

3. These published poems can be found under the date indicated in two contemporary Nauvoo newspapers, *Times and Seasons* or the *Neighbor* (or, in some instances, both). Eliza R. Snow's poetry was reprinted in *Poems, Religious, Historical, and Political* (Liverpool, England: F. D. Richards, 1856). Poems in the unpublished journals of William I. Appleby, William Hyde, and Nelson W. Whipple are in the Archives, Historical Department, Church of Jesus Christ of Latter-day Saints, Salt Lake City, Utah (hereafter LDS Archives). The Rogers and Lewis poems appeared in *The Prophet* (New York, N.Y.) on August 10, 1844, and September 28, 1844, respectively.

4. Warren Foote, Journal, June 28, 1844, LDS Archives. Descriptions and synopses of unpublished diaries and journals cited here can be found in my *Guide to Mormon Diaries and Autobiographies* (Provo, Utah: Brigham Young University Press, 1977).

5. Jacob Gibson, Journal, n.d., LDS Archives. When exact dates are not given, the relevant passages can be readily found in the entries for late June or early July 1844.

6. Benjamin Franklin Cummings, Journal, n.d., Special Collections, Harold B. Lee Library, Brigham Young University, Provo, Utah.

7. Arouet Lucius Hale, Journal, n.d., LDS Archives.

8. John Lyman Smith, Journal, n.d., LDS Archives.

9. Vilate Kimball to Heber C. Kimball, June 30, 1844, quoted in Stanley B. Kimball, *Heber C. Kimball: Mormon Patriarch and Pioneer* (Urbana: University of Illinois Press, 1981), 108.

10. Almira Mack Covey to Temperance Mack, July 18, 1844, quoted in John C. Cumming, *The Pilgrimage of Temperance Mack* (Mount Pleasant, Mich.: n.p., 1967), 41–43.

11. Lucy Walker Kimball, Letter, Autobiographical Sketch (n.d.), LDS Archives.

12. "Autobiography," *Utah Genealogical and Historical Magazine* 14 (July 1923): 110.

13. Parley P. Pratt, *Autobiography of Parley P. Pratt* (New York: Russell Brothers, 1874), 331–34.

14. John D. Lee, Diary, July 6, 1844, LDS Archives.

15. Quoted in Joseph Smith, *History of the Church of Jesus Christ of Latter-day Saints,* ed. B. H. Roberts (Salt Lake City: Deseret News Press, 1902–12; 6 vols., a seventh volume was published in 1932; reprinted by Deseret Book, 1976, and reissued in paperback in 1978), 7:132.

16. Wilford Woodruff, Journal, July 9, 1844, LDS Archives; published in Scott G. Kenney, ed., *Wilford Woodruff's Journal,* 9 vols. (Midvale, Utah: Signature Books, 1983).

17. Ibid., July 17, 1844.

18. Heber C. Kimball, Journal, July 9, 1844, LDS Archives; published in Stanley B. Kimball, ed., *On the Potter's Wheel: The Diaries of Heber C. Kimball* (Salf Lake City: Signature Books, 1987).

19. Ibid., July 12, 1844.

20. Ibid., July 18, 1844.

21. Alfred Cordon, Journal, July 26, 1844, LDS Archives.

22. James Madison Fisher, Journal, LDS Archives.

23. Harvey Harris Cluff, Journal, LDS Archives.

24. William Hyde, Journal, LDS Archives.

25. William I. Appleby, Journal, July 10, 1844, LDS Archives.

26. Brigham Young to Vilate Young, August 11, 1844, LDS Archives.

27. Benjamin F. Grouard, Journal, February 25, 1845, microfilm, LDS Archives.

28. Quoted in Kenneth W. Godfrey, Audrey M. Godfrey, and Jill Mulvay Derr, *Women's Voices: An Untold History of the Latter-day Saints* (Salt Lake City. Deseret Book, 1982), 141.

29. Ibid., 141–42.

30. W. H. C. Frend, *Martyrdom and Persecution in the Early Church* (Oxford: Blackwell, 1965).

31. Smith, *History of the Church,* 3:330.

32. The C. C. A. Christensen painting, the original of which is at Brigham Young University, is reproduced in *Art in America* 58 (May–June 1970): 52–65. See also *Ensign* 9 (December 1979).

33. *The Doctrine and Covenants of the Church of Jesus Christ of Latter-day Saints* (Salt Lake City: Deseret Book, 1981), 135:4. See also Smith, *History of the Church,* 6:555.

34. Godfrey, Godfrey, and Derr, *Women's Voices,* 142.

12

The Lion and the Lady:
Brigham Young and Emma Smith

VALEEN TIPPETTS AVERY AND
LINDA KING NEWELL

During the nineteenth century Brigham Young's power grew until it was felt throughout the western areas of the United States. For the most part his followers revered him, and his enemies kept respectful distance, yet to his extreme annoyance he was never successful in extending that same power over Emma Smith. She neither revered him nor kept her adult sons a respectful distance from him, and her opposition plagued him from the time he became head of the Church of Jesus Christ of Latter-day Saints. Brigham and Emma freely expressed their opinions of each other but never understood the other's position; they were victims of circumstance, personality, and differing doctrinal views. Their mutual inability to resolve their differences cemented the division of the Latter-day Saints.

On October 6, 1866, Brigham Young, "the Lion of the Lord,"[1] president of the Mormon church, ex-governor of the Utah Territory, colonizer of a vast area of the West, and spiritual leader to 100,000 Mormons, was in the midst of one of his usually pointed tabernacle sermons. As he approached the end of his remarks, he remembered an unsettling incident. Alexander Hale Smith, a son of Joseph Smith Jr., the founder of Mormonism, had recently visited Salt Lake City. He came, however, not as the son of a beloved old friend who wanted to renew acquaintances but as a missionary for a rival church, whose president was the eldest of Joseph Smith's sons, Joseph Smith III. Attempting to explain the origins of so peculiar a situation, Brigham said:

> I will now speak upon a subject which I think I ought to notice for the benefit of a few who are inclined to be giddy-headed.... You are already apprized of the fact that a son of Joseph Smith the prophet

was here in our city. . . . The sympathies of the Latter-day Saints are with the family of the martyred prophet. I never saw a day in the world that I would not almost worship that woman, Emma Smith,[2] if she would be a saint instead of being a devil. . . . [We] would have been exceeding glad if the prophet's family had come with us when we left Nauvoo. . . . We would have fed them on milk and honey. Emma is naturally a very smart woman; she is subtle and ingenious . . . she has made her children inherit lies. To my certain knowledge Emma Smith is one of the damnest liars I know of on this earth; yet there is no good thing I would refuse to do for her, if she would be a right-eous woman.[3]

By implication Brigham Young laid the troublesome activities of the sons of Joseph at the feet of their mother.

Emma Hale Smith had refused to go west with the main body of Mormons and remained aloof from the western settlement. Instead, she raised her children in Nauvoo, Illinois, far removed in distance and philosophy from the Mormon church and the kingdom established in the valley of the Utah mountains. Spokesmen for the loosely knit group of Saints remaining in the general Illinois area contacted Emma's son, Joseph III, in 1856 and asked him to assume the leadership of their organization—later known as the Reorganized Church of Jesus Christ of Latter Day Saints (RLDS Church). After four years of deliberation, he became prophet and president of the RLDS Church at their Amboy, Illinois, conference on April 6, 1860. Emma Smith was received unanimously as a member of the group on the same day.

Two months before Brigham Young's conference address in 1866, Emma wrote to her son, "Joseph Dear. . . . Now you must not let those L.D.S.'s trouble you too much. If they are determined to do evil, they will do it, and such are anxiously willing to make you trouble are not worth laboring over hard to save from the dogs."[4]

Three years after Brigham's conference address, Alexander returned to Utah on a second mission. With him as his companion was his youngest brother, David. Apprehensive about their experiences in Utah, Emma wrote again to her son Joseph, "I tried before they left here to give them an idea of what they might expect of Brigham and all of his ites, but I suppose the impression was hardly sufficient to guard their feelings from such unexpected falsehoods and impious profanity as Brigham is capable of. . . . I do not like to have my children's feelings abused, but I do like that Brigham shows to all, both Saint and sinner that there is not the least [particle of] friendship existing between him and myself."[5]

Historians have assumed considerable enmity must have existed between Brigham and Emma during the twelve years that spanned their meeting in Kirtland, Ohio, on November 8, 1832, to the death of Joseph in 1844.[6] There is, however, no supporting evidence of such antagonism until a year or so before Joseph's death.

Brigham Young had arrived in Kirtland that November day in 1832 in search of a prophet. That he found one chopping wood might have surprised him, but once confident that Joseph Smith spoke for the Lord, Brigham arranged his affairs to join the Mormons. He was thirty-one years old and an accomplished painter, carpenter, and glazier. He came as a seeker, anxious to know more, willing to assist, eminently able, and awed to be in the association of his prophet.

That same day Joseph Smith took Brigham Young inside the Gilbert and Whitney store to a room on the second floor to meet his wife Emma. She rested in bed, a two-day-old son at her side. The first child of Emma and Joseph to live beyond infancy,[7] the baby was named after his father and grandfather and called "young Joseph" in his youth and Joseph III as an adult. This day marked the first meeting of these most influential people in the history of the LDS churches.

Emma was three years younger than Brigham. Already married nearly six years to Joseph Smith, she lived singled out by an 1830 revelation her prophet-husband received that titled her the "elect lady" and commissioned her to compile the first Latter-day Saint hymnal.[8] Less than two years later, Joseph charged William W. Phelps with correcting and printing the hymns Emma had selected.[9]

Diligent in completing the church assignments given him, Brigham knew that Emma too had fulfilled hers. He took with him a copy of Emma's *Sacred Hymns* on his 1839–41 mission to England. He included some of her hymns in a new hymnal printed for the English Saints and commented on his efforts when he wrote to his wife Mary Ann Angell in June 1840: "We are printing 3,000 copes of a hym book 5,000 copes of the Book of Mormon. . . . I have now got through with the hym book. I have had perty much the whole of it to doe my self . . . so it has made my labor so hard that it seems as though it would be imposable for me ever to regane my helth."[10] Thoughtful of Emma after knowing her for over eight years, he sent a copy of the hymnal to her and checked on its safe arrival when he wrote to Mary Ann. Brigham instructed his wife, "Tell *Br* Joseph Smith that I send as much love to him and Emma and famely . . . as I can get carid a cross the water."[11]

Brigham Young named a daughter after Emma Smith. The first child born to him and Mary Ann was a son they named Joseph—perhaps not revealing whether the namesake was his brother or his prophet. Their twins were called Brigham and Mary Ann, but the daughter born ten days before Brigham departed for his English mission was named Roxy

Emma Alice. He wrote plaintively of his sixteen-month-old daughter as he expressed his homesickness to Mary Ann in a letter of January 15, 1841: "My little daughter Emma she dos not know eny thing a bout me."[12] After 1847, when the relationship between Emma and Brigham had disintegrated, Roxy Emma Alice became known as Alice.[13]

If Emma resented the men who took Joseph's time from her, there was little reason for her to extend those feelings to Brigham Young. Absent from Kirtland much of the time that the Saints spent there, Brigham was not knocking on Joseph's door with constant demands that Joseph meet the needs of the Mormon kingdom. In addition, Brigham was away nearly three of the five years from 1839 to 1844. There were others besides Brigham who might have earned her animosity. William Marks, as president of the Nauvoo Stake, president of the high council, and regent of the University of Nauvoo, required much more of Joseph's time but remained Emma's friend.

Young stayed in Nauvoo from the summer of 1841 to July 1843, but John C. Bennett's meteoric rise to power as Bennett became mayor of Nauvoo, major general of the Nauvoo Legion, and de facto counselor in the church presidency certainly eclipsed Brigham's presence the first of those years. According to her son, Emma distrusted Bennett from the first.[14] When he was stripped of his power and forced from office, he launched a vituperative campaign against Joseph. Brigham's support in ridding the church of Bennett and his influence might have made Brigham an ally of Emma rather than an antagonist.[15]

If Emma had any reservations about Brigham's character, she did not express them in her pre-1844 correspondence. She neither commented about him negatively nor influenced her young children to dislike him. For example, young Joseph was well aware his mother did not like or trust John C. Bennett, yet he did not acquire negative feelings about Brigham Young during that same period. By the time Joseph III wrote his memoirs, the temptation to discredit Young might have been very strong, but he remembered, "I saw but little of [Brigham] before Father's death, though, I did know him. . . . I often saw him upon the stand, in the streets, and in his home, and thought him a pleasant man to meet, neither liking nor disliking him particularly as I now recall, until a short time after my father's death."[16]

Both Brigham and Emma had great affection for Joseph but naturally had differing views about some of his actions. Brigham commented about his own attitude toward Joseph: "Though I admitted in my feelings and knew all the time that Joseph was a human being and subject to err, still it was none of my business to look after his faults." He admitted to only one uncertainty about Joseph, but the thought was quickly put down: "A feeling came over me that Joseph was not right in his financial management, though I presume the feeling did not last sixty seconds." Brigham Young surveyed Joseph Smith's dealings, all of them, with a detachment that was truly remarkable. He never distinguished Joseph's personal life and human mistakes from the divine dictation of the Lord: "It was not my prerogative to call him into question with any regard to any act of his life. He was God's servant, and not mine . . . and if He should suffer him to lead the people astray, it would be because they ought to be led astray . . . because they deserved it, or to accomplish some righteous purpose."[17]

Emma recognized Joseph's prophetic calling, but the realities of marriage forced her to deal more directly with Joseph's faults. His inability to farm and translate at the same time caused an estrangement between the Smiths and Emma's parents. If there was a scandal because of Joseph, Emma felt the sting. If there was no money, Emma took in boarders. When Joseph was arrested, Emma bore the loneliness. She played the roles accorded her by tradition: wife, mother, hostess, nurse, companion, figurehead. She also assumed roles that were not part of Brigham Young's relationship with women: roles as partner, agent, spokesperson. Inasmuch as Joseph assigned her these roles himself, she felt confident in assuming them.

Emma also felt free to address Joseph as a business partner. "The situation of your business is such as is very difficult for me to do anything of any consequence," she complained from Kirtland. "Partnership matters give everybody such an unaccountable right to every particle of property or money that they can lay their hands on." She requested further information from him about the state of his affairs and ended her letter with a little free legal advice in the form of a postscript, "If you should give anyone a power of attorney, you had better give it to brother Knight, as he is the only man that has not manifested a spirit of indifference to your temporal interest."[18]

From Liberty Jail, Joseph made Emma his spokesperson to the Mormon church in seeking redress for the property lost in Missouri: "I want all the Church to make out a bill of damages and apply to the United States Court as soon as possible. . . . You emphasize my feelings concerning the order."[19] In later years her son too recognized her business acumen. Joseph Smith III had been president of the Reorganized Church for thirteen years when he wrote his sixty-nine-year-old mother, "So much was your mind like my own upon the matter that I at once wrote to Kirtland, offering the temple for sale. Should I be able to sell for the price offered, I will be able to get out of debt."[20]

Emma sympathized with her son's concern for getting out of debt;

financial difficulties plagued her for most of her years. During the Kirtland era, Emma sometimes had problems obtaining food for her family. "There is no prospect of my getting one dollar of current money or even get the grain you left for our bread, as I sent to the French place for that wheat and brother Strong says that he shall let us only have ten bushel, he had thus sold the hay and keeps the money . . . it is impossible for me to do anything, as long as every body has so much better right to all that is called yours than I have," she wrote to Joseph.[21] Brigham knew of the monetary plight of Joseph's family and assisted them on several occasions.

On the morning of December 22, 1837, Brigham fled Kirtland. He went as far as Dublin, Indiana, where several Mormon families were spending the winter. Joseph and Emma and their three children joined them, "destitute of means," and Joseph asked Brigham's advice in the matter. "You rest yourself and be assured, brother Joseph, you shall have plenty of money to pursue your journey," Brigham replied. Brother Tomlinson, who lived in the area, planned to sell a tavern stand he owned and had already approached Brigham for his opinion. "I told him if he would do right and obey counsel, he should have opportunity to sell soon, and the first offer he would get would be the best." Not long after this, Tomlinson sold his place for "$500 in money, a team, and $250 in store goods. I told him that was the hand of the Lord to deliver President Joseph Smith from his present necessity. . . . Brother Tomlinson . . . gave the Prophet three hundred dollars, which enabled him comfortably to proceed on his journey."[22]

Brigham also came to the Smiths' financial aid in Nauvoo. The Quorum of the Twelve Apostles, under the direction of Brigham, made a request to the Mormon church in La Harpe. They informed the members there that foodstuffs available in La Harpe could not be obtained in Nauvoo and that they could decide whether their prophet should spend his time earning a livelihood for his family or meeting the spiritual needs of the church.[23] The apostles issued a second plea only five days later to the church members in Ramus: "Brethren, we are not unmindful of the favors our President has received from you in former days but a man will not cease to be hungry this year because he eat last year."[24]

Emma was a spirited woman who did not sit back helplessly and let events take their course, and there were two aspects of her relationship with Joseph to which she never became resigned. The first was the relentless attempts by legal authorities to imprison her husband. There were needless warrants for his arrest and constant attempts to extradite him to Missouri as he tried to administer the affairs of church and state. This was a constant source of anxiety to her, and she resolved to do something about it. By 1842 she had personally visited the governor of

Illinois on Joseph's behalf, and following that visit she and the governor exchanged a series of letters. With Eliza R. Snow acting as scribe, Emma wrote, "To His Excellency Gov. Carlin . . . I much regret your ill health, and still hope that you will avail yourself sufficient time to investigate our cause, and thoroughly acquaint yourself with the illegality of the Prosecution instituted against Mr. Smith . . . we do believe that it is your duty to allow us in this place, the privileges and advantages guaranteed to us by the laws of this State and the United States."[25] Emma then outlined for him the provisions of the city charter and reminded the governor that those powers existed over his own signature. The overall tone of the Carlin letters indicates that Emma was not likely to drop the issue simply because of the state's inertia. She clearly intended to do something about the precarious legal situation in which Joseph lived.

The second unresolved aspect of Emma's relationship with Joseph centered on his attempts to establish polygamy. Here Joseph felt Emma's strong determination, formerly used in his behalf, now turned against him. It was Joseph's reaction to Emma's efforts to stop plural marriage that forced Brigham Young to choose sides. As long as Joseph approved of Emma's activities, Brigham also accepted them. Until Joseph complained about Emma, Brigham held his tongue and kept his feelings in check.

The first covert conflict between Brigham Young and Emma Smith probably came when Brigham's loyalty to Joseph led Brigham to accept polygamy both as a doctrine and a practice, while it was apparently Emma's loyalty to her traditional concept of Christian morality that led her to reject it. When Joseph resorted to subterfuge in order to take other wives, Emma vacillated, first agreeing to his marrying other women, then recanting her decision, and finally confronting him.[26]

When Joseph recruited his brother to assist him in convincing Emma to change her mind, Hyrum came home cowed from an interview with her. That this incident was reported by William Clayton[27] argues that other apostles, including Brigham Young, knew about the Smiths' domestic difficulties. It exasperated Emma to realize that other people knew more about her husband's matrimonial affairs than she did. Suspicions and speculations that knew no bounds added to her anxiety. Brigham's exasperation was that, despite her obvious inside knowledge of plural marriage, Emma denied to her death its painful existence in her life.

The real irony of the whole polygamous affair came later for Emma. On December 23, 1847, she married a non-Mormon businessman named Lewis C. Bidamon. He had delivered new carriages to Joseph and Hyrum Smith before their deaths. The first correspondence between the "Major" and Emma was a request from him to lease the Mansion House.[28] Emma's marriage to Bidamon was a problem for the Saints in 1847 and has remained so to this day. Many preferred to believe that he married her for her money and that she married him for convenience. Their letters attest that she loved him, however, and their union lasted thirty-two years.[29]

Their life together was not without its difficulties for Emma, though. In the fifteenth year of their marriage, Lewis Bidamon sired a son as the result of a liaison with a widow named Nancy Abercrombie, who lived with her three children in the Nauvoo area. When the son, named Charles, was four years old, Emma took him into her home to be reared. Charles Bidamon's own words establish that this alien child received love and affection: "I was raised in her home and knew what kind of a woman she was.... [I] was as one of the family until her death.... She was a person of very even temper. I never heard her say an unkind word, or raise her voice in anger."[30]

When Emma was on her deathbed in 1879, her son Joseph came to Nauvoo to be at her side. His journal entry for April 22 reads, "Found Alex here at Nauvoo and Julia in care of Mother. *Mrs. Abercrombie doing the work of the house.*"[31] There were women in Utah who could sympathize with both Emma's and Nancy Abercrombie's positions. Emma lived the practice, if not the principle, of polygamy.

The first open conflict between Brigham and Emma occurred when Young as president of the Quorum of the Twelve was successful in his bid for leadership of the church after Joseph was killed. Emma opposed him, and he was embarrassed and frustrated to have the prophet's widow in another camp. Her feelings on the succession to the presidency were recorded by James Monroe, a young schoolteacher who lived with the Smith family. His diary entry of April 24, 1845, reveals:

My time ... has been occupied chiefly in conversing with Aunt Emma from whom I have obtained several new and interesting ideas concerning the organization and government of the church.... Now as the Twelve have no power with regard to the government of the Church in the Stakes of Zion, but the High Council have all power, so it follows that on removal of the first President, the office would devolve upon the President of the High Council in Zion.... Mr. Rigdon is not the proper successor of President Smith, being only his counselor, but Elder Marks should be the individual.... And according to the ordination pronounced upon him by Br Joseph he is the individual contemplated by him for his successor. The Twelve never received any such instructions or commands or ordinations as would author-ize them to take that office. They were aware of these facts but acted differently.[32]

The rift over succession widened when Emma offered hospitality to William Smith—Joseph's only surviving brother—when the apostles, under Brigham's leadership, excommunicated him. William was an unstable character and sought to be installed as guardian of the Mormon church until young Joseph was old enough to assume his father's role. There is little evidence that Emma ever supported William in his bid for leadership, but he did stay in Emma's house, and his presence was enough to raise a question in Brigham's mind about Emma's loyalty to the church.

Emma's home served as a central meeting place for the surviving members of the Smith family during this period. Because the threat of violence was great in Nauvoo, armed men periodically guarded several of the church leaders' homes, including Emma's. Reports by Joseph III and Samuel Smith's daughter Mary reveal that the Smiths regarded this action as a hostile house arrest. Whether the family was unaware of the danger or whether the guard represented hostility on the part of Young is not clear. Communication had broken down enough between Brigham and Emma that explanations for the guard were not satisfactory.

Brigham's suspicions about Emma were not eased when a man named Van Tuyl took up quarters in the Mansion House when Emma fled from Nauvoo during the anti-Mormon attack. She returned just in time to stop the man from stealing everything she owned, but it was discovered that he was a spy from the anti-Mormon forces and had used his position in the house to report not only on the Mormons but also on those Gentiles friendly to the Saints. Emma certainly did not knowingly harbor a spy, but the incident was not one to effect an increase of love and affection in the hearts of those already suspicious of her.

Brigham's and Emma's disagreement over the doctrine of polygamy and the succession to the Mormon church presidency, almost as a matter of course, opened the way to argument over Joseph's estate. During Joseph's lifetime, Emma had enjoyed a practical, quiet, businesslike approach to life, seasoned by theatrical military performances and other occasions for fancy dress. After Joseph's death, however, when Brigham Young assumed that Joseph's trappings went along with his office, Emma took offense.

In preparation for a parade of the Nauvoo Legion, Brigham sent a note to Emma requesting use of the prophet's uniform, sword, and his favorite horse, a sorrel named Jo Duncan. Twelve-year-old Joseph had recently nursed the animal back to health. The boy obediently fitted out the horse with the requested saddle, housings, holsters, and bridle.

After the parade, Brigham's clerk rode the horse to exhaustion, which infuriated young Joseph, who resolved never again to put a saddle on a horse for Brigham Young.[33]

Brigham accused Emma of taking a portrait and ring from Hyrum's widow, Mary Fielding, and a ring from Don Carlos Smith's widow and never returning them.[34] Brigham and the other apostles took most of Joseph's papers. Emma was furious over the absence of Joseph's long wool cloak. In reality both Brigham and Emma were caught in the classic struggle to determine the disposal of a loved one's properties. Emma, as widow, and Brigham, as successor, each asserted authority the other was unwilling to concede.

The struggle soon escalated into a major dispute between them over the disposal of Joseph's real property and the payment of his debts. Joseph had made little distinction in his efforts to provide for his family, on the one hand, and the Mormon converts who came to Nauvoo, on the other. A case in point is the Hotchkiss Purchase, five hundred acres of land bought by the First Presidency (Joseph Smith, Hyrum Smith, and Sidney Rigdon). It was clear that these men had purchased land for Mormon church members to live on, but they had pledged their personal credit to do so.[35]

In addition to land purchases, Joseph had become involved in business ventures that ranged from stores to steamboats, and he included members of the Mormon church in all his various dealings. By 1841 Joseph was elected sole trustee-in-trust for the Mormon church, but Brigham Young became officially involved when Joseph asked him and the other apostles to assist in managing the lands and settling the immigrants.

The Smiths' financial situation was not entirely dependent on Joseph As far back as Kirtland, Emma took in boarders whenever the family was in financial difficulty. When she assessed Joseph's estate, whatever it consisted of and however it was titled, she viewed the assets not only as the fruit of her husband's work but also as properties that she as a businesswoman had helped buy with money she herself had earned. At Joseph's death, the question facing Emma, with five children to raise, was how to preserve for herself and her family the inheritance that was rightfully theirs. The question facing Brigham, with thousands of destitute church members to look after, whose tithing and labor had helped build the city, was how to preserve for them what was rightfully theirs as church members.

Emma was made administrator of Joseph's estate but after two months was replaced by Joseph W. Coolidge when she failed to post the bond required by the court. By 1848 Coolidge was replaced by a man named Ferris at the request of Almon Babbitt, one of the lawyers retained by

Brigham Young. The settling of the estate then provided the setting for another classic struggle—the widow versus the executor.

Coincidental with her marriage to Lewis C. Bidamon, Emma decisively won the first major round. Almon Babbitt wrote from Nauvoo to Heber C. Kimball, "On my arrival home I found considerable excitement in Nauvoo from the fact that *Emma Bidamon* had made a Quit Claim deed of all the Lands in the City that she conveyed to the church. . . . It operates as a perfect Estopel to the sale of any more City property until the matter is tested in the courts of *Law.*"[36] It was a blow, and it left Brigham helpless and frustrated in his attempts to secure capital for the trek west. He felt for the rest of his life that Emma had usurped properties paid for by the labor and tithes of the members of the Mormon church.[37]

When the exodus west began, everyone was forced to sell fine homes and beautiful farms for a pittance to outfit a wagon. It was easy for those crossing the river to look back at the expansive Mansion House, the Homestead, the Red Brick Store, and the foundations of the Nauvoo House, which Emma was *not* abandoning, and make their private judgments about her generosity. Brigham anxiously looked at her holdings in terms of the cash equity the church so desperately needed.

Emma was in for an equally great disappointment. When Joseph was alive, there had been a great deal of entertaining; Emma herself commented that he never liked to eat alone. There were military parades in spectacular uniforms, and only ten months before Joseph's death the Smith family had seen the completion of their new home and hostelry. Where, then, was all the money? Emma was to learn that the legacy of debt she had inherited would plague her for a long time and that Nauvoo city lots were of little cash value. She was land rich and money poor, and the only explanation she could find for the situation was that somehow Brigham Young must have swindled her out of what should rightfully have been hers.

Neither Brigham nor Emma fully understood where the riches had gone. In fact, there were no riches. Nauvoo had been built in a speculative economy, and when the Mormons left, the remaining inhabitants of the desolated city could not generate the thriving, bustling economy that had characterized the building up of Zion.

Five months before Joseph Smith's death, Jacob Scott in Nauvoo had written to his daughter in Canada:

> Many hundreds come in to Nauvoo, from different parts of the union, and a great number from Europe, & the brick laying continued, plastering & chimney building, until a few days ago—Nauvoo is now a splendid spectacle to view from any point in sight, hundred of ele-

gant brick buildings, after the mode of different countries and the taste of the owners—and the Saints of other climes, in their respective costumes, is to me a novel & interesting sight.... We confidently expect before long to witness the arrival of Saints from every country in Europe. And the time is not far distant when the *Arabians* will arrive with their tents & their camels & dromedaries, "And *Etheopia* will soon stretch out her hands to God."[38]

Emma could not bring herself to leave the dream; Brigham confidently believed he could take it with him. They both erred in assuming that Nauvoo could finance it.

Brigham Young was right—Emma was smart and ingenious—but he underestimated her. She was smart enough to know that he did not always appreciate those qualities in her. He did not understand the relationship Emma had with Joseph. An independent woman, she would have scorned the offer of a "cradle" to carry her across the plains. The Relief Society she had presided over had been dissolved, leaving her without a base of influence. If she went west, she probably would have gone as a plural wife of one of the Twelve. She did not choose that future. "I have no friend but God," she said, "and no place to go but home."[39]

With the passage of time, both Brigham and Emma might have seen that their struggle was not entirely of their own making, but their opposition to each other polarized the uncomfortable emotions that many of the early Mormons felt as they embraced an unorthodox religion. The "moderate Mormons"[40] who remained in Illinois shed such encumbering practices as temple activities and plural marriage, and they blamed Brigham Young for whatever embarrassment they felt about being Latter Day Saints. Among Brigham Young's followers, a gradual sentiment developed that there was something sinister about Emma Smith. It became an undercurrent of anticipation: what would be learned about Emma, could the depths of hell be probed for an interview?[41] Whether Emma raised her sons on falsehoods or Brigham ineptly handled his beloved friend's wife, the most unfortunate result of their conflict was the institutionalized rancor that developed between two churches that claimed the same founder.

Brigham Young and Emma Smith centered their lives on the charismatic Joseph. Brigham loved him and did his bidding; Emma loved him and challenged him. Both died calling his name.[42]

Notes

An earlier version of this essay appeared in the *Utah Historical Quarterly* 48 (Winter 1980): 81–97.

1. The Quorum of the Twelve Apostles in 1845 had some elegant names: Brigham Young, the Lion of the Lord; Heber C. Kimball, the Herald of Grace; Orson Hyde, the Olive Branch of Israel; Willard Richards, the Keeper of the Rolls; John Taylor, the Champion of Right; William Smith, the Patriarchal Jacob's Staff; Wilford Woodruff, the Banner of the Gospel; Parley P. Pratt, the Archer of Paradise; George A. Smith, the Establisher of Truth; Orson Pratt, the Gauge of Philosophy; John E. Page, the Sun Dial; Lyman Wight, the Wild Ram of the Mountains. Brigham Young and Lyman Wight were the only two whose names were well known, perhaps because they were so apt (Alan H. Gerber, "Church Manuscripts," microfilm, vol. 11, 122, Harold B. Lee Library, Brigham Young University, Provo, Utah).

2. Emma Hale married Joseph Smith in 1827 and Lewis C. Bidamon in 1847. Brigham Young refused to call her Emma Bidamon, although she used that name and lived under it for thirty-two years.

3. Brigham Young, Address, October 7, 1866, Brigham Young Papers, Archives, Historical Department, Church of Jesus Christ of Latter-day Saints, Salt Lake City, Utah (hereafter LDS Archives). Some punctuation and spelling have been previously corrected in this manuscript.

4. Emma Smith Bidamon to Joseph Smith III, August 19, 1866, Emma Smith Bidamon Papers, Library-Archives, Reorganized Church of Jesus Christ of Latter Day Saints, Independence, Mo.

5. Ibid., August 1, n.d. Three of Emma's sons, Joseph, Alexander, and David, served missions in Utah for the RLDS church.

6. Our thanks to Gene Sessions of Weber State College, who challenged us on this point, and to Ronald K. Esplin of the LDS Church Historical Department, for his valuable assistance in documenting it. Both of these men have given valuable insights and assistance in the preparation of this essay.

7. Joseph and Emma's first three children did not survive their birth: a son Alvin, born in Harmony, Pennsylvania, on June 15, 1828; and twins, Thaddeus and Louisa, born in Kirtland, Ohio, on April 30, 1831. An adopted son, Joseph Murdock, died April 21, 1832, at the age of eleven months. His twin sister, Julia, was the only surviving child in the Smith household when Joseph Smith III was born.

8. *The Doctrine and Covenants of the Church of Jesus Christ of Latter-day Saints* (Salt Lake City: Deseret Book, 1968), sect. 25; *Book of Doctrine and Covenants* (Independence, Mo.: Herald Publishing House, 1970), sect. 24.

9. Joseph Smith, *History of the Church of Jesus Christ of Latter-day Saints*, ed. B. H. Roberts (Salt Lake City: Deseret News Press, 1902–12; 6 vols., a seventh volume was published in 1932; reprinted by Deseret Book, 1976, and reissued in paperback in 1978), 1:217. For a more detailed account of the publication of the hymnal, see Peter Crawley, "A Bibliography of the Church

of Jesus Christ of Latter-day Saints in New York, Ohio, and Missouri," *Brigham Young University Studies* 12 (Summer 1972): 503–5.

10. Brigham Young to Mary Ann Angell Young, June 12, 1840, Phillip Blair Collection, Special Collections, Marriott Library, University of Utah, Salt Lake City.

11. Ibid.

12. Ibid., January 15, 1841.

13. Dean C. Jessee, "Brigham Young's Family: Part I, 1824–1845," *Brigham Young University Studies* 18 (Spring 1978): 321.

14. Mary Audentia Anderson and Bertha Audentia Anderson Hulmes, eds., *Joseph Smith III and the Restoration* (Independence, Mo.: Herald Publishing House, 1952), 57–58.

15. Brigham Young did take an active part in negating John C. Bennett's influence. He and others assisted Joseph in preparing and printing the anti-Bennett affidavits that appeared in the *Times and Seasons* (Nauvoo, Ill.) 3 (July 2, 1842): 839–43. He was also among 308 elders of the Mormon church who volunteered to go to the eastern states to help neutralize Bennett's influence in the eastern press. Our thanks to Peter Crawley for this information.

16. Anderson and Hulmes, *Joseph Smith III and the Restoration*, 87.

17. *Journal of Discourses*, 26 vols. (Liverpool, England: F. D. and S. W. Richards, 1854–86), 4:297–98.

18. Emma Smith to Joseph Smith Jr., May 3, 1837, Joseph Smith Jr. Collection, LDS Archives.

19. Joseph Smith Jr. to Emma Smith, March 21, 1839, Joseph Smith Jr. Collection.

20. Joseph Smith III to Emma Bidamon, March 8, 1873, Emma Smith Bidamon Collection. Joseph III was not the first to offer the LDS temple for sale. Under the signatures of Babbitt, Heywood, and Fullmer, who were Brigham Young's attorneys, the temple in Nauvoo had been advertized for sale in 1846, being "admirably designed for Literary or religious purposes" (*Hancock Eagle* [Nauvoo, Ill.], April 10, 1846). In the same newspaper, the Kirtland Temple, "this splendid edifice," was also offered "on advantageous terms."

21. Emma Smith to Joseph Smith Jr., May 3, 1837, Joseph Smith Jr. Letterbooks, LDS Archives.

22. Elden Jay Watson, ed., *Manuscript History of Brigham Young, 1801–1844* (Salt Lake City: Smith Secretarial Service, 1968), 24–25.

23. Twelve to the Church at La Harpe, February 18, 1843, Brigham Young Papers, LDS Archives.

24. Twelve to Ramus, February 23, 1843, Brigham Young Papers.

25. Emma Smith to Governor Carlin, August 27, 1842, Emma Smith Bidamon Papers.

26. Among the wives that Emma agreed to give Joseph were two sets of sisters—Emily and Eliza Partridge, and Sarah and Maria Lawrence. Danel W. Bachman's "A Study of the Practice of Plural Marriage before the Death

of Joseph Smith" (M.A. thesis, Purdue University, 1975) contains one of the most comprehensive studies of plural marriage during Joseph Smith's lifetime. It documents Emma's agonizing participation in the practice of plural marriage. See also Fawn M. Brodie, *No Man Knows My History: The Life of Joseph Smith, the Mormon Prophet* (New York: Alfred A. Knopf, 1945), 434–65.

27. Bachman, "A Study of the Practice of Plural Marriage," 160.

28. Lewis Crum Bidamon to Emma Smith, January 11, 1847, Emma Smith Bidamon Papers.

29. See letters in the Emma Smith and Lewis Bidamon Collections, RLDS Library-Archives.

30. Charles E. Bidamon to L. L. Hudson, August 10, 1940, Special Collections, Harold B. Lee Library.

31. Joseph Smith III, Journal, April 22, 1879, Joseph Smith III Papers, RLDS Library-Archives (emphasis added).

32. James Monroe, Diary, April 24, 1845, Beineke Library, Yale University, New Haven, Conn.; microfilm copy at the Utah State Historical Society, Salt Lake City. For a detailed account of the organizational structure that could have been the basis for Emma's support of Marks, see D. Michael Quinn, "The Mormon Succession Crisis of 1844," *Brigham Young University Studies* 16 (Summer 1976): 187–233.

33. Anderson and Hulmes, *Joseph Smith III and the Restoration*, 87.

34. Brigham Young, Statement, Liverpool, April 1, 1867, Brigham Young Papers.

35. Joseph I. Bentley and Dallin H. Oaks, "Joseph Smith and the Legal Process: In the Wake of the Steamboat *Nauvoo*," *Brigham Young University Law Review* 6 (Fall 1976): 745.

36. Almon W. Babbitt to Heber C. Kimball, January 31, 1848, LDS Archives.

37. Brigham Young, Address, October 7, 1866. Such accounts as the following illustrate the frustrations Brigham's agents felt and communicated to him as they tried to sell Nauvoo properties and found them in Emma's name: Joseph L. Heywood to Heber C. Kimball, March 17, 1846; John M. Bernhisel to Brigham Young, June 10, 1846; Almon W. Babbitt to Heber C. Kimball, January 31, 1848, all in the LDS Archives.

38. Jacob Scott to Mary Scott Warnock, January 5, 1844, RLDS Library-Archives.

39. Quoted in E. Cecil McGavin, *Nauvoo the Beautiful* (Salt Lake City: Stevens and Wallis, 1946), 191.

40. "Moderate Mormons" is Alma Blair's term for members of the RLDS Church and stems from his article, "The Reorganized Church of Jesus Christ of Latter Day Saints: Moderate Mormons," in *The Restoration Movement: Essays in Mormon History*, ed. F. Mark McKiernan, Alma R. Blair, and Paul M. Edwards (Lawrence, Kan.: Coronado Press, 1973), 207–30.

41. Mormon folklore has Joseph stating he would go to hell for Emma and Brigham commenting that that's where he would find her.

42. For an account of Brigham's death by his daughter, see Susa Young Gates and Leah D. Widtsoe, *The Life Story of Brigham Young* (New York: Macmillan, 1930), 362; for an account of Emma's death by her son Alexander Hale Smith, see *Zion's Ensign* (Independence, Mo.), December 31, 1903.

13

From Assassination to Expulsion: Two Years of Distrust, Hostility, and Violence

MARSHALL HAMILTON

The murders of Joseph Smith and Hyrum Smith on June 27, 1844, marked the beginning of the end of the presence of the Latter-day Saints in Illinois. Conflict with their neighbors had begun three years earlier,[1] but even after the murders of the church leaders, it was by no means a foregone conclusion that the Smiths' deaths would mean the departure of their followers. As one scholar put it, "One should avoid viewing the final expulsion of the Mormons from Hancock County as the inexorable effect of the killings,"[2] although in some minds no other alternative ever became acceptable.

This essay deals with the movements and countermovements undertaken by the Latter-day Saints and their neighbors from the time of the Smith's assassination until the day, a little over two years later, when the last party of church members left Nauvoo, Illinois. Those movements are chronicled in the media and public records of the day—especially in the pro-Mormon newspapers published in Nauvoo and in the anti-Mormon press in Warsaw, Illinois, twelve miles downriver from Nauvoo. One wonders whether the eventual outcome of the conflict between the Latter-day Saints and their neighbors might have been different if the Saints had been more successful at what we now call external communications. Although the Saints might have left Nauvoo eventually of their own choice, could the expulsion of the church as a body have been avoided? Answers to these questions about the experiences of Nauvoo Mormons suggest lessons that members of modern belief-driven organizations might learn about dealing with outsiders or opponents.

Within days after the assassinations of Joseph and Hyrum Smith, both the Mormons and the anti-Mormons had published extra newspaper issues describing the killings and offering opinions on what the future held. In Warsaw, two days after the assassinations, Thomas Sharp's *Signal* issued an extra that included the following editorial comment: "Our opinion is, that either the old citizens or the Mormons must leave. The county cannot be quieted, until the expulsion of one or the other is effected."[3] One day later, a crew at John Taylor's *Neighbor* got out an extra edition, which included the following advice attributed to Willard Richards: "The people of the county are greatly excited and fear the Mormons will come out and take vengeance—I have pledged my word the Mormons will stay at home as soon as they can be informed, and no violence will be on their part, and say to my brethren in Nauvoo, in the name of the Lord—be still—be patient."[4]

In the days just after the Smiths' deaths, non-Mormons in Hancock County expected a "general attack all over the country" in retaliation for the killings.[5] Thomas Ford, the governor of Illinois, had been in Nauvoo at the time of the attack on the jail. Rumors flew that he was besieged in a house in Nauvoo, so a force of over two hundred men set out by steamboat from Quincy to Nauvoo to rescue him. However, Governor Ford, while initially fearful himself—especially since the Mormons had been represented to him as a "lawless, infatuated, and fanatical people, not governed by the ordinary motives which influence the rest of mankind" —soon tried to maintain order. He countermanded the march to Hancock County of at least two overly eager state militia units in the neighborhood, and he tried to keep informed about events in Hancock County from a listening post in Quincy.[6]

In Nauvoo, the Saints' initial reaction was grief. In the extra the *Neighbor* published three days after the assassinations, along with the plea from Willard Richards, the editorial staff included a reassurance to the governor that intentions were peaceful: "We assure the governor, if he can manage human butchers, he has nothing to fear from *armless*, timid, and law abiding Latter-day Saints."[7] The following day the Nauvoo City Council met and resolved to discourage "private revenge" by Nauvoo residents.[8] In a Sunday church meeting held a week and a half after the killings, W. W. Phelps read to the congregation an angry letter written by Governor Ford to a group of avowed anti-Mormons.[9] Church leaders seemed intent on controlling the anger of individual members and ensuring that the Saints' reaction would not be violent. They tried to assure church members that state power would protect their interests.

Among the anti-Mormons, however, no effort to control anger or thwart violence was exerted. Calls for expulsion of the church had been heard earlier. The Anti-Mormon Party, a political group, had been running candidates for public office since 1841. When Nauvoo's population grew to the point that the Saints controlled local elections, the anti-Mormons had begun to call for their expulsion.[10] One of the leaders of the anti-Mormons was Thomas Sharp, the publisher and editor of the Warsaw *Signal.*

The *Signal* missed its usual publication date the day before the killings, most likely because its editor was busy with the intrigues in Carthage, but a special issue was published on June 29. It includes a useful compilation of documents issued in the days leading up to the assassinations—letters and agreements between Governor Ford and church leaders. Sharp also provided a chronology of the events of the week. After giving his editorial opinion that the Saints must leave, he recorded that the Nauvoo Legion's small arms and cannon had been taken from them, thereby pointing out to his readers the vulnerability of Nauvoo.

A public meeting, whose attendees called themselves the Warsaw Committee of Safety, was called in Warsaw. Sharp was designated to draft a letter to Governor Ford urging the Mormons' expulsion. The letter, which was hand-carried to Ford in Quincy, reviews with approval the Mormons' previous expulsion from Missouri and says that expulsion from Illinois would be not only a "measure of wise expediency but one of absolute necessity." The Saints in Nauvoo were charged with murder, arson, and theft by their non-Mormon neighbors; with abusing the forms of justice to free Mormon criminals; with building a military force that had no legitimate defensive purpose; and with using Mormon votes to bargain shamelessly for favors from corrupt politicians.[11] These four themes were elaborated by anti-Mormons over the next two years.

Pervasive accusations of Latter-day Saint criminal behavior, particularly theft, characterize the anti-Mormon press throughout the Illinois period of church history. Such accusations were a major tool of the anti-Mormons to justify the repression or expulsion of the church. In fact, the charges of theft were used explicitly to persuade the public some distance from Hancock County that expulsion was merely the last resort of a long-suffering group of victims of Mormon thievery.[12]

The accusations of theft suggest a fertile area for further research into the Nauvoo era—the church generally either denied the accusations[13] or minimized the presence of thieves among the Saints,[14] while anti-Mormons continued to accept the accusations as true.[15] During the period following the assassinations of Joseph and Hyrum Smith, those accusations were redoubled. The Warsaw *Signal* included articles headed "Mormon Thieves" in eight of the fourteen issues published from September 18, 1844, until the end of the year.[16] Beginning on Christmas Day 1844 and running for several weeks into 1845,[17] Sharp included a special column headed "Mormon Stealing," rendered in ornate block lettering, followed by a quotation from the "Mormon Book of Doctrine and Covenants,"[18] which purported to justify thefts from non-Mormons.

Accusations of theft by the Mormons were one reason Governor Ford left Carthage for Nauvoo on the day the prophet and his brother were murdered. The purported thefts were also used to justify a proposed encampment of independent companies of militia near Warsaw on October 26, 1844. This encampment was quickly dubbed a "wolf hunt" by its organizers; it was understood by Mormons and non-Mormons alike that the "wolves" to be sought were alleged Mormon thieves.[19]

Church members were, of course, extremely worried about the "wolf hunt."[20] Governor Ford was convinced the only purpose of the proposed encampment was to expel or murder Mormons. The governor called out the state militia to assist him in suppressing the encampment. The militia then marched under General Hardin to Hancock County. Ford's posse proved to be too much for the anti-Mormons. Although Ford could round up a force of only about two hundred men, the anti-Mormons thought better of their plans and canceled the "wolf hunt."[21]

The accusations of theft by church members may not be valid, but there is no question that the period from the death of Joseph and Hyrum to the departure of the Latter-day Saints was a time of considerable lawlessness in the environs of Hancock County. Five church members in an outlying community were arrested for larceny in February 1845,[22] and two men were murdered in Lee County, Iowa, in May 1845.[23] In June the father of the two suspects in the Iowa murders was killed in Nauvoo,[24] and on July 4 another murder took place on an island in the Mississippi.[25] Later, a man was accidently shot and killed near the Nauvoo Temple, apparently through careless gunfire in the city itself.[26]

With the increase in lawlessness, the year 1845 was a difficult one for Hancock County sheriffs. In June, Minor Deming, a church member who was elected to the office in August 1844 just after the martyrdom, shot and killed Samuel Marshall, an anti-Mormon county court clerk.[27] Deming claimed self-defense, but he was indicted for murder, and he resigned the office. Before he could come to trial, Deming died of fever.[28]

Deming's replacement as sheriff, Jacob Backenstos, was also involved in a killing. Only weeks after taking office, Backenstos, a non-Mormon who was known as a friend of the Saints, was present at the killing of Frank Worrell, who had commanded the guard on duty at Carthage Jail when Joseph and Hyrum were murdered.[29] Backenstos was among those indicted for this murder but was acquitted in a trial held in Peoria.[30] Curiously, even while under indictment, Backenstos continued to act as sheriff. His alleged part in the killing of Worrell earned Backenstos the anti-Mormons' hatred, which continued even after he left the county to serve in the Mexican War.[31]

The only topic sure to stir up more heated discussion than lawlessness in Hancock County was local politics. As previously mentioned, non-Mormons were so frustrated about the growing number of Mormon voters that they formed a political party to try to elect non-Mormon county officers. One problem the "old citizens" faced was alien franchise, allowed by the 1818 Illinois Constitution, section 27. The Latter-day Saints were quite successful in encouraging British converts to immigrate to Nauvoo, and the law allowed new residents to vote immediately upon arrival. One scholar, in analyzing the political status of Nauvoo, notes that "the exercise of their franchise brought the Mormons many enemies but few friends."[32]

The first local election following the martyrdom was scheduled for just forty days after the assassination. Initially, the Saints planned not to participate in the election, but eventually a political meeting was held in Nauvoo, and in the election all the Mormon-backed candidates won. As the *Signal* glumly put it, "Though [the winning candidates] are not all Mormons in name [all] are yet so in heart. One of the representatives, [Almon] Babbitt, is a Mormon. The coroner is a Mormon, but had not the courage to say so, and as for the ballance we would sooner trust Mormons than either of them."[33] Other anti-Mormons were equally disappointed.[34]

Despite the presence of Representative Babbitt in the 1844–45 session of the Illinois state legislature, the house and senate took up repeal of the Nauvoo city charter. The anti-Mormons believed that the charter's repeal would help solve two problems: (1) Mormon use of the Nauvoo city court system to defeat writs and warrants issued by courts outside of Nauvoo, and (2) the existence of the Nauvoo Legion, a militia force reported to number about three thousand men.[35]

The bill for the repeal of the Nauvoo charter was introduced in early December 1844 by Senator John Henry.[36] As debate proceeded on the repeal motion, the Hancock County sheriff Deming committed a serious blunder. One of the senators, Jacob Cunningham Davis, was among those indicted for the murders of Joseph and Hyrum Smith.[37] At the time of the indictment, the defendants and prosecution had made an agreement that no attempt would be made to arrest the defendants prior to the May 1845 term of the circuit court. Notwithstanding that agreement, arrest warrants were issued in November for all nine defendants. Sheriff Deming, acting on one of the warrants, went to Springfield and tried to arrest Davis on the floor of the state senate. Deming's action, which violated Davis's legislative immunity, infuriated the state assembly and undoubtedly hurt the prospects for retaining the Nauvoo charter.[38] The charter was in fact repealed on January 29, 1845.

The next local election, in August 1845, also saw the Mormon vote carry every office. The anti-Mormons made little effort to affect the result, and the Nauvoo *Neighbor* commented, "The people knew how to act, and acted."[39]

By the election of August 1846, the prospect that there would be any Mormon votes at all in Hancock County prompted a near outbreak of civil war. In early June, a meeting of anti-Mormons was held in Carthage calling for the remaining church members to leave Nauvoo.[40] By that time, thousands of Saints were on the march in Iowa, and one observer found Nauvoo "desolate, houses empty, and inhabitants gone. Prairies deserted of cattle & people."[41] The anti-Mormons sent a delegation to Nauvoo, and many of the remaining Saints fled in the face of these threats.

By this time, a new group of people was involved in Nauvoo civic affairs: the "new citizens." These non-Mormons bought property from the exiled Saints and were living in Nauvoo. The "old citizens" of the anti-Mormon camp reportedly whipped some new citizens who refused to join in driving the remaining Latter-day Saints out of town.[42] The anti-Mormons gathered nearly six hundred men in an encampment about six miles from Nauvoo.[43] Sheriff Backenstos came to Nauvoo to organize the residents for a defense of the city. The anti-Mormons, not anticipating resistance, lost their taste for attack, and the encampment, with its threat of violence and civil war, dissolved.

Still, the anti-Mormons did not want any of the Saints to vote in the August 1846 election, and they continued to harass those who remained. In July a few church members were whipped by a group of thirty men for being troublemakers.[44] Very few Mormons were left to vote in the election, and the outcome was much more to the anti-Mormons' liking.[45]

It seems clear, however, that despite the non-Mormons' resentment of what they considered to be crimes perpetrated by church members and their frustration over their inability to win elective office, some catalyst was required—some call to action—to bring about the actual expulsion of the Saints. That call was provided by Thomas Sharp through his newspaper, the Warsaw *Signal*.

Sharp had provided a similar call to action earlier. He is perhaps best known among Latter-day Saints for his stirring call to arms after the destruction of the Nauvoo *Expositor* in June 1844.[46] In the immediate aftermath of the assassination of Joseph and Hyrum, Sharp continued his extremist rhetoric, as evidenced by the call for the expulsion of the Saints and his role as spokesman for the Warsaw Committee of Safety.[47]

During the summer of 1844, it had become increasingly evident that Sharp himself would be indicted for the murder of the Smiths—not because evidence placed him at Carthage Jail but because he had incited others, in his newspaper and especially in his speeches, to go there. As that prospect loomed, Sharp let up on his claim that the killings were completely justified. That claim was based on a theory of "community self-defense," which Sharp elaborated on at length in the *Signal*,[48] and on his claim that the execution of the Smiths was actually the fulfillment of the verdict of thousands, superior even to the verdict of a panel of only twelve peers.[49] Instead of pursuing those claims, Sharp took increased pains to describe the thievery of church members and the uncertain nature of the Saints' voting to make the case that the Saints were undesirable neighbors. The level of his vehemence did not change, but the topics of discussion did.[50]

Although Sharp was the principal catalyst inciting non-Mormons to urge expulsion of the church, it should be noted that he was not guilty of everything attributed to him by Latter-day Saints then or by some current scholars. For example, the Nauvoo *Neighbor* of November 13, 1844, reprinted a letter that had originally appeared in the *Illinois State Register*, claiming that Sharp had published an anti-Masonic paper in upstate New York, that he had invented the terms *jack-Mason* and *jack-Mormon* to describe nonadherents who nevertheless advanced the goals of the organization, and that he was the mouthpiece for a group of Warsaw real-estate speculators. None of these statements about Sharp is true, although they still occasionally find their way into otherwise careful studies.

How did church leaders react to charges of lawlessness and political chicanery and to Sharp's drumbeat of expulsion? The first order of business for the remaining leaders was to ensure succession in the church to keep the organization alive. Just fifteen days after the martyrdom, a council was held among church leaders in Nauvoo—most of the Quorum of Twelve had not yet returned to Nauvoo—to discuss the establishment of a new trustee-in-trust for the church to replace Joseph Smith.[51] Such concerns for the very survival of the organization help explain church leaders' reluctance, mentioned previously, to hold a political meeting that summer.

On August 8, the famous conference on succession was held, which finally settled leadership of the church on the Quorum of the Twelve. The next day, the Twelve met to appoint trustees for the church.[52] With those details cleared up, there remained challenges by Sidney Rigdon, Lyman Wight, and James Strang to be dealt with, although time became available to consider how the church should interact with their neighbors and with civil authorities.

Church leaders decided early on to rely on their own forces, rather than legal authority, to protect the interests of church members. Reports of the planned "wolf hunt" were received in Nauvoo on Friday, September 13, 1844; on the following Monday, the church publicly dedicated ground for an arsenal.[53] When the governor's forces came to Nauvoo seeking volunteers for a posse to visit Warsaw to prevent the "wolf hunt," the Saints declined to participate. At the same time, church leaders continued to fill vacancies in the Nauvoo Legion.[54]

By spring 1845, church leaders had decided to ignore, as much as possible, the civil court system. Since the repeal of the Nauvoo charter, Nauvoo had no authorized police force. By the April 1845 general conference, the Saints had begun to employ a "whistling and whittling brigade" to unnerve outsiders and discourage non-Mormons from coming to Nauvoo.[55]

John Taylor, speaking at a Sunday church meeting, announced that the Saints should resist "gentile" (non-Mormon) processes.[56] About the same time, the leaders decreed that men for whom writs had been issued should go on missions to avoid service. Church leaders actually wanted to align themselves with the legal government, but they saw the issuance of warrants as an attempt by anti-Mormons to drive a wedge between the Saints and the state. By not allowing church leaders to stand trial or be imprisoned, they hoped to avoid the appearance that the state and the church were on opposite sides of the issue.[57] Unfortunately, this policy, intended to promote church interests, produced the opposite effect—it convinced some non-Mormons, including the editor of the *State Register* in Springfield, that the church was lawless.[58]

In May, church members, except those required to go to court as witnesses or jurors, avoided going to the trial of Joseph Smith's accused assassins. The verdict of innocent, reached after two and a half hours of jury deliberations, was met with a shrug in Nauvoo. John Taylor's *Neighbor* commented that the Saints would refer the case to God for a righteous judgment.[59] Four weeks later, when the trial for Hyrum Smith's murder was dismissed for want of prosecution, the *Neighbor* ignored the proceedings entirely. As the Saints completed work on their temple, they seemed to ignore earthly institutions; their expected endowment from on high caused them to assume an otherworldly perspective. The last shingles were nailed on the temple roof on August 13, 1845.[60]

As the year 1845 wore on, the Saints' temporal situation became more tenuous. On August 11, with the endorsement of the Nauvoo *Neighbor,* Jacob Backenstos became county sheriff in a special election. Within a month of his election, the anti-Mormons met in a schoolhouse near the southern border of the county to discuss problems some had experienced in executing civil judgments against church members. During the meeting, shots were fired into the school building by persons unknown.[61] Although no one was injured, the anti-Mormons resolved to take revenge on the Saints for the shooting, a move that led to near civil war conditions in Hancock County. A small Latter-day Saints settlement called Morley's Settlement, or Yelrome (from *Morley* spelled backwards), was near Lima, in Adams County. The day after the shooting incident at the schoolhouse, the anti-Mormons collected en masse at Morley's and burned houses to the ground, apparently after residents were warned to vacate. Estimates of the number of houses burned vary widely. Sharp admits "two or three houses burned."[62] Thomas Gregg said that "two Mormon cabins" were burned the first night and that within a week "the whole of Morley-Town was in ashes."[63] The Nauvoo *Neighbor* stated eight houses and three outbuildings were destroyed the first day and forty-four buildings within the first three days. The *Neighbor* also claimed that the provocative shots had been a ruse, actually fired by anti-Mormons to provide a pretext for future violence.[64]

Newly elected Sheriff Backenstos responded by issuing a proclamation reciting the Illinois law against arson and commanding "rioters and other peace-breakers to desist forthwith, disperse, and go to their homes."[65] Opponents dismissed the proclamation as "very exaggerated."[66] Backenstos called all law-abiding citizens to serve as a *posse comitatus,* but he was unable to stop the burning. It was at this time that Frank Worrell was shot outside of Warsaw, further elevating the almost fever pitch of emotion in the county.

Anti-Mormons turned their attention briefly from the Mormons to those they considered jack-Mormons—non-Mormons who advanced the interests of the Saints. The Warsaw postmaster, E. A. Bedell, was threatened by a group outside his home; he left through a back door and paddled across the river to Iowa in a canoe. In Carthage, the county treasurer and county recorder, who had been elected to office with Mormon support, received warnings to leave town.

The next day, September 16, Sheriff Backenstos rode into Carthage with an armed force to remove his family from their home, since they had also been subjected to threats.[67] On September 17, the Warsaw *Signal* featured a call to arms in the wake of Worrell's killing, including the observation that Worrell had been "one of our best men."[68] The call to arms must have been eerily reminiscent of the similar call in an issue of the *Signal* fifteen months earlier, when the call to arms inflamed emotion throughout the county and helped lead to the killing of Joseph and Hyrum Smith.[69]

After Sharp's call to fight, the civil war heated up. On Friday, September 19, Backenstos went to Carthage with an armed force and occupied the courthouse. Many of the reported four hundred armed men accompanying the sheriff were Latter-day Saints.[70] Rumors spread that the Saints had taken four prisoners away to Nauvoo.[71] Backenstos led a search through Carthage for weapons, seizing them from anti-Mormons and requiring passes for anyone trying to enter or leave Carthage.[72]

Naturally, such activity in Hancock County caused consternation throughout the region and the state. On Monday, September 22, a public meeting was held in Quincy, at which many of Adams County's leading citizens gathered to search for an end to the hostilities.[73] The meeting became known as the Quincy Committee and eventually played a leading role in producing a cease-fire. In Springfield, Governor Ford worked on assembling a force of militiamen to restore order, and he issued a proclamation warning all other outsiders to stay out of Hancock County.[74]

The Quincy Committee wrote the church asking about its intentions. Brigham Young responded with a conciliatory letter, explaining that the Latter-day Saints wished only for peace and that they planned to leave Nauvoo as soon as proper arrangements could be made.[75]

It took until Sunday, September 28, nine days after Carthage was commandeered by Backenstos's posse, for Governor Ford's army under General Hardin to reach Carthage and dismiss the occupying posse.[76] Governor Ford himself and other political leaders, including Congressman Stephen A. Douglas, accompanied the state force.

Although the constitutional forces of law and order were nearby, Brigham Young decided to communicate with the ad hoc Quincy Committee to defuse the situation. The committee asked for a written guarantee the Mormons would leave, which the Twelve Apostles provided on October 1, 1845, in a famous letter promising to leave "when grass grows and water runs" the next spring.[77] The Quincy Committee wrote back to the church the next day accepting the church's offer to leave.[78]

Although General Hardin accepted the offer on October 3, placating the anti-Mormons took a little more time. Hardin wrote them on October 6. One of the terms of the agreement was that General Hardin would designate a force to remain in Hancock County through the winter to enforce the peace.[79]

At regular October general conference sessions, church leaders apprised the membership of the coming move. At that conference, committees were created to dispose of property left in Nauvoo.[80] An uneasy peace settled over the county, with three groups trying to coexist: an armed force of occupation, a group preparing to move the next spring, and another group unwilling to believe the agreements reached between the other two.

Long before the agreement was reached, the Saints had been investigating the possibility of at least part of them leaving. Before his death, Joseph sent Lyman Wight to investigate the possibility of moving members to Texas, then an independent nation. In 1844, shortly after the prophet's death, Wight established a colony in Texas with about 150 Saints. But the rest of the church never joined this group, and the colony lasted only through 1857.[81] As early as January 7, 1845, the Quorum of the Twelve had discussed sending scouts west to California.[82] In April 1845, letters were sent to the president of the United States and governors of all the states except Illinois and Missouri asking their advice on where to relocate the church.[83] There is no evidence any useful advice was received in return. Reports suggest that in September 1845 the Council of Fifty called for fifteen hundred pioneers to go to the Salt Lake Valley.[84] The decision to depart Nauvoo for a location west of the Rockies obviously did not occur in a vacuum.

As the winter of 1845–46 wore on, the church began organizing their emigration companies. At the same time, warrants were issued for Brigham Young and other church leaders on charges of counterfeiting. In December, a federal marshal spent over a week in Nauvoo but was unable to find Brigham.[85]

When reports surfaced in Nauvoo that federal and state agents might try to prevent the exodus, the church decided to begin the migration ahead of schedule. The first wagons headed west on February 4, 1846. Brigham Young himself left on the fifteenth.[86] By February 11, the Warsaw *Signal* reported that a thousand Mormons had left.

By June 2, Thomas Bullock, secretary to the Twelve, described the country as "desolate," with nothing but empty houses.[87] On the second anniversary of the martyrdom, Bullock lamented that the empty city contained little more than "whorehouses" and "lawyers."[88] Notwithstanding the efforts thousands had made to leave Nauvoo, some Latter-day Saints still remained. As described previously, the anti-Mormons stepped up their harassment of the remaining church members in advance of the August election, and civil war was only narrowly averted.

In early July, a group of three or four church members hired themselves out to work a farm north of Nauvoo. They behaved obnoxiously and were accused of petty theft. Anti-Mormons whipped them and sent them back to Nauvoo.[89] Sharp later described this act as "tickling with the hickory."[90] The Saints and the new citizens raised a posse and arrested two anti-Mormons who had participated in the vigilantism. The anti-Mormons responded by taking five Saints hostage. At this point, an anti-Mormon deputy sheriff called out a posse to go to Nauvoo to arrest one figure in the incident, and the crisis seemed destined to escalate out of control.[91]

The citizens of Nauvoo appealed to Governor Ford for military force to restore order. Ford complied but withheld funds; only volunteers were sent to Hancock County. Finally, on September 10, 1846, a force of about seven hundred anti-Mormons faced off against a group of about three hundred Saints, new citizens, and state militia volunteers.[92] There followed a few days of skirmishing, with the Battle of Nauvoo, a seventy-five-minute barrage of rifle and cannon fire, occurring on Saturday, September 12, 1846.[93] As they had done the previous year, the citizens of Quincy, acting once again as the Quincy Committee, agreed to mediate a solution. A treaty was negotiated with seven points. Paragraph five read, "The Mormon population of the city [is] to leave the State, or disperse, as soon as they can cross the river."[94]

The anti-Mormons had at last achieved the goal they had set in early June 1844—they had expelled the Mormons. Those Saints who left under the September 1846 treaty were among the poorest residents of Nauvoo. Their suffering at the "poor camp" in Montrose, Iowa, has taken on mythic proportions among their descendants.[95]

My examination of the records of this two-year period indicates that the Saints could not have prevented their forcible expulsion by responding in more favorable ways to the circumstances after the assassination of Joseph and Hyrum. This is not to say that the Saints were blameless. It is clear that the decision announced in the spring of 1845 not to honor "gentile process" alienated some previously sympathetic non-Mormons. Since one of the principal charges against the Saints during Joseph Smith's tenure as mayor of Nauvoo was lack of respect for laws and judicial proceedings from outside Nauvoo, it seems particularly naive for the Saints to have announced their intentions not to honor future writs.

It could also be argued that the Twelve Apostles should have responded more effectively to the charges of thievery and political chicanery. Because the anti-Mormon charges went unrefuted outside of Nauvoo, those charges came to be widely accepted as true, and as a result, the Saints' claims of persecution were vitiated to a considerable extent in the minds of political leaders and the general public.

There were also some among the Mormons who were widely believed to be guilty of many crimes, whether or not they actually were. The Hodges brothers, for example, who were hanged for a double murder in Lee County, Iowa, in 1845, claimed to be Mormons. Another such church member was Porter Rockwell, who was widely thought to have pulled the trigger firing the shot that killed Frank Worrell. Although Sheriff Backenstos was present and took the responsibility and political heat, Rockwell's antics were well known in Hancock County, and he was greatly feared. Nonetheless, not everyone seems to have been willing to accept anti-Mormon charges at face value. Governor Ford, for example, mocked the charges of Mormon theft as groundless, at a time when he himself was concerned about his political standing.[96]

The Saints' responses to the murder of their leaders, to the revocation of their city charter, to the acquittal of the alleged assassins of the Smiths, and to the burnings at Morley's Settlement appear to be exemplary—the sort of "turning the other cheek" that might be expected of people calling themselves "saints." However, no matter how peaceful the Mormons might have been, the anti-Mormons would not be mollified. Thomas Sharp appears to have been correct in saying that the anti-Mormons resolved even before the killings to expel the Saints and that nothing changed that determination. No population of church members would be tolerated in the county, even if it took a military force with cannons to besiege the city and drive out the last thousand poorest Saints.

What can the members of modern organizations who are under attack learn from the expulsion of the Saints from Illinois? It seems clear that simply ignoring charges or addressing refutations only to the organization's members will not be enough to defuse a threat from a determined group of opponents. Such charges must be refuted, and the refutations must be disseminated beyond the organization's boundaries. The anti-Mormons developed their arguments along four themes: Mormon lawlessness, Mormon disrespect for legal proceedings, Mormon militarism, and Mormon political corruption. These themes were repeated again and again but were never effectively challenged.

In addition, the Latter-day Saints did not use established channels to redress their grievances. The letters of the Twelve Apostles to the U.S. president and state governors betray a breathless kind of naiveté—the same naiveté shown time and again by the Saints throughout their early years in dealing with governments. This is not to say that they would have been more successful had they used more orthodox lobbying methods, but a modern organization might conclude from the Nauvoo Saints' experience that making up new ways of approaching civil authorities has a low probability of success.[97]

Among modern members of the church, many believe that the departure from Nauvoo immediately followed the assassination of Joseph Smith, when actually more than two years elapsed before the departure was complete. Even in historical studies, there often seems to be confusion over the sequence of events—perhaps because terms are often confusing. For example, several different events are called the "Battle of Nauvoo," and a group named the Quincy Committee played a role in settling potential civil wars in two different years. I hope this essay helps dispel the confusion and increases our understanding of and interest in those turbulent times.

Notes

An earlier version of this essay appeared in *Brigham Young University Studies* 32 (Winter/Spring 1992): 95–118.

1. Marshall Hamilton, "Thomas Sharp's Turning Point: Birth of an Anti-Mormon," *Sunstone* 13 (October 1989): 16–22.

2. Annette P. Hampshire, *Mormonism in Conflict: The Nauvoo Years* (New York: Edwin Mellen Press, 1985), 227.

3. *Signal* (Warsaw, Ill.), June 29, 1844.

4. *Neighbor* (Nauvoo, Ill.), June 30, 1844.

5. Thomas Ford, "Message from the Governor in Relation to the Disturbances in Hancock County," published in the *Neighbor,* January 1, 1845, and *Signal,* January 15, 1841. See also Thomas Ford, *A History of Illinois: From Its Commencement as a State in 1818 to 1847* (Chicago: S. C. Griggs, 1854), 348. Note that 329–54 are also reprinted in Joseph Smith, *History of the Church of Jesus Christ of Latter-day Saints,* ed. B. H. Roberts (Salt Lake City: Deseret News Press, 1902–12; 6 vols., a seventh volume was published in 1932; reprinted by Deseret Book, 1976, and reissued in paperback in 1978). See also Thomas Gregg, *History of Hancock County, Illinois* (Chicago: Charles C. Chapman, 1880), 323.

6. Ford, "Message"; Ford, *History of Illinois,* 348.

7. *Neighbor,* June 30, 1844.

8. Ibid., July 2, 1844.

9. Smith, *History of the Church,* 7:169. For a text of the letter, see Smith, *History of the Church,* 7:160–62; *Neighbor,* July 10, 1844; and *Signal,* July 10, 1844.

10. Marshall Hamilton, "Strange Bedfellows in Hancock County: The Anti-Mormon Party, 1842–46" (Paper delivered at the Mormon History Association annual meeting, Quincy, Illinois, May 13, 1989).

11. *Signal,* July 10, 1844.

12. See, for example, *Signal,* October 27, 1841, September 18, 1844; and *Warsaw Message,* September 13, 1843.

13. See, for example, *Neighbor,* August 6, 1845; and Smith, *History of the Church,* 7:56.

14. See, for example, Samuel W. Taylor, *Nightfall at Nauvoo* (New York: Macmillan, 1971), 317–18; and Samuel W. Taylor, "The Nauvoo Everyone Should Know," *Restoration Trail Forum* 14 (October 1988): 4.

15. See, for example, William Wise, *Massacre at Mountain Meadows* (New York: Thomas Y. Crowell, 1976), 49; Clark Roland [Thomas Sharp's great-grandson], telephone interview by Marshall Hamilton, September 1988;

and Kenneth W. Godfrey, "Crime and Punishment in Mormon Nauvoo, 1839–1846," *Brigham Young University Studies* 32 (Winter/Spring 1992): 195–227.

16. *Signal,* September 18, October 16 and 20, November 13, 20, and 27, December 4 and 18, 1844.

17. Ibid., December 25, 1844; January 1 and 22, 1845.

18. *The Doctrine and Covenants of the Church of Jesus Christ of Latter-day Saints* (Salt Lake City: Deseret Book, 1968), sect. 64:27–28, states, "Behold it is said in my laws, or forbidden, to get in debt to thine enemies; But behold it is not said at any time that the Lord should not take when he please, and pay as seemeth him good."

19. Ford, "Message"; Ford, *History of Illinois,* 340, 364; Gregg, *History of Hancock County,* 327; Dallin H. Oaks and Marvin S. Hill, *Carthage Conspiracy: The Trial of the Accused Assassins of Joseph Smith* (Urbana: University of Illinois Press, 1975), 36.

20. Smith, *History of the Church,* 7:270.

21. Ford, *History of Illinois,* 365; Hampshire, *Mormonism in Conflict,* 231.

22. Smith, *History of the Church,* 7:373.

23. *Neighbor,* May 5, 1845.

24. Ibid., June 25, 1845.

25. Ibid., July 16, 1845.

26. Thomas Bullock, "Journal of Thomas Bullock (1816–1885): 31 August 1845 to 5 July 1846," *Brigham Young University Studies* 31 (Winter 1991): 20. The killing was reported in the entry of September 19, 1845.

27. *Neighbor,* June 26, 1845.

28. Smith, *History of the Church,* 7:439.

29. Thomas C. Sharp, "Manuscript History of the Mormon War" (unfinished), n.d., Thomas C. Sharp and Allied Anti-Mormon Papers, Coe Collection of Western Americana, Beinecke Rare Book and Manuscript Library, Yale University, New Haven, Conn., published in Roger D. Launius, ed., "Anti-Mormonism in Illinois: Thomas C. Sharp's Unfinished History of the Mormon War, 1845," *Journal of Mormon History* 15 (1989): 27–49; *Signal,* September 17, 1845.

30. Gregg, *History of Hancock County,* 341.

31. *Signal,* January 16, 1847.

32. Robert Bruce Flanders, *Nauvoo: Kingdom on the Mississippi* (Urbana: University of Illinois Press, 1965), 221.

33. *Signal,* August 7, 1844.

34. See, for example, Frank Worrell to Thomas Gregg, 1844, Thomas C. Sharp and Allied Anti-Mormon Papers, published in Hampshire, *Mormonism in Conflict.*

35. *Signal,* July 17, 1844; Flanders, *Nauvoo,* 153, 232, and 324.

36. Hampshire, *Mormonism in Conflict,* 235.

37. Gregg, *History of Hancock County,* 329; Oaks and Hill, *Carthage Conspiracy,* 51.

38. Oaks and Hill, *Carthage Conspiracy,* 65–66.

39. *Neighbor,* August 6, 1845.
40. *Signal,* June 17, 1846.
41. Bullock, "Journal," June 2, 1846, 64.
42. Ibid., June 10, 1846, 67.
43. *Signal,* June 14, 1846.
44. Ibid., November 14, 1844.
45. Ibid., August 4 and 11, 1846.
46. Ibid., June 12, 1844.
47. Ibid., July 10, 17, and 31, 1844.
48. Ibid., July 10, 1844.
49. Ibid., July 27, 1844.
50. Because of Sharp's importance and his role in defining the debate during this crucial period, I believe there is a need for further research into the evolution of his arguments, but such research is beyond the scope of this essay.
51. Smith, *History of the Church,* 7:183.
52. Ibid., 7:247.
53. Ibid., 7:720–71.
54. Ibid., 7:274, 271.
55. *Neighbor,* April 16, 1845.
56. Ibid., April 23, 1845.
57. Smith, *History of the Church,* 7:380.
58. Hampshire, *Mormonism in Conflict,* 238.
59. *Neighbor,* June 4, 1845.
60. Ibid., August 13, 1845.
61. Sharp, "Manuscript History"; Gregg, *History of Hancock County,* 340.
62. Sharp, "Manuscript History."
63. Gregg, *History of Hancock County,* 340.
64. *Neighbor,* September 10, 1845. This issue was evidently published several days late since it includes the text of documents dated as late as September 13.
65. *Neighbor,* September 10, 1845; *Signal,* September 24, 1845. This and four other proclamations from Backenstos have been gathered and published in B. H. Roberts, *A Comprehensive History of the Church of Jesus Christ of Latter-day Saints,* 6 vols. (Salt Lake City: Deseret News Press, 1930), 2:490–503.
66. Sharp, "Manuscript History."
67. Ibid.
68. *Signal,* September 17, 1845.
69. Ibid., June 12, 1844.
70. Sharp, "Manuscript History."
71. Bullock, "Journal," September 19, 1845, 20.
72. Sharp, "Manuscript History."
73. *Neighbor,* September 24, 1845.
74. Ibid., October 1, 1845.
75. Ibid., September 24, 1845.

76. Sharp, "Manuscript History."

77. *Neighbor,* October 1, 1845.

78. Smith, *History of the Church,* 7:450–51.

79. *Neighbor,* October 29, 1845.

80. Ibid., October 8, 1845.

81. "The Historian's Corner," *Brigham Young University Studies* 17 (Autumn 1976): 108. See also n. 1.

82. Smith, *History of the Church,* 7:350.

83. Ibid., 7:402–404.

84. Ibid., 7:439.

85. Bullock, "Journal," December 24 and 25, 1845, 38–39; Smith, *History of the Church,* 7:549–57.

86. Smith, *History of the Church,* 7:585; Oaks and Hill, *Carthage Conspiracy,* 205.

87. Bullock, "Journal," June 2, 1846, 64.

88. Ibid., June 27, 1846, 72.

89. *Signal,* July 16, 1846.

90. Ibid., November 14, 1846.

91. Ibid., July 16, 1846.

92. Ibid., November 14, 1846.

93. Gregg, *History of Hancock County,* 350.

94. *Signal,* November 14, 1846; Gregg, *History of Hancock County,* 353.

95. For a recapitulation of the Latter-day Saints' sufferings in Montrose, see Carol Lynn Pearson, "Nine Children Were Born: A Historical Problem from the Sugar Creek Episode," *Brigham Young University Studies* 21 (Fall 1981): 441–44.

96. Ford, "Message"; Ford, *History of Illinois,* 331.

97. I have already suggested a couple of avenues of further study on the period from the assassination to the expulsion. In addition, much work remains to be done on the topics discussed in this essay. For example, numerous extant Mormon journals date back to the last years of Nauvoo, and many shed new light on these topics. I have only glanced at these resources for this essay. In addition, detective work is needed to locate papers or journals from non-Mormons. For example, no journal has been located for Thomas Sharp, and only a few of his letters have been located. There may also be primary documents still to be found and studied from Jacob Backenstos, members of the Quincy Committee, or other non-Mormons.

14

The Awesome Responsibility: Joseph Smith III and the Nauvoo Experience

ROGER D. LAUNIUS

For the inheritors of the legacy of early Mormonism, Nauvoo and the activities that took place there hold a special place. Of the more than fifty organizations arising out of Mormonism currently in operation, nearly all draw important lessons in the form of analogies about their church's organization, doctrine, and weltanschauung from the Nauvoo experience between 1839 and 1846.[1] Robert Bruce Flanders remarked in 1973 that "Utah began in Nauvoo, as did the 'dissenting' sects of Mormonism such as the Reorganized Church in a different way." He added that "Nauvoo was a volatile mixture of elements—American patriotism, immigrant dreams of the promised land, displaced-person desperation, religious mysticism and fanaticism, free experimentation with new social, ethical, and politico-economic modes, optimism, opportunism, energy—and escalating violence within and without."[2] Whether those lessons are positive or negative matters not; the compelling factor of seeking an order from the experience makes the issue worth exploring.[3]

An individual heading one of the factions of the church emerging after the death of the Mormon prophet on June 27, 1844, was Joseph Smith III, the eldest son of Mormonism's founder.[4] Although only a boy of eleven at the time of his father's death, by 1860 Smith had been ordained president of the Reorganized Church of Jesus Christ of Latter Day Saints, an organization composed of individuals of moderate Mormon tendencies and in time the second-largest faction of the splintered Mormon movement.[5] He presided over that church until his death in 1914, establishing it as a viable and positive force within the Christian mainstream. Smith grew to manhood in Nauvoo, he witnessed firsthand many of the events taking place there during his father's reign, and he drew important conclusions about the meaning of the Mormon stronghold on the Mississippi for the church's future development. These conclusions were applied in his presidential activities with the Reorganized Church and affected, perhaps fundamentally, the direction of that movement.[6]

It is the contention of this essay that the Nauvoo experience represented a conflicting set of ideals for Joseph Smith III. It was both a triumph and a tragedy, the lessons of which Smith applied throughout his career. He was attracted to the success and image of the city; it was the closest approximation the church had to the ideals of Zion carried in scripture and doctrine. The political power and secular authority also served Smith as reminders of the ultimate goal of the church, the merging of church and state into a benevolent theocratic democracy. At the same time, Smith was repelled by the darker side of political power —corruption, influence-peddling, and the difficulty of political choices. Much the same was true when considering the other aspects of the Nauvoo experience, such as the development of theology, the growth and development of church institutions and ecclesiastical quorums, some individuals' treatment of others both in terms of group loyalty and dissident elements, and the promotion of peace instead of the warrior mentality. Each of the reactions contributed to the formation of Smith's style of leadership in the Reorganized Church. While these factors were not the sole determinants of his method of presidential leadership, they were important ingredients in the development of Smith's approach to problems. In turn, Smith pushed the Reorganized Church along paths that partly reflected his reactions to the Nauvoo experience.[7]

One indicator of Joseph Smith III's reaction to the events of the Nauvoo years was his cautious and deliberate approach to community-building in the early Reorganization.[8] The establishment of what the Saints referred to as Zion had been the most persistent goal of the early Mormon movement. The early Latter Day Saints believed they were commissioned from among the world to help usher in the triumphal Second Coming of Christ and the advent of the millennial reign by building a community from which Christ could rule the world. Accordingly, during the 1830s and 1840s they had established Mormon communities to serve as utopian centers, places that were a refuge from a world of sin and where they could foster a new, righteous social order that would be ready for the return of the Lord. Settlements at Kirtland, Ohio, and Independence and Far West, Missouri, however, were less than successful and eventually dissolved in failure and disillusionment.[9]

The gathering Saints in Nauvoo followed on the heels of these earlier efforts with little change in approach except insofar as it related to the scale of the experiment. Indeed, Nauvoo represented the height of the church's standing in the secular world. In terms of size and importance, Nauvoo during the Mormon heyday was the epitome of the Mormon kingdom, the forerunner of the zionic/utopian mission of the church. Without question, the community was the fullest expression of the Mormon ideal of the literal kingdom of God with towns, organizations, and governments. It represented the most thorough model, thought the Saints, of what the millennium would be like.

Nauvoo, of course, met a fate similar to that of earlier Mormon communities because it was perceived, perhaps rightly, as a political, economic, and military threat to settlers in neighboring communities. Many reasons for this conclusion on the part of outsiders are apparent from a review of the records. One example should suffice. Benjamin F. Morris was the minister of the Congregational church in Warsaw, Illinois, during the early 1840s and offered this assessment of the Mormon situation in Hancock County on August 15, 1843:

> In regards to the County, the prospects for successful labor in the moral fields is indeed dark and forbidding enough. The frogs of egypt are utterly covering the whole land. The Mormons now have all the power, elect whom they please and have taken the entire government of the County into their own hands. This election they got all but one or two petty offices. They are still increasing and will do so. They are insolent, lawless, and unchecked. . . . The result of all this is to unsettle every thing pertaining to education and true religion. People are disposed to go out of the county as soon as they can. They are now under pretty high pressure of excitement, and I expect the scenes of Mo. to be acted over again.[10]

Eventually the non-Mormons of Hancock County rose up against the Saints in Nauvoo. In spite of the political, economic, and military might of the Mormons, less than a year after Morris's commentary their prophet had been killed, and by 1846 anti-Mormons had destroyed Nauvoo's viability as a church stronghold and forced its Mormon inhabitants to leave Hancock County.[11]

Joseph Smith III never directly commented on the failure of Nauvoo as a utopian experiment, but some of his statements alluded to his negative reaction to it. Moreover, his actions as president clearly demonstrated his use of the fate of Nauvoo as an analogy for later Reorganized Church policy concerning community-building endeavors. When Smith assumed leadership of the Reorganized Church, his followers believed that he would begin the long-anticipated regathering of the Saints for the building of another zionic community. But because of the young president's background, his perceptions of the movement's zionic mission, and his essentially practical nature, Smith disappointed most of his followers.

Although convinced that his father's basic approach to organizing utopian communities was correct, Smith realized that the early Mormons had tried to accomplish too much too quickly. He believed that neither the early church members nor the non-Mormons of Hancock County had been sufficiently prepared to overcome their fundamentally selfish human nature and accept an all-sharing utopian lifestyle: the Saints had lacked the mutual respect necessary for a communitarian society as well as the personal piety and desire for perfection crucial to the successful establishment of such a Christian utopia; non-Mormons did not understand the significance of such a society and mistook the theocratic-democratic ideal for pure political takeover.[12]

Joseph Smith III believed that the Reorganization's community-building effort should be more liberal and all-encompassing than it had been during the Nauvoo period. He maintained that the millennial kingdom of God could be initiated only through personal righteousness and moral perfection and would reach full fruition only if the righteous attacked evil in society at large. In contrast to the Nauvoo approach to Zion, which sought to *remove* the Saints from secular society, Smith's emphasis called for the church to be *involved* in the affairs of the world in the hope that it would assist in changing it. Young Joseph's belief that the Saints would purify themselves and become moral crusaders in the world therefore represented an alteration of his father's policies as implemented in Nauvoo. The logical conclusion of Joseph Smith III's philosophy was an emphasis on Zion's spiritual nature rather than its physical, community-building aspects.[13]

Smith summarized his basic approach to church-sponsored communities in an editorial in the Reorganization's newspaper, the *True Latter Day Saints' Herald,* in 1865: "The church should begin to take a high moral ground in regard to the very many abuses in society, which can only be reached, to correction, by a strong setting upon them of the current of public opinion."[14] Smith repeatedly stated, as in one of his earliest epistles to the Saints in November 1860, that he would deemphasize the gathering of the Saints into one community as had been done at Nauvoo. "There is no command to gather," he wrote, "at any given locality." Before any gathering could take place, he continued, "there are many obstacles to be met by us, which are to be overcome, not the least of which is . . . prejudice."[15] He counseled the Saints to live righteously wherever they resided and to serve as a force for good in their communities.[16]

Even as Smith was developing this approach to the issue of zionic community, partly in reaction to the analogy provided by the Nauvoo sojourn, his followers were pressing ever more passionately for the establishment of a church community. Smith parried these efforts for several years with arguments that the Saints were not morally prepared for the effort and that any such community-building experiment would end in failure, as had Nauvoo. "Strife and contention, with disobedience," he chided in 1868, "are sure fruit that the gospel, with great witness, had not wrought in us the work of peace, and without peace in our heart we predict that *no perfectness will come in Zion*." He claimed that only when the Saints cease "evil of any and every kind, become champions of truth, there will be no want of definite action or policy" in establishing a church community.[17]

About 1870 Smith acquiesced in the establishment of a religious community, where members of the Reorganized Church could practice their unique beliefs. He was never particularly excited by this effort and at best was involved to ensure that the effort did not go awry. Indicative of his caution and hesitancy in this effort, in contrast to his father's "God will provide regardless" approach in founding Nauvoo, were the much more tentative activities associated with the Order of Enoch and the founding of Lamoni, Iowa. The organization founding Lamoni was not officially sponsored by the church, it was a joint-stock company that shed most of the millennial overtones of earlier Mormon community efforts, and it established and managed the Lamoni experiment for more than ten years before Joseph Smith III moved there.

Smith, moreover, never viewed Lamoni as the penultimate in church zionic endeavors. At best, he understood it as a small step in the moral perfection of the Saints, an example to nonmembers, and a tiny experience in the attainment of understanding about the zionic mission of the church. The establishment of Zion, he believed, could be accomplished not in one fell swoop, as his father had attempted in Nauvoo, but in a series of halting steps aimed at spiritual development and proper relationships one with another. The effort would take years, perhaps even centuries, but the Saints should be content with small advances and not long for the spectacular. Nauvoo had failed because no one was prepared for its promise and they made too many mistakes. Too much hope had been attached to it. Smith did not allow the Reorganization to repeat the community-building mistakes of Nauvoo.[18]

Along similar lines, Smith considered two of the most important problems with the Nauvoo experiment of his father to be the church's involvement in political matters and military affairs. Although he undoubtedly understood that political involvement was inextricably related to the establishment of any church community, he sought to mitigate against any negative effects bloc voting and other partisan activities on the part of his followers might engender. Unlike his father, and principally because of the lessons of Nauvoo, Smith refused to endorse candidates, make political speeches for or against anything but accepted moral issues, and refrained from discussing political parties and candidates in any public forum. He wrote in the church newspaper in 1876 that "no subject is of less importance to the Saints than politics."[19] His approach was aimed at avoiding the needless excitement of the types of mobs that had killed his father and ruined the Nauvoo community. Seeking to demonstrate a bipartisan spirit and an apolitical posture, he emphasized caution. While not always successful, Smith nevertheless ensured that political questions did not excite outside interests to violence as they had in Nauvoo.[20]

Smith also drew lessons about military issues from his Nauvoo experiences. The early Mormons had created a massive militia known as the Nauvoo Legion, which had been most successful in terrifying other residents of Hancock County in the mid-1840s. Whether the Nauvoo Legion was a viable military organization is a moot question; that the Saints were serious about using it as a means of defending themselves and were diligent in training and equipping it cannot be denied. Thomas C. Sharp, editor of the Warsaw *Signal*, formed his first really negative impressions of the Saints when he was invited to Nauvoo on April 6, 1841, for the laying of the cornerstones of the Nauvoo Temple and the commemoration of the eleventh anniversary of the organization of the church. The military power exhibited on that occasion terrified Sharp, who went back to Warsaw with the impression that the Mormons were a warmongering horde that would decimate the county.[21]

As a small boy, Joseph Smith III participated in the children's unit of the Nauvoo Legion and enjoyed practicing martial tactics with wooden swords and toy rifles. At its height, there were some five hundred boys in this unit, and they were a prominent part of the public ceremonies of Mormon Nauvoo, leading parades and other festivities. Smith said that he benefited from the experience of participating in this unit but that some questioned the apparent love of war demonstrated by the prominent place of the Nauvoo Legion and its children's counterpart in Nauvoo.

Emma Smith, Joseph's mother, for one, opposed this militarism and encouraged her son to withdraw from the boys' troop. Joseph Smith III did so, acknowledging the suzerainty of his mother, but not without mixed feelings because of the friendships he had created in it. In later years, however, Smith came to understand his mother's concern, not just for himself but for the entire military aspect of Nauvoo society. "Looking back along the pathway," he wrote in his memoirs, "I feel it was a pity that such a [martial] spirit crept in among them, however, and a still greater one that the leading minds of the church partook of it."[22] He recognized that this approach was detrimental to the spiritual welfare of the Saints and to outsiders' perceptions of the church. He tried to maintain a flexibility on all issues relating to the military and to adopt a practical position that was both legitimate and responsive to the biblical dictum "Thou Shalt Not Kill."[23]

Joseph Smith III essentially rejected the standard Mormon idea of a political kingdom of God brought about by a unification of church and state in the here and now through the creation of a religious commonwealth. He stressed that whenever people of like mind gathered in one location, the potential for controversy increased. As the head of a small and not respected religious organization, Smith sought harmony and order. He recognized, as few others of his movement did, that unlike the portion of the church that followed Brigham Young to the refuge of the Great Basin, the Reorganized Church lived in the middle of the United States. It had to conform, to appear to outsiders to fit the accepted notions of what a Christian church should be. It had to do so to establish its own identity apart from the Utah Mormons and to ensure that it did not repeat the problems associated with Nauvoo and other Mormon communities.[24] The Utah Saints, ensconced in their Rocky Mountain hideaway, were able to defer an accommodation with the larger American society until the end of the nineteenth century.[25] Joseph Smith III had neither the opportunity nor the inclination to do likewise, and he rejected the patently secular aspects—the political, economic, and military power—of Mormon society as expressed in Nauvoo. The result was a moderate and much more accommodating social policy on the part of the Reorganization—a position that has remained to the present.[26]

From a theological perspective, the Reorganized Church under Joseph Smith III's leadership also essentially rejected the unique religious ideas that were developed and promulgated in Mormon Nauvoo. The theological thinking of the Mormon divines evolved between 1830 and 1844 from a doctrinal position of relative simplicity to one of incredible sophistication. The Nauvoo period was the most fertile time for the development of Joseph Smith Jr.'s doctrinal ideas; at least it was the time when his most esoteric speculations were publicly stated. During that era the unique ideas of eternity, the multiplicity of gods, the possibility of progression to godhood, celestial and plural marriage, baptism for the dead, and other temple endowments all came to fruition.[27] Some of these ideas were well outside the mainstream of American religious thought. A few of them were simply considered quaint by non-Mormons;

others, such as plural marriage, aroused volatile emotions and became rallying points for opposition to the movement.

Joseph Smith III questioned the validity of several doctrines arising from the Nauvoo experience. Essentially, Smith either denied that they had any place in the church, usually challenging the notion that they had ever been practiced in early Mormonism, or found a theological compatibility that allowed them to be adopted in principal but not in practice. During his presidency, Smith steered the Reorganization down a middle path that emulated the early Mormon movement's theology and policy accepted during the Kirtland era of the mid-1830s. He took a variety of approaches and a number of years to accomplish his task, but over a period of time, with the skill of a master politician, Smith directed the church into the formal adoption of his moderate doctrinal beliefs. Without question, he loathed the temple concept of the Mormons as developed in Nauvoo and sought to discourage the creation of a *temple cultus* in the Reorganization, although the impetus for one existed during his early presidency. He believed and publicly called temple endowment ceremonies "priestcraft" of the worst order. "I would not value going through the temple a dollar's worth," he wrote to L. L. Barth in 1893. "I cannot see anything sacred or divine in it." More than that, he thought that it had become an obsession in Nauvoo, distracting the members and detracting from the goals of the church.[28] It never became a part of the Reorganized Church.

Smith adopted a very cautious, long-term policy in dealing with doctrinal issues arising from Nauvoo. The manner in which he dealt with the doctrine of a plurality of gods is a case in point. It was both delicate and subtle, effective and harmonious. The Book of Abraham, supposedly translated from ancient Egyptian papyri by Joseph Smith Jr. and first published in Nauvoo in 1842, was accepted by several influential leaders in the early Reorganization as legitimate in its theological teachings, although it had no official status in the canon of scripture. The book very clearly taught the concept of a plurality of gods. According to that record, the gods formed a council presided over by a supreme Lord. This council "organized" the universe, placed human beings on the earth, and offered a plan of salvation that allowed them to become gods, provided they adhered to the proper ideals.[29]

While Smith refused to accept such doctrine as correct, he recognized that it had strong support from several of the church's leading officials. For instance, he was present in a Quorum of Twelve meeting in 1865 when the members of the quorum debated the issue and voted that they considered the doctrine scriptural. He succeeded, however, in having inserted into the meeting's minutes the statement that belief in the doctrine could not be considered a test of fellowship within the organization and demanded that it not be taught, except on rare occasions necessary to show the overall "plan of salvation."[30] As time passed, those rare occasions grew even rarer. Instead of inciting a heated doctrinal debate that would have been of long duration and unfathomable controversy within the movement, Smith waited out the proponents of the theory. Gradually, the church came around to the concept that he proposed—the more prevalent Christian view of God and the Godhead.[31]

Very early in the movement's history, Smith also moved the Reorganized Church to adopt an official position about baptism for the dead, an 1842 practice originated in Nauvoo by his father, which allowed for its eventual rejection. The policy Smith promoted viewed the doctrine as permissive. God had allowed its practice for a time in Nauvoo during the 1840s, but without additional divine guidance the Reorganized Church was not prepared to teach or practice the temple ritual. It was, in official church parlance, a doctrine of "local character" that had been directed by God to be practiced at a specific time and specific place under strict control of the church leadership. At a joint council of ruling quorums in May 1865, William Marks, the one man in the Reorganization to have been "in the know" concerning doctrinal ideas of the Nauvoo period, stated that the doctrine had originally been considered a permissive rite, to be practiced only under the most restricted conditions in a temple built especially for the purpose. Marks asserted that Joseph Smith Jr. "stopped the baptism for the dead" in Nauvoo, at least for a time, and Marks "did not believe it would be practiced any more until there was a fountain built in Zion or Jerusalem."[32] At the conclusion of this meeting, the joint council affirmed a cautious policy, resolving "that it is proper to teach the doctrine of baptism for the dead when it is necessary to do so in order to show the completeness of the plan of salvation, but wisdom dictates that the way should be prepared by the preaching of the first principles."[33]

Perhaps the clearest expression of the Reorganized Church's position on baptism for the dead can be seen in a *True Latter Day Saints' Herald* editorial written by Joseph Smith III in 1874:

> For the Doctrine of Baptism for the Dead, we have only this to write; it was by permission, as we learn from the history, performed in the river until the font should be prepared. The font and the temple which covered it are gone, not a stone remains unturned, the stranger cultivates the soil over the places where the corner stones were laid; and when memory paints in respondent hues the rising light of the glorious doctrine, the mind should also remember how sadly sombre and dark are the clouds lying heavily over the horizon where this

light was quenched; "You shall be rejected with your dead, saith the lord your God."

The practice of "Baptizing for the Dead" was made a part of the practice of the Church only after years of suffering and toil; was not taught nor practiced until a place of rest was supposed to have been found; does not add to, nor diminish the promises made to the believer in the gospel proclamation; and while it was permitted, was of so particular form in its observance, that a settled place, and only one, was essential to the keeping of the records of baptism. . . .

Baptism for the dead is not commanded in the gospel; it is at best only permitted, was so by special permission, and we presume that should we ultimately prove worthy, it may be again permitted. . . .

In conclusion on this subject, let those who are most anxious for the reinstating of the doctrine and practice of baptism for the dead remember, that there is but little of direct scriptural proof that can be adduced in support of the doctrine; and that left mainly to the direct institution of it among the Saints, we must be fully prepared to meet all the consequences attendant upon its introduction, or we shall rue the mooting of the subject.[34]

Smith went on to say that the Saints should live justly and not concern themselves with such practices as baptism for the dead until God directed them.

Smith was even more forceful in his personal writings. He wrote to Alfred Ward in May 1880 that "baptism for the dead, temple building, and gathering are not rejected; and what you may see laying on the shelf, remains to be seen." He commented, however, that baptism for the dead was at best a permissive doctrine that might or might not be practiced again. In a similar manner, he told Job Brown in 1886 that he believed in the principle of universal salvation and that baptism for the dead was one means of achieving it, "but [I] do not teach it; having as I understand it no command to do so."[35]

Joseph Smith's opposition to Mormon plural marriage has been well documented, and he spent a lifetime trying unsuccessfully to clear his father's name of any connection with its origination. At his inaugural address, given when he accepted leadership of the Reorganized Church on April 6, 1860, Smith encapsulated most of his central ideas on the subject. He denounced the practice of plural marriage that had been adopted by Brigham Young's movement as well as by some other Mormon-oriented organizations. He declared unequivocally that those involved in it were doing so without divine authority. Indeed, God explicitly opposed these practices, Smith concluded. He added that some had charged his father with teaching and practicing plural marriage but that did not square with what he remembered of his father, and he always denied that the practice had been introduced by Joseph Smith, the Mormon prophet, and practiced with official church sanction.[36]

Smith's rejection of plural marriage led him to adopt a missionary policy aimed at correcting what he perceived as the errors introduced into the church by Brigham Young and his associates and to call those who had followed them to repent and to return to a more reasonable Mormon religious vision. Smith inaugurated a vigorous missionary program to "rescue" those Latter-day Saints enmeshed in what the Reorganized Church believed were the "evil practices" Young began in Nauvoo. Simplistically, he believed that all the Reorganized Church had to do to redeem these people was to offer an alternative, pointing out the errors of plural marriage.[37] Smith sent the first Reorganization mission to Utah in 1863 with the express mission of teaching "orthodox Mormonism."[38] Thereafter, the Reorganization maintained a missionary effort in Utah for the purpose of showing the errors of Young and the apostles on plural marriage. These efforts, much to the chagrin of the Reorganization's leadership, were not particularly effective.[39]

Joseph Smith III also became involved in the political antipolygamy crusade in the latter decades of the nineteenth century. He was a vocal advocate of legislation to prohibit plural marriage, and, as the son of the Mormon prophet, he held a special place in the effort. At one point in the early 1880s Smith was even considered a serious contender for appointment to territorial governor of Utah because he would enforce enthusiastically the antipolygamy laws. When the Utah Mormon leader, Wilford Woodruff, announced in 1890 that the church would no longer countenance the performance of plural marriages, Smith was overjoyed. It was for him a vindication of his efforts since becoming the president of the Reorganized Church in 1860.[40] In recent years, Reorganized Church historians have seriously investigated this issue and have found there is ample reason to believe Joseph Smith III was wrong in seeking to establish his father's innocence in the practice of plural marriage. Few would now dispute that polygamy was practiced during the lifetime of Joseph Smith Jr. or would challenge the contention that he had originated it.[41]

If Joseph Smith III inherited from the early Latter Day Saint movement in Nauvoo a unique set of sometimes confusing and often controversial theological ideas, he also embraced some theological conceptions that continued to be a part of the church in the era. In addition to the cherished conceptions of mainstream Christianity, Smith emphasized four basic doctrinal conceptions. The first was his forceful belief in the divine nature of the Book of Mormon. It was, for Smith, nothing more or less than the religious *history* of the inhabitants of ancient America.

Second, Smith accepted the role of prophets and divine revelation throughout the ages. He ranked himself and his father with the biblical prophets. The third fundamental for Smith was a firm belief that Jesus Christ would return to earth and usher in the millennial reign and that the Latter Day Saints must work to make the world ready for that Second Coming. Finally, Smith believed that the Reorganized Church must remain true to the legitimate ideals of the early Mormon church and that he specifically had been called by God for the special purpose of teaching the essential elements of the Restoration.

To ensure that these ideals remained at the epicenter of the Reorganized Church's existence in the nineteenth century, Joseph Smith III used the organization's general conferences, another legacy from the early Mormon experience. He made these conferences the most important policy-making bodies of the church, meeting twice annually during the first part of the prophet's career and annually thereafter, and in every case he ensured that the Saints were heard on all matters relating to church government. A remarkable set of resolutions arising out of these conferences, some 725 by the time of Smith's death in 1914, dealt with all manner of issues, many of them doctrinal. Through this process, as well as his reliance on revelation (something else inherited from the earlier era), Smith guided the Reorganized Church into a place somewhere between the radicalism of Utah Mormonism and the conservatism of traditional American Protestantism. Joseph Smith III was remarkably successful in orienting the Reorganization along lines that were, to use the apt phrase of Clare D. Vlahos, both "reasonable to gentiles and legitimate to Mormons."[42] Although it could not be both in all instances, the Reorganization by the end of Smith's presidency was a movement that rested somewhere in the middle, neither Protestant nor Mormon but with enough ingredients of both to be marginally acceptable as a distant cousin to each.

One final point regarding Smith's reaction to the Nauvoo experience. Smith was by temperament and inclination a person who took a legalistic perspective on issues. This approach held the potential for him to draw power to himself and to wield it arbitrarily, as his father had done, especially in Nauvoo. Joseph Smith III trained himself to be patient and tolerant and to make practical decisions based on solid evidence. He exercised care and restraint throughout his presidential career in dealing with individuals and rendering decisions affecting his religious movement. He was always open to the opinions of others, although he understood and accepted responsibility for his own actions.[43] Richard P. Howard correctly observed that "this notable blend of courage and humility enabled Joseph III to promote the policy of 'an open pulpit' wherever the RLDS church existed." In both a figurative and literal sense, the open pulpit ideal served the Reorganized Church well in allowing it to take a place in the American Christian community.[44]

While other factors certainly contributed, Joseph Smith III took this approach partly because of his remembrance of Nauvoo and the events that had taken place there. He associated those unique doctrinal developments with negative images. Probably they also rested somewhat on his reactions to the events in Nauvoo immediately after the death of his father in 1844. Brigham Young and Smith's mother represented opposing positions on these doctrinal issues. Young embraced Joseph Smith Jr.'s unique theological speculations and incorporated them into the Mormon movement that settled in Utah. Emma Smith never fully accepted them, especially plural marriage, even if she occasionally participated in some of the rituals associated with them while her husband was still alive.[45]

After Joseph Smith Jr.'s murder, the two clashed over several issues, one of them the doctrinal direction of the church. A battle of wits ensued, and the Smith family, at least in its collective remembrance, suffered enormously at the hands of Brigham Young and his associates. Because of the negative connotations Joseph Smith III associated with this episode in Nauvoo, because Young and his followers were proponents of these doctrinal ideas, and because his mother taught him the horrors of these conceptions, the reaction of the Reorganized Church prophet could be predicted.[46] Much the same can be argued for Smith's reaction to the Nauvoo issues associated with secular authority and the use of ecclesiastical power. I do not want to make too much of this, but interpreting Smith's basic approach to the Nauvoo experience as a reaction against Brigham Young and his leadership style after June 1844 offers intriguing possibilities. This is only a preliminary assessment, and much additional research remains to be conducted before any authoritative assessment can be rendered.[47]

Even so, it seems likely that many of the themes of Joseph Smith III's career were born out of the images of the Nauvoo experience, most of which were negative. Smith guided, by both principle and practicality, the direction of the Reorganization's missionary activities, its ministerial and administrative functions, and its organizational apparatus in a way that was both reasonable and farsighted for more than fifty years. Joseph Smith III forged a dynamic, moderate, and active organization that always viewed the earlier activities in Nauvoo with skepticism.

Most of the themes present in Smith's presidential career have some background in the Nauvoo he remembered from the 1840s. He reaffirmed many of them throughout the rest of his life. His inaugural address, given when he accepted leadership of the Reorganized Church on April 6, 1860, encapsulated most of the central ideas of his presidency and the attitudes he had adopted from his youthful experiences.[48] On that occasion Smith explained his position and beliefs regarding the gospel. "I believe in the doctrine of honesty and truth," he said. "The Bible contains such truth, and so do the Book of Mormon and the Book of Covenants, which are auxiliaries to the Bible." He embraced moderate Mormon ideas and rejected those that aimed at a powerful theocracy.

Smith also denied the temporal nature of Nauvoo as a community by reaffirming his commitment to the government of the United States and contending that the church was subservient to civil authority. There can be no antagonism between the two, he continued, no attempts to supplant civil with religious authority. He explicitly commented on his commitment to legal institutions, both civil and spiritual.[49] This framework of legalism guided Smith in every decision, enabling him to separate, as least in his own mind, right from wrong. It structured his principles and guided his actions. He also demonstrated in his inaugural address a strong commitment to the principles of the Restoration gospel as he understood them based on his background and understanding. Furthermore, he developed a remarkable humility, forbearance, and tolerance of others, tempering his legalistic frame of reference.

With issues of all types, Smith carefully considered the ramifications and took actions that could be considered compromises in the many cases. Almost instinctively, Smith inclined to a middle-of-the-road position on issues. He was willing to listen to alternative positions and did not assume that he was necessarily right on every issue. This was a learned trait, however, and Smith's leniency toward other positions had limits. Smith's responses recognized that if the Reorganized Church was to accomplish anything of worth, it had to unify and focus its efforts along a concentrated path. To do so required enough centralized direction for the system to function with a degree of efficiency. Tolerance and sympathy could be accepted, even demanded, but when they significantly impinged on the accomplishment of church objectives, then they had to be curtailed. He expressed this basic belief about limited freedom in a letter to Jason W. Briggs in 1877: "I assume no right to dictate, but have supposed from the action of all the conferences since 1852, that if a matter was decided by the plain teaching of the books it was settled for all members of the Church. If this is not correct, nothing is gained by organization, for the word alone means nothing. However, I am a man for free speech and free inquiry, howbeit, he who mistakes *belief* for liberty will have a hard row to hoe."[50] If this was not clear enough, Smith wrote around the same time to the president of Briggs's quorum about what was required of members. "I acknowledge the 'right of conscience' and I believe in its exercise," he commented, "but to allow that to dictate to, and dominate the rights of fellowship and ignore the bonds of Association, I cannot." Then he offered the clincher, which stated what he thought should happen to persistent malcontents: "If a man wants to retain and exercise *all* his individual rights, let him get by himself, where his elbows and knees will not hurt his neighbors."[51] Smith understood very well that the Saints had to give up some liberty for the sake of the movement's larger goals.

This measured response he first began to appreciate because of his experiences in Nauvoo. Smith rejected the Nauvoo experience's excessive use of authority to control others in the community but still understood the need to ensure that some commonality of belief and practice existed. Such a leadership style was critical to the continued success of what had begun as a loosely organized, extremely heterogeneous movement started by strikingly nonconformist dissenters of the early Mormon church. As an ingredient in the manner in which Joseph Smith III conducted his presidential office in the Reorganized Church between 1860 and 1914, his reaction to the development of the church during the earlier Nauvoo sojourn cannot be overlooked.

Notes

An earlier version of this essay appeared in *Western Illinois Regional Studies* 11 (Fall 1988): 54–68.

1. The principal book-length study on Mormon Nauvoo is Robert Bruce Flanders, *Nauvoo: Kingdom on the Mississippi* (Urbana: University of Illinois Press, 1965).

2. Robert Bruce Flanders, "Dream and Nightmare: Nauvoo Revisited," in *The Restoration Movement: Essays in Mormon History*, ed. F. Mark McKiernan, Alma R. Blair, and Paul M. Edwards (Lawrence, Kan.: Coronado Press, 1973), 145, 165.

3. An excellent source discussing the uses of history in drawing analogies and lessons is Richard E. Neustadt and Ernest R. May, *Thinking in Time: The Uses of History for Decision Makers* (New York: Free Press, 1986).

4. For information on the life of Joseph Smith III, see Roger D. Launius, *Joseph Smith III: Pragmatic Prophet* (Urbana: University of Illinois Press, 1988).

5. The moderate nature of the Reorganization is explained in Alma R. Blair, "The Reorganized Church of Jesus Christ of Latter Day Saints: Moderate Mormons," in *The Restoration Movement*, ed. McKiernan, Blair, and Edwards, 207–30.

6. The effect of childhood experiences on the actions of adults has been discussed and debated for half a century with little consensus. A strong

school of historiography has emerged that presents compelling arguments for believing past events significantly affect adult actions. For discussions of this issue, see Lloyd deMause, ed., *The New Psychohistory* (New York: Psychohistory Press, 1975); Peter Gay, *Freud for Historians* (New York: Oxford University Press, 1985); Phyllis Greenacre, *The Quest for a Father: A Study of the Darwin-Butler Controversy, as a Contribution to the Understanding of the Creative Individual* (New York: Harper and Row, 1963); George M. Kren and Leon H. Rappoport, eds., *Varieties of Psychohistory* (New York: Spring Publishing, 1976); William L. Langer, "The Next Assignment," *American Historical Review* 63 (January 1958): 283–304; Howard Dwight Lasswell, *Power and Personality* (New York: W. W. Norton, 1948); and Benjamin B. Wolman, ed., *The Psychological Interpretation of History* (New York: Basic Books, 1971). One should also see the pathbreaking *History of Childhood Quarterly: The Journal of Psychohistory* as the best means of gaining a feel for the scholarly output of the field.

7. Many of the ideas in this essay have been presented in earlier work, including Blair, "Reorganized Church of Jesus Christ of Latter Day Saints," 205–30; Richard P. Howard, "The Reorganized Church in Illinois, 1852–1882: Search for Identity," *Dialogue: A Journal of Mormon Thought* 5 (Spring 1970): 63–75; W. Grant McMurray, "The Reorganization in Nineteenth-Century America: Identity Crisis of Historiographical Problem," *John Whitmer Historical Association Journal* 2 (1982): 3–11; and Richard P. Howard, "The Emerging RLDS Identity," in *Restoration Studies III,* ed. Maurice L. Draper (Independence, Mo.: Herald Publishing House, 1986), 44–53.

8. For a discussion of Smith's community-building ideas, see Launius, *Joseph Smith III,* 168–89.

9. The best published analysis of Mormonism's zionic commitment is Leonard J. Arrington, Feramorz Y. Fox, and Dean L. May, *Building the City of God: Community and Cooperation among the Mormons,* 2d ed. (Urbana: University of Illinois Press, 1992).

10. Quoted in Roger D. Launius, ed., "American Home Missionary Society Letters and Mormon Nauvoo: Selected Letters," *Western Illinois Regional Studies* 8 (Spring 1985): 26.

11. For an analysis of this development, see Annette P. Hampshire, "The Triumph of Mobocracy in Hancock County, 1844–1846," *Western Illinois Regional Studies* 5 (Fall 1982): 17–35.

12. Joseph Smith III to J. J. Pressley, March 31, 1880, Joseph Smith III Letterbook #3, Library-Archives, Reorganized Church of Jesus Christ of Latter Day Saints, Independence, Mo. (hereafter RLDS Library-Archives); "The Location of Zion," *True Latter Day Saints' Herald* (Cincinnati, Ohio) 3 (October 1862): 74; "Questions and Answers," *Saints' Herald* (Lamoni, Iowa) 38 (September 26, 1891): 616.

13. Joseph Smith III to Alfred Hart, May 9, 1880, Joseph Smith III Letterbook #3; Joseph Smith III to William H. Kelley, March 22, 1871, William H. Kelley Papers, RLDS Library-Archives.

14. *True Latter Day Saints' Herald* (Plano, Ill.) 8 (September 1, 1865): 67.

15. Joseph Smith III, "An Address to the Saints," *True Latter Day Saints' Herald* 1 (November 1860): 254–56.

16. This whole approach to the communal aspects of early Mormonism was anticipated by William Marks in 1839 when a church conference debated the establishment of Nauvoo as a gathering point. Marks commented that "from the circumstances of being driven from the other places, he almost was led to the conclusion that it was not wisdom that we should not do so" (Joseph Smith, *History of the Church of Jesus Christ of Latter-day Saints,* ed. B. H. Roberts [Salt Lake City: Deseret News Press, 1902–12; 6 vols., a seventh volume was published in 1932; reprinted by Deseret Book, 1976, and reissued in paperback in 1978], 3:260). Marks, of course, was an early member of the Reorganized Church and served as Joseph Smith III's counselor in the First Presidency between 1863 and his death in 1872.

17. Joseph Smith III, "Pleasant Chat," *True Latter Day Saints' Herald* 13 (June 1, 1868): 168–69.

18. Roger D. Launius, "The Mormon Quest for a Perfect Society at Lamoni, Iowa, 1870–1890," *Annals of Iowa* 47 (Spring 1984): 325–42.

19. Joseph Smith III, "Editorial," *True Latter Day Saints' Herald* 23 (November 15, 1876): 262.

20. The difficulties associated with avoiding secular issues once a church community has started are analyzed in Alma R. Blair, "A Loss of Nerve," *Courage: A Journal of History, Thought, and Action* 1 (September 1970): 29–36. Blair argued persuasively "that although the early Reorganized Latter Day Saints were not always conscious of it, and would certainly have denied it, they were in fact a very 'political' group. The reason they were is simple: Certain values they held important enough to act on were also of concern to others outside the church" (34).

21. Norton Jacobs, "Record of Norton Jacobs," April 6, 1841, Mormon Collection, Huntington Library, San Marino, Calif.; Donna Hill, *Joseph Smith: The First Mormon* (Garden City, N.Y.: Doubleday, 1977), 288–89.

22. Joseph Smith III, "The Memoirs of President Joseph Smith (1832–1914)," *Saints' Herald* 82 (January 1, 1935): 15–16. See also Ebenezer Robinson, "Items of Personal History of the Editor," *The Return* (Davis City, Iowa) 2 (February 1890): 210–11.

23. Launius, *Joseph Smith III,* 134–35.

24. This approach has been convincingly explained in Claire D. Vlahos, "Images of Orthodoxy: Self-Identity in Early Reorganization Apologetics," in *Restoration Studies I,* ed. Maurice L. Draper (Independence, Mo.: Herald Publishing House, 1980), 176–86.

25. Klaus J. Hansen, "Mormonism and American Culture: Some Tentative Hypotheses," in *The Restoration Movement,* ed. McKiernan, Blair, and Edwards, 1–25, especially 2–3; Thomas G. Alexander, *Mormonism in Transition: A History of the Latter-day Saints, 1890–1930* (Urbana: University of Illinois Press, 1986).

26. The mainstream approach of the Reorganized Church down to the present can be glimpsed by reviewing such representative books as Peter Judd and A. Bruce Lindgren, *Introduction to the Saints Church* (Independence, Mo.: Herald Publishing House, 1976); and Clifford A. Cole and Peter Judd, *Distinctives: Yesterday and Today* (Independence, Mo.: Herald Publishing House, 1984).

27. The literature on many of the theological developments in Nauvoo is extensive. For general introductions, see T. Edgar Lyon, "Doctrinal Development of the Church during the Nauvoo Sojourn, 1839–1846," *Brigham Young University Studies* 15 (Summer 1975): 435–46; Marvin S. Hill, "Mormon Religion in Nauvoo: Some Reflections," *Utah Historical Quarterly* 44 (Spring 1976): 170–80; and Larry C. Porter and Milton V. Backman Jr., "Doctrine and the Temple in Nauvoo," *Brigham Young University Studies* 32 (Winter/Spring 1992): 41–56.

28. Joseph Smith III to L. L. Barth, May 26, 1893, Joseph Smith III Letterbook #4, RLDS Library-Archives.

29. "The Book of Abraham," *Times and Seasons* (Nauvoo, Ill.) 3 (March 15, 1842): 720–22. The development of the Book of Abraham within the Reorganized Church has been documented in Richard P. Howard, "Joseph Smith, the Book of Abraham, and the Reorganized Church in the 1970s," in *A Decade of the Best: The Elbert A. Smith Award Winning Articles* (Independence, Mo.: Herald Publishing House, 1972), 186–211.

30. Quorum of Twelve Minutes, May 2–5, 1865, 12, RLDS Library-Archives.

31. Numerous instances of Smith's position on the Godhead can be found in Joseph Smith III to J. Jeremiah, September 8, 1877, Joseph Smith III Letterbook #1, RLDS Library-Archives; Joseph Smith III to Othilla Grabske, February 10, 1904, and Joseph Smith III to J. W. Peterson, June 10, 1902, both in Miscellaneous Letters and Papers, RLDS Library-Archives; and Joseph Smith III, "The Memoirs of President Joseph Smith (1832–1914)," *Saints' Herald* 82 (23 April 1935): 527.

32. Council of Twelve Minutes, May 2–5, 1865, 12.

33. Council of Twelve Resolutions, May 5, 1865, 3, RLDS Library-Archives.

34. "Editorial," *True Latter Day Saints' Herald* 21 (July 15, 1874): 434.

35. Joseph Smith III to Alfred Ward, May 9, 1880, Joseph Smith Letterbook #3; Joseph Smith III to Job Brown, January 5, 1886, Joseph Smith III Letterbook #4.

36. The speech of Joseph Smith III is most conveniently available in Joseph Smith III and Heman C. Smith, *The History of the Reorganized Church of Jesus Christ of Latter Day Saints,* 4 vols. (Lamoni, Iowa: Herald Publishing House, 1896–1911), 3:247–50. I have verified it against the original publication appearing in the *New York Times,* April 11, 1860.

37. Joseph Smith III to Caleb Parker, August 14, 1895, Joseph Smith III Letterbook #6, RLDS Library-Archives; Samuel H. B. Smith to George A. Smith, July 10, 1860, George A. Smith Papers, Special Collections, Harold B. Lee Library, Brigham Young University, Provo, Utah. See also Charles W.

Turner, "Joseph Smith III and the Mormons of Utah" (Ph.D. diss., Graduate Theological Union, 1985).

38. "News from Utah," *True Latter Day Saints' Herald* 2 (June 1861): 92–93; Joseph Smith III, "The First General Epistle of the President of the Reorganized Church of Jesus Christ of Latter Day Saints, to All the Scattered Saints," *True Latter Day Saints' Herald* 2 (August 1861): 121–24.

39. Space prevents a full recitation of this effort. For a fuller discussion, see Launius, *Joseph Smith III,* 218–46; and Richard Lyle Shipley, "Voices of Dissent: The History of the Reorganized Church of Jesus Christ of Latter Day Saints in Utah, 1863–1900" (M.A. thesis, Utah State University, 1969).

40. Launius, *Joseph Smith III,* 247–72; Roger D. Launius, "Politicking against Polygamy: Joseph Smith III, the Reorganized Church, and the Politics of the Antipolygamy Crusade, 1860–1890," *John Whitmer Historical Association Journal* 7 (1987): 35–44; Roger D. Launius, "Methods and Motives: Joseph Smith III's Opposition to Polygamy, 1860–90," *Dialogue: A Journal of Mormon Thought* 20 (Winter 1987): 105–21.

41. For outstanding analyses of this subject, see Alma R. Blair, "RLDS Views of Polygamy: Some Historiographical Notes," *John Whitmer Historical Association Journal* 5 (1985): 16–28; and Richard P. Howard, "The Changing RLDS Response to Mormon Polygamy: A Preliminary Analysis," *John Whitmer Historical Association Journal* 3 (1983): 14–29.

42. See the seminal essay by Vlahos, "Images of Orthodoxy," 176.

43. This aspect of Smith's character is ably discussed in Claire D. Vlahos, "Moderation as a Theological Principle in the Thought of Joseph Smith III," *John Whitmer Historical Association Journal* 1 (1981): 3–11.

44. Howard, "Emerging RLDS Identity," 50.

45. For discussions of Emma Smith's response to theological developments in Nauvoo, see Linda King Newell and Valeen Tippetts Avery, *Mormon Enigma: Emma Hale Smith,* 2d ed. (Urbana: University of Illinois Press, 1994); Linda King Newell, "Emma Hale Smith and the Polygamy Question," *John Whitmer Historical Association Journal* 4 (1984): 3–15; and Maureen Ursenbach Beecher, Linda King Newell, and Valeen Tippetts Avery, "Emma, Eliza, and Stairs: An Investigation," *Brigham Young University Studies* 20 (Winter 1980): 51–62.

46. A discussion of this period can be found in Roger D. Launius, "Joseph Smith III and the Mormon Succession Crisis, 1844–1846," *Western Illinois Regional Studies* 6 (Spring 1983): 5–22. The general relationship between Emma Smith and Brigham Young is deftly analyzed in Linda King Newell and Valeen Tippetts Avery, "The Lion and the Lady: Brigham Young and Emma Smith," *Utah Historical Quarterly* 48 (Winter 1980): 81–97.

47. Perhaps I have made too much of the Nauvoo experience's effect on Joseph Smith III's presidency of the Reorganization. Clearly, there were other compelling factors that contributed to his background and to the direction of the movement. His mother and his friends and his colleagues in the church, some of whom shared the Nauvoo experiences with him,

clearly affected his outlook. The coincidence of geographical location and membership ideals also informed the direction of the Reorganization, as did the direction of the Mormon movement of the Great Basin itself. A careful reading of the documentation, however, convinces me that Smith, although a boy in his formative years, was fundamentally affected by his recollections of Nauvoo. He used the Nauvoo experience as an analogy many times in formulating policy. The elucidation of exactly how each of these factors contributed to Smith's policies I gladly leave to others.

48. Smith and Smith, *History of the Reorganized Church*, 3:247–50.

49. Joseph Smith III, Jason W. Briggs, and W. W. Blair, "The Declaration of Loyalty to the Government of the United States, by the Church of Jesus Christ of Latter Day Saints," *True Latter Days Saints' Herald* 3 (May 1863): 201–202; Joseph Smith III et al., "Memorial to Congress from a Committee of the Reorganized Church of Jesus Christ of Latter Day Saints, on the Claims and Faith of the Church," *True Latter Day Saints' Herald* 17 (April 1870): 321–27.

50. Joseph Smith III to Jason W. Briggs, January 22, 1877, Joseph Smith III Letterbook #1.

51. Joseph Smith III to William H. Kelley, January 22, 1880, William H. Kelley Papers.

Bibliographical Essay

ROGER D. LAUNIUS AND
JOHN E. HALLWAS

This essay mentions some of the more significant secondary materials available for anyone seeking information on the Mormon church in Illinois during the 1840s. Without question, the "new Mormon history," a descriptive term with a multitude of meanings and a divergent set of practitioners, has rejuvenated the study of the Mormon past and made it possible for scholars to explore church history free from the "polemics designed as either attacks on or defense of the Mormon movement" (Paul M. Edwards, "The New Mormon History," *Saints Herald* 133 [November 1986]: 13). Not all Mormon scholars have achieved a functional objectivity in their writing, but clearly many are striving in that direction.

For anyone entering into a study of the Mormon experience in Hancock County, there are several general studies that are good starting points. The best introduction to the Mormon experience in Nauvoo remains Robert Bruce Flanders, *Nauvoo: Kingdom on the Mississippi* (Urbana: University of Illinois Press, 1965), although it is now more than thirty years old. Flanders applies many of the themes found elsewhere in Jacksonian American urban history to the Mormon stronghold and emphasizes its political and economic development. In the process, he depicts in bold relief the details of the city's development. David E. Miller and Della S. Miller, *Nauvoo: The City of Joseph* (Santa Barbara, Calif.: Peregrine Smith, 1974), is a much less satisfactory narrative survey, but it does try to explain the social and religious development of the city. It also contains useful sections on land transactions and the operation of city government during its Mormon period but deemphasizes the political conflict between the Mormons and their neighbors. Both of these works represent a "middle ground" of historical inquiry, but *Nauvoo: The City of Joseph* is decidedly defensive in tone. Finally, Samuel W. Taylor,

Nightfall at Nauvoo (New York: Macmillan, 1971), while a historical work that employs fictional techniques, contains many insights that should be pondered by serious students of Mormonism and the conflict in Illinois. Glen M. Leonard is working on a new synthesis of the Nauvoo experience. A glimpse of the major themes to be explored in it are highlighted in Glen M. Leonard and T. Edgar Lyon, "The Nauvoo Years," *Ensign* 9 (September 1979): 10–15.

Several older works also deal with the crisis in a defensive manner, while fostering the myths of Mormon innocence and religious persecution. Joseph Smith, *The History of the Church of Jesus Christ of Latter-day Saints,* ed. B. H. Roberts (Salt Lake City: Deseret News Press, 1902–12; 6 vols., a seventh volume was published in 1932; reprinted by Deseret Book, 1976, and reissued in paperback in 1978), contains a wealth of primary source materials but must be used with caution since it takes a decidedly apologetic approach to documenting the history of the church. Useful in determining the weaknesses of this work are Dean C. Jessee, "The Reliability of Joseph Smith's History," *Journal of Mormon History* 3 (1976): 23–46; and Dean C. Jessee, "The Writing of Joseph Smith's History," *Brigham Young University Studies* 11 (Spring 1971): 439–73. Synthesizing works are B. H. Roberts, *The Rise and Fall of Nauvoo* (Salt Lake City: Bookcraft, 1900; reprint, 1965); E. Cecil McGavin, *Nauvoo the Beautiful* (Salt Lake City: Stevens and Wallis, 1946); Mabel A. Sanford, *Joseph's City Beautiful: A Story of "Old Nauvoo"* (Independence, Mo.: Herald Publishing House, 1939); and Elbert A. Smith, *Timbers for the Temple: A Story of Old Nauvoo in the Days of Her Glory* (Independence, Mo.: Herald Publishing House, 1922), all of which are sympathetic and sentimental treatments.

For non-Mormon perspectives, see Thomas Gregg, *The History of Hancock County, Illinois* (Chicago: Charles C. Chapman, 1880); Thomas Ford, *History of Illinois: From Its Commencement as a State in 1818 to 1847* (Chicago: S. C. Griggs, 1854; reissued with annotations and introduction by Rodney O. Davis and bibliographical notes by Terence A. Tanner, Urbana: University of Illinois Press, 1995); Alexander Davidson and Bernard Stuve, *Complete History of Illinois from 1673–1884* (Springfield: Illinois Journal, 1884); Adelaide Albers, Virginia Van Pappelendam, and Marie Worth, *History of Warsaw* (Warsaw, Ill.: Warsaw Bulletin, 1960); Newton Bateman, J. Seymour Curvey, and Paul H. Selby, eds., *Historical Encyclopedia of Illinois and History of Hancock County,* 2 vols. (Chicago: Munsell Publishing, 1921); Harry M. Beardsley, "The Mormons in Illinois," in *Transactions of the Illinois State Historical Society for the Year 1933,* Illinois State Historical Library Publication, no. 40 (Springfield: Illinois State Historical Society, n.d.), 45–54; Orville F. Berry, "The Mormon Settle-

ment in Illinois," in *Transactions of the Illinois State Historical Society for the Year 1906,* Illinois State Historical Library Publication, no. 11 (Springfield: Illinois State Historical Society, 1906), 88–102; Clyde E. Buckingham, "Mormonism in Illinois," *Journal of the Illinois State Historical Society* 32 (June 1939): 173–92; *History of Hancock County, Illinois* (Carthage, Ill.: Board of Supervisors of Hancock County, 1968); W. Gerard Huslamp, "The Mormon Colony at Nauvoo, Illinois, *Journal of the West* 2 (October 1963): 470–90; Thomas Rees, "Nauvoo, Illinois, under Mormon and Icarian Occupation," *Journal of the Illinois State Historical Society* 21 (January 1929): 506–24; and John E. Hallwas, *Western Illinois Heritage* (Macomb: Illinois Heritage Press, 1983).

For perceptive reviews of the general literature on Mormon Nauvoo, see Richard D. Poll, "Nauvoo and the New Mormon History: A Bibliographical Survey," *Journal of Mormon History* 5 (1978): 105–23; and Glen M. Leonard, "Recent Writing on Mormon Nauvoo," *Western Illinois Regional Studies* 11 (Fall 1988): 69–93. A useful formal bibliography can be found in Richard Neitzel Holzapfel and T. Jeffery Cottle, *Old Mormon Nauvoo, 1839–1846: Historic Photographs and Guide* (Provo, Utah: Grandin Books, 1990), 237–53.

Two general histories of early Mormonism offer intriguing possibilities for interpreting Mormonism in Illinois. Marvin S. Hill's *Quest for Refuge: The Mormon Flight from American Pluralism* (Salt Lake City: Signature Books, 1989) describes the early Saints as generally destitute and the social and economic policies of the church they embraced as radical, in part because there was little for the Saints to lose in a complete restructuring of society. In an environment where the major values of society were not accepted by a people, conflict was virtually inevitable, and Hill traces this as far as the removal of the Saints from the settled parts of the United States and their retreat to the Great Basin, where their accommodation to the American mainstream was not immediately required. Kenneth H. Winn's *Exiles in a Land of Liberty: Mormons in America, 1830–1846* (Chapel Hill: University of North Carolina Press, 1989) carries some of these same ideas into a study of the use of rhetoric and the theme of "republicanism" in Jacksonian America. Both add significantly to an understanding of Mormon warfare with the larger American society.

The most thorough study of the Illinois frontier environment of Nauvoo is still Theodore Calvin Pease, *The Centennial History of Illinois,* vol. 2, *The Frontier State, 1818–1848* (Chicago: A. C. McClurg, 1919), which includes the chapter "The Mormon War," 340–62. The book also has chapters on important contextual matters, including "The Rise of Jacksonian Democracy," 114–35, and "State Politics, 1840–1847," 278–302, which are directly related to the political situation that evolved in Hancock County.

Studies of aspects of Mormonism in Illinois can be found in several other recent works. The motivating force behind the establishment of Nauvoo as a Mormon political entity sprang from a concept of utopia, called Zion by the Mormons, in which the church and the state were one. The concept of a Mormon theocracy has been a subject of great interest to historians. Among the better works are Rex Eugene Cooper, *Promises Made to the Fathers: Mormon Covenant Organization* (Salt Lake City: University of Utah Press, 1990); Leonard J. Arrington, Feramorz Y. Fox, and Dean L. May, *Building the City of God: Community and Cooperation among the Mormons*, 2d ed. (Urbana: University of Illinois Press, 1992); Gordon Douglas Pollock, *In Search of Security: The Mormons and the Kingdom of God on Earth, 1830–1844* (Kingston, Canada: Queen's University at Kingston, 1977); Richard T. Hughes and C. Leonard Allen, "Soaring with the Gods: Early Mormons and the Eclipse of Religious Pluralism," in *Illusions of Innocence: Protestant Primitivism in America, 1630–1875*, ed. Richard T. Hughes (Chicago: University of Chicago Press, 1988), 133–52; and Warren David Hansen, "Re-establishing Community: An Analysis of Joseph Smith's Social Thought in the Context of Philosophical Tradition" (Ph.D. diss., Rutgers University, 1980). An apologia for Mormon theocracy is Edwin Brown Firmage and Richard Collin Mangrum, *Zion in the Courts: A Legal History of the Church of Jesus Christ of Latter-day Saints, 1830–1900* (Urbana: University of Illinois Press, 1988).

Several historians have focused on the Mormon institutions created to make the new theocratic order a reality. The specific expression of theocracy in Nauvoo came with the laying out of the community in 1839. Most of the land was acquired on easy terms from speculators. One of them is profiled in Lyndon W. Cook, "Isaac Galland—Mormon Benefactor," *Brigham Young University Studies* 19 (Spring 1979): 261–84. The physical dimensions of the community are discussed in Donald L. Enders, "Platting the City Beautiful: A Historical and Archaeological Glimpse of Nauvoo Streets," *Brigham Young University Studies* 19 (Spring 1979): 409–15; Donald Q. Cannon, "The Founding of Nauvoo," in *The Prophet Joseph: Essays on the Life and Mission of Joseph Smith*, ed. Larry C. Porter and Susan Easton Black (Salt Lake City: Deseret Book, 1988), 246–60; Richard H. Jackson, "The Mormon Village: Genesis and Antecedents of the City of Zion Plat," *Brigham Young University Studies* 17 (Winter 1977): 223–40; Donald L. Enders, "A Dam for Nauvoo: An Attempt to Industrialize the City," *Brigham Young University Studies* 18 (Winter 1978): 246–54; and Dennis Rowley, "Nauvoo: A River Town," *Brigham Young University Studies* 18 (Winter 1978): 255–72. An interesting analysis of demographics in Nauvoo can be found in James E. Smith, "Frontier Nauvoo: Building a Picture from Statistics," *Ensign* 9 (September 1979): 16–19.

That Mormonism in the area was not limited to Nauvoo but spread out elsewhere can be seen in the following studies: Donald Q. Cannon, "Spokes on the Wheel: Early Latter-day Saint Settlements in Hancock County, Illinois," *Ensign* 16 (February 1986): 62–68; Stanley B. Kimball, "Nauvoo West: The Mormons of the Iowa Shore," *Brigham Young University Studies* 18 (Winter 1978): 132–42; Marshall Hamilton, " 'MONEY–DIGGERSVILLE'—The Brief, Turbulent History of the Mormon Town of Warren," *John Whitmer Historical Association Journal* 9 (1989): 49–58; and Susan Sessions Rugh, "Conflict in the Countryside: The Mormon Settlement at Macedonia, Illinois," *Brigham Young University Studies* 32 (Winter/Spring 1992): 149–74. That many residents of Nauvoo were British immigrants is noted in M. Hamlin Cannon, "Migration of English Mormons to America," *American Historical Review* 52 (April 1947): 436–55; P. A. M. Taylor, *Expectations Westward: The Mormons and the Emigration of Their British Converts in the Nineteenth Century* (Edinburgh: Oliver and Boyd, 1965); and Conway B. Sonne, *Saints on the Seas: A Maritime History of the Mormon Migration, 1830–1890* (Salt Lake City: University of Utah Press, 1983).

More ominous was the Council of Fifty, organized in Nauvoo in the spring of 1844 to bring about the political kingdom of God, presided over by the coronated Joseph Smith Jr. as the ruler of God's kingdom on earth. Although the secret Council of Fifty was mentioned as early as 1844 in George T. M. Davis's *An Authentic Account of the Massacre of Joseph Smith, the Mormon Prophet, and Hyrum Smith, His Brother, Together with a Brief History of the Rise and Progress of Mormonism, and All the Circumstances Which Led to Their Death* (St. Louis: Chambers and Knapp, 1844), the first thorough discussion of his body was Klaus J. Hansen, whose *Quest for Empire: The Kingdom of God and the Council of Fifty in Mormon History* (East Lansing: Michigan State University Press, 1967) presented a compelling interpretation of the empire-building designs of Joseph Smith. Hansen explicitly used this interpretation to explain conflict in other important writings: "The Metamorphosis of the Kingdom of God," *Dialogue: A Journal of Mormon Thought* 1 (Autumn 1966): 63–83; and *Mormonism and the American Experience* (Chicago: University of Chicago Press, 1981), especially 113–46. Robert B. Flanders offered a similar analysis in "Dream and Nightmare: Nauvoo Revisited," in *The Restoration Movement: Essays in Mormon History*, ed. F. Mark McKiernan, Alma R. Blair, and Paul M. Edwards (Lawrence, Kans.: Coronado Press, 1973), 141–66. It should be mentioned that the interpretation that the Council of Fifty was a shadow theocratic government seeking to overthrow the United States has had its challengers. See D. Michael Quinn, "The Council of Fifty and Its Members," *Brigham Young University Studies* 20 (Winter 1980): 163–97; Marvin S. Hill, "Quest for Refuge: An Hypothesis as to the Social Origins and Nature of the Mormon Political Kingdom," *Journal of Mormon History* 2 (1975): 3–20; and Andrew F. Ehat, " 'It Seems Like Heaven Began on Earth': Joseph Smith and the Constitution of the Kingdom of God," *Brigham Young University Studies* 20 (Spring 1980): 253–79.

The bulwark of the community was the Nauvoo city charter, which was passed in 1840 and repealed in 1845. An analysis of this charter that is sympathetic to the Mormon cause is Edward L. Kimball Jr., "A Study of the Nauvoo Charter, 1840–1845" (M.A. thesis, University of Iowa, 1966), from which "A Wall to Defend Zion: The Nauvoo Charter," *Brigham Young University Studies* 15 (Summer 1975): 491–97, was drawn. Both emphasize that the legal apparatus was not different from other charters passed in Illinois during the era but that it was logically used by the Mormons as a means of defending themselves from abuses and persecutions such as they perceived in Missouri. The central means of maintaining order in the city was the Nauvoo Legion; neither the local police nor the Nauvoo Legion were sufficient to maintain order, however, and the Nauvoo Mormons organized a paramilitary outfit to intimidate unwanted strangers. On this guard, see Thurmon Dean Moody, "Nauvoo's Whistling and Whittling Brigade," *Brigham Young University Studies* 15 (Summer 1975): 480–90, but much additional work is required on this subject.

In addition to the Mormons' use of the charter, the involvement of the church in politics was an important element of activity in Nauvoo. The work of Ford, Gregg, Hansen, Flanders, Hampshire, Hallwas, and Pollock deal with this issue in detail, but one should also review the literature on the 1844 attempt of Joseph Smith to attain the U.S. presidency. See Richard D. Poll, "Joseph Smith and the Presidency, 1844," *Dialogue: A Journal of Mormon Thought* 3 (Autumn 1968): 17–21; Martin B. Hickman, "The Political Legacy of Joseph Smith," *Dialogue: A Journal of Mormon Thought* 3 (Autumn 1968): 22–27; James B. Allen, "The American Presidency and the Mormons," *Ensign* 2 (October 1972): 46–56; George R. Gaylor, "The Mormons and Politics in Illinois, 1839–1844," *Journal of the Illinois State Historical Society* 49 (Spring 1956): 48–66; and two biographies of Joseph Smith: Fawn M. Brodie, *No Man Knows My History: The Life of Joseph Smith, the Mormon Prophet*, rev. ed. (New York: Alfred A. Knopf, 1971); and Donna Hill, *Joseph Smith: The First Mormon* (Garden City, N.Y.: Doubleday, 1977). Two important primary source works add much to any effort to understand Joseph Smith's political goals in Nauvoo: Andrew F. Ehat and Lyndon W. Cook, eds., *The Words of Joseph Smith:*

The Contemporary Accounts of the Nauvoo Discourses of the Prophet Joseph (Provo, Utah: Religious Studies Center, Brigham Young University, 1980); and Dean C. Jessee, ed., *The Personal Writings of Joseph Smith* (Salt Lake City: Deseret Book, 1984). There is, however, need for a fully reasoned analysis of Mormon/non-Mormon political issues in the 1840s.

The political issues at play in western Illinois in the 1840s found expression in publications, especially newspapers, appearing in the region. Studies of two central literary figures in the region and players in the Mormon conflict are John E. Hallwas, *Thomas Gregg: Early Illinois Journalist and Author*, Monograph Series (Macomb: Western Illinois University, 1983); Marshall Hamilton, "Thomas Sharp's Turning Point: Birth of an Anti-Mormon," *Sunstone* 13 (October 1989): 16–22; and Roger D. Launius, ed., "Anti-Mormonism in Illinois: Thomas C. Sharp's Unfinished History of the Mormon War, 1845," *Journal of Mormon History* 15 (1989): 27–46. The debate between William B. Smith, Mormon editor of the *Wasp*, and Thomas C. Sharp, anti-Mormon editor of the Warsaw *Signal*, has been discussed in Jerry C. Jolley, "The Sting of the *Wasp*: Early Nauvoo Newspaper—April 1842 to April 1843," *Brigham Young University Studies* 22 (Fall 1982): 487–96. Much remains to be done in this analysis, however, especially through studies documenting the roles of editors and what they printed in shaping public opinion.

The political dimension found ready expression in Joseph Smith's adoption of Masonry and the incorporation of some of its ideas into Mormon theological conceptions. A relatively straightforward narrative of Mormonism and Masonry can be found in Kenneth W. Godfrey, "Joseph Smith and the Masons," *Journal of the Illinois State Historical Society* 64 (Spring 1971): 79–90. More suggestive of the connections between the church's theology and Masonic practices are Jack Adamson and Reed C. Durham Jr., *Joseph Smith and Masonry: No Help for the Widow's Son; Two Papers on the Influence of the Masonic Movement on Joseph Smith and His Mormon Church* (Nauvoo, Ill.: Martin Publishing, 1980); D. Michael Quinn, *Early Mormonism and the Magic World View* (Salt Lake City: Signature Books, 1987); and Mervin B. Hogan, *Mormonism and Freemasonry: The Illinois Episode* (Salt Lake City: Campus Graphics, 1980). A fine study of relationships between Mormon and non-Mormon Masons is Kent L. Walgren, "James Adams: Early Springfield Mormon and Freemason," *Journal of Illinois State Historical Society* 75 (Summer 1982): 121–36.

The non-Mormons' concern about Mormon lawlessness is another significant area in need of scholarly attention. What has been published is at best only partially illuminating. For instance, Mormon theft seems to have sprung from the destitute nature of the Saints in Nauvoo, a theme virtually unexplored. Some of this can be ascertained from Joseph Smith's scheme to declare bankruptcy in 1842, treated in M. Hamlin Cannon, ed., "Bankruptcy Proceedings against Joseph Smith in Illinois," *Pacific Historical Review* 14 (December 1945): 424–33, and 15 (June 1946): 214–15. In addition, see Dallin H. Oaks and Joseph I. Bentley, "Joseph Smith and Legal Process: In the Wake of the Steamboat *Nauvoo*," *Brigham Young University Studies* 19 (Winter 1979): 167–99; and Donald L. Enders, "The Steamboat *Maid of Iowa:* Mormon Mistress of the Mississippi," *Brigham Young University Studies* 19 (Spring 1979): 321–35. That theft would emerge from such a situation is not surprising. Harold Schindler's *Orrin Porter Rockwell: Man of God, Son of Thunder* (Salt Lake City: University of Utah Press, 1966) contains some discussion of law enforcement issues, as does the diary of Hosea Stout, the head of the Mormon police, in Juanita Brooks, ed., *On the Mormon Frontier: The Diary of Hosea Stout, 1844–1861,* 2 vols. (Salt Lake City: University of Utah Press, 1964). See also the overview in Kenneth W. Godfrey, "Crime and Punishment in Mormon Nauvoo, 1839–1846," *Brigham Young University Studies* 32 (Winter/Spring 1992): 195–227. On an important murder trial emerging from this lawlessness in 1845, see Barbara Howard and Junia Braby, "The Hodges Hanging," *Palimpsest* 60 (March–April 1979): 49–58.

While politics and economics and lawlessness were critical components of Mormon relations with the larger community, some religious ideas certainly adversely affected perceptions in the outside community. Non-Mormons, of course, had little sympathy for the religious practices of the Mormons, but that did not motivate violence. The reactions of other religious figures to Nauvoo Mormonism can be found in Myron J. Fodge, "Primitivism and Paternalism: Early Denominational Approaches in Western Illinois," *Western Illinois Regional Studies* 3 (Fall 1980): 105–40; Donald Q. Cannon, "Reverend George Moore Comments on Nauvoo, the Mormons and Joseph Smith," *Western Illinois Regional Studies* 5 (Spring 1982): 5–16; and Roger D. Launius, ed., "American Home Missionary Society Ministers and Mormon Nauvoo: Selected Letters," *Western Illinois Regional Studies* 8 (Spring 1985): 16–45. A broader discussion can be found in William Mulder, "Nauvoo Observed," *Brigham Young University Studies* 32 (Winter/Spring 1992): 95–118.

Specific practices did, however, spark their ready opposition. The most important of these was polygamy, about which much has been written in recent years. The most important works on this subject include Lawrence Foster, *Religion and Sexuality: Three American Communal Experiments of the Nineteenth Century* (New York: Oxford University Press, 1981; reprint, Urbana: University of Illinois Press, 1984); Louis J. Kern, *An Ordered Love: Sex Roles and Sexuality in Victorian Utopias—the Shakers, the Mormons, and the Oneida Community* (Chapel Hill: University of North

Carolina Press, 1981); Richard S. Van Wagoner, *Mormon Polygamy: A History* (Salt Lake City: Signature Books, 1986); B. Carmon Hardy, *Solemn Covenant: The Mormon Polygamous Passage* (Urbana: University of Illinois Press, 1992); and Danel W. Bachman, "A Study of the Mormon Practice of Plural Marriage before the Death of Joseph Smith" (M.A. thesis, Purdue University, 1975). Richard S. Van Wagoner, "Mormon Polyandry in Nauvoo," *Dialogue: A Journal of Mormon Thought* 18 (Fall 1985): 67–83, describes the less than lofty liaisons that resulted from the practice and leads one to the conclusion that much of the supposedly religious practice was motivated by lust. This conclusion was also offered in 1842 by John C. Bennett, *The History of the Saints; or, an Expose of Joe Smith and Mormonism* (Boston: Leland and Whiting, 1842). An exceptionally useful study that employs a diary inaccessible to other researchers is James B. Allen, "One Man's Nauvoo: William Clayton's Experience in Mormon Illinois," *Journal of Mormon History* 6 (1979): 37–59, which discusses at length Smith's polygamous relations. A larger study of William Clayton is James B. Allen, *Trials of Discipleship: The Story of William Clayton, a Mormon* (Urbana: University of Illinois Press, 1987).

Some have denied that polygamy had any true place in early Mormonism and that Joseph Smith was never involved in its practice, a decidedly simplistic, unsubstantiated perception. See, for example, Richard Price, *The Polygamy Conspiracies* (Independence, Mo.: Cumorah Books, 1984); Roy A. Cheville, *Joseph and Emma Companions: For Seventeen and a Half Years, 1827–1844* (Independence, Mo.: Herald Publishing House, 1977); and Maurice L. Draper, *Marriage in the Restoration* (Independence, Mo.: Herald Publishing House, 1969). Richard P. Howard, "The Changing RLDS Response to Mormon Polygamy: A Preliminary Analysis," *John Whitmer Historical Association Journal* 3 (1983): 14–29, offered an analysis of the development of polygamy in Nauvoo as an "accident of history."

Besides plural marriage, family and sex roles underwent changes among the Mormons in Nauvoo. See M. Guy Bishop, "Preparing to 'Take the Kingdom': Childrearing Directives in Early Mormonism," *Journal of the Early Republic* 7 (Fall 1987): 275–90; William G. Hartley, "Joseph Smith and Nauvoo's Youth," *Ensign* 9 (September 1979): 26–29; and M. Guy Bishop, "Sex Roles, Marriage, and Childrearing in Nauvoo," *Western Illinois Regional Studies* 11 (Fall 1988): 30–45, on this subject. Women's roles and gender relations in Nauvoo have received significant study. Among the important work done on this subject, see Linda King Newell, "A Gift Given, a Gift Taken: Washing, Anointing, and Blessing the Sick among Mormon Women," *Sunstone* 6 (September–October 1981): 16–25; L. Madelon Brunson, *Bonds of Sisterhood: A History of the RLDS Women's Organization, 1842–1983* (Independence, Mo.: Herald Publishing House,

1985); John Heeren, Donald B. Lindsay, and Marylee Mason, "The Mormon Concept of Mother in Heaven: A Sociological Account of Its Origins and Development," *Journal for the Scientific Study of Religion* 23 (December 1984): 396–411; Maureen Ursenbach Beecher and Lavina Fielding Anderson, *Sisters in Spirit: Mormon Women in Historical and Cultural Perspective* (Urbana: University of Illinois Press, 1987); and Richard Neitzel Holzapfel and Jeni Bramberg Holzapfel, *Women of Nauvoo* (Salt Lake City: Bookcraft, 1992). For a discussion of the development of Mormon women's history, see Carol Cornwall Madsen and David J. Whittaker, "History's Sequel: A Source Essay on Women in Mormon History," *Journal of Mormon History* 6 (1979): 123–45; and Patricia Lyn Scott and Maureen Ursenbach Beecher, "Mormon Women: A Bibliography in Progress, 1977–1985," *Journal of Mormon History* 12 (1985): 113–28.

The Nauvoo period was the most fertile period for the promulgation of Smith's unique theological ideas, and most were much less controversial than plural marriage. The development of a *temple cultus* in Nauvoo, only one connection of which was to masonry, can be studied using Laurel B. Andrew, *The Early Temples of the Mormons* (Albany: State University of New York Press, 1978); Lisle G. Brown, "The Sacred Departments for Temple Work in Nauvoo: The Assembly Room and the Council Chamber," *Brigham Young University Studies* 19 (Spring 1979): 361–74; David John Buerger, "The Development of the Mormon Temple Endowment Ceremony," *Dialogue: A Journal of Mormon Thought* 20 (Winter 1987): 33–76; Joseph Earl Arrington, "Destruction of the Mormon Temple at Nauvoo," *Journal of the Illinois State Historical Society* 40 (1947): 414–25; J. Earl Arrington, "William Weeks, Architect of the Nauvoo Temple," *Brigham Young University Studies* 19 (Spring 1979): 337–59; Andrew F. Ehat, "Joseph Smith's Introduction of Temple Ordinances and the 1844 Mormon Succession Question" (M.A. thesis, Brigham Young University, 1982); Roger D. Launius and F. Mark McKiernan, *Joseph Smith, Jr.'s, Red Brick Store,* Monograph Series (Macomb: Western Illinois University, 1985); Armand L. Mauss, "Culture, Charisma, and Change: Reflections on Mormon Temple Worship," *Dialogue: A Journal of Mormon Thought* 20 (Winter 1987): 77–83; Virginia S. Harrington and J. C. Harrington, *Rediscovery of the Nauvoo Temple* (Salt Lake City: Nauvoo Restoration, 1971); Stanley B. Kimball, "The Nauvoo Temple," *Improvement Era* 66 (November 1963): 973–84; Mark P. Leone, "The Mormon Temple Experience," *Sunstone* 10 (May 1985): 4–7; and Marcus von Wellnitz, "The Catholic Liturgy and the Mormon Temple," *Brigham Young University Studies* 21 (Winter 1981): 3–35. Building the temple was difficult at best, and a community of Saints was sent to Wisconsin to cut lumber for the construction effort there and in the rest of Nauvoo. This has been described in Dennis

Rowley, "The Mormon Experience in the Wisconsin Pineries, 1841–1845," *Brigham Young University Studies* 32 (Winter/Spring 1992): 119–48.

The temple was really an outgrowth of Smith's larger thinking about humanity's relationship with God. The general parameters of this subject have been outlined in Willis G. Swartz, "Mormon Life and Doctrine in Illinois and Utah (1840–1860)," in *Transactions of the Illinois State Historical Society for the Year 1926* (Springfield: Illinois State Historical Society, 1926), 65–74; T. Edgar Lyon, "Doctrinal Development of the Church during the Nauvoo Sojourn, 1839–1846," *Brigham Young University Studies* 15 (Summer 1975): 435–46; and Larry C. Porter and Milton V. Backman Jr., "Doctrine and the Temple in Nauvoo," *Brigham Young University Studies* 32 (Winter/Spring 1992): 41–56. Much of this was encapsulated in the Mormon scriptures, the Inspired Version of the Bible, the Book of Mormon, the Doctrine and Covenants, and the Pearl of Great Price. On these scriptures, see Richard P. Howard, *Restoration Scripture: A Study of their Textual Development* (Independence, Mo.: Herald Publishing House, 1969); Robert J. Matthews, "The Bernhisel Manuscript Copy of Joseph Smith's Inspired Version of the Bible," *Brigham Young University Studies* 11 (Spring 1971): 253–74; Robert J. Matthews, *"A Plainer Translation": Joseph Smith's Translation of the Bible; A History and Commentary* (Provo, Utah: Brigham Young University Press, 1975); Philip L. Barlow, *Mormons and the Bible* (New York: Oxford University Press, 1991); and Stanley B. Kimball, "New Light on Old Egyptiana: Mormon Mummies, 1848–71," *Dialogue: A Journal of Mormon Thought* 16 (Winter 1983): 72–90.

Specific theological teachings have been discussed in several articles. Perhaps the most significant explanation Joseph Smith ever gave in Nauvoo was the King Follett discourse, where he laid out his conception of the nature of God and the possibility of humanity's eternal progression. On this subject, see Donald Q. Cannon, "The King Follett Discourse: Joseph Smith's Greatest Sermon in Historical Perspective," *Brigham Young University Studies* 18 (Winter 1978): 179–92; Van Hale, "The Doctrinal Impact of the King Follett Discourse," *Brigham Young University Studies* 18 (Winter 1978): 209–25; Van Hale, "The King Follett Discourse: Textual History and Criticism," *Sunstone* 8 (September–October 1983): 5–12; Stan Larson, "The King Follett Discourse: A Newly Amalgamated Text," *Brigham Young University Studies* 18 (Winter 1978): 193–208; and Robert E. Paul, "Joseph Smith and the Plurality of Worlds Idea," *Dialogue: A Journal of Mormon Thought* 19 (Summer 1986): 12–38. Central to Smith's theology was the concept of a preexistence with God before life on earth, as explained in Charles R. Harrell, "The Development of the Doctrine of Preexistence, 1830–1844," *Brigham Young University Studies* 28 (Spring 1988): 75–96; and Blake Ostler, "The Idea of Preexistence in the Development of Mormon Thought," *Dialogue: A Journal of Mormon Thought* 15 (Spring 1982): 59–78. Other related theological ideas have been discussed in Fred C. Collier, "The Nauvoo Doctrine on Priesthood," *Restoration* 6 (January 1987): 8–15; Gordon Irving, "The Law of Adoption: One Phase of the Development of the Mormon Concept of Salvation, 1830–1900," *Brigham Young University Studies* 14 (Spring 1974): 291–314; D. Michael Quinn, "Latter-day Saint Prayer Circles," *Brigham Young University Studies* 19 (Fall 1978): 79–105; D. Michael Quinn, "The Practice of Rebaptism at Nauvoo," *Brigham Young University Studies* 18 (Winter 1978): 226–32; M. Guy Bishop, "To Overcome the 'Last Enemy': Early Mormon Perceptions of Death," *Brigham Young University Studies* 26 (Summer 1986): 63–79; M. Guy Bishop, " 'What Has Become of Our Fathers?' Baptism for the Dead at Nauvoo," *Dialogue: A Journal of Mormon Thought* 23 (Summer 1990): 85–97; and M. Guy Bishop, Vincent Lacy, and Richard Wixom, "Death in Mormon Nauvoo, 1843–1845," *Western Illinois Regional Studies* 9 (Fall 1986): 71–77.

Much work remains to be done on the social history of the Saints in Nauvoo; however, a start as been made. Kenneth W. Godfrey, "Some Thoughts regarding an Unwritten History of Nauvoo," *Brigham Young University Studies* 15 (Summer 1975): 417–24, opened the area for consideration. His "A Note on the Nauvoo Library and Literary Institute," *Brigham Young University Studies* 14 (Spring 1974): 386–89, provides some detail on the subject. Other publications on the subject include Leonard J. Arrington and Jon Haupt, "The Missouri and Illinois Mormons in Ante-Bellum Fiction," *Dialogue: A Journal of Mormon Thought* 5 (Spring 1970): 37–50; Richard Neitzel Holzapfel and T. Jeffery Cottle, "The City of Joseph in Focus: The Use and Abuse of Historic Photographs," *Brigham Young University Studies* 32 (Winter/Spring 1992): 249–68; Gary L. Bunker and Davis Bitton, *The Mormon Graphic Image, 1834–1914: Cartoons, Caricatures, and Illustrations* (Salt Lake City: University of Utah Press, 1983); and John E. Hallwas, "The Midwestern Poetry of Eliza Snow," *Western Illinois Regional Studies* 5 (Fall 1982): 136–45. There is ample room for additional work on this subject, however.

Dissension in Nauvoo, especially over polygamy, developed by at least 1842. John C. Bennett split from the church and wrote his exposé, and while Smith survived his defection, the case of the Nauvoo reformers led by William Law was another story. Law, a very attractive but tragic figure in Mormon history, has been the subject of several articles: Lyndon W. Cook, "William Law, Nauvoo Dissenter," *Brigham Young University Studies* 22 (Winter 1982): 47–62; John Frederick Glaser, "The Disaffection of William Law," in *Restoration Studies III,* ed. Maurice L. Draper and Debra Combs (Independence, Mo.: Herald Publishing House, 1986),

163–75; and Lyndon W. Cook, ed., " 'Brother Joseph Is Truly a Wonderful Man, He Is All We Could Wish a Prophet to Be': Pre-1844 Letters of William Law," *Brigham Young University Studies* 20 (Winter 1980): 207–18. His group published the Nauvoo *Expositor* challenging Smith's direction for the church, and Smith retaliated by destroying the press. This has also been discussed in some detail in George R. Gaylor's "The 'Expositor' Affair: Prelude to the Downfall of Joseph Smith," *Northwest Missouri State College Studies* 25 (February 1961): 3–15; Dallin H. Oaks's apologetic study "The Suppression of the Nauvoo *Expositor*," *Utah Law Review* 9 (Winter 1965): 862–903; and John Hallwas's essay in this volume.

The destruction of the *Expositor* led directly to the lynching of Joseph Smith and Hyrum Smith in Carthage in 1844. This episode has attracted serious historical investigation. The most important work on the subject, as well as on its aftermath, is Dallin H. Oaks and Marvin S. Hill, *Carthage Conspiracy: The Trial of the Accused Assassins of Joseph Smith* (Urbana: University of Illinois Press, 1975). Studies of the governor's role in this episode include George R. Gaylor, "Governor Ford and the Death of Joseph and Hyrum Smith," *Journal of the Illinois State Historical Society* 50 (Winter 1957): 391–411; and Keith Huntress, "Governor Thomas Ford and the Murderers of Joseph Smith," *Dialogue: A Journal of Mormon Thought* 4 (Summer 1969): 41–52. Interesting analyses of the meaning of the murders can be found in Kenneth W. Godfrey, "Non-Mormon Views of the Martyrdom: A Look at Some Early Published Accounts," *John Whitmer Historical Association Journal* 7 (1987): 12–20; Dean C. Jessee, "Return to Carthage: Writing the History of Joseph Smith's Martyrdom," *Journal of Mormon History* 8 (1981): 3–21; Clifton H. Jolley, "The Martyrdom of Joseph Smith: An Archetypal Study," *Utah Historical Quarterly* 44 (Fall 1976): 329–50; Michael Hicks, " 'Strains Which Will Not Soon Be Allowed to Die': 'The Stranger' and Carthage Jail," *Brigham Young University Studies* 23 (Fall 1983): 389–400; George F. Partridge, ed., "The Death of a Mormon Dictator: Letters of Massachusetts Mormons, 1843–1848," *New England Quarterly* 9 (December 1936): 583–617; Paul D. Ellsworth, "Mobocracy and the Rule of Law: American Press Reaction to the Murder of Joseph Smith," *Brigham Young University Studies* 20 (Fall 1979): 71–82; and Richard C. Poulsen, "Fate and the Persecutors of Joseph Smith: Transmutations of an American Myth," *Dialogue: A Journal of Mormon Thought* 11 (Winter 1978): 63–70. Contemporary accounts can be found in Keith Huntress, ed., *Murder of an American Prophet: Materials for Analysis* (San Francisco: Chandler Publishing, 1960); Dan Jones, "The Martyrdom of Joseph Smith and His Brother Hyrum," *Brigham Young University Studies* 24 (Winter 1984): 78–109; Steven G. Barnett, "The Canes of the Martyrdom," *Brigham Young University Studies* 21 (Spring 1981): 205–11; Ronald

K. Esplin, "Life in Nauvoo, June 1844: Vilate Kimball's Martyrdom Letters," *Brigham Young University Studies* 19 (Winter 1979): 231–40; and Richard S. Van Wagoner and Steven C. Walker, "The Joseph/Hyrum Smith Funeral Sermon," *Brigham Young University Studies* 23 (Winter 1983): 3–18. A useful perspective on violence in America can be found in David Grimstead, "Rioting in Its Jacksonian Setting," *American Historical Review* 77 (April 1972): 361–97.

Immediately after the murders at Carthage, there was relative quiet in the county, but the institutional church began to disintegrate. Dissension among leaders over theology, policy, and a host of other issues resulted in a splintering. Emma Smith, the prophet's widow, for one, broke with the leadership that emerged in Nauvoo under Brigham Young. By far the best works on this are Linda King Newell and Valeen Tippetts Avery, *Mormon Enigma: Emma Hale Smith,* 2d ed. (Urbana: University of Illinois Press, 1994); Linda King Newell and Valeen Tippetts Avery, "New Light on the Sun: Emma Smith and the *New York Sun* Letter," *Journal of Mormon History* 6 (1979): 23–35; and Linda King Newell, "The Emma Smith Lore Reconsidered," *Dialogue* 17 (Autumn 1984): 87–100. Useful principally because it contains previously unpublished recollections is Buddy Youngreen, *Reflections of Emma: Joseph Smith's Wife* (Orem: Grandin Book, 1982).

Only a few scholars have worked directly on the overall history of the conflict in Illinois. An early work on the subject is Herbert Spencer Salisbury, "The Mormon War in Hancock County," *Journal of the Illinois State Historical Society* 8 (Fall 1915): 281–87 One of the best works is unpublished: Kenneth W. Godfrey, "Causes of Mormon–Non-Mormon Conflict in Hancock County, Illinois, 1839–1846" (Ph.D. diss., Brigham Young University, 1967). Godfrey published a political summary from this larger study, "The Road to Carthage Led West," *Brigham Young University Studies* 8 (Winter 1968): 204–15, but it suffered from common Mormon biases. In addition, the British scholar Annette P. Hampshire's *Mormonism in Conflict: The Nauvoo Years* (New York: Edwin Mellen Press, 1985), drawn from her "Mormonism in Illinois, 1839–1847: A Study of the Development of Socio-Religious Conflict" (Ph.D. diss., University of Durham, 1979), takes a sociological perspective on the conflict in Illinois. She summarized her findings in Annette P. Hampshire, "The Triumph of Mobocracy in Hancock County, 1844–1846," *Western Illinois Regional Studies* 5 (Spring 1982): 17–37; and she presented some valuable primary source materials found in the Coe Collection of Western Americana at the Bienecke Library at Yale University in Annette P. Hampshire, "Thomas Sharp and Anti-Mormon Sentiment in Illinois," *Journal of the Illinois State Historical Society* 72 (May 1979): 82–100. A recent account is contained in John E. Hallwas and Roger D. Launius, *Cultures in Conflict: A Documentary History of the Mormon War in Illinois* (Logan: Utah State University Press, 1995).

While the succession was not easy, Brigham Young eventually gained the greatest following. For discussions of this, see Leonard J. Arrington, *Brigham Young: American Moses* (New York: Alfred A. Knopf, 1985; reprint, Urbana: University of Illinois Press, 1986); and Newell G. Bringhurst, *Brigham Young and the Expanding Frontier* (Boston: Little, Brown, 1986). Not all of the ranking members of the hierarchy accepted Young's control, including three apostles. One of these was William B. Smith, the only surviving brother of the prophet. See Irene M. Bates, "William Smith, 1811–1893: Problematic Patriarch," *Dialogue: A Journal of Mormon Thought* 16 (Summer 1983): 11–23; Irene M. Bates, "Uncle John Smith, 1781–1854: Patriarchal Bridge," *Dialogue: A Journal of Mormon Thought* 20 (Fall 1987): 79–89; Paul M. Edwards, "William B. Smith: The Persistent 'Pretender,'" *Dialogue: A Journal of Mormon Thought* 18 (Summer 1985): 128–39; and E. Gary Smith, "The Patriarchal Crisis of 1845," *Dialogue: A Journal of Mormon Thought* 16 (Summer 1983): 24–35. The others were John E. Page and Lyman Wight, who are profiled in John Quist, "John E. Page: An Apostle of Uncertainty," *Journal of Mormon History* 12 (1985): 53–68; and Davis Bitton, "Mormons in Texas: The Ill-Fated Lyman Wight Colony, 1844–1858," *Arizona and the West* 11 (Spring 1969): 5–26.

The succession crisis following the death of Joseph Smith was significant to the development of the Mormon conflict in Illinois. Anti-Mormons believed that internal dissension over leadership would destroy the organization. They underestimated the drive of Brigham Young, however, whose forceful and dynamic challengers were unable to wrest control from him. Studies of the three members of the Quorum of Twelve who did not follow Young and studies of Emma Smith are appropriate here, as is the biography of the only surviving member of the Mormon First Presidency: F. Mark McKiernan, *The Voice of One Crying in the Wilderness: Sidney Rigdon, 1796–1876, Religious Reformer* (Lawrence, Kan.: Coronado Press, 1971); and Richard S. Van Wagoner, *Sidney Rigdon: A Portrait of Religious Excess* (Salt Lake City: Signature Books, 1994). A biography of one who sided with Brigham Young is Stanley B. Kimball, *Heber C. Kimball: Mormon Patriarch and Pioneer* (Urbana: University of Illinois Press, 1981). Blatant apologies for the Mormon approach to succession can be found in Reed C. Durham and Steven C. Heath, *Succession in the Church* (Salt Lake City: Deseret Book, 1970); Steven C. Heath, "Notes on Apostolic Succession," *Dialogue: A Journal of Mormon Thought* 20 (Summer 1987): 44–57; T. Edgar Lyon, "Nauvoo and the Council of Twelve," in *The Restoration Movement: Essays in Mormon History,* ed. F. Mark McKiernan,

Alma R. Blair, and Paul M. Edwards (Lawrence, Kan.: Coronado Press, 1973), 167–205; and Ronald K. Esplin, "The Emergence of Brigham Young and the Twelve to Mormon Leadership, 1830– 1941" (Ph.D. diss., Brigham Young University, 1981), from which was taken "Joseph, Brigham, and the Twelve: A Succession of Continuity," *Brigham Young University Studies* 21 (Summer 1981): 301–41. Much more useful are D. Michael Quinn, "The Mormon Succession Crisis of 1844," *Brigham Young University Studies* 16 (Winter 1976): 187–233; H. Michael Marquardt, "Some Interesting Notes on Succession at Nauvoo in 1844," *Restoration* 5 (January 1986): 17–20; D. Michael Quinn, "Joseph Smith III's 1844 Blessing and the Mormons of Utah," *Dialogue: A Journal of Mormon Thought* 15 (Summer 1982): 69–90; and Roger D. Launius, "Joseph Smith III and the Mormon Succession Crisis, 1844–1846," *Western Illinois Regional Studies* 6 (Fall 1983): 5–22. For studies of two of the alternatives to Young's leadership, see Roger Van Noord, *King of Beaver Island: The Life and Assassination of James Jesse Strang* (Urbana: University of Illinois Press, 1988); and Roger D. Launius, *Joseph Smith III: Pragmatic Prophet* (Urbana: University of Illinois Press, 1988).

Almost nothing about the Mormon experience after the deaths of Joseph Smith and Hyrum Smith has been thoroughly examined. General works provide only imprecise discussions. Detailed studies are flawed and shy away from important questions. In addition to the work of Flanders, the Millers, Hill, Winn, Hampshire, and Godfrey, see Marshall Hamilton's essay in this volume; and the apologetic and myth-making essay by William A. Sheldon, "Why the Latter-day Saints Were Driven from Nauvoo," *Restoration* 1 (January 1982): 10–11.

The exodus from Nauvoo has usually been treated as part of the story of Mormon settlement in the Rocky Mountains. There are several important studies of the subject, including Stanley B. Kimball, *Historic Sites and Markers along the Mormon and Other Great Western Trails* (Urbana: University of Illinois Press, 1988); Joseph E. Brown, *The Mormon Trek West: The Journey of American Exiles* (Garden City, N.Y.: Doubleday, 1980); Richard E. Bennett, *Mormons at the Missouri, 1846–1852: "And We Should Die . . ."* (Lincoln: University of Nebraska Press, 1987); and Wallace Stegner, *The Gathering of Zion: The Story of the Mormon Trail* (New York: McGraw-Hill, 1964). Richard E. Bennett, "Eastward to Eden: The Nauvoo Rescue Missions," *Dialogue: A Journal of Mormon Thought* 19 (Winter 1986): 100–108, describes the removal of last remaining Mormons from Nauvoo.

In general, there has been an enormous imbalance in the scholarship on the Mormon experience in Illinois. The lives and documents of many Mormons have been discussed, but there are no thorough studies of such key non-Mormons as Thomas Ford and Thomas Sharp, while such lesser figures as Jacob Backenstos and Levi Williams have received virtually no attention. Furthermore, while Nauvoo has been studied from every angle, the important non-Mormon towns of Carthage and Warsaw have been all but neglected.

Contributors

VALEEN TIPPETS AVERY is an associate professor of history at Northern Arizona University, Flagstaff. She coauthored (with Linda King Newell) the award-winning *Mormon Enigma: Emma Hale Smith, Prophet's Wife, "Elect Lady," Polygamy's Foe*.

DAVIS BITTON is a professor of history at the University of Utah. A distinguished scholar, he is the author or editor of more than ten books, including *The Mormon Experience: A History of the Latter-day Saints* (with Leonard J. Arrington); *Guide to Mormon Diaries and Autobiographies; Mormons and Their Historians* (with Leonard J. Arrington); and *The Ritualization of Mormon History and Other Essays*.

KATHRYN M. DAYNES is an assistant professor of history at Brigham Young University. Her specialties are American social history and family history, and her research has focused on Mormon plural marriage.

RONALD K. ESPLIN is the director of the Joseph Fielding Smith Institute for Church History at Brigham Young University. He is the author of several articles on Mormon subjects and *Men with a Mission, 1837–1841: The Quorum of the Twelve Apostles in the British Isles* (with James B. Allen and David J. Whittaker).

ROBERT BRUCE FLANDERS is the director of the Center for Ozark Studies and a professor of history at Southwest Missouri State University, Springfield. Well known for numerous articles on the history of Mormonism, he is also author of the seminal study *Nauvoo: Kingdom on the Mississippi*.

HAMILTON GARDNER was a lawyer and a member of the Utah legislature before his death in 1961. He published articles on military history in a variety of journals. His interest in the Nauvoo Legion sprang from his research on the history of the Utah Territorial Militia.

KENNETH W. GODFREY recently retired as the area director of the Latter-day Saints Institutes of Religion, Logan, Utah. He is the author of numerous articles and coauthor of *Women's Voices: An Untold History of the Latter-day Saints, 1830–1900.*

JOHN E. HALLWAS is a professor of English and the director of Regional Collections at Western Illinois University, Macomb. He is the author or editor of fifteen books related to Illinois history and literature, including *Western Illinois Heritage* and *Cultures in Conflict: A Documentary History of the Mormon War in Illinois* (with Roger D. Launius).

MARSHALL HAMILTON is a businessman in Frederick, Maryland, who has published several articles on the history of the Mormon war in Hancock County, Illinois, in the 1840s.

KLAUS J. HANSEN is a professor of history at Queens University, Kingston, Canada. A distinguished scholar of Mormon studies, he is the author of two seminal books, *Quest for Empire: The Kingdom of God and the Council of Fifty in Mormon History* and *Mormonism and the American Experience.*

MARVIN S. HILL was a professor of history at Brigham Young University until his retirement in 1993. A distinguished historian of Mormonism, he has written several important articles and books. His books include *Mormonism and American Culture* (edited with James B. Allen); *Carthage Conspiracy: The Trial of the Accused Assassins of Joseph Smith* (with Dallin H. Oaks); and *Quest for Refuge: The Mormon Flight from American Pluralism.*

JAMES L. KIMBALL JR. is the senior librarian at the Church of Jesus Christ of Latter-day Saints Library in Salt Lake City.

ROGER D. LAUNIUS is the chief historian of the National Aeronautics and Space Administration, Washington, D.C. He is the author or editor of *Joseph Smith III: Pragmatic Prophet; Differing Visions: Dissenters in Mormon History; Cultures in Conflict: A Documentary History of the Mormon War in Illinois* (with John E. Hallwas), and nine other books.

LINDA KING NEWELL is an independent writer, editor, and research who divides her time between Salt Lake City and Deep Springs College in

California. She is coauthor (with Valeen Tippets Avery) the award-winning *Mormon Enigma: Emma Hale Smith, Prophet's Wife, "Elect Lady," Polygamy's Foe.*

TERENCE A. TANNER is a rare-book dealer in Skokie, Illinois, who has done extensive research on early Illinois imprints and newspapers.

Index

Abercrombie, Nancy, 205
Abraham (Prophet), 25, 31, 83, 104, 131
Acadians, 6
Adams, George J., 81
Ajzen, Icek, 134
Allen, Elihu, 182–83
Alton, Ill., 40, 42, 43
Alton (Ill.) *Telegraph,* 4–5, 166
Amana Church Society, 148
Anderson, Moses K., 53, 54, 59
Anderson, Richard Lloyd, 27
Angell, Mary Ann, 200
Anti-Mormons, 3, 12, 160–63, 173–75,
    215–16; and Battle of Nauvoo, 5, 225,
    226–27; and conflict with Mormons, 2–3,
    8–9; and death of Joseph Smith, 5, 9, 12,
    13, 27–28, 32, 58, 68, 109, 124, 141–42,
    181–95, 214–15, 216, 225, 231; and
    Expositor affair, 57–58, 67, 108–9, 168–72,
    173, 219; and expulsion of Mormons,
    12, 110–11, 214–30; and Hancock
    County Circuit Court, 42; and Jacksonian
    democracy, 4, 12, 146, 148, 160–63,
    173–75; and Jacob Backenstos, 155,
    217–18, 219, 221–22, 225–26; and Joseph
    Smith's presidential campaign, 108, 185;
    and Mormon abuse of habeas corpus,
    42–43, 58, 149; and Mormon authori-
    tarianism, 4–5; and Mormon crime,
    86–88, 216–17; and Mormon militia,
    50–51; and Mormon occupation of
    Carthage, 222–23; and Mormon politi-

cal kingdom of God, 11, 62–71, 107, 120,
    141, 147–59, 160–75, 237; and Mormon
    settlement in Hancock County, 2; and
    Mormon theocracy, 3–4, 8–9, 12, 147–59,
    160–75, 237; and Nauvoo charter, 11,
    39–47, 149, 221; and Nauvoo Legion, 11,
    12, 43–44, 48–61, 66, 122, 154, 166, 172,
    183, 201, 206–7, 216, 221, 235–37; party
    of, 215–16; and persecution of
    Mormons, 1–2, 8, 11, 19–33; and politics,
    120, 125, 147–59, 166–68, 218–20; and
    pro-Mormon sheriff, 155, 217–19,
    221–22, 225–26; republicanism of, 12,
    160–75; and trial of Joseph Smith's
    accused murderers, 218–21; and "wolf
    hunts," 217, 219, 221
Apostles, Quorum of the Twelve. *See* Quo-
    rum of the Twelve Apostles
Appleby, William I., 182, 187
"The Assassination of Gen'ls Joseph Smith
    and Hyrum Smith" (Eliza Roxley Snow),
    180, 188–89, 190, 193
Avery, Valeen Tippetts, 12–13

Babbitt, Almon W., 84, 207–8, 218
Backenstos, Jacob, 155, 217–18, 219,
    221–22, 225–26
Badlam, Alexander, 65, 68
Baptism for the dead, 3, 239–40
Barlow, Israel, 82, 85
Barth, L. L., 238
Bates, Eliza Jane, 103–4